The Street Porter and the Philosopher

The Street Porter and the Philosopher

Conversations on Analytical Egalitarianism

13 July/08

Edited by Sandra J. Peart and David M. Levy

To Jonathan with best wishes from Sandy and David

THE UNIVERSITY OF MICHIGAN PRESS • Ann Arbor

Published in the United States of America by
The University of Michigan Press
Manufactured in the United States of America
⊗ Printed on acid-free paper

2011 2010 2009 2008 4 3 2 1

A CIP catalog record for this book is available from the British Library.

Library of Congress Cataloging-in-Publication Data

The street porter and the philosopher : conversations on analytical egalitarianism / edited by Sandra J. Peart and David M. Levy.
p. cm.
Includes index.
ISBN-13: 978-0-472-11644-7 (cloth : alk. paper)
ISBN-10: 0-472-11644-4 (cloth : alk. paper)
1. Equality. I. Peart, Sandra. II. Levy, David M., 1944–
JC575.S77 2008
320.01'1—dc22 2008008260

Contents

PART 3 • The Role of the Expert

PART 4 • Literature, Biology, and Economics

PART 5 • The Buchanan-Rawls Correspondence

Acknowledgments

The Summer Institute for the Preservation of the History of Economics owes its existence to our belief that economists benefit from the ability to read the texts of past economists. The classical liberal tradition itself cannot be understood without knowledge of the writings of the great British classical liberal economists. David Kennedy, then President of the Earhart Foundation, suggested that we apply to the Foundation for a grant to support a meeting in the summer of 2000. The generosity of the Earhart Foundation continues to help support the Summer Institute. We are particularly grateful for a grant that helped make this book possible.

During the first five years, from which the contributions in the book are drawn, David Levy received additional financial support and encouragement from the Center for Study of Public Choice and the Department of Economics at George Mason. The last years have seen many changes at the Center. Carol Roberts and Janet Byrd, who were both here when the Summer Institute began, have passed away. We miss them.

Sandra Peart received summer support from Baldwin-Wallace College; her sabbatical in 2004–5, when much of the initial work for the collection was done, was supported by the Earhart Foundation and the Mercatus Center.

The conversation between James Buchanan and Warren Samuels (Chapter 2), and Warren Samuels's "Adam Smith's Invisible Hand" (Chapter 8), were taped during the Summer Institute of 2004 and transcribed by Jo Ann Burgess. Chapter 3, David Levy and Sandra Peart's "The Theory of Economic Policy is British Classical Political Economy," is reprinted with the permission of Duke University Press from *The History of Political Economy,* where it appeared in 2005, volume 37 (Suppl. 1). Chapter 4, Samuel Hollander's "Economic Organization, Distribution and the Equality Issue," is reprinted with the permission of Springer from *The Review of Austrian Economics,* where it appeared in 2004, volume 17 (1).

Chapter 6, "Sacred Economics," is an early version of Deirdre McCloskey's *Bourgeois Virtues,* reprinted with permission of the University of Chicago Press, where it appeared in 2006. Chapter 9, Maria Pia Paganelli's "*In Medio Stat Virtus,*" is reprinted with the permission of Duke University Press from *The History of Political Economy,* where it appeared in 2003, volume 35 (1). Sandra Peart and David Levy's "Attitudes Toward Race, Hierarchy and Transformation in the Nineteenth Century" is reprinted with the permission of the editors of *The History of Economic Thought,* where it appeared in 2005, volume 47. Chapter 12, Andrew Farrant's "Frank Knight, Worst-Case Theorizing, and Economic Planning," is reprinted with the permission of Duke University Press from *The History of Political Economy,* where it appeared in 2004, volume 36 (3). Chapter 16, Sandra Peart and David Levy's "Denying Human Homogeneity," is reprinted with the permission of the *Journal of the History of Economic Thought,* where it appeared in 2003, volume 23. Chapter 17, Thomas Leonard's "More Merciful and Not Less Effective," is reprinted with the permission of Duke University Press from *The History of Political Economy,* where it appeared in 2003, volume 35 (4). Gordon Tullock's "Evolution and Human Behavior" is reprinted with the permission of Springer from the *Journal of Bioeconomics,* where it appeared in 2002, volume 4 (2). Finally, the letters between James Buchanan and John Rawls are published with the gracious permission of James Buchanan and the estate of John Rawls.

For this volume, we have been fortunate to deal with a fine economics editor at the University of Michigan Press, Jim Reische, who found helpful reviewers for the manuscript. Sarah Remington assisted with the production. Marcia La Brenz once again served as senior copyeditor coordinator. The bulk of the proof reading was borne by Michael D. Thomas. Emily Jane Perry checked the transcription of the Buchanan-Rawls correspondence with very sharp eyes. Lisa Hill-Corley kept track of the finances and helped with the permissions.

The Summer Institute takes time. David thanks Nicholas and Milton for their support and remembers his mother's. Sandra Peart thanks her two sons, Nathan and Matthew, and husband Craig, for many weeks away from home while at the Summer Institute. Nathan and Matthew enjoyed meeting Daniel Hammond, Steven Medema, and Warren Samuels over lox and bagels at the Institute breakfast and Summer Institute barbeques on the lawn of the Buchanan House.

1 • Introduction

The Street Porter and the Philosopher Contextualized

What Is Analytical Egalitarianism?

Analytical egalitarianism is our term for the theoretical system that abstracts from any inherent difference among persons. Here is an example from within this tradition, a statement that the argument pays no attention to natural differences.

> [A]ssume that these persons have roughly similar needs and interests, or needs and interests in various ways complementary, so that fruitful cooperation amongst them is possible; and suppose that they are sufficiently equal in power and ability to guarantee that in normal circumstances none is able to dominate the others. This condition . . . may seem excessively vague but . . . there seems no reason for making it more exact here. (171)

We postpone identifying the author in order to spell out why analytical egalitarianism is a useful organizing principle for economists and philosophers alike.

A second, perhaps more familiar, organizing principle for thinking about theoretical systems is the sort of socio-political-economic egalitarianism that advocates a normative goal of equalizing income ex post. In order to distinguish this policy-oriented approach from the analytical approach, we shall refer to this form of egalitarianism in what follows as practical egalitarianism. It is in the context of such a practical egalitarianism that debates over the merits of income transfers from one person to another by political means are frequently conducted. Those who favor such income transfers are typically located on the left of the political spectrum while those who oppose them are generally on the political right. Because the reading public is frequently familiar with the debates over practical, but not analytical, egalitarianism, we often confuse one with the other. And we often think that those who are on the left of the political spectrum can have little or nothing in common with those on the political right. A major theme that emerged from the research presented at the Summer Institute for the Preservation of the History of Economics during its early years, however, has been that in point of fact those on the left and right may share a deep commitment to analytical egalitarianism. Such a shared commitment may align such seemingly politically distant speakers as James Buchanan and John Rawls who, as it turns out, are much closer intellectually *and* in policy space than many of us imagine.[1]

It is therefore fitting that a volume featuring contributions by James Buchanan, edited by those associated with him, begins with a passage from John Rawls's 1958 "Justice as Fairness." Rawls and Buchanan, who are politically at some distance, are nonetheless two key voices in the revival of analytical egalitarianism after the Second World War. It is equally fitting that we conclude the collection with previously unpublished correspondence between Rawls and Buchanan. The correspondence concludes with a letter from Rawls to Buchanan thanking him for a copy of the lecture given as a consequence of his being awarded the Nobel Prize for Economics.

The Forgotten Context of Analytical Egalitarianism

As we read the record, a worldview that abstracts from human differences flourished in the roughly one-hundred-year period bounded by Adam Smith's two great books (1759, 1776) and John Stuart Mill's death (1873). By the time Rawls revived analytical egalitarianism, its historical context had been lost. Rawls put forward recommendations that flow from his view of justice as the "fair" relationship between equals in which all inequalities are justified: "[I]t is also necessary that the various offices to which special benefits or burdens attach are open to all" (1958, 169). But he failed to point out that his recommendations would be satisfied by the view of an equilibrium in a competitive labor market advanced by Adam Smith in *The Wealth of Nations.* Perhaps only specialists in the history of economic ideas know that an equalization of the net advantages of employment was held out as a policy goal throughout the period of classical political economy.

Smith, and those who followed in his tradition, assumed that people were natural equals. Smith's analytical egalitarianism is based on a factual claim of natural equality that is more precise than Rawls's statement above, denying obvious natural inequality. Indeed, at the beginning and throughout much of the nineteenth century, social scientists endorsed the presumption that humans are the same in their capacity for language and trade (Peart and Levy 2005). Observed differences are then

1. Buchanan presented an early version of his "influences" paper at the 2003 Summer Institute: "Influences on My Work." Many in attendance, but not the editors of this volume, were surprised to see John Rawls listed there.

explained by incentives, luck, and history, and it is the "vanity of the philosopher" to conclude, incorrectly, that ordinary people are somehow different from the expert (Smith [1776] 1976, 1.2 § 4).

In Smith's account, competition gives all persons potential access to every position.[2] The notion of equilibrium allows us to abstract from random events and to allow for time to make adjustments. From these assumptions we obtain Smith's famous theorem that the net advantages of employment are equalized in a competitive market. Of course, pecuniary gain is not equalized but all pecuniary differences are compensated. One of the compensating factors is the approbation that results from employment in different occupations. We shall have much to say about the desire for approbation—sympathy—throughout this collection.

What might be appropriate treatment for a person who has been subjected to a sequence of unhappy random events? Smith worried about this possibility in his statements about the unfortunate lot of beggars and prostitutes, but he had nothing other than economic growth and private charity to recommend. Later writers in classical political economy proposed what we now call a social safety net, a guaranteed minimum existence with sufficient strings attached to attenuate moral hazard. Part 1 of this volume, "Politics, Markets and Equality," examines contemporary and classical economic policy with an eye to whether or not markets serve to effect economic reforms and practical equality. Here the conversation between Warren Samuels and James Buchanan in chapter 2 is most interesting; although both endorse analytical egalitarianism, the two scholars come to very different conclusions about the efficacy of democratic politics to effect reform. Acknowledging that Samuels is no "social-welfare maximizer," Buchanan points to the "hard question": "[T]he world's out there; it's a complex set of interacting people and institutions and behavior and everything else going on and . . . social science, generally, or economics, in particular, has a hard time getting a handle on how to look at that world. . . .We're looking almost necessarily, it seems to me . . . we're looking at that world from a window, a perspective, a predisposition on the way to look at it." Samuels adds that the real question that separates them is "whether we privilege the existing law or the opportunity to change the existing law." In Samuels's view, exchange pre-

2. This, of course, leaves aside the issue of those who are not included as "persons." The 2006 Summer Institute was much preoccupied with this theme, considering Mill's work to obtain the franchise for women. In fact, that year's Summer Institute T-shirt features an 1867 *Punch* caricature of Mill captioned "Pray clear the way there for these—a—persons." *Our* T-shirt caption reads "We Are All Persons Now."

supposes a distribution of rights and power: "If you want to talk about the rights structure of whose interests count, you should be doing that because that's this power structure within which trade takes place. And that power structure, in part—the part that I'm interested in at any rate—is legal rights, and legal rights come about in different ways. Whether you want that or not, whether you like it or not, that's the way it is." Hence the concern with the status of the status quo.[3]

One might well suggest that Rawls is a philosopher and, as such, he is correctly careful not to trespass on the discipline of economics.[4] This book provides a great deal of evidence to suggest that such demarcations—across time or space—are unhelpful. In economics, there is a familiar proposition from general equilibrium theory that if one market is out of equilibrium others must be as well. We argue here and elsewhere (Peart 2004; Peart and Levy 2005) that ideas and interpretations are similarly interrelated. If we do not understand how the classical economists, qua economists, analyzed a competitive equilibrium among natural equals, we will not be able to appreciate their work qua moral theorists. Rawls is careful to point out that his view of a just society requires a recognition of others as persons "with similar interests and feelings as oneself" (1958, 182). But if the desire for approbation from one's fellow creatures is part of the working toolkit of classical political economists, then it will be in their toolkit when they operate as moral philosophers. The desire for approbation recognizes that there is something that others, insofar as we regard them as our equals or peers, have to give us that differs from material goods.

The story that unfolds in this collection, however, is that both analytical egalitarianism and the reliance on sympathetic judgments were overthrown sometime after 1850. Thereafter, as the contributions to this volume by Peart and Levy and Leonard attest, notions of race and hierarchy came to infect economic and social analysis. The book sketches out some disastrous consequences of the transition to hierarchical thinking, and it makes the case that political economy in the classical tradition *rightly* presupposed human homogeneity and *rightly* rejected hierarchical presuppositions of any sort. Hence we celebrate the contributions by Buchanan and Rawls, who, we suggest, *rightly* helped revive the analytical equality presumption in the twentieth century.

The questions at issue between analytical egalitarians and their crit-

3. Buchanan presented the paper entitled "Status of the Status Quo" at the 2003 Summer Institute. References to Samuels's contributions are provided in the chapter 2.

4. We shall have more to say about this in our comments on the Buchanan-Rawls correspondence in chapter 19.

ics are whether everyone's preferences count equally and whether everyone is equally capable of making economic decisions.[5] In Smith's account, all people, philosophers and subjects alike, are motivated by fame and fortune, and we are all equally capable of making decisions. Since Smith is so important to our story, part 2 is explicitly concerned with "Smithian Themes." Here we take up the role of sympathy and the market in Smith, the nature of Smithian policy regarding the laboring poor, and, of course, the nature and significance of Smith's "invisible hand."

By contrast, the oppositional view holds that some among us are different from others. Since "difference" implies "superiority" in the period we study, we call this doctrine analytical hierarchicalism.[6] Difference may be within the public—as races or ethnic groups—or between the public and its advisers, the economic "experts." Part 3 therefore attends to the significance of the nature and role of experts in society. In the period we study, those who opposed the classical economists' presumption of homogeneity focused on two purported heterogeneities between the expert and his subject. First, the expert was presumed to be untainted by considerations of self-interest, while his subject is motivated by self-interest. Second, perhaps because of superior self-control or some other inherent difference, the expert is supposed to be "superior" to or smarter than the subject he studies. And it is important to note that this intellectual superiority is not merely a matter of better information; the expert with whom we are concerned is someone who simply doesn't trust all subjects, who holds that some will always be hopelessly prone to making persistent mistakes no matter how much we educate, train, and inculcate.

Since the attacks on analytical egalitarianism were mounted from

5. The notion of the "expert" is deliberately left broad here. The key feature of those we refer to as experts is that they are people who make recommendations about how others might achieve human happiness. Depending on the specific context involved in what follows, experts may be social commentators, biologists, or political economists. We provide a more restrictive, formal definition of an expert in Peart and Levy 2005 so that we can distinguish between an expert's direction and the advice that flows from "universal experience" by way of proverbial wisdom. In Adam Smith's account, philosophy is a *social* enterprise that begins with universal experience. His proverbial wisdom confirms the advice of financial theorists not to "put all their eggs in one basket." When *expert* and *proverb* point in different directions, we need to be precise.

6. We prefer the broader term, *postclassical* to the more familiar *neoclassical.* On the origin of the term *neoclassical,* see Colander 2001, 154ff.; on the transition to early "neoclassicism"—the "Marginal Revolution"—see the collection in Black, Coats, and Goodwin (1973). We find that the transition entailing the rise of hierarchical thinking, the loss of sympathy, and the endorsement of eugenic remaking infects a broad set of economists, not all of whom would be considered neoclassical. In Peart and Levy 2005, we argue that traditions within and outside of neoclassical economics—the Austrian School scattered by the coming of the Hitler era, as well as the London School and Chicago—revived the presupposition of equal competence.

outside economics—in literature, anthropology, and biology—part 4 examines the relationships among literature, biology, and economics. F. Y. Edgeworth captured the difference between the classical egalitarian framework in J. S. Mill and post-Darwinian ideas, which implied that education and other institutional changes would fail to produce the desired social good. In 1881, he wrote that "the authority of Mill, conveying an impression of what other Benthamites have taught openly, that all men, if not equal, are at least *equipotential,* in virtue of equal educatability" would "probably result in the ruin of the race" because it failed to take into account "*difference of quality*" among men (1881, 132).[7]

It is precisely this supposition of superiority that Smith opposed as the "vanity of the philosopher"; such vanity implies that the subject is in need of guidance from the expert.[8] It also implies that the expert will be predisposed to disapprove of (and even disallow) the subject making unfettered choices in a marketplace or in the direction of his or her affections in the household and elsewhere. As long as experts maintain that they possess insight into the sorts of preferences people "should" possess—if only people knew better—they must also accept, and may perhaps even demand, responsibility for directing those preferences until the subjects gain the sort of sophistication they enjoy. We suggest in this volume that the "science" of eugenics operationalizes this doctrine. By contrast, the classical economists' egalitarian notion of homogeneity—motivational and otherwise—and choices unfettered by the direction of one's "betters," go hand in hand.

Famously, Rawls objected that "classical utilitarianism" might have been used to justify slavery to the extent that slavery was a more efficient social system than free labor (Rawls 1958, 188). Rawls is, of course, careful to point out that it would be an "absurdity" (188) to think that the classical utilitarians actually made such an argument. But he fails to realize that his general statement against utilitarianism *is* a fair representation of F. Y. Edgeworth's neoclassical utilitarianism in which, in fact, Edgeworth *does* mount a utilitarian defense not of slavery but of eugenic policy. For Edgeworth, this was a way to replace low-capacity people with high-capacity ones to maximize social utility. It is important to realize that Edgeworth vigorously objects to the egalitarianism of the classical writers, Mill in particular, for whom everyone "counts as one." Classical utilitarianism is based on counting—decisions are made on the

7. Edgeworth calls Mill's equal educability argument "pre-Darwin prejudice" (1881, 132).

8. In Peart and Levy 2005 we examine Smith on how proverbs might provide such guidance, and we develop a technical account of how ordinary people might obtain much of the advice they require from the experience of others.

basis of majority—and the only way that doctrine has normative weight is if something akin to sympathy restrains the stronger from grabbing. And, of course, the slavery that most incensed the classical utilitarians was simply the grabbing of a weaker person by a stronger.

The Conversations

We now turn to the essays in this collection. We begin with the sequence "Politics, Markets, and Equality," which opens with what is arguably the most important twentieth-century conversation on the nature and significance of analytical egalitarianism to policy analysis—that between James Buchanan and Warren Samuels on the role of government. If society is composed as equals, then, as Buchanan has argued, reform and government might be conceived of as exchange. The social contract is the ratification of exchange. Here, as J. S. Mill held in the nineteenth century, the status quo constitutes a starting point for reform and reform requires compensation. On the other side of this, if power is unequally distributed in society, we have Samuels's insistence that exchange occurs on an unequal footing or not at all.

Continuing on with the role of government, David Levy and Sandra Peart examine the classical origins of Buchanan's government as exchange, emphasizing the role of sympathy in the classical theory of economic policy, the sympathetic process that helps both to motivate and to constrain economic policy as a type of exchange. Samuel Hollander examines Marx's analysis of transitions from one economic system to another when the individuals (and policymakers) who inhabit those systems are equally self-interested. He proceeds to highlight some common ground relating to market processes between Marx and Engels and the modern "classical liberals," Mises and Hayek. Eric Crampton and Andrew Farrant revisit the socialist calculation debate in the tradition of Buchanan and Hume's worst-case political economy. Rather than questioning the information or knowledge available (or otherwise) to economic planners or other public choosers, Crampton and Farrant focus on worst-case motivational suppositions: private and public chooser alike are Homo economicus always and everywhere. The authors argue that worst-case theorizing about government à la Buchanan necessitates adherence to a principle of motivational homogeneity or symmetry: private and public chooser alike are modeled as pursuing their private interest. Failure to model private and public chooser symmetrically will, of course, unduly bias one's analysis in favor of private or public choice per se.

Not unsurprisingly, since, as noted earlier, Adam Smith is perhaps the most famous forceful proponent of analytical egalitarianism, part 2 is entitled "Smithian Themes." We begin the section with a provocative selection from Deirdre McCloskey's new book, *Bourgeois Virtues,* in which McCloskey celebrates the Smithian propensity to "truck, barter, and exchange." She defends the capitalist system as a system of fair exchange. Rather than corrupting bourgeois life, as is the fashion in some circles to suggest, McCloskey holds that Smithian self-interest is essentially fulfilling, productive, and cooperative for "the capitalist system provides a field in which ordinary people can exercise their abilities harmlessly." She points out how poorly noneconomists among the self-declared intellectual élite understand that fair exchange is a positive-sum affair. Perhaps the actions of the American rich, who give away the wealth they struggled to acquire, vividly described by McCloskey, are exchanges of another sort, attempts to obtain approbation. This is an ill-understood exchange. One hundred and fifty years ago J. S. Mill wrote that if a rich British person attempted to follow this admirable American practice his relatives would have him declared mad.

As we have come to more fully appreciate the role of the cooperative element in Smith, a natural question follows. Why has Smith's emphasis on sympathy been so neglected? Leonidas Montes tackles this question by examining how the separation of Smith's two great works, *Wealth of Nations* and *Theory of Moral Sentiments,* occurred, a puzzle widely known as Das Adam Smith Problem. Montes argues that the economic hegemony of Great Britain played an important role in shaping the reception of Smith in Germany as the founder of the school of self-interest and laissez-faire. Warren Samuels introduces us to his project on what is possibly the most famous of all Smithian themes, the invisible hand. The invisible hand is frequently invoked as the equilibrating mechanism that facilitates the attainment of wage equality, alluded to earlier. Samuels shows us just how deeply and broadly the phrase is ingrained in economic discourse today. Maria Pia Paganelli examines how Smith's position on usury makes sense in the context of a moral philosophy that acknowledges systematic bias and, as a consequence, prefers a middling estimate. Eric Schliesser argues for a sort of "practical egalitarianism" in Smith with the suggestion that the analytical core of the *Wealth of Nations* aims at aiding large numbers of working poor.

If the presumption that we are all the same has any claim to analytical teeth, then a question arises: what is the role of the expert in an economy?[9]

9. William Easterly put this question to us when we sent him a copy of our book (Peart and Levy 2005).

This, too, has been a recurring theme at the Summer Institute, and we devote part 3, "The Role of the Expert," to it. Here a contribution by Sandra Peart and David Levy examines how, historically, the expert economist has been exempted from the presupposition of analytical egalitarianism by those who opposed the classical economists' presumption of homogeneity. The expert was presumed to be untainted by considerations of self-interest while his subject was motivated by self-interest. Second, perhaps because of superior self-control or some other inherent difference, the expert was supposed to be "superior" to or smarter than the subject he or she studies. Andrew Farrant reexamines Frank Knight's political critique of planning with an eye on the expert, arguing that Knight's critique of planning is predicated on a worst-case logic that anticipates public choice arguments concerning the motives of planners. According to Farrant, Knight recognized that the incentives in "planned" economies were such that planners, like the rest of us, was self-interested. M. Ali Khan attempts to untangle the role of the expert in a free society as he reads *The Road to Serfdom* some sixty years after its publication. In this attempt, Khan identifies a need for (arbitrary) judgment beyond some threshold of analysis as a result in part of the impartial and local knowledge of any so-called expert. Juan Pablo Couyoumdjian focuses on the problem of hiring a foreign expert when advice seekers have imperfect knowledge. As long as advice seekers are unable adequately to determine and screen the most relevant attributes of a potential expert, their decision will involve nontrivial risks. In Couyoumdjian's view, this was the predicament faced by advice seekers in nineteenth-century Chile.

Much of the resistance to the classical economist's presumption of analytical homogeneity resided in other disciplines, notably anthropology, biology, and literature. It is therefore appropriate to include a section in the book on "Literature, Biology, and Economics." Rather than include what are becoming widely known discussions of the attacks on economics by literary figures, we begin the section with a call for something of the opposite. Tyler Cowen defends the notion that we can gain from trade and the relevance of fiction to social science investigation. He suggests that novels are more like economic models than is commonly believed. Some novels present verbal models of reality, while others might be something like a simulation akin to how simulations are used in economics.

In the account of Peart and Levy, the opposition to economics in Britain occurred largely as a result of the attacks on the presumption of human homogeneity from biology. The authors trace the opposition to race-blind accounts from Thomas Carlyle to the cofounder (with Francis Galton) of eugenics, W. R. Greg, and then to James Hunt and the Anthropological Society of the 1860s. Early eugenicists' characterization of race influenced economic analysis in the postclassical period. Next comes a contribution by Thomas Leonard that takes the history of eugenics to America. As he attempts to fill a gap in the history of eugenics and Progressive era American economics, which have so far been separate and seemingly unrelated entities, Leonard shows how American eugenicists supported policy interventions such as minimum wage legislation in order to "thin the herd" and get rid of inferior workers. By contrast, Gordon Tullock's reflections on economics, sociobiology, and sympathy find common themes where historically there has been much opposition. These are precisely the confusions that arise when simple-minded right/left labels are applied to policy analysis without much real information: the view that "progressive" economics must be unrelated to eugenic thinking is simply incorrect. Moreover, those whose presuppositions lean toward the dismissal of the "Chicago School" as simple-minded right-wing politics might be surprised by our history: the analytical egalitarian arguments that were revived by Chicago, the London School of Economics, and the Austrian School provided a key means by which economic analysis may be insulated from eugenic or otherwise hierarchical analyses. Such was the importance of the Rawls-Buchanan attempt to revive and operationalize analytical egalitarianism.

And so we return to the Rawls-Buchanan connection. Part 5 lets the theorists speak for themselves. Readers who have made their way through this introduction will perhaps come to appreciate why the conversation turns, early on, to a comparison of Rawls and Adam Smith. They will also, perhaps, no longer be surprised to read in Buchanan's words that (jointly with Geoffrey Brennan) he has been working on "some very interesting Rawls-like applications to normative tax theory" and that he characterizes himself as developing "the spirit of your [Rawls's] original position" in such a way as to "offer a good response to some of your critics."

Bibliography

Black, R. D. Collison, A. W. Coats, and Craufurd D. W. Goodwin. 1973. *The Marginal Revolution in Economics.* Durham: Duke University Press.

Colander, David. 2001. *The Lost Art of Economics: Essays on Economics and the Economics Profession.* Cheltenham: Edward Elgar.

Edgeworth, F. Y. 1881. *Mathematical Psychics.* London: C. Kegan Paul.

Peart, Sandra J. 2004. "On the 'Bitter Quarrel' between Economics and Its Enemies." *History of Economic Ideas* 12 (2004): 75–84.

Peart, Sandra J., and David M. Levy. 2005. *"The Vanity of the Philosopher": From Equality to Hierarchy in Post-classical Economics.* Ann Arbor: University of Michigan Press.

Rawls, John. 1958. "Justice as Fairness." *Philosophical Review* 67 (April): 164–94.

Smith, Adam. [1776] 1976. *An Inquiry into the Nature and Causes of the Wealth of Nations.* Edited by W. B. Todd. Oxford: Clarendon.

PART 1 • Politics, Markets, and Equality

2 • Politics as Exchange or Politics as Power
Two Views of Government

James M. Buchanan
Warren J. Samuels

SJP: We're all in for a real treat this morning.

When we first invited Warren to give some talks at the Summer Institute, he enthusiastically agreed. And then we got the additional idea of asking him to have a conversation with Jim Buchanan, and he, again, enthusiastically agreed.

He did ask me . . . or remind me . . . that he thought the Summer Institute was about preserving the history of economic thought and this was rather present. And I responded to him that, "We're gonna make history on preserving economic thought today."

This has been one of the most interesting intellectual debates of the twentieth century. And so today Warren and Jim are going to talk about their differences and perhaps some commonalities.

JMB: The reason I think that . . . David [Levy] and Sandra [Peart] had the idea of inviting us to have this conversation, after Warren had kindly agreed to participate in the whole session, is based on a dialogue/discussion that Warren and I have had for . . . going on a long time now, for over thirty years now. . . . He published a piece . . . no doubt we'll get into that . . . he published a piece in the *Journal of Law and Economics* (Samuels 1971) and then I wrote a piece in response (more or less a criticism of it) (Buchanan 1972) and then we had a *long* correspondence about that afterwards . . . back and forth. . . . I give Warren full credit for entrepreneurship here, what he did after a few years, which bottled up that correspondence and put it together and published it as an exchange between Warren Samuels and Jim Buchanan (Buchanan and Samuels 1975).

Actually, as it turns out—now this is sort of my lesson to the rest of

---

James M. Buchanan [JMB], Distinguished Professor Emeritus of Economics, George Mason University, and University Distinguished Professor Emeritus of Economics and Philosophy, Virginia Polytechnic and State University; Warren J. Samuels [WJS], Professor Emeritus of Economics, Michigan State University; Sandra J. Peart [SJP]; Q = Questioner. 29 July 2004. Summer Institute for the Preservation of the Study of the History of Economics 26–30 July 2004.

you—it turns out that has been a very, very well-received piece, the fact that . . . that exchange of correspondence where both of us are representing our side, and the idea [that this was] in an open way in which we didn't have any idea that it would ultimately be published—this was just back and forth. . . . And the fact that that has appealed to many people . . . we've had, at least I have had, a lot of comments on that exchange. And that's happened to me another time, and this is the lesson I'm sort of suggesting.

About six years ago or so the people at Munich, Hans-Werner Sinn, had been trying for years to get Richard Musgrave and I to have a debate, and finally we organized one at that center for economic studies in Munich. And so we had a weeklong dialogue/debate/discussion. And at that time we didn't have any idea that they planned to publish the thing, but then they published it. And it's been published in this little book MIT Press printed called *Public Finance and Public Choice* (Buchanan and Musgrave 1999), and that, again, like the one with Warren, has been very popular actually; that has sold . . . that book has sold extremely well.

And so the idea is that people seem to like discussion amongst people who can join issues and approach the issues in a one-on-one way without either talking past each other or, in effect, just simply criticizing each other. It seems to me there is enough commonality of discussion in both those cases—both with Dick Musgrave, on the one hand, and with Warren, on the other—that it makes for an interesting exchange, and people enjoy the sort of dialogue part; they enjoy the dialogic aspects of these discussions. At least in this experience, in both cases it's been very salutary. So anytime you have a chance, in a way an opportunity to do this kind of thing, I think I'd suggest that you try it out, because it has . . . it has certainly worked for me in both of these cases.

Now in some cases it won't work because [in] some cases you have people who really talk past each other. Jim Tobin, who was a friend of mine, was . . . one of the nicest economists I've ever known. On public debt, for example, he and I just talked past [each other]; we could not join, we could never join the argument, just simply talking past each other. We could never have carried out a dialogue comparable to the one that Warren and I had like . . . like this. So it requires particulars of the two people. But, on the other hand, if you have a chance to organize it, it's worth doing.

And I do think it fits in with the . . . it has already shown up in Warren's comments on my . . . presentation the other day (Buchanan 2004). The difference between us *does* lie in this basic fundamental way of how we look at the world and how we can conceive the world of the political economy that we live with. And no doubt we will get into that, and that is . . . central, but I did want to mention at the outset this usefulness of having this kind of a dialogue. . . .Warren, do you want to take over?

WJS: I appreciate the opportunity to be here. . . .

Well, when we talked yesterday about what we were doing here, I . . . I had interpreted what we were saying was to make a short presentation about where we came from. So let me tell you where I come from.

I may be one of the very few people who got through the 1950s inoculated against extreme "isms." When we were driving over here, it was said that somebody shifted from Marxism to Austrianism. Well, I never had an "ism" of any kind to shift to any other "ism." Why was that? . . .

Well, when I was in high school, I learned several things. I learned that there was Euclidean geometry and there was non-Euclidean geometry, and that it wasn't a question of truth or falsity. It was a question of logic . . . and as long as the logic worked, it was no problem; it was a question of different premises. And that (1) under certain circumstances Euclidean geometry worked, and (2) under other circumstances Lobachevskian and Reimannian geometry worked. So there is a kind of relativism here.

I also learned, because of a teacher I had who gave me a book by James Harvey Robinson, that you could tell different stories of American history, particularly constitutional history. That opened my mind, and I'm sure that was her intention, to . . . be careful about buying into anything . . . whole hog without knowing what you were doing. And if you did that, you probably weren't buying into it whole hog.

Now another thing that happened to me since I became a young adult in the late 1940s and the early 1950s was [I gained] experience with liberalism versus conservatism. And it struck me, in summary, that liberalism meant different things to different people, conservatism meant different things to different people, that there was an awful lot of potential overlap, that these were not definitions of the world in any meaningful sense other than sentiments, and that the sum of all of this was utter confusion and . . . one could not rely upon either of these, or any version of these, as a reliable definition of reality.

And then, probably because I was going through adolescence . . . [I had] the desire to be independent and autonomous and, the other hand, to have the confidence of knowing you're under the family wing, and that's why you have all the tension between that gives rise to teenage rebellion. . . . I understood that there was this conflict in society . . . generated in part by virtue of individuals going through all this and working it out differently and also because you have the problem of reconciling the individual to society.

My inclination throughout my life has been, contrary to the perceptions of many other people, libertarian to the point of anarchist. But that has been tempered by an enormous, deep, strong recognition that what anybody calls libertarianism or anarchism carries with it its own system of social control, and that without recognition of that, and doing something about it . . . or doing something with it, it was simply another matter of sentiments.

So, by the time I finished college, I was inoculated against all of this, about things that were bothering other people, and I understood . . . why they were being bothered by it—it didn't bother me because I didn't feel a need to become this or that. What I wanted was essentially a nonideological approach to the economic role of government. And when I was an undergraduate taking a course in government and business, the textbook that was used was not an ordinary textbook (in fact, I don't think it was really a textbook at all); it was Dahl and Lindblom's *Politics, Economics, and Welfare,* which really hasn't gone very far in influencing the profession, but it had a big influence on me. And the influence was precisely this: it convinced me that you could take a strongly positive, as opposed to normative, approach to the economic role of government—that you didn't have to absorb and give effect to antecedent normative assumptions called liberalism or conservatism or anarchism or what have you. At the same time . . . you could call this schizophrenia if you like . . . I was aware that there were normative premises . . . ideology or what Schumpeter called vision or what have you . . . that w[ere] inevitable, and today, of course, I would attribute that to the hermeneutic circle problem.

So I am sensitive to that, [and] I wrote in one autobiographical piece, near the end, that I . . . strongly believe in what I've . . . had to say about the economic role of government, but I am sensitive to the fact that . . . it's a subject of the hermeneutic problem.

What I wanted . . . was not just to give effect to some sentimental belief system, but I wanted to understand what really was going on whatever one's beliefs; whatever one's ideological presumptions. And then I eventually came to understand, since I was anarchistically inclined (I was very much a fan of Thomas Jefferson and yet . . . the Jeffersonian ideal of every man being a property owner, and every . . . body having a piece of property, and . . . participating in the government that controlled them), that the reason why that didn't work, unfortunately, was not because somebody had a different ideology but because we had forces in the country of economic development in which we no longer were gonna have local markets that were isolated; we were going to have national markets, that the logic of what we'll call the merger solution to externalities brought about larger and larger systems of social control, if you like, so that the Hamiltonian approach to development was empirically—not normatively—was empirically more correct than Jefferson, *as it turned out*. And that convinced me, since I thought this was a correct analysis, that I *was* right, that one should *not* define the world in terms of how you would prefer it to be but rather in terms of what is really going on.

So arguments over constitutional interpretation, I thought, were very fascinating—I was a very intense student of constitutional law—but it made no difference to me which side won; it made no difference to me whether the arguments seemed good to me or interesting or persuasive—what really impressed me was that, however the court held, it was establishing, in Commons's words, "the legal foundations of the economic system." And that was really what was going on—that it was structuring the economic system, it was changing the economic system, that no matter what the ideology of the people was, what happened in the . . . eighteenth and nineteenth centuries was the transformation of law, the legal system in this country, from a rural, agrarian, landed property system to an urban, industrial, nonlanded property system. And ideology was simply the false consciousness, if you like, through which we viewed this.

Well, then, . . . in my last year I was exposed to Commons's work, and that's why I went to Wisconsin. . . . I wasn't turned off by neoclassicism, but it seemed to me that it was inadequate . . . in other words, I liked, if I had known it at the time, Abba Lerner's second thing—that politics goes on forever and economics is not just . . . exchange once you've solved the political problems. But, as I learned later, I could quote from Paul Samuelson that "politics is economics by other means"—that [if] you can't maximize within the market, you use the law to change the market, okay? So I was really very much taken with Commons, . . . and fortunately I had the tail end of the regime of his students, and we were not told to hate neoclassicism but that neoclassicism had its place, but . . . there were other variables involved.

Q: Where did you go to undergraduate school?

WJS: At University of Miami. I was going to go to Princeton and study astronomical physics, but I didn't do that for two reasons: I met my wife

. . . or I had met my wife and decided that I didn't want to be a thousand miles away from her, and, secondly, I was not terribly happy with the kind of jobs theoretical physicists were going into at that time.

So . . . what I've done since then is to try to develop what I will call a positive welfare economics as to whose interests count—not what is the optimal solution because I don't buy optimality analysis, because you have to constrain everything to reach that, and the work that I've done in . . . the economic role of government or law and economics or whatever you want to call it—the economics of property rights—is just a continuation of this . . . attitude that I've had: to try to minimize the impact of ideology. I didn't need ideology in my work; I tried to minimize it. I'm sure it's there, but . . . the tersest statement I can make of it is that I believe in openness to change. As an empirical fact. And therefore, since I agree that . . . there's a role for normative and subjective motivations and movements, that there not only is but should be these, . . . I did not feel myself driven by the need to promote a particular "ism."

Now, having said that, I will . . . conclude with another schizophrenic view . . . which is very apropos of the present situation in the United States.

On the one hand . . . the short version of this is that sometimes I see the United States as a narrow plutocracy and, on the other hand . . . at other times, I see the United States, as several people have called it, as man's last great hope for enlightened democracy. The schizophrenia is that the United States . . . is exactly that—but I can enlarge upon it by saying that there are two strands at least of . . . America: one is the vision of Jefferson and others of a philosophy of live and let live—a philosophy of democracy and pluralism, of progress—but then, on the other hand, you have the history of a war party, of the United States as . . . just like any other country . . . trying to extend its influence in the world. So, even more narrowly, I would say it's whether you have American exceptionalism or you don't have American exceptionalism. I am caught on that, and today, with regard to the terrorist threat, it's a very, very different world. But . . . I'll stop there.

JMB: Well . . .

WJS: . . . How have I disturbed you?

[Laughter]

JMB: Well . . . you haven't disturbed me very much. I . . . was very interested in that autobiographical sketch because it's given me an insight into . . . where you're coming from, that I had never quite appreciated before, and certainly I think this may explain why you and I, although we categorically disagree along several dimensions, can also have a good dialogue because basically I think we start at a very deep foundational level, from very similar roots here in the sense that I, too, like you, am . . . at the really deepest level, basically I'm a philosophical anarchist, or libertarian, if you want to call it that. So that's where we're ultimately coming from, and, knowing that, I think we share a common starting point in a certain sense.

But the real question is . . . that we diverge once we go beyond that. Now, I think, if you remember, that I did acknowledge, in that correspondence, that I had falsely accused you at one point in my article of . . . belonging to the group of the social welfare-function maximizers—and you're not that at all; . . . it was just a misreading of your whole position, and it was based on my view that anybody who didn't agree with me was a social welfare maximizer. . . .

[Laughter.]

But the question comes down—the really hard question, and there are lots of hard questions here, but the real question comes down, as I've said many times and said the other day, too, that is, the world's out there; it's a complex set of interacting people and institutions and behavior and everything else going on and . . . social science, generally, or economics, in particular, has a hard time getting a handle on how to look at that world. And I . . . come back to . . . and cite Nietzsche all the time on this, and he talked about looking at this world . . . through different windows. Now that's sort of acknowledging, in one sense, that the world is there—we're not getting into this sort of idea that the world is strictly what we make it up in our mind—the world is there, there is something there. But the question is: how do we look at this world? We're looking almost necessarily, it seems to me . . . at that world from a window, a perspective, a predisposition on the way to look at it. And if you look at it differently you get different aspects of that world, you stress different aspects, and you look at it differently, and the question is, and my inclination is to say, that at one level . . . I think using the word *ideology* is not very proper here in the sense that . . . it doesn't carry much meaning here. It seems to me it's a sort of a normative vision that we sort of have—and maybe it's something we *can't* choose, maybe we *can* choose. (And this gets into something I mentioned the other day—whether or not we can choose to look at the world a certain way or is that just sort of preprogrammed . . . it's a difficult question.) But the point is that we get differing aspects of the way we look at this complex world depending on which window we are looking at it from.

Now, where Warren and I reach our main differences is, I argue that you are necessarily going to look at that world through what I would call a kind of a normative vision, one way or the other, and he seems to think, and he expressed it again today and he has in his other work and this was our basic little . . . controversy, really, is that somehow or another there is one window that is pure. That is, there's a window out here that doesn't require this sort of precommitted disposition, that somehow or another there is an antiseptic vision that is possible that he has tried to achieve. And we might say, well, you really haven't got there, and it's impossible, and there are implications of your vision and therefore we can read back into . . . the way you look at the world, we can read a normative vision into it. Yet he wants to seem somehow to stay with this, what I would call an illusion, that, in fact, he can look at the world as an "antiseptic scientist" in the purer sense, whereas I am much more willing to acknowledge that the way I look at the world is in a sense a precommitment to look at the world that way. And this is not necessarily a conscious *choice* of a way to look at the world—it's not a *chosen* ideology and then moving toward the ideology. It's rather that you're sort of preprogrammed to look at the world that way. I . . . don't really think I could look at the world much differently from the way I do look at the world given my conversion, and it was a conversion, as I said the other day; it was akin to a religious-type conversion when I looked at the world . . . started looking at the world as a set of interacting individuals. And that appealed to my fundamental libertarian anarchist roots here, because, until Frank Knight really changed my world, I couldn't see the world that way. And the world seemed chaotic, it seemed confused, and all of a sudden things clicked, and I began to see the world that way. And now that becomes a kind of a normative vision, I must acknowledge, and it's a desirable world. And that's the way I look at the world, and I interpret the world in that framework, and that's the fundamental difference, I think, between us.

Now what I think is another aspect of it that he touched on right at the end that is very interesting. I think . . . go back to my Nietzsche metaphor again. I think it's possible, and this came up a little bit yesterday, not quite, but it's possible that we can simultaneously hold views by looking at the world differently through differing windows. We don't necessarily *strictly* stay within one predisposition; we can sort of back off and say, well, I don't like that and that way of looking at the world, but I can see what you're talking about, you see. And I can see Warren's position in this. I can see how he looks at the world as essentially people exercising power over each other through the . . . legal institutions that exist and carry on or, as he said, as we can see the American structure as a kind of a plutocracy. And we can see that people are exploiting other people, and we can see that people take advantage of other people, and we can examine the unfairness that is proceeded. One thing that has driven me in a normative sense more strongly than anything else is I *can't stand* unfairness and I *can't stand* people getting ahead of the game unfairly. I hate the rich; everybody knows that. I hated the Kennedys with a passion—absolute utter and total passion, and I don't like people buying their way through some politics. So I can see an aspect of the world that's very close to Marx in a very differing sort of framework, but, on the other hand, I don't *like* to look at the world that way, I *want* to look at the world differently. And somehow or another, it seems to me that I, personally, have a kind of a moral obligation, if you want to call it that, to look at the world from a window that does, in fact, emphasize the positive features. . . .

And I go back . . . we were all surprised, I think, . . . a month ago . . . with the Reagan funeral celebrations. It seemed to me as if the American people were just *longing* for something that would bring them together—that would somehow bring back a kind of a spirit of . . . of our whole civility, civil order, civic order that Reagan, himself, was able to tap into, and his success was based on that. Now, sure, you can look at Reagan in lots of different ways, but he did convey to the people, generally, a kind of a *spirit* of America, and I surely share the view . . . that, when you get down to this break that Warren mentions, I think America *is* exceptional. I am a *firm* advocate of American exceptionalism, and I think we are diverging more and more from Europe in . . . many respects here.

But my point is I have a moral obligation to look at the world through one window, and I think this distinguishes me from Warren here—he wants to shed himself of his moral obligation to look at the world through any particular window. And the main struggle I have with that is the idea that there can be a window in which that's not in there one way or the other. There is no doubt degrees in which we can do that.

But . . . that's sort of where we come down and split off here, after having started from . . . commonality.

WJS: I agree with much of what Jim says descriptively and even, to some extent, normatively. I, too, don't like unfairness; I don't feel a moral obligation to adopt any particular system of morality or ethics or justice or whatnot and view the world through that. My feeling is, given the limits . . . hermeneutic and otherwise . . . I don't think in terms of moral obligation . . . but my preference is for a division of labor. There is no reason why people can't do what Jim does and look through a particular normative pane of glass, but I also think that if you're going to have a grasp on what's really going on in the world (I think this is Hayek's rationale as well in part) you need to have . . . as solid knowledge as you can get as to what is really going on. Even though there are going to be normative premises, biases, or ideologies, or whatever you want to call it, that one . . . can extirpate, that one should try as much as one can to develop this body of knowledge without any pretense that it is going to be pure. So . . . the "pure" version of this I don't like, I can't accept. But I do think the effort should be there, consciously, to find out what is really going on.

I am going to return to that in a minute.

I once published an article in a German journal on three paradigms of distribution. One was the productivity paradigm, the second was the exploitation paradigm, and the third was the Max Weber appropriation paradigm that had no normative assumptions—it's just people jockeying for a position to get at the dinner table to get more or less out of the income stream. Okay? But without any attribution of exploitation, Marxist or otherwise, or you deserve what you got because you're productive. Okay. And I think that approach is . . . really mutual and enables you to isolate, but not necessarily to exclude, considerations of justice.

Now . . . how did I get to my present position? I guess there's one thing I should have said earlier. As an undergraduate, I had, in effect, three courses in the history of economics, and [in] graduate school I had another three or four courses in the history of economics. Why? Because I had Jim Early's year long course in it; Martin Bronfenbrenner taught distribution theory . . . to a large extent that way; Gene Rotwein taught imperfect competition [theory] that way. So, if I hadn't been . . . even a middling sort of an historian of economic thought, having had it so much, it would have been . . . almost a miracle. So what I'm getting at is I've had a lot of training in the history of economic thought and what came from this . . . this is egoism, now, and immodesty . . . what came . . . and it may be false as well—but what came from this, I think, is the ability to juggle different schools of thought, different bodies of thought, different definitions of reality at the same time. I believe I can think like an Austrian. think like a Marxist. think like an Ayresian. think like a common person, think like a mercantilist—without buying into them, okay? I can hold them at arm's length.

Now, with regard to this business about the dichotomy of Abba Lerner . . . let me give you a couple examples. Consider maternal benefits, or maternity benefits. I don't care what your view is on that. I would say this: maternity benefits can be accomplished either by individual negotiation with an employer, through collective bargaining, through legislation, or through litigation. Okay. If you want to talk about the rights structure of whose interests count, you should be doing that because that's this power structure within which trade takes place. And that power structure, in part—the part that I'm interested in at any rate—is legal rights, and legal rights come about in different ways. Whether you want that or not, whether you like it or not, that's the way it is. There's going to be something with regard to whose interests count with regard to maternity benefits, okay?

Now, I'll give you another example: surrogate motherhood. Along comes technology that enables us to have surrogate motherhood. You can approach that, as I am sure most of you are aware, in a number of different ways—legally, philosophically, morally. One thing is ubiquitous, and that is the feeling that everyone who's involved in surrogate motherhood should have their rights protected.

Now what are those rights? You're gonna have litigation, you're gonna have legislation . . . *something will come of this.* The child's rights, the biological parents' rights, the surrogate mother's rights . . . I personally have no particular feeling on this. I am not an expert on this except to the extent that I'm telling you about it. What I insist upon, and I think this is *absolutely nonideological*— okay?—is that there is going to be a law governing the respective rights of the parties, who are parties, and what their respective rights are gonna be. Who haven't I mentioned? Grandparents, okay? The courts, and legislation, will ultimately determine who has a piece of this pie, whose interests are exposed to others' interests, whose interests are gonna count. This is going to happen. You may not like it, but it's a fact of life, and it's going to be a body of covering law. This is an empirical statement just like the fact that we had bagels, lox, and cream cheese for breakfast. . . . There's no ideology involved.

[Laughter.]

I do not believe that this is a conservative view or a liberal view, an anarchical view; it may run against certain people's sentiments, but I would insist that we try to develop a legal/economic analysis of things like that in this way, and I believe that is . . . not subject to the hermeneutic circle. I may be wrong; I still have the asterisk about that.

Now, when I wrote this article that Jim was telling you about in the *Journal of Law and Economics,* about red cedar trees, I knew that some people might get exercised about red cedar trees, others might get exercised about . . . apple trees. And I knew this was Virginia and it was an apple-growing state, etc., but I didn't think it would bother so many people as it bothered Jim.

What can I say? There's going to be a law governing whose interests count. Okay? Whether you like it or not, whether you like one tree or another tree, there's going to be a law. In a broader model there's going to be morals, there's going to be mores, there's going to be custom, but I'm just talking about the law here.

I think I'll stop there.

Oh, one other thing.

[Laughter.]

In that wonderful—I have it here, I forgot to mention it—in that wonderful exchange of lectures and comments with Musgrave, two things came out. Jim . . . said that he was motivated to hate the federal government because of what happened in the Civil War, the Civil War period. And this is the same federal government of the United States that attracted Musgrave to North America to escape from Hitler. This is the same America of American exceptionalism that Jim has this reservation about. I can sympathize with both of these guys because I think that the South should have had the right to secede; I . . . did not then and do not now support slavery, and I certainly sympathize as . . . my father came to this country and my mother's parents came to this country to escape the crap of the Old World. So I can sympathize with Buchanan, I can sympathize with Musgrave.

What I'm smiling about is that I think, as much as I can sympathize with both of them, I think that having this reaction or any reaction to the Civil War or having Musgrave's reaction to Hitler or anything like that is a too-thinned, slender basis on which to develop a theory, even an ideology, of government. And he [Buchanan] doesn't buy it either because he thinks about American exceptionalism, and this is the same America that includes the North having beat up on the South.

[Laughter.]

JMB: Well, I acknowledge that I'm split down the middle on a lot of these things.

[Laughter.]

. . . I don't deny that. But, for purposes of clarification, let me . . . just summarize the red cedar case because then it'll show you where we . . . did differ in that one context.

This was in 1927 as I remember . . . I've got it here, but we'll see, a 1927 case that went up to all the way to the Supreme Court. What had happened was . . . there had been a development, a natural event, a development of this kind of fungus that grew on cedar trees, and it didn't harm cedar trees at all. But if the fungus grew on the cedar trees, if there was an apple tree within . . . oh, a half a mile of the cedar tree, it would kill or damage, severely damage, the apple tree. So . . . all of a sudden there was an interaction between the apple growers and the cedar tree growers that hadn't happened before. And so this came up . . . and so the Virginia state legislature, upon petition by the apple growers, simply passed legislation that allowed the state entomologists to go and look and condemn the cedar trees and force the cedar tree owners to cut down the cedar trees if they were . . . near the apple orchards without compensation.

Now, Warren's reading of that case—and it went all through the courts, and it was approved, and the courts approved this legislative action—Warren's reading of that case was the courts . . . the legislature and the courts . . . simply had to make a decision between the values of the damages to the apple growers . . . and the damages to the . . . to the cedar tree owners for having to cut their trees down. And they made a decision—now this is more or less arbitrary—that the law, in a sense, is going to decide one or the other . . . there's going to be a clarification here, clarify[ing] this particular interaction or interdependence that emerged.

The reason I didn't agree with that, and my criticism of Warren's position on that, was that . . . what happened was there was in existence a set of property rights—there was a law—and that the apple tree owners did not have any property right in the cedar trees prior to this happening. This happened. It created interdependence, but that also created a potential for gains-from-trade. And the proper way for this to have been resolved would have been for the apple growers . . . either themselves, voluntarily or through collective action, to have organized in such a way that they would, in fact, either buy off . . . or compensate the cedar tree owners, and if it's a gain, if the damage to the apple crop was much more than the damage to the [apple] trees, then there would have been a Coase-type bargain, and they would have bought off the cedar tree owners, and you would have had a voluntaristic Wicksell-Pareto-type solution to the problem. As opposed to coming and bringing politics in . . . anytime that there's a conflict here and saying, "Well, there's got to be a law and, therefore, whoever has the most authority can get the legislature, the majority in the legislature, to pass the law; that, in fact, is the way it should come out." That's the way it comes out, quite arbitrarily in certain situations.

Well, that's the basis for our discussion. . . . [H]e wrote a piece, then I wrote a piece, and then that correspondence emerged, but it always goes back to . . . whether or not there is a kind of a legitimacy in that which is, and we got into this . . . discussion about the status quo—we had a conference in Blacksburg last year about this . . . the relevance and the status of the status quo, and I think you circulated your piece [Samuels 2004]. . . . So that is the fundamental debate between us—whether or not you look at the world in that sort of different way.

But, I want to switch off that now and go back a little bit to what Warren was saying. . . .

WJS: Can I comment on this . . .

JMB: Sure.

WJS: . . . so we don't lose it?

JMB: Yeah.

WJS: There's gonna be . . . we agree there's going to be a law. The question is whether we privilege the existing law or the opportunity to change the existing law. The fact of the matter is that I did not argue in the paper, as Jim . . . acknowledges, what was the right thing to do. What I described was what happened and then went on to interpret this. The law changed from L_1 to L_2, and that meant that under the circumstances of this red cedar rust the bargaining power in the market changed from the red cedar tree owner to the apple orchard owner. And . . . generalizing that, I suggested that . . . one thing that law does is structure, what I called, in a nonpejorative sense, mutual coercion in the market.

Now, apropos . . . there's a footnote . . . the Wicksell-Pareto connection here: one difference between Jim and me is that he buys Wicksell with regard to his use of it—the emphasis on gains-from-trade—but does not buy what Wicksell himself says should be anterior to that, namely, agreement on distribution, which I take to be agreement on the structure of rights. And I insist that in the real world that, too, is an issue, in other words, the political part of Lerner's statement.

Let me allude to a different example between Jim and me. He [and Gordon Tullock] published an article in the AER [*American Economic Review,* Buchanan and Tullock 1975], and I, with Al Schmid, wrote a response to that, and the AER turned it down. I sent it to Gordon, who may or may not remember this, and he published it [Samuels and Schmid 1976]. Our argument was that the Paretian analysis that Jim used was fine, but we wondered why, in setting out the rights within which Pareto optimality was developed through trade, . . . he always assigns the rights to the producer and not to the consumer?

Now, the point that I am making here is exactly the same point . . . that I . . . [was] trying to make in the red cedar tree case—that whoever has the rights is gonna have their interest protected in the structuring of mutual coercion in the market, period. . . . [A]nd therefore I could not see why Jim assigned the rights . . . in his article always to the producer. Conceivably there could be justification for this; I personally wasn't interested in whether it was one party or the other party that had the rights but simply in establishing that choosing one party over the other structured mutual coercion in its favor. Therein, too, is this difference between us, which goes, I think, beyond the Lerner dichotomy—Jim never responded to that. Maybe he wants to now, I don't know.

JMB: I don't understand it. I don't understand the producer point; I don't understand what you're making there. I don't remember . . .

WJS: Okay . . . with regard to externalities . . .

JMB: Yeah . . .

WJS: . . . you basically said let the affected parties bargain and—the Coase solution—

JMB: Yeah . . .

WJS: . . . but you always gave the right to the . . . producer of the good and of the pollution. Why not give the protection to the consumer or the "innocent" third party, innocent in the Coasean sense—why not them? Now, I have no particular view why they should have it, but why always to the producer?

JMB: What . . . My position has never been directional in the sense of saying they ought to have it or not ought to have it, it's just whatever is. You start from . . . this goes back to the status quo point . . . you start from whatever is . . .

WJS: . . . I'm not sure that that was the issue in your piece. It may have been . . .

JMB: . . . yeah, yeah . . .

WJS: . . . If it was, then I missed it, but you invariably in that case assume that the right was with the producer. And that may not be the case, that was my point.

JMB: Yeah . . . [unclear] . . .

WJS: In fact in the real world it's not nice . . . if you start where it is, you now have consumer protection laws—or third-party protection laws. So we do have these innocent differences . . .

JMB: Yeah [chuckle].

WJS: . . . and Gordon was very nice to publish that piece . . . because the AER wasn't interested in doing that. On that matter, I agree with you; I'm not sure about everything else. . . . I'm teasing you.

JMB: I want to go back, though, a little bit further . . . to one thing you raised earlier, where you talked about the way that you look at distribution in terms of the Max Weber thing. You said that there're ways you could look at it as distribution; you could say as Max Weber . . . you've cited Max Weber here . . . but simply a conflict, people trying to get their share of the pie, just in a kind of a . . . with no normative overtones is just the way you put it, or you could view it as people exerting authority over each other, that is, exploitation with a kind of Marxist perspective. Or you could think of it in terms of, you know, productivity, that is, you get out what you put in type of thing.

Now, I want to change that example a little bit . . . the reason why I don't think you really get much by taking the Max Weber view. . . . Let's take the way we look at politics—get a little bit away from the distributional question—but let's just look at politics now . . .

WJS: I think that politics is distributional . . .

JMB: . . . Okay, fine, that's fine. I have no objection, but let's make it general about politics. Well, it seems to me there are three . . . at least three ways we can look . . . at politics—and, again, it's a complex matter, and we have to somehow . . . be a reductionist and force something on this; I have no objection to that—they're three ways: basically we can take the position that political theorists have taken through the centuries since Plato. That is, they say you can look on politics as the search for the good and the true and the beautiful, that is . . . we're searching for *truth* out there or *beauty* out there, whatever the summum bonum. . . . And they model the behavior of politicians as seeking this court of mystical public interest out there and sort of the collective goal of what I call the "truth/judgment" politics. And, of course, I reject that categorically—that's what's been *wrong* with the way people think about politics.

Or you can think of politics . . . this gets back close to the Max Weber point . . . as simply conflict—conflict among people . . . groups forming themselves (individuals *and* groups *and* parties *and* coalitions and various things) and simply a form of conflict . . . a war by peaceful means, so to speak, which includes distributional aspects. . . . It . . . seems to me that's not a very healthful way to look at politics, and here it seems to me you're obligated to look at politics—and, again, this comes back to a kind of moral obligation of having this vision of politics as a means through which people are . . . trying to get together to accomplish purposes . . . individual purposes . . . that cannot be accomplished by their own separate anarchistic developments. . . . You have to have a legal structure; you have to have a constitutional structure. But to look at that as basically what . . . in a broader sense, I've said . . . that one-half of public choice is politics as exchange, in this ultimate sense—that people are getting together . . . to . . . try to accomplish shared purposes that they couldn't accomplish on their own. And it seems to me that if you view politics that way . . . you can offer a meaningful understanding/explanation which *does have* normative implications, as opposed to looking at this as pure conflict or this illusory looking at it as a truth/judgment thing.

Now, and I think you can make a *case* for looking at politics that way, *even though,* if you want to take this scientific, antiseptic view, politics is just simply people fighting with each other or pure conflict—I'm taking . . . I'm trying to get more of my share. It seems to me this is a categorically different way of looking at politics, and I think that if you stick to your way of looking at it you have some normative implications here . . . that personally I don't like and I don't think you like either, really.

WJS: Let me . . . let me say this about that. Let me say that I would assume . . . let me assume that I agree with you that politics would be healthier if people were trying to work together to achieve goals. I submit . . . that . . . when they're working together to achieve goals, they're going to differ as to the goals; differ as to the means. And it is conflict in the sense. . . . I believe this is conflict in the *same* sense that I've been talking about here. I don't believe *conflict by coercion* need be a pejorative term; I find that even in the healthy, to use your phrase (which I like), in a healthy world in which people are trying to work things out together—and I think that's what we *are* doing—they're going to conflict as to ends and means, so you must inevitably come back to what I would call "the Weberian view" if you want to know what is going on. So we have two good guys who love each other, who happen to disagree as to ends and/or means, and somehow, given these conflicts, they have to work it out. I don't see that the fact of conflict is bad; I don't think the fact that there's a structure of mutual coercion is bad or that law protects *alpha*'s interest rather than *beta*'s interest, or vice versa, is bad. I think this is just the way of the world. I think there is an awful lot of pretense, not by you, that my way is *the right way* and anybody else's is wrong; I think that is kind of like hand-on-the-door bargaining—you either accept my offer or I'm out of here.

So what I'm saying is that I'm prepared to accept your view that healthy-minded people, nobly motivated people, can still disagree, and in these disagreements you're going to have a conflict model. Not because I like it or I want it; it's just there as an empirical fact. Now, it may be that morally I would agree with you it would be better if we all agreed, but then, what the hell, life would be dull—but that's another matter.

JMB: Well, let's go back to the . . . good example we're talking about here . . . this red cedar versus the apple growers case. Now, you see, the way you interpret that—. . . this conflict where one side or the other is gonna win—you don't have conflicts, [which is] not necessarily bad. So they go to the legislature and they both lobby and the apple growers win and so they impose their solution without compensation on the . . . red cedar growers. Now, my argument in the critique of that view was, in fact, if you accept *that* view, if you start looking at the world *that* way, you preclude the incentive and the possibilities of these people . . . get[ing] together and work[ing] out a bargain. Now there're obviously mutual gains as there is this interdependence; either it is or isn't worthwhile for the apple growers to fully compensate the cedar tree owners. . . . And if you start . . . if you impose too quickly the *conflict* vision on this, then you encourage these apple growers to go and just [say] . . . as long as they can get a majority in the legislature . . . to hell with the cedar tree owners. That's the point—where voluntarism, looking at it from the point of view of working out a compromise, is a quite different thing from starting and say[ing], "Well, it's a conflict, therefore whoever is the strongest wins." You see, it's a quite different way of looking at it, it seems to me.

WJS: I agree that there is that difference; I do not believe that my . . . position supports . . . an improper solution. What it does is say this is what happened, and, indeed, I illustrated this by saying, "Consider the reverse case of an apple orchard rust that had adverse effects on red cedar trees" . . . it's the opposite solution but to the same effect. . . . I do not . . . this is a normative subject, now, I do not believe that we should foreclose legal change of law . . . or [see] simply changing the law as an option, which Jim's approach does . . . nor, as a positive matter, do I see in the real world that law is adopted once and for all time. I . . . have a friend who's a professor of criminal procedure, and we were talking about some recent Supreme Court cases, and the really funny thing is that every time I talked about law, he interjected, "and legal change." I'm the one who emphasizes legal change in my work or opportunity for it or the fact of it; he felt the need to inject it because I was just saying law, not legal change. . . . Pareto and Knight, as I indicate in the preface to my book on Pareto, both wrote that if this . . . their work, in which they wrote this, was going to be widely read they would perhaps not have published it because it would induce the kind of behavior that . . .

JMB: (chuckle)

WJS: . . . you don't like. . . . I sympathize with that a little bit, but I guess my position is, if I had moral . . . if I was in your shoes and adopted Moral View 1, I would hope to be smart enough to know that somebody else had Moral View 2—which leads me to the conflict model—and that I would not so push my Moral View 1 as to foreclose the possibility of Moral View 2, even though I prefer [Moral View] 1. So what I'm saying here is I don't want to foreclose people from . . . buying each other off under the status quo law, but that's not really my problem. If I thought it was gonna do that, and throw everything into . . . up, topsy-turvy (everybody could run to court every time we turn around . . . I mean *real* litigation oriented), I might have the Pareto-Knight sense that, well, if everybody's gonna read this, I wouldn't publish it, but I don't . . . the sales weren't that big . . .

[Laughter.]

. . . I'm trying to describe, if describing something has the effect of influencing people's behavior, I suspect we'll influence people's behavior both ways. I don't know. But, you know, there's a . . . limit to how far one can say, "I'm not gonna publish" . . . But especially I want a model to accept the fact of legal change. . . .

What are we talking about here? We're talking about a world that you can reduce to a model: X equals the function of $A, B, C, D \dots N$. Now, if we each adopt a model on normative grounds because it incorporates certain normative grounds, that only has X as a function of A, B, C and drops all the rest, then that model has serious defects; it's not gonna fully explain, and it's gonna prejudice the normative process by only focusing on A, B, and C. I would prefer a wide range of variables—all of them that's manageable—so as not to preclude recognizing what is going on in the world.

Now, let's just go back to traditional, turn of the century, neoclassical theory. There was a belief in 1900, that there was a governing law for everything. There were . . . read the textbooks . . . a law governing rent, law governing wages, interest, property, etc. There was a fellow, whose name escapes me right now [Gustav Kleene] whom Taussig published in the QJE [*Quarterly Journal of Economics*], who argued the Weberian approach that there was no governing law of anything but rather the meeting in the marketplace and in . . . politics—politics as exchange maybe—in which the gathering forces of the one side met the gathering forces of the other and somehow something was worked out. Taussig was not entirely . . . he wrote on this, okay? So I'm not interpreting; I'm telling you what he said . . . he was not happy with this, but he was not able to rebut it. And now what do we have? . . . We don't have governing laws; we have models—models amplified by . . . specific theories (so one specific theory might be that of a particular law.) But my point is that if you narrow it down to *A, B,* and *C,* and forget about *D, E, F . . . N,* you bias the view of the world the way it is. And, furthermore, if you want to achieve a certain moral state of the world, okay? . . . it seems to me you're better off knowing what really is going on so that you can take the right kind of action. Now, it may be, it certainly will be, that there're gonna be unintended and unforeseen consequences. I don't question that. But it seems to me the more knowledge you have the more sophisticated the legal change or the moral change you want to bring about will be and the greater chance you will have ceteris paribus to bring about the moral order that you prefer. In other words, the issue is not the end of the moral order but . . . the means appropriate thereto which has operational value; the greater operational value the more consonant it is with what really is going on. Unless you pull . . . the people pull the wool over other people['s eyes]. And that's what politics is all about, and that's why I don't like it either.

JMB: Well, I'm under instruction here to open it up for questions, now, for the next fifteen minutes . . .

WJS: That's a good idea. We've talked to each other.

* * * * *

JMB: Sam.

Q: [Unclear]

WJS: It tells me a lot. It does not . . . many students have said to me, but so what? It doesn't tell me . . . whose interest should be protected. Why should I go out on a limb and assume that I know whose interest should be protected?

Q: [Unclear]

WJS: I couldn't agree more. . . . I agree with Hicks, who says, "no theory can answer every question you have." I don't deny other people doing their thing; I'm just doing my thing.

Q: [Unclear]

WJS: I think my approach has a place for competing moral views or competing interests. I'm not prejudicing it saying it should be under the existing law, and there should be no pressure on people to bargain under the existing law because of the threat of legal change. I am simply asserting that there is in fact legal change.

Now, if I thought, and this would be the ultimate ego trip, if I thought that what I wrote was gonna convince people to go to the legislature and litigate, you would . . . you should have me institutionalized. . . . In this world, what Warren Samuels writes—describing what's going on—is not going to encourage people to litigate.

Well, I haven't given you the full story. . . . I haven't told [you] anything about . . . the sources of law. I haven't told you anything about . . . the question as to what is law. I haven't said anything about a theory—and I do have a theory—of judicial interpretation. . . . I haven't told you that I think that at the level of our conversation . . . the concept of the rule of law is vacuous, though I've published a piece on that already. I do have . . . what you want, and it does provide [an] opportunity to examine the kinds of questions that you are alluding to, and I . . . in part what . . . I think Sam was . . .

Q: [Unclear]

WJS: It *isn't* a normative enterprise—that's my point. You see . . . my version of postmodernism does not say that you cannot choose; my point is that what you think is that an absolute is really a choice . . . editorial you . . . is that an absolute is really a choice. That the Supreme Court, for example, doesn't follow precedent because there is a whole set . . . there; oh, in every case there're rival sequences of precedent. They reach the decision they want, and then they explicate it in terms of this case . . . and this precedent . . . or sequence rather than the other. So I . . . I do have that theory. . . . I spell it out and teach it, have taught it in great detail.

JMB: Let me just. . . . I can't refrain from making one comment here. . . . [Y]ou said the rule of law is vacuous. . . . That to me is a perfect exemplar of what we're talking about here, and let me just instance one personal account that I think . . . most of you would agree with had you experienced it.

In 1981, I visited Dennis Mueller in Berlin, and we went over into the East [Berlin] section. We went through Checkpoint Charlie, gave up our passports—everything—went through this East [Berlin], came back. I have never experienced in my life quite the feeling as when I walked . . . when I came back from that barrier. It gave . . . a sense that you are back where the rule of law would prevail, where people mattered, but when you went back behind that [Iron] Curtain you had a sense it was absolutely vanished. You were vulnerable—totally vulnerable. Now, to me the rule of law, then, is surely not vacuous; it has a *meaning*—it has a *meaning* . . .

WJS: Jim, I said . . . at the level in which we're considering it here . . .

JMB: [Laughing] Oh, all right . . .

WJS: Let me illustrate. . . . In my book *Economics, Governance, and Law* [2002], there is a chapter on the rule of law. I commend it to you so you can understand what I'm talking about. Okay?

I obviously agree with Jim, but that phrase . . . at the level we're dealing with it here. . . . Let me illustrate this.

In that chapter I cite several, and summarize the content of several, books that talk about the founding fathers—the Adams, Jefferson, Madison, and whatnot—and how . . . they . . . formulated words in the Constitution that deferred issues to be worked out by the courts, how, in their own careers, they misstated what transpired at the Constitutional Congress, how they used one interpretation of a clause in one context because it was politically efficacious for them and, in another context, ten years later, they used a different . . . interpretation of a clause. Okay? Now if you want to invoke original intent, if you want to invoke rule of law, these are the people who you need to deal with. Okay?

Now let me take up the really interesting case of the Clinton impeachment. The one view is that he committed a "high crime and misdemeanor" by lying to the grand jury about "not having sex with that woman"—or not having sexual relations with that woman—and differing as to what *is* means. But he lied; there's no question about it. Whether that rises to high crimes and misdemeanors is a matter of judgment—which is my point. So one group says that the rule of law requires that the president be impeached if he lies to a grand jury; the other interpretation of the rule of law is that politics, which they believe was the driving force behind the impeachment, should not drive the rule of law.

So you have two different views of the rule of law—I'm not going to sit here and debate with you over this—all I'm trying to establish is that just as at the time of Madison, in the time of Rehnquist, you have different views of what the rule of law means. And that is true of everything. Take, for example, the commerce clause. Is manufacturing . . . interstate commerce? The original interpretation was that it was, the E. C. Knight case and a whole string of cases; it wasn't—and then it becomes again. What is this? What law is the rule here? It is a matter of interpretation. What we would like—morally, normatively, sentimentally—is a given, strict law that's easily applied. But there is no such thing at this level of discourse, okay? *There is no such thing.* Every clause is subject to interpretation and is going to be interpreted by people who have interests.

Q: [Unclear]

JMB: No, but . . . this is a very important point; we could spend a lot of time going into this, but, let me just see if I can sketch out a little bit of response here.

I think it is . . . you're right in a certain sense that even children . . . that's one thing they develop quite early on—a sense of fairness. I mean . . . Piaget's sum of all his experiments, it's very, very early on—but I do think it does require, and I think it's a very important driving force in the way we think about the world, and so forth and so on, and it is behind all of the Rawlsian enterprise. And . . . I have a lot of affinity for John Rawls and what he was trying to accomplish here in this context. But it does require—you say everybody—it's not quite everybody, because you can't have—and this gets directly into the stuff that Sandy [Peart] and David [Levy] are working on—you cannot have a conceptualization of the world in which people are classified hierarchically and have a sense of fairness. You can have justice . . . in the sense you define justice there, totally differently. There you define justice in terms of a kind of a compassion, an altruism, benevolence . . . you can talk about [how] you are just to the man who is poor, but if you classify him totally differently from yourself . . . you can't apply fairness criteria. Fairness criteria, and the fact that you say everybody honors this, mean that you're accepting this idea that basically we're natural equals out there to be considered in the normative sense as natural equals. And so I think that's an important distinction to make, and it does separate these two conceptually.

WJS: I . . . agree with what Jim is saying . . . it really is a vastly difficult topic. We're all professors here—well, most of us are—and others are exposed to our machinations . . .

JMB: . . . at this level of discourse . . .

[Laughter.]

WJS: Let . . . me give you an example. . . .

You can argue that the only fair exam is one that goes over the assigned material. Most of you would say, yes. I once had a class in mathematical logic in which the exam did not cover the assigned material but went to the next step in the development of the mathematical logic—basically asking on each question, "If you understand what we've done thus far, what do you need to do to get to the next step?" (Now, it wasn't quite as blunt as that, but this was an unusually good class . . . [and there were] a lot of scholarship students in it.)

Now, is that fair? . . . Fairness is a very complex subject, but I agree. I don't believe that my focusing on the importance of a solid, nonnormative picture of what actually is going on is inconsistent with having a part of your model . . . one of the elements in *A, B, C, D* . . . the normative inputs here. And, as I said to Jim, if you have more than one person with a normative input you're gonna have a conflict, and that's going to have to be worked out. And that is really what I think is going on out there. And that's why I believe that the position that I'm taking here is good old American pragmatism. We all come to it with our own highfalutin' sentiments, our highfalutin' moral principles, but in reality what is going on is working out solutions to problems. . . . Whether we do it nicely or nastily, that's a different matter.

Now, on this question of fairness. I can remember, when I was a young professor at University of Miami in the early 1960s. . . . The first person who called me a communist in public was a student . . . (he [indicates Buchanan] called me a statist) . . . who was the head of Young Americans for Freedom. And he didn't like my spiel about social control and that, whether you like it or not, government is important. . . . But I was close to him—he eventually went to law school and became a judge. I once ran into him, and he said, "You know, you were right on all those issues about law; at Young Americans for Freedom, we were a bunch of nuts."

[Laughter.]

At any rate, I was close to them; I was close to a number of other groups, including the Cuban Student Directorate and . . . a couple of other Cuban groups, right wing, from the first wave of Castro émigrés, and I was also close to students on the left, who were vastly outnumbered, but you had an SDS [Students for a Democratic Society] group there. The people on the right were fearful of a coup d'état from the left, and the people from the left were afraid of a coup d'état from the right, okay? And it was my picture . . . and I don't think I imagined this . . . that if there had been one, either one of those coups, the people on the other side would have been "freedom fighters/terrorists." And I could have imagined myself joining them, okay?

Now, what's fair? It depends upon whether it is Moral View 1 or Moral View 2; that has to be worked out in the minds of each individual. Now, if I was a single person, I might have reacted differently under the circumstances . . . the hypothetical circumstances . . . than if I had been a father and a husband with two children . . . as I was, in fact. But if there had been a coup, I'm sure that I would [have] . . . joined in. I would have been an enemy of the people to those . . . in office; I'd have been a wonderful freedom fighter to the other. Now, if you call this moral relativism, fine; I don't care what you call it. I believe the moral absolute here, if you want to call it an absolute, is good old Americanism, pluralism, meaningful civil rights, and markets. But believing that does not keep me from understanding that law shapes markets and you don't have markets given by nature, which is the problem of neoclassicism.

SJP: Jim, do you want to have the last word?

JMB: No, no.

[Laughter.]

SJP: Please join me in thanking Warren and Jim.

Bibliography

Buchanan, James M. 1972. "Politics, Property, and the Law: An Alternative Interpretation of *Miller et al. v. Schoene*." *Journal of Law and Economics* 15 (October): 439–52.

Buchanan, James M. 1987. *Economics: Between Predictive Science and Moral Philosophy.* Edited by Robert D. Tollison and Viktor J. Vanberg. College Station: Texas A&M University Press.

Buchanan, James M. 2004. "Saving the Ideas." Summer Institute for the Preservation of the Study of the History of Economics. 26 July.

Buchanan, James M., and Richard A. Musgrave. 1999. *Public Finance and*

Public Choice: Two Contrasting Visions of the State. Cambridge: MIT Press.

Buchanan, James M., and Warren J. Samuels. 1975. "On Some Fundamental Issues in Political Economy: An Exchange of Correspondence." *Journal of Economic Issues* 9 (March): 15–38.

Buchanan, James M., and Gordon Tullock. 1975. "Polluters' Profits and Political Response: Direct Controls versus Taxes." *American Economic Review* 65 (March): 139–47.

Dahl, Robert A., and Charles E. Lindblom. 1953. *Politics, Economics, and Welfare: Planning and Politico-Economic Systems Resolved into Basic Social Processes.* New York: Harper.

Samuels, Warren J. 1971."Interrelations between Legal and Economic Processes." *Journal of Law and Economics* 14 (October): 435–50.

Samuels, Warren J. 2000. "Buchanan and Musgrave on Public Finance and Public Choice: A Review Essay." *Journal of the History of Economic Thought* 22: 499–507.

Samuels, Warren J. 2002. *Economics, Governance, and Law: Essays on Theory and Policy.* Cheltenham: Edward Elgar.

Samuels, Warren J. 2004. "The Problem of the Status of the Status Quo: Some Comments." *Research in the History of Economic Thought and Methodology* 22A: 235–56.

Samuels, Warren J., and A. Allan Schmid. 1976. "Polluters' Profits and Political Response: The Dynamics of Rights Creation." *Public Choice* 29 (winter): 99–105.

3 • The Theory of Economic Policy in British Classical Political Economy
A Sympathetic Reading

David M. Levy and Sandra J. Peart

How selfish soever man may be supposed, there are evidently some principles in his nature, which interest him in the fortune of others, and render their happiness necessary to him.

—Adam Smith, *The Theory of Moral Sentiments* (1759)

Bentham's followers . . . may have been led by Bentham's incautious use of the phrase ["greatest happiness of the greatest number"] into exaggerating the democratic or isocratic tendencies implicit in Utilitarianism.

—F. Y. Edgeworth, *Mathematical Psychics* (1881)

Introduction

In his 1952 *Theory of Economic Policy in English Classical Political Economy,* Lionel Robbins rightly maintained that the English classical economists were reformers in a utilitarian tradition.[1] To make utilitarianism operational, they needed to specify the weights for individuals' capacities for happiness. Classical economists held that everyone counted as one. And, although Robbins (1938) himself accepted that as a *norm,* the strictures that he advanced in his *Nature and Significance* against such weights as *science* spoke against the scientific status of

An earlier version of this essay received helpful comments from Warren Samuels, Richard Wagner, Steve Meardon, Roger Backhouse, and Andrew Farrant. The mistakes that remain are our responsibility.

1. Although there are later studies of classical economic policy (e.g., Samuels 1966), we focus on Robbins's because his criticism of the scientific status of classical economic policy is a criticism of all economic policy recommendations. "The criterion the English Classical Economists found in the principle of utility, the principle that the test of policy is to be its effect on human happiness. . . . This attitude is common to all the English Classical Economists. We get the picture badly out of focus if we conceive that reliance on the principle of utility was confined to Bentham and his immediate circle" (Robbins 1952, 177–78).

classical policy.[2] In this essay, we add one significant element to Robbins's account: we argue that the economic policy of the classical economists constitutes a variation of the theory of exchange.[3] What we find missing in Robbins's discussion is an appreciation of the role of sympathy in the classical economists' theory of economic policy because Robbins supposes that utilitarianism is bereft of appeals to sympathetic motivation. On the contrary, we argue that motivation through a sympathetic process is a vital component of the classical utilitarian tradition that helps both motivate and constrain economic policy as a type of exchange.

Sympathy allows complicated exchanges to proceed through the political process. By restraining individuals from injustice, it allows the well-being of majorities, utilitarianism by counting (Peart and Levy 2005a), to have a semblance of plausibility. Sympathy connects spectators with actors in such a way that spectators might be willing to trade something of theirs to prevent harm to actors. Adam Smith's ([1759] 2004, III.i.46) account of a European without a personal stake in the matter who is willing to give up a little finger to save China is well known. The trade that concerns us is the payment by British taxpayers to make slavery disappear from the empire.

To make our assertion that later classical economists see reforms as akin to sympathetic exchanges, we need to provide evidence at the outset that sympathy was viewed as important by the later classical economists in the utilitarian tradition. In *Utilitarianism* John Stuart Mill claimed that

2. "It is a fundamental difficulty of utilitarian ethics that it appears to involve the comparability and summation of the satisfactions of different individuals. . . . the weighting which is given to the satisfactions of different individuals is another element which partakes of the nature of an ethical postulate rather than a principle established by observation or introspection. Among the English utilitarians the assumption was that each man's capacity for happiness was to be counted as equal. But it is easily possible to think of other assumptions which might be held to be equally binding" (Robbins 1952, 180). F. Y. Edgeworth's hedonic calculus made Robbins uneasy (Robbins 1938; Peart and Levy 2005c). Edgeworth's consideration of people with such a low capacity for happiness that their total happiness might integrate out as zero or even negative is discussed in Peart and Levy 2004. His eugenic conclusion is blocked by the "weak" Pareto principle, which, as Robbins (1981) recognized, is not a value-free foundation for economics.

3. "I had not thought it necessary to observe that, in speaking of exchanges, I did not mean to limit myself to *voluntary* exchanges;—those in which the whole transaction takes place with the full consent of both parties to all the terms of it. Most exchanges, indeed, are of this character; but the case of taxation,—the revenue levied from the subject in return for the protection afforded by the sovereign, constitutes a remarkable exception; the payment being compulsory, and not adjusted by agreement with the payer. Still, whether in any case it be *fairly* and reasonably adjusted, or the contrary, it is not the less an exchange. And it is worth remarking, that it is just so far forth as it is an exchange,—so far forth as protection, whether adequate or not, is afforded in exchange for this payment,—that the payment itself comes under the cognizance of this science. There is nothing else that distinguishes *taxation* from *avowed robbery*" (Whately [1831] 2002, lecture 1, n. 5).

education and "a complete web of corroborative association" serve to extend sympathy. In the process of a moral education, the well-being of others becomes akin to the "physical conditions of our existence."

> Not only does all strengthening of social ties, and all healthy growth of society, give to each individual a stronger personal interest in practically consulting the welfare of others; it also leads him to identify his *feelings* more and more with their good, or at least with an even greater degree of practical consideration for it. He comes, as though instinctively, to be conscious of himself as a being who *of course* pays regard to others. The good of others becomes to him a thing naturally and necessarily to be attended to, like any of the physical conditions of our existence. ([1861] 1969, 231)

Mill's phrase, "the contagion of sympathy," locates his notion of sympathy in a tradition older than Smith's, one that emphasizes the unreflective, automatic aspects of sympathy:[4] "Consequently the smallest germs of the feeling are laid hold of and nourished by the contagion of sympathy and the influences of education; and a complete web of corroborative association is woven round it, by the powerful agency of the external sanctions" (232).

In our understanding, the 1833 Act of Emancipation is an important example because Mill viewed it as the paradigm of reform. As such, we begin with a discussion of the exchange that abolished slavery. As Robbins does not discuss the role of economists in the antislavery movement, we quote some unfamiliar texts at length.[5]

4. The difference between Hume's and Smith's treatments is discussed in Levy and Peart 2004 and Fleischaker 2004. Fleischaker's use of "contagion" to describe Hume's sympathetic machinery and distinguish it from Smith's "projection" machinery is most helpful.

5. The topic of antislavery seems to be absent from Robbins's book on Robert Torrens, as Thomas Fowell Buxton's name is not found, although Edward Gibbon Wakefield's position on slavery and colonial development is discussed at some length (Robbins 1958, 155–60). Torrens's role in the antislavery debates is featured in the new specialist account of the debates leading up to emancipation. Here is an instance of both the importance of sympathetic compensation and the race-neutral procedure of classical economists for which we have argued elsewhere (Peart and Levy 2005b): "Torrens drew his [evidence] from the new experiments in colonization by Britons in the South Pacific. He asked the House of Commons to base its expectations on the actual behavior of 'men of the British race,' already placed in circumstances quite similar to those in which Buxton contended, freed Africans would work for wages. On any frontier, Englishmen 'immediately ceased to work for wages' and sought to cultivate on their own" (Drescher 2002, 134). In the 1840 *Prospectus of the Society for the Extinction of the Slave Trade,* we find the name "Colonel Torrens" as a member of the "Provisional Committee" (Buxton [1840] 1968, 13). Torrens also appears in the *Anti-Slavery Reporter*'s list of the famous who gathered at the great Exeter Hall meeting in preparation for the final push for passage of the Act of Emancipation.

Second, if policy is viewed as exchange, then the notion of a quid pro quo is obvious. As Richard Whately says, one trades taxes for protection against murder and theft.[6] He left unsaid that the governmental protection agency would insist that the taxpayer contribute to the cause by, say, putting valuables inside the house and not on the lawn. We consider how the classical analysis of poor relief relies on the quid pro quo of sumptuary controls in exchange for protection against extreme destitution.

Third, if policy is an act of exchange, then one might insist on having a representative at the table when deals are done. Thus, political representation would be an important component of an economic theory of policy. In our third section, we provide testimony for the importance of political representation in Mill.[7] Mill was a member of Parliament during the Eyre controversy and the Fenian violence, and he was often caricatured in *Punch* during these years. As far as we can see, the only policy issue given visual form is that of political representation.

Finally, we close with a natural question. What happened to the view of politics as exchange? We have argued elsewhere that sympathy collided with the theological interpretation of natural selection (Peart and Levy 2003a, 2004). Although W. H. Hutt revived politics as exchange in his 1943 *Plan for Reconstruction,* the idea was not recognized until decades later. Hutt drew on a tradition, lost to the rest of the profession, of sympathy and the well-being of majorities to explain what he called "consumer sovereignty."[8] In the collision with the theology of

---

6. "Many are apt to think Taxes quite a different kind of expense from all others, and either do not know, or else forget, that they receive any thing in *exchange* for the Taxes. But, in reality, this payment is as much an exchange as any other. You pay money to the baker and butcher for feeding you, and to the tailor for clothing you; and you pay the King and Parliament for protecting you from being plundered, murdered, or cheated. Were it not for this, you could be employed scarcely half your time in providing food and clothing, and the other half would be taken up in guarding against being robbed of them; or in working for some other man, whom you would hire to keep watch and to fight for you. This would cost you much more than you pay in Taxes" (Whately 1833, 66–67).

7. We have elsewhere (Peart and Levy 2003b) discussed how J. E. Cairnes emphasized the importance of the political representation of the freed American slaves as a way to ensure that their interests were protected. Elsewhere we have considered how Mill, in *Representative Government,* viewed a minimal amount of sympathy as a necessary condition for a representative form of government (Peart and Levy 2005a).

8. "Because the moral principle of 'sympathy for the greater number at the expense of sympathy for the lesser number' formed the essence of their teaching, the Utilitarian economists have, moreover, been brought into a permanent clash with reformers and philanthropists. For the latter are commonly aware of and moved by the interests of the few only with whom they are in direct contact" (Hutt 1936b, 131–32). Hutt's shaky command of the texts was noted by Viner (1938), who missed Hutt's insight into the majoritarian aspect of the utilitarian tradition, which may well have come via Graham Wallas (e.g., 1898). Testimony from Malthus ([1798] 2004, XVI.1) shows that Smith was read by his contemporaries as a majoritarian.

natural selection, utilitarianism lost its majoritarian interpretation. Perhaps the last great economic theorist who saw the majoritarianism in utilitarianism, if only to oppose it in service to Darwinian science, was F. Y. Edgeworth.[9]

Abolishing Slavery by Exchange

We have noticed that Richard Whately viewed taxation as an exchange for the government enforcement of justice. The text we quoted from in note 6 is titled *Easy Lessons on Money Matters; for the Use of Young People* (R. Whately 1833). In the instance Whately considers, protection from violence, the resources provided for taxation more than pay for themselves in terms of output gained. This is indeed an easy problem.

Now let us consider how he addressed a hard problem, one in which the policy is costly in the sense that it is not self-financing. This we view as a signature of a sympathetic exchange, what we might say reveals a willingness "to do the right thing" even if one receives nothing in return for doing so. On 28 February 1833, Whately, then archbishop of Dublin, wrote a letter to the Anti-Slavery Society in which he considered how to get rid of slavery. As this has not been widely discussed, we quote large extracts with references to the account given by Seymour Drescher in his *The Mighty Experiment: Free Labor versus Slavery in British Emancipation* (2002).

Whately begins with a moral claim and the illusion of freedom from culpability of those who are not slave owners.

> I perfectly concur with you in thinking the existence of slavery in our empire a national sin, and that justice demands, therefore, that we should be ready to bear our fair proportion of the evils consequent upon it.
>
> Though this, however, is the case *really,* the persons most closely connected with the sinful act will often *appear* the chief or the sole perpetrators. One who has planned, for instance, and authorised a murder, will often fancy himself innocent, compared with him whose hands were actually imbrued with blood. (Quoted in E. J. Whately 1866, 183)

9. "Bentham's followers . . . may have been led by Bentham's incautious use of the phrase ["greatest happiness of the greatest number"] into exaggerating that democratic or isocratic tendencies implicit in *Utilitarianism*" (Edgeworth 1881, 117). Robbins's strictures in *Nature and Significance* block the scientific status of Edgeworth's appeal to the differential capacity for happiness and prepare the way for the Paretian interpretation of utilitarianism (Peart and Levy 2005c).

Drescher (2002, 108) reports discussions of the importance of habitual behavior. Whately stresses this at the outset: "Most of those who swell the cry for immediate emancipation are ignorant of the chief evil of slavery—viz., its making and keeping the slave unfit for freedom, by completely separating in his mind the two ideas habitually associated in the minds of free labourers, properly so called (not parish paupers), of labour and maintenance" (E. J. Whately 1866, 184).

As is common in classical economics, Whately appeals to proverbial wisdom (Peart and Levy 2005b): "The greatest of the ancient moralists lays it down, that a man is *naturally* a slave as long, and *only* as long, as he is unfit for freedom,—*i.e.*, incapable of taking care of himself, and requiring to be guided like a child."[10] Then Whately refers to his teaching on fallacies in *Elements of Logic* (R. Whately [1827] 1975, 145–56), in which he explains how difficult it is to separate inference from desire: "Unhappily for the *application* of this excellent principle, the person who alone is well qualified both to *know* when a slave is fit for freedom, and to train him to that fitness, is the very person who is interested in keeping him as slave" (Quoted in E. J. Whately 1866, 184).

Leaping a century ahead to discussions of self-assessed taxation, Whately proposes a truth-revealing process.

> If any way can be devised which can make it the *master's* interest to free his slaves, that, it appears to me, and that alone, will solve the difficulty. And the only way I can conceive in which this can be effected is, to take off a portion of the duties on colonial produce, to be replaced by an equivalent tax on slaves; that the tax to be *ad valorem,* the price of each slave to be fixed by the *master,* and each slave to be redeemable at the price fixed. (Quoted in E. J. Whately 1866, 184)

One can trust homeowners to truthfully assess their own homes' value for tax purposes—"Why my tiny Georgetown townhouse couldn't possibly be worth more than $5,000!"—if and only if that assessment is an offer to sell: "Oh, never mind."

> Thus the slaves best *qualified* to become independent labourers for wages, being the most costly, would be those the master would, for his own interest, be the most anxious to set free; and

10. Quoted in E. J. Whately 1866, 184. W. H. Hutt—who introduced the term *consumer sovereignty*—tells us how it came to be: "I am not sure whether I coined the term myself. Marketing literature contains phrases like 'the customer is always right,' and I am told that a proverbial expression in High Dutch is 'De klant is koning' (the customer is king)" (1940, 66).

> it is probable he would be ready himself to *lend* such a slave the price of his freedom, allowing him to *work out* the debt at a stipulated rate of wages. Such an intermediate state between slavery and freedom would, I think, prove the best preparatory to an independence advantageous to both parties. (185)

A test for sympathetic compensation is whether the reform would be self-financing in any short time horizon. If it were, then there might as well be only two parties to the transaction. For Whately, it was clear that emancipation would not be self-financing.

> Of course, in proportion as this plan succeeded, the revenue from the West Indian Islands would for the present diminish. This I would reckon as one of its advantages, as relief would thus be afforded to a class peculiarly in need of it. And if the English people grudged a trifling and temporary defalcation of revenue for the accomplishment of such an object as the gradual extinction of slavery, in the only way in which it can be effected without cruelty to the negroes themselves, it is plain their clamour in the cause of humanity must be the grossest hypocrisy. (Quoted in E. J. Whately 1866, 185)

Thus, the compensation to be paid in exchange for freedom was from the spectator/consumer who benefited from slavery past. The slave was not supposed to provide compensation for his freedom. The emancipation would not be self-financing.

Thomas Fowell Buxton was the parliamentary wizard who, as floor manager later in the year, negotiated the Act of Emancipation for William Wilberforce and the antislavery movement. As such, Buxton crafted the complicated compensation package that ended imperial slavery (Drescher 2002). In *The African Slave Trade and Its Remedy,* Buxton ([1839] 1968, 11–12) found the sympathetic compensation embodied there a "sublime" act by the "disinterested."

> One noble sacrifice in behalf of the negro race has already been made. In the words of the most eloquent citizen of another nation [Dr. Channing]—"Great Britain, loaded with an unprecedented debt, and with a grinding taxation, contracted a new debt of a hundred million dollars, to give freedom, not to Englishmen, but to the degraded African. I know not that history records an act so disinterested, so sublime. In the progress of ages England's naval triumphs will shrink into a more and more

> narrow space in the records of our race. This moral triumph will fill a broader, brighter page."

This principle would later become embodied in John Stuart Mill's *The Principles of Political Economy* as the doctrine of compensation for reform. In Mill's statement of the principle of compensation, the paradigm was the 1833 Act of Emancipation, "whether the object be education; a more efficient and accessible administration of justice; reforms of any kind which, like the Slave Emancipation, require compensation to individual interests" ([1848] 2004, bk. 5, chap. VI, sec. V.6.2).

The obvious question, to which we have no answer, is whether Whately's views on the matter had an impact on the discussions in Wilberforce's circle.

Poor Laws

Protection against violence is not the only protection discussed in the period. Protection against the vagaries of life in a commercial society is much discussed by Robbins. A defining characteristic of a sympathetic agent is a willingness to share. The natural policies one might expect from sympathetic agents would be akin to what we would call a "safety net."[11] We glance at the discussion of poor relief in British economics with an eye toward conditionality. What sort of responsibilities do those asking for assistance bear? If policy is an exchange, each party has to expect to give up something in order to get something else. Without giving up something valuable, there is no exchange; the policy is a gift. What the taxpayers give up is easy enough. Perhaps their rewards are sympathetic, perhaps not. Our authorities have different views on that matter. What is the person who applies for charity expected to give up?

The idea that a minimum existence, a protection against extreme distress, can be guaranteed occurred to Thomas Robert Malthus in the paragraph immediately following his 1798 argument that the poor laws of Britain had the perverse consequence of helping create the poor that they maintained. One could, however, solve this unintended consequence by attaching conditions.

> Lastly, for cases of extreme distress, county workhouses might be established, supported by rates upon the whole kingdom,

11. Hutt's *Plan for Reconstruction* (1943, 8) begins with the safety net: "The Board shall, with the advice and assistance of the Trustee, determine a guaranteed minimum income for every person from whom a form . . . is received."

> and free for persons of all counties, and indeed of all nations. The fare should be hard, and those that were able obliged to work. It would be desirable that they should not be considered as comfortable asylums in all difficulties; but merely as places where severe distress might find some alleviation. A part of these houses might be separated, or others built for a most beneficial purpose, which has not been infrequently taken notice of, that of providing a place, where any person, whether native or foreigner, might do a day's work at all times and receive the market price for it. Many cases would undoubtedly be left for the exertion of individual benevolence. ([1798] 2004, V.25)

When Nassau W. Senior reviewed European experience with the safety net, he paid close attention to these conditions. What were the terms of trade?

> We have now given a very brief outline of the institutions of those portions of the Continent which appear, from the returns, to have adopted the English principle of acknowledging in every person a right to be supported by the public. It will be observed that in no country, except, perhaps, the Canton de Berne, has compulsory relief produced evils resembling, either in intensity or in extent, those which we have experienced; and that in the majority of the nations which have adopted it, the existing system appears to work well. (1835, 84)

There are several cases to consider that are not germane to the existing British situation. First, there are quasi slave societies.[12]

> Among some of the nations in question villeinage still exists. Now where slavery, in any of its forms, prevails, the right of the slave or villein to support is a necessary and a safe consequence. I[t] is necessary, because a person who is not a free agent cannot

12. Senior ([1841] 1865, 2:46–47) would later argue that the old poor law of England was an attempt by the masters to reintroduce a system akin to slavery: "We believe that the English poor laws originated in selfishness, ignorance, and pride. Better motives, without doubt, though misdirected by almost equal ignorance, dictated the changes which were made in the laws during the eighteenth century—the fourth which elapsed from their commencement; but we are convinced that the origin was an attempt substantially to restore the expiring system of slavery." This view of older policy is akin to that of Smith ([1776] 2004, III.iv.10): "All for ourselves and nothing for other people, seems, in every age of the world, to have been the vile maxim of the masters of mankind."

> provide for himself. It is safe, because one of the principal evils of pauperism, improvidence, can scarcely exist among slaves. (84)

Second, there are countries in which the compulsory system has just started (84–85). Third, there are countries where people would lose a good deal, either in property or in social standing, by applying for public relief (85–87). Then Senior turns to the remaining cases, which are comparable. There is no cost of applying for public assistance in Britain.

> But the conditions on which parochial assistance is afforded in the countries in question, form perhaps the principal difference between their systems and that which we have adopted. In England, where the scale and allowance system prevail, no condition whatever can be said to be imposed on the pauper. What he receives is a mere gratuitous addition to his income. Even where work is required, the hours are in general fewer, and the labour less severe than those of the independent labourer. And the workhouse, the most powerful of our instruments of repression, affords, in general, food, lodging, clothing, and warmth, better than can be found in the cottage, *and may be quitted at a day's notice.* (87–88)

On the Continent, by contrast, there is a real cost of being a pauper, so this is an exchange: "But in all the countries which we have been considering, except the Canton de Berne and perhaps Denmark, the great object of pauper legislation, that of the rendering the situation of the pauper less agreeable than that of the independent labourer, has been effectually attained" (88). Senior then reviews the various conditions that different countries attach to the right of assistance such as restrictions on marriage and the like (88–94).

Famously, when John Stuart Mill reviewed Harriet Martineau's *Illustrations of Political Economy,* he found only "one point of importance" with which to differ. Her work on population was behind the times: "The recent investigation of the poor-law commission, with which Miss Martineau is familiar, seem to us as conclusive in support of the *principle* of a poor-rate, as they are in condemnation of the existing practice" ([1834] 1967, 227–28).

A View from *Punch*

We have discussed elsewhere how *Punch* opposed the classical economists' views of human homogeneity during the 1850s and 1860s (Peart and Levy 2005b).[13] There were many issues on which *Punch* took issue with Mill. The verse "A Fenian on His Friends," printed on 7 March 1868, blames the Fenian violence on Mill's support of the former slaves in Jamaica in his failed attempt to bring Governor Eyre to justice.[14] Racial cartoons are impossible to miss in *Punch* at the time. Images refer to Mill's *On Liberty, Logic,* and *Political Economy.* He is often pictured in the company of John Bright. Nonetheless, we have not found a single one in which Mill is pictured in a racial context.

When there is a political issue pictured in association with Mill, it invariably concerns the extension of the franchise. If policy were viewed as an act of exchange, then political representation would be required to protect one's interests.[15] This suggests that, from the point of view of a well-informed opposition, what is most important about Mill's policy is the extension of the franchise.

The role of sympathy in self-government is explained in Mill's *Considerations on Representative Government* ([1861] 1977). Mutual sympathy plays a critical role in the argument, being a necessary condition for representative self-government.[16]

As a source of moral obligation, sympathy constrains people and forms a barrier to injustice (Mill [1861] 1977, 547). Mutual sympathy creates the boundaries of successful association.[17] Government must take people "as they are," but some sympathy with others is requisite for representative government.[18] Competition and a sufficient number of

13. While the race-neutral accounts in Adam Smith and John Stuart Mill are clear, the position of Senior is debated. This statement from his *Outline of the Science of Political Economy* suggests that he is in line with Smith and Mill: "Almost all the differences between the different races of men, differences so great that we sometimes nearly forget that they all belong to the same species, may be traced to the degree in which they enjoy the blessings of good government" ([1836] 1938, 76). Here is his application of that principle to poor-law reform: "The able-bodied pauper is the result of art; he is not the natural offspring of the Saxon race" (Senior [1841] 1865, 2:98).

14. Mill's statement on the role of sympathy in the enforcement of justice in *Utilitarianism* ought to be read as the explanation of his actions as the head of the Jamaica Committee. Packe's discussion (1954, 470–71) is unhelpful. Robbins's (1957) unhappiness with Packe is well merited.

15. James Mill's ([1820] 1978, 79) view of virtual representation—the interests of a woman being represented by the men in her life—had been criticized by Macaulay ([1829] 1978, 116) four decades before.

16. "Among a people without fellow-feeling, especially if they read and speak different languages, the united public opinion, necessary to the working of representative government, cannot exist" (Mill [1861] 1977, 547).

17. "To render a federation advisable, several conditions are necessary. The first is, that there should be a sufficient amount of mutual sympathy among the populations. The federation binds them always to fight on the same side" (ibid., 553).

18. "Governments must be made for human beings as they are, or as they are capable of speedily becoming: and in any state of cultivation which mankind, or any class among them, have yet attained, or are likely soon to attain, the interests by which they will be led, when they are thinking only of self-interest, will be almost exclusively those which are obvious at first sight, and which operate on their present condition. It is only a disinterested regard for others, and especially for what comes after

disinterested sympathetic individuals to influence the election will prevent factional injustice.[19]

As evidence of how well *Punch* was informed on these matters, it provided testimony that a test for representation was the efficacy of sympathetic motivation, the ability to cooperate: "One of the reasons, Mr. Mill, why the working classes ought to have the elective franchise, is said to be the capacity which they evince for organization" (8 April 1867, 144).

Figures 3.1–3.8 are the images of Mill we have found in *Punch.* We reproduce sections of the caricatures that feature him. Figure 3.1 (10 February 1866) has Mill, the author of *On Liberty,* with the dancing bear of reform, John Bright, on a chain.[20] Figure 3.2 (2 February 1867) is a double-page imagining of the parliamentary debaters as gladiators. It shows Mill again, but now with *Logic,* in conjunction with Bright as the great adversaries of aristocracy. Figure 3.3 (16 February 1867) shows Mill and Bright now in the role of seconds in the debates to come. Figure 3.4 (30 March 1867) reacts to Mill's proposal to make men and women equal persons in the eyes of the law. It now gives Mill a cartoon of his own.

Continuing the theme on 1 June 1867, figure 3.5 remarks on the defeat of Mill's proposal with another such cartoon. Figure 3.6, the two-page plate of 15 July 1867, marking the triumph of the reform bill, deserves to be reproduced in full because even on this small scale we can appreciate Mill's central role in the reform. The detail in figure 3.7 is the image of Mill himself. Figure 3.8 (21 March 1868) shows the author of *Political Economy* with a new baby in his arms.

Hutt's Politics as Exchange

When James Buchanan revived the theory of politics as exchange, he proceeded from Knut Wicksell's nineteenth-century work. As far as Buchanan recognized, there was nothing in the English-language dis-

---

them, for the idea of posterity, of their country, or of mankind, whether grounded on sympathy or on a conscientious feeling, which ever directs the minds and purposes of classes or bodies of men towards distant or unobvious interests" (ibid., 445).

19. "The reason why, in any tolerably constituted society, justice and the general interest mostly in the end carry their point, is that the separate and selfish interests of mankind are almost always divided; some are interested in what is wrong, but some, also, have their private interest on the side of what is right: and those who are governed by higher considerations, though too few and weak to prevail against the whole of the others, usually after sufficient discussion and agitation become strong enough to turn the balance in favour of the body of private interests which is on the same side with them. The representative system ought to be so constituted as to maintain this state of things" (ibid., 447).

20. We owe the "dancing bear" reading to Andrew Farrant.

Fig. 3.1. *Punch,* 10 February 1866.

cussion that made this suggestion. Hutt's descent to obscurity explains why it was not until 1988 that his 1943 *Plan for Reconstruction* was recognized as in the tradition of politics as gains from trade (Buchanan 1988).[21]

There are several components to the framework of democratic politics as exchange. First, one must suppose something akin to competition inside the political process. Second, one must have a way to deal with the possibility of majoritarian taking. We argue elsewhere that the classics supposed sufficient sympathy (Peart and Levy 2005a); the modern

21. Buchanan (1988, 135–52) notes that F. A. Hayek called his attention to Hutt's connection with Buchanan's larger project.

Fig. 3.2. *Punch,* 2 February 1867.

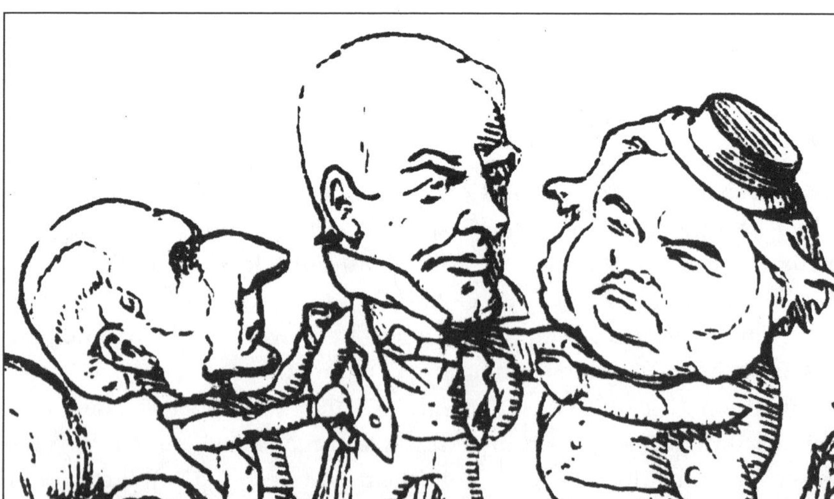

Fig. 3.3. *Punch,* 16 February 1867.

PUNCH, OR THE LONDON CHARIVARI.—March 30, 1867.

MILL'S LOGIC; OR, FRANCHISE FOR FEMALES.

"PRAY CLEAR THE WAY, THERE, FOR THESE—A—PERSONS."

Fig. 3.4. *Punch,* 30 March 1867.

Rawls-Buchanan approach supposes the constraint of impartiality at the constitutional level. It is not clear whether these approaches are fundamentally different, although one emphasizes imagination across people and the other emphasizes imagination across time.[22] Third, one must be comfortable with the outcome of a majority-rule process. Here Buchanan and Tullock (1962) are clearly not, since majority rule is only one of many decision rules that might be selected at the constitutional stage.[23]

22. "The cosmopolitanism of the early orthodox writers is in itself evidence of a certain scientific aloofness; for whilst it might be unjust to regard nationalism as springing from the struggle for political and economic power and prestige, the universal exploitation of the national and racial feeling in the cause of vested interests are clearly responsible for the repulsion which the economist felt towards the expression of nationalistic aspirations" (Hutt 1936b, 56). "The 'bloated capitalist' with his cigar and diamond rings, or the 'sweater' with foreign or Semitic features, were essential creations" (59).

23. Hutt's 1966 review of Buchanan and Tullock's *The Calculus of Consent* (1962) is wonderfully interesting in this regard: "It is at the 'operational' level, how-

PUNCH, OR THE LONDON CHARIVARI.—June 1, 1867.

THE LADIES' ADVOCATE.

Mrs. Bull. "LOR, MR. MILL! WHAT A LOVELY SPEECH YOU *DID* MAKE. I DO DECLARE I HADN'T THE SLIGHTEST NOTION WE WERE SUCH MISERABLE CREATURES. NO ONE CAN SAY IT WAS *YOUR* FAULT THAT THE CASE BROKE DOWN."

Fig. 3.5. *Punch,* 1 June 1867.

ever (in the process of legislating within the limits of the constitution), that it may be the most important to prevent blocking by minorities. But if the constitution (a) forbids discrimination *except after some form of unanimous consent* . . . and (b) enshrines the principle of compensation (when legislation—assumed to be for the common gain—harms the few in favouring the many), there seems to be no other surviving purpose for the unanimity principle at the 'operational' level. Given the entrenchment of these two qualifying rules, it seems to us that simple majority decisions would be acceptable" (Hutt [1966] 1975, 28). We owe our knowledge of this review to Richard Wagner.

Fig. 3.6. *Punch,* 15 July 1867.

Fig. 3.7. *Punch,* 15 July 1867 (detail).

Fig. 3.8. *Punch,* 21 March 1868.

Hutt's larger work, in particular his disagreement with Joan Robinson about the efficiency of price discrimination, is revealing in this context. Robinson's defense of discrimination depends on the utilitarian tradition in which one counts units of utility not people being helped or harmed. This is siding with Edgeworth against Spencer and the classical utilitarians (Peart and Levy 2005b). Robinson developed Edgeworth's mean-utilitarianism via A. C. Pigou, for whom an income transfer from producer to consumer is of no social consequence.

Hutt proposes to reformulate welfare judgments based on the well-being of consumers, who are, of course, the *majority* in any choice. Consumer sovereignty was intended by Hutt to continue the tradition of the classical economists, to make explicit what they took for granted. For Hutt, this tradition explains their unpopularity.

> It cannot be denied that if economists had confined themselves to the purely formal or logical side of their science they would have been less unpopular in society. But all along, orthodox writers in this field have, in fact, been concerned with "the general good" or "the social welfare." They have been constantly stressing the opposition between social advantage and the benefits accruing to particular individuals or particular groups. (1936b, 130)

So what is this "general good"?

> There was nothing subtle about the notion in the economists' minds. It was pure common sense to them. They knew that a tariff on corn would benefit farmers but spread a diffused burden on consumers. There was nothing question-begging about it. The notion of the conflict of interest had been understood by several eighteenth-century pamphleteers and economists. They regarded it in terms of the opposition between organized groups and the community as consumers. It was reflected in the attacks of Turgot and his contemporaries on "the spirit of monopoly," it was stated forcibly by Tucker, it was found in the *Wealth of Nations,* it was implied in subsequent economic writings, and it again crystalized clearly in the mind of Ricardo, who held that the consumers' interests should be paramount. (130–31)

To see the difference between median- and mean-based utilitarianism, consider the now familiar argument that perfect price discrimination and competition are equally efficient. This supposes that a transfer from consumer to producer is of no social concern. But what if one regards an income transfer from one person to another as injustice? Hutt is perhaps the last exemplar of median-based utilitarianism who makes a social decision by counting those helped and those harmed; the many consumers or the few producers.

> The existence of most of the differential charging that we find is based either (in the short run) on the exploitation of co-operant producers possessing immobile resources; or else (in the long run) at the consumers' expense through bringing about an un-

> favourable distribution of investment of productive resources. It is an arbitrary private benefit that is obtained from discrimination in the majority of classes. There are no grounds for assuming that it produces an ideal distribution of investment adjusted to the existence of different scales of preferences on the part of consumers. It represents a pricing system developed in the interests of private profit and based mainly on chance facts arising out of the relations of many co-operating agents in the productive process. (1936a, 77–78)[24]

Hutt asserts that this insistence on distinguishing the interests of the few from the interests of the many caused the great attacks on classical economics.

> We need to look no further than this for the causes of that attitude of mind which has so early seized on Carlyle's condemnation of economics as "the dismal science"; which enabled Kingsley's unscrupulous caricature of an economist [*Alton Locke,* chap. 10] to be accepted as authentic by the public opinion of his day; which led Napoleon to say that if an empire were built of granite, political economy would grind it to powder; which has led to that general dislike and misrepresentation of the Classical economists lasting right down to the present day. "No real Englishman," said Bagehot, "in his secret soul was ever sorry for the death of an economist." (1936b, 131)[25]

Hutt knew much that has been lost.

Bibliography

Bagehot, Walter. 1858. *Estimates of Englishmen and Scotchmen.* London: Chapman and Hall.

Buchanan, James M. 1988. "Economists and the Gains-from-Trade." In *The Collected Works of James M. Buchanan,* vol. 19. Indianapolis: Liberty Fund.

---

24. Thus, in Hutt's *Plan for Reconstruction,* price discrimination was outlawed except in the Joan Robinson case, in which the commodity would not exist at all without discrimination (Hutt 1943, 34–39).

25. So much is right with this paragraph: the Jewish "sweaters" that Hutt mentioned are featured in *Alton Locke* (Levy 2001; Peart and Levy 2005b). But the line from Bagehot is misquoted. It reads: "No real English gentleman, in his secret soul, was ever sorry for the death of a political economist: he is much more likely to be sorry for his life" (Bagehot 1858, 22). "English gentleman" is more to Hutt's point than the "Englishman" that he misremembered

Buchanan, James M., and Gordon Tullock. 1962. *The Calculus of Consent.* Ann Arbor: University of Michigan Press.

Buxton, Thomas Fowell. [1839] 1968. *The African Slave Trade and Its Remedy.* London: Dawsons of Pall Mall.

Buxton, Thomas Fowell [1840] 1968. *Prospectus of the Society for the Extinction of the Slave Trade and of the Civilization of Africa.* London: Dawsons of Pall Mall.

Drescher, Seymour. 2002. *The Mighty Experiment: Free Labor versus Slavery in British Emancipation.* Oxford: Oxford University Press.

Edgeworth, F. Y. 1881. *Mathematical Psychics.* London: C. Kegan Paul.

Fleischaker, Samuel. 2004. "Hume and Smith on Sympathy." Paper presented at the Summer Institute for the Preservation of the History of Economics, George Mason University, Fairfax, Virginia, July.

Hutt, W. H. 1936a. "Discriminating Monopoly and the Consumer." *Economic Journal* 46 (March): 61–79.

Hutt, W. H. 1936b. *Economists and the Public.* London: J. Cape.

Hutt, W. H. 1940. "The Concept of Consumers' Sovereignty." *Economic Journal* 50 (March): 66–77.

Hutt, W. H. 1943. *Plan for Reconstruction: A Project for Victory in War and Peace.* London: Kegan Paul, Trench, Trubner.

Hutt, W. H. [1966] 1975. "Unanimity versus Non-discrimination (as Criteria for Constitutional Validity)." In *Individual Freedom: Selected Writings of William H. Hutt,* edited by Svetozar Pejovich and David Klingman. Westport, Conn.: Greenwood.

Levy, David M. 2001. *How the Dismal Science Got Its Name: Classical Economics and the Ur-Text of Racial Politics.* Ann Arbor: University of Michigan Press.

Levy, David M., and Sandra J. Peart. 2004. "Sympathy and Approbation in Hume and Smith: A Solution to the Other Rational Species Problem." *Economics and Philosophy* 20:331–49.

Macaulay, T. B. [1829] 1978. *Mill's Essay on Government: Utilitarian Logic and Politics.* In *Utilitarian Logic and Politics,* edited by Jack Lively and John Rees. Oxford: Clarendon.

Malthus, T. R. [1798] 2004. *An Essay on the Principle of Population, as It Affects the Future Improvement of Society, with Remarks on the Speculations of Mr. Godwin, M. Condorcet, and Other Writers.* http://www.econlib.org/library/ Malthus/malPop.html.

Mill, James. [1820] 1978. *On Government.* In *Utilitarian Logic and Politics,* edited by Jack Lively and John Rees. Oxford: Clarendon.

Mill, John Stuart. [1834] 1967. "Miss Martineau's Summary of Political Economy." In *Collected Works of John Stuart Mill,* vol. 4. Edited by John M. Robson. Toronto: University of Toronto Press.

Mill, John Stuart. [1848] 2004. *The Principles of Political Economy with Some of Their Applications to Social Philosophy.* 7th ed. Edited by William J. Ashley. http://www.econlib.org/library/Mill/mlP.html.

Mill, John Stuart. [1861] 1969. *Utilitarianism.* In *Collected Works,* vol. 10. Edited by John M. Robson. Toronto: University of Toronto Press.

Mill, John Stuart. [1861] 1977. *Considerations on Representative Government.* In *Collected Works,* vol. 19. Edited by John M. Robson. Toronto: University of Toronto Press.

Packe, Michael St. John. 1954. *The Life of John Stuart Mill.* New York: Macmillan.

Peart, Sandra J., and David M. Levy. 2003a. "Denying Human Homogeneity: Eugenics and the Making of Postclassical Economics." *Journal of the History of Economic Thought* 25, no. 3: 261–88.

Peart, Sandra J., and David M. Levy. 2003b. "Post-Ricardian Political Economy, 1830–1870." In *The Blackwell Companion to the History of Economic Thought,* edited by Warren J. Samuels, John Davis, and Jeff Biddle. Oxford: Blackwell.

Peart, Sandra J., and David M. Levy. 2004. "Sympathy and Its Discontents: 'Greatest Happiness' versus 'General Good.'" *European Journal of History of Economic Thought* 11, no. 3: 453–78.

Peart, Sandra J., and David M. Levy. 2005a. "A Discipline without Sympathy: The Happiness of the Majority and Its Demise." *Canadian Journal of Economics* 38, no. 3: 937–54.

Peart, Sandra J., and David M. Levy. 2005b. *The "Vanity of the Philosopher": From Equality to Hierarchy in Post-classical Economics.* Ann Arbor: University of Michigan Press.

Peart, Sandra J., and David M. Levy. 2005c. "From Cardinal to Ordinal Utility Theory: Darwin and Differential Capacity for Happiness." *American Journal of Economics and Sociology* 64, no. 3: 851–80.

Robbins, Lionel. 1938. "Interpersonal Comparisons of Utility: A Comment." *Economic Journal* 48 (December): 635–41.

Robbins, Lionel. 1952. *Theory of Economic Policy in English Classical Political Economy.* London: Macmillan.

Robbins, Lionel. 1957. "Packe on Mill." *Economica,* n.s., 24 (August): 250–59.

Robbins, Lionel. 1958. *Robert Torrens and the Evolution of Classical Economics.* London: Macmillan.

Robbins, Lionel. 1981. "Economics and Political Economy." *American Economic Review* 71 (May): 1–10.

Samuels, Warren J. 1966. *The Classical Theory of Economic Policy.* Cleveland: World.

Senior, Nassau W. 1835. *Statement of the Provision for the Poor.* London: B. Fellows.

Senior, Nassau W. [1836] 1938. *An Outline of the Science of Political Economy.* London: Allen and Unwin.

Senior, Nassau W. [1841] 1865. "English Poor Laws." In *Historical and Philosophical Essays.* London: Longman, Green, Longman, Roberts and Green.

Smith, Adam. [1759] 2004. *The Theory of Moral Sentiments.* 6th ed http://www.econlib.org/library/Smith/smMS.html.

Smith, Adam. [1776] 2004. *An Inquiry into the Nature and Causes of the Wealth of Nations.* 5th ed. Edited by Edwin Cannan. http://www.econlib.org/library/Smith/ smWN.html.

Viner, Jacob. 1938. Review of *Economists and the Public: A Study of Competition and Opinion. Journal of Political Economy* 46, no. 4: 571–75.

Wallas, Graham. 1898. *The Life of Francis Place, 1771–1854.* London: Longmans, Green.

Whately, E. J. 1866. *Life and Correspondence of Richard Whately, D.D.* London: Longmans, Green.

Whately, Richard. 1833. *Easy Lessons on Money Matters; For the Use of Young People.* London: J. W. Parker.

Whately, Richard. [1827] 1975. *Elements of Logic.* 2nd ed. Delmar, N.Y.: Scholars' Facsimiles and Reprints.

Whately, Richard. [1831] 2002. *Introductory Lectures on Political Economy.* 2nd ed. http://www.econlib.org/library/Whately/whtPE.html.

4 • Economic Organization, Distribution, and the Equality Issue
The Marx-Engels Perspective

Samuel Hollander

Introduction

My first concern is the treatment of distribution by Marx and Engels within the general framework of "historical materialism." After a brief review of their rejection of egalitarian schemes based on "justice" or "morality," I proceed to their objections on grounds of the impossibility of divorcing distribution from conditions of production and the related exchange system. I demonstrate first that growing *inequality* is accorded a strategic and essential role in the evolution of a capitalist-exchange economy. (In any event, Marx and Engels seem to have downplayed the quantitative significance for labor even of major transfers.) That the pattern of distribution could not be altered unilaterally without damaging consequences for production is then shown to govern their hostility to schemes of *communist* organization entailing wages paid according to "equal right" and "the undiminished proceeds of labour." In brief, Marx's communism in its first phase (sometimes referred to as the socialist phase), when there remains a residual influence exerted by the preceding institution,[1] would recognize the essential *inequality* of labor on grounds of efficiency and growth; the celebrated dictum "from each according to his abilities to each according to his needs" applied only in a utopian phase. Engels's rendition of these themes is approached in terms of his critique of Dühring.

Throughout this chapter MECW refers to the *Marx-Engels Collected Works* (New York: International Publishers).

I thank the participants at a Ben-Gurion University departmental seminar, 9 May 2001; a University of Nice seminar, 20 June 2001; the Summer Institute for the Presentation of the History of Economic Thought, George Mason University, 13 July 2001; and Peter Boettke's Political Economy Seminar at George Mason University, 2 November 2001. This chapter, in an earlier version, appeared in Carleton Economic Papers (C. E. P. 02–05) February 2002 and was presented at the History of Economics Society meetings, Atlanta, 4 January 2002. I am particularly indebted to Bridget Butkevich, John Davis, Ragip Ege, Andrew Farrant, David Levy, and Joe Persky for their generous and helpful criticisms.

1. Engels's *Principles of Communism*, and the *Communist Manifesto* are shown in what follows to apply to an earlier period involving communist *political* control but allowance for a residual private sector. The socialist phase, by contrast, entails full-fledged public ownership and central control.

A high degree of respect for the allocative role of markets is then brought into the picture to explain Marx's rejection of contemporary rent-confiscation and price-control schemes. I seek in this context to understand the championship of a full-fledged control system—social ownership of the means of production, central planning, abolition of markets for labor and goods, consumer rationing—notwithstanding such respect, and notwithstanding Engels's severe condemnation of Rodbertus and Dühring for neglecting the role of competition in their socialist schemes. Essentially, the system would ideally be simplified to the point that a sophisticated allocation mechanism would not be required.

I draw some unexpected parallels entailing common ground on the approach to distribution and market process between Marx and Engels and the modern "conservative" or "classical liberal" writers Mises and Hayek.

An overview focuses on the cautious *evolutionary* nature of the Marx-Engels perspective: the development *within* capitalism of forces preparing the ground for a political takeover by the proletariat, preeminently nationalization of industry; the period of transition to full communism with continued though diminishing reliance on a capitalist sector, to which period the *Communist Manifesto* applied; and the *two* phases of communism, the first of which would entail a measure of inequality reflected in differential wage rates.

Objections to Egalitarian Reform

1. The Rejection of Claims Based on Justice

Marx insisted that his case for socialism did not turn on the immorality or inequity of capitalist wage setting in particular or the pattern of distribution in general (Baumol 2001, 231).[2] To the contrary, "[W]e must assume throughout that the wages being paid are *economically* just, i.e. determined by the general laws of political economy" (*Grundrisse* 1857–58, in MECW 28:354). Or again: "[I]s [present-day distribution] not, in fact, the only 'fair' distribution on the basis of the present-day mode of production?" (*Critique of the Gotha Programme* 1875, in MECW 24:84). In his manuscript notes (completed after January 1881) on

2. John Davis has brought to my attention the debate over the status of moral standards in Marx's analysis: whether postcapitalist moral standards can be used to evaluate capitalism (represented to some extent in the actual *proletarian* form of consciousness) consistently with the perspective on morals as reflecting the ruling mode of production. (See, e.g., Tucker 1969 and Wood 1972 on the position that moral standards are determined uniquely in terms of the mode of production; and Husami 1978 for the alternative position.) Even if one accepts that reference to postcapitalist standards—such as that encapsulated in the rule "from each according to his abilities, to each according to his needs"—is almost certainly in the background as an *ultimate* ideal, this was not made the basis of the public case for socialism, as will now become clear.

Adolphe Wagner's *Lehrbuch der politischen Ökonomie,* Marx protests that he was falsely represented by Wagner as maintaining that profit was "a *deduction from,* or *robbery of,* the worker," whereas his position was the precise opposite.

> On the contrary, I depict the capitalist as the necessary functionary of capitalist production and demonstrate at great length that he not only "deducts" or "*robs*" but enforces the *production of surplus value,* thus first helping to create what is to be deducted; what is more, I demonstrate in detail that even if *only equivalents* were exchanged in the exchange of commodities, the capitalist—as soon as he pays the worker the real value of his labour-power—would have every right, i.e. such right as corresponds to this mode of production, to *surplus-value.* (MECW 24:535)

He adds:

> The obscure man falsely attributes to me the view that "the *surplus-value* produced by the workers alone remains, *in an unwarranted manner,* in the hands of the capitalist entrepreneurs." . . . In fact I say the exact opposite: that the production of commodities must necessarily become "capitalist" production of commodities at a certain point, and that according to the *law of value* governing it, the "surplus-value" rightfully belongs to the capitalist and not the worker (558).

And in *Capital* itself Marx referred to "a very cheap sort of sentimentality which declares [the] method of determining the value of labour-power, a method prescribed by the very nature of the case, to be a brutal method" (1965, 173).

Engels read Marx to this same effect in his preface to the first German edition of *Poverty of Philosophy* (1885).

> According to the laws of bourgeois economics, the greatest part of the product does *not* belong to the workers who have produced it. If we now say: that is unjust, that ought not to be so, then that has nothing immediately to do with economics. We are merely saying that this economic fact is in contradiction to our sense of morality. Marx, therefore, never based his communist demands upon this, but upon the inevitable collapse of the capitalist mode of production which is daily taking place before

our eyes to an ever growing degree; he says only that surplus value consists of unpaid labour, which is a simple fact. (MECW 26:281–82)

We may add that in his contribution to *The Labour Standard,* "A Fair Day's Wages for a Fair Day's Work" (7 May 1881), Engels defined the very concept "a fair day's wages" as the subsistence wage, namely, "under normal conditions . . . the sum required to procure to the labourer the means of existence necessary, according to the standard of life of his station and country, to keep himself in working order and to propagate his race" (MECW 24:376–77).

2. The Economic Role of Inequality

I turn now to a strictly economic objection to egalitarian reform. Marx, in his *Poverty of Philosophy* (1847), objected to Proudhon's egalitarianism partly on the grounds of a technical error involving confusion of labor embodied with labor commanded: "Let us see to what extent the application of labour time as a measure of value is incompatible with existing class antagonism and the unequal distribution of the product between the individual worker and the owner of accumulated labour," that is, to what extent "exchange of products measured by labour time results in an equality of payment for all the producers"—as Proudhon maintained (MECW 6:125–26). Proudhon had in fact *proven* nothing: "All the 'equalitarian' consequences which M Proudhon deduces from Ricardo's doctrine are based on a fundamental error. He confounds the value of commodities measured by the quantity of labor embodied in them with the value of commodities measured by '*the value of labour*' " (127). The identification in question implied that *labor was the sole factor*—an error compounded by the further notion that labor was of uniform quality (129)—and could be seen in the invalid identification of production costs with wage costs: "M. Proudhon makes the value of labour the 'determining cause' of the value of products to such an extent that for him *wages,* the official name for the 'value of labour,' form the integral price of all things" (129).[3]

Beyond this there is the principle of historical materialism—that "the mode of production" corresponding to each particular form of class antagonism governed the mode of exchange (including products and factors) rather than the reverse. Consider from this perspective the eco-

3. Marx's objection that Proudhon had failed to appreciate the source and nature of nonlabor income is striking since the 1844 documents had actually commended *Qu'est que la proprieté* (1840) for hitting on a notion of surplus value in a private property system (MECW 4:31–33).

nomic role of income inequality insisted on in reaction to Proudhon's observation in 1846 that "with the progress of collective industry, every day's individual labour produces a greater and greater product, and whereas therefore by a necessary consequence, the worker with the same wage ought to become richer every day, there actually exists estates in society which profit and others which decay" (cited in MECW 6:158). Proudhon's question, "Why was not the English worker of 1840 twenty-seven times as rich as the one of 1770?"—assuming a corresponding productivity increase—implied a failure to appreciate the positive necessity in a class-organized private-property society of "classes which profited and classes which decayed"—*the economic role of income inequality*—such decay, or *dépérissement,* being a condition for "the development of productive forces" and the corresponding "surplus left by labour."

> In raising such a question one would naturally be supposing that the English could have produced this wealth without the historical conditions in which it was produced, such as: private accumulation of capital, modern division of labour, automatic workshops, anarchical competition, the wage system—in short, everything that is based upon class antagonism. Now, these were precisely the necessary conditions of existence for the development of productive forces and of the surplus left by labour. Therefore, to obtain this development of productive forces and this surplus left by labour there had to be classes which profited and classes which decayed. (MECW 6:159)[4]

Moreover, Proudhon's model, designed to explain the source of surplus in terms of a "person society," missed the point entirely. The true "Prometheus" was *class* based, and any program of redistribution in the class-based society implied the undermining of productive capacity and the ability to produce a surplus.

> What then, ultimately, is this Prometheus resuscitated by M. Proudhon? It is society, social relations based on class antagonism. These relations are not relations between individual and individual but between worker and capitalist, between farmer and landlord, etc. Wipe out these relations and you annihilate

4. Marx seems implicitly to assume throughout differential savings propensities between classes.

> all society, and your Prometheus is nothing but a ghost without arms or legs; that is, without automatic workshops, without division of labour—in a word, without everything that you gave him to start with in order to make him obtain this surplus left by labour. (MECW 6:159)

Of this consequence, Proudhon seemed unaware: "If then, in theory, it sufficed to interpret, as M. Proudhon does, the formula of the surplus left by labour in the equalitarian sense, without taking into account the actual conditions of production, it should suffice, in practice, to share out equally among the workers all the wealth at present acquired, without changing in any way the present conditions of production"—which was inconceivable (MECW 6:159).[5] In any event, Marx here added the estimate that "[s]uch a distribution would certainly not assure a high degree of comfort to the individual participants."

3. The Case for Inequality under Communism

Marx's general methodological objection to the party program of 1875 is that to focus on *distribution* at all was to put the cart before the horse since the distributional pattern in any system is a necessary outcome of "the mode of production."[6]

> Quite apart from the analysis so far given, it was in general a mistake to make a fuss about so called *distribution* and put the principle stress on it.
>
> Any distribution whatever of the means of consumption is only a consequence of the distribution of the conditions of production themselves. The latter distribution, however, is a feature of the mode of production itself. The capitalist mode of production, for example, rests on the fact that the material conditions of production are in the hands of nonworkers in the form of capital and land ownership, while the masses are only owners of the personal condition of production, of labour power. If the elements of production are so distributed, then the

5. In his "Wages," in this same period, Marx had written of the "crazy relationship" between capital and labor in the light of which "all Fourierist and other attempts at mediation"—an obvious allusion to redistribution measures—"appear in their true absurdity" (MECW 6:429).

6. *Inequality* in the preceding heading refers specifically to labor's claim to private consumption goods or "individual means of consumption." Other sources of inequality would be eliminated in communist society considering the absence of private ownership of land and capital.

> present-day distribution of the means of consumption results automatically. If the material conditions of production are the collective property of the workers themselves, then there likewise results a distribution of the means of consumption different from the present one. The vulgar socialists (and from them in turn a section of the Democrats) have taken over from the bourgeois economists the consideration and treatment of distribution as independent of the mode of production and hence the presentation of socialism as turning principally on distribution. After the real relation has long been made clear, why retrogress again? (*Critique of the Gotha Programme,* in MECW 24:87–88)

Marx's more specific concern was the party's failure to recognize that the principle applied to *any* system—including a communist system—with particular reference to the "first phase," not the "higher phase,"of communist society.[7] In the higher phase, the distributive rule "from each according to his abilities to each according to his needs" would apply, the division of labor would be abolished, and in general the scarcity problem would be greatly diminished, though apparently not obliterated.

> In a higher phase of communist society, after the enslaving subordination of the individual to the division of labour, and thereby also the antithesis between mental and physical labour, has vanished; after labour has become not only a means of life but life's prime want; after the productive forces have also increased with the all-round development of the individual, and all the springs of common wealth flow more abundantly—only then can the narrow horizon of bourgeois right be crossed in its entirety and society inscribe on its banners: From each according to his abilities, to each according to his needs! (MECW 24:87).

Now the program itself is described by Marx as "altogether deplorable as well as demoralising for the party" (Karl Marx to Wilhelm

---

7. Marx specifically refers to the circumstance that "[b]etween capitalist and communist society lies the period of the revolutionary transformation of the one into the other," corresponding to which "is also a political transition period in which the stage can be nothing but *the revolutionary dictatorship of the proletariat*" (MECW 24:95). He points out that the Gotha Programme "deals neither with this nor with the future state of communist society." On the "period of transition," see Duncan 1973, 170–81.

Bracke, 5 May 1875, reprinted in MECW 24:78). And in the *Critique* itself he actually refers to the program's references to distribution based on the "undiminished proceeds of labour" and on "equal right" and "fair distribution" as a *crime.*

> I have dealt at greater length with the "undiminished proceeds of labour," on the one hand, and with "equal right" and "fair distribution," on the other, in order to show what a crime it is to attempt, on the one hand, to force on our Party again, as dogmas, ideas which in a certain period had some meaning but have now become obsolete verbal rubbish, while again perverting, on the other, the realistic outlook, which it cost so much effort to instill into the Party but which has now taken root in it, by means of ideological, legal and other trash so common among the Democrats and French Socialists. (MECW 24:87)

Consider, then, Marx's response to item 1 of the program: "Labour is the source of all wealth and all culture, and since useful labour is possible only in society and through society, the proceeds of labour belong undiminished with equal right to all members of society" (MECW 24:81). Marx rejected the initial declaration: "*Nature* is just as much the source of use values (and it is surely of such that material wealth consists!) as labour, which itself is only the manifestation of a force of nature, human labour power." As for "*an undiminished distribution,*" there is first the general objection that "If useful labour is possible only in society and through society, the proceeds of labour belong to society—and only so much therefrom accrues to the individual worker as is not required to maintain the 'condition' of labour, society" (82). Marx adds that "the whole paragraph, bungled in style and content, is only there in order to inscribe the Lassallean catchword of the 'undiminished proceeds of labour' as a slogan at the top of the party banner" (83). He promises to "return later to the 'proceeds of labour,' 'equal right,' etc., since the same thing recurs in a somewhat different form further on," alluding to the third item of the program: "The emancipation of labour demands the raising of the means of labour to the common property of society and the collective regulation of the total labour with a fair distribution of the proceeds of labour."

Now it is specifically to the so-called fair distribution that Marx objects, not to "collective regulation," which implies central planning of activity. Before proceeding to his objections to the program we should confirm the support for central control since it is alluded to only in scattered remarks rather than systematically and cannot simply be taken for granted in what follows.

Brief mention is made of "co-operative societies" in the *Critique of the Gotha Programme* (MECW 24:93–94) but with no suggestion that Marx favored them as a feature of communist society. Central planning is apparently alluded to in *The German Ideology* (1845–46)—a joint product of Marx and Engels. They wrote that "with the abolition of . . . private property, with the communist regulation of production . . . the power of the relation of supply and demand is dissolved into nothing, and men [will] once more gain control of exchange, production" (MECW 5:48). In *The Communist Manifesto,* Marx affirms that the outcome of the proposed transitional program would be that "all production [is] concentrated in the hands of a vast association of the whole nation" (MECW 6:698–99). This is the formulation in the 1888 English edition, namely, Samuel Moore's translation edited by Engels. The German editions, however, have "in the hands of associated individuals," which may suggest some form of cooperative organization. But central planning seems to be the favored solution for we also read in the *Manifesto* of the *centralisation* of "all instruments of production in the hands of the State" (504). In *Capital II,* Marx refers to "collective" as distinct from capitalist production, implying central organization (MECW 36:149, 450), and he points out that with the elimination of "money capital"—including preeminently credit—"[*s*]*ociety* distributes labour power and means of production to the different branches of production" (356, emphasis added). *Capital III* points to the situation in which "production is under the actual, predetermining control of society," such control "establish[ing] a relation between the volume of social labour time applied in producing definite articles, and the volume of the social want to be satisfied by these articles" (MECW 37:186). There is also reference to "Asocialised man, the associated producers, rationally regulating their interchange with Nature, bringing it under their common control" (807). Even when explicit allowance is made for cooperation, it is not J. S. Mill's competing cooperatives that Marx had in mind but some form of cooperation under central control.

> If co-operative production is not to remain a sham and a snare; if it is to supersede the Capitalist system; if *united* co-operative societies are to regulate national production *upon a common plan,* thus taking it under their own control, and putting an end to the constant anarchy and periodic convulsions which are the fatality of Capitalist production—what else, gentlemen, would

> it be but communism . . . ? (*The Civil War in France* [1871], in MECW 22:335, emphasis added)[8]

With this frame of reference regarding desirable organization in mind, we turn to Marx's specific objection to the distribution of an "undiminished product" proposed in the party program of 1875. Marx insists first on the deductions that would have to be made from the social product on purely *economic* grounds—deductions for capital maintenance, net investment, and insurance—before distribution for consumption purposes could be allowed.

> But "all members of society" and "equal right" are obviously mere phrases. The crucial point is this, that in this communist society every worker must receive his "undiminished" Lassallean "proceeds of labour."
>
> Let us take first of all the words "proceeds of labour" in the sense of the product of labour; then the collective proceeds of labour are the *total social product*. From this must now be deducted: *First*, cover for replacement of the means of production used up. *Secondly*, additional portion for expansion of production. *Thirdly*, reserve or insurance funds to provide against accidents, disturbances caused by natural factors, etc.

---

8. See note 25 for a similar conclusion regarding Engels on cooperation.

That Engels wished to *abolish the market* entirely and replace its allocative function with a full-fledged central plan relating to production and distribution is suggested already in *Principles of Communism*, question 14, which explains the general conception of the "new social order." The key feature is *central planning "for the social good"* (referred to as "association"), "community of property," and income distribution "by common agreement." "Above all," he writes, " it will have to take the running of industry and all branches of production in general out of the hands of separate individuals competing with each other and instead will have to ensure that all these branches of production are run by society as a whole, i.e., for the social good, according to a social plan and with the participation of all members of society. It will therefore do away with competition and replace it by association. Since the running of industry by individuals had private ownership as its necessary consequence and since competition is nothing but the manner in which industry is run by individual private owners, private ownership cannot be separated from the individual running of industry and competition. Hence, private ownership will also have to be abolished, and in its stead there will be common use of all the instruments of production and the distribution of all products by common agreement, or the so-called community of property. The abolition of private ownership is indeed the most succinct and characteristic summary of the transformation of the entire social system necessarily following from the development of industry, and it is therefore rightly put forward by the Communists as their main demand" (MECW 6:348).

And at the close of his twelve proposals for the communist system listed under question 18, there is mention of *the abolition of money:* "[W]hen all capital, all production, and all exchange are concentrated in the hands of the nation, private ownership will have ceased to exist, money will have become superfluous, and production will have so increased and men will have so much changed that the last forms of the old social relations will also be able to fall away" (351).

> These deductions from the "undiminished proceeds of labour" are an economic necessity and their magnitude is to be determined according to available means and forces, and party by computation of probabilities, but they are in no way calculable by equity. (MECW 24:84)

In essence, labor must be subject to the same "deductions" to meet gross and net investment requirements as under capitalism. The objections to Proudhon would thus not apply. And that is not all, for after the investment-related deductions there were further deductions.

> *First, the general costs of administration not directly appertaining to production.* This part will, from the outset, be very considerably restricted in comparison with present-day society and it diminishes in proportion as the new society develops.
>
> *Secondly, that which is intended for the common satisfaction of needs,* such as schools, health services, etc. From the outset this part grows considerably in comparison with present-day society and it grows in proportion as the new society develops.
>
> *Thirdly, funds for those unable to work,* etc., in short for what is included under so-called official poor relief today. (85)

We come now to the matter of "fair" in the sense of "equal" distribution. It is readily allowed that "what the producer is deprived of in his capacity as a private individual benefits him directly or indirectly in his capacity as a member of society." Nevertheless, Marx presumes that the "equal" distribution—"which the Programme, under Lassallean influence, has alone in view in its narrow fashion"—applies specifically "to that part of the means of consumption which is divided among the individual members of the collective" or to distribution for *private* ends. What follows points to Marx's adherence to a system involving labor certificates and the absence of markets.

> The social working day consists of the sum of the individual hours of work; the individual labour time of the individual producer is the part of the social working day contributed by him, his share in it. He receives a certificate from society that he has furnished such and such an amount of labour (after deducting his labour for the common funds), and with this certificate he draws from the social stock of means of consumption as much as the same amount of labour costs. The same amount of labour

> which he has given to society in one form he receives back in another. (MECW 24:86)[9]

But Marx goes a step further. What matters is the application of an "equal standard," not the crude equality envisaged by the party, and such application implies recognition of *the essential inequality of labor.*

> But one man is superior to another physically or mentally and so supplies more labour in the same time, or can work for a longer time; and labour, to serve as a measure, must be defined by its duration or intensity, otherwise it ceases to be a standard of measurement. This *equal* right is an unequal right for unequal labour. It recognises no class distinctions, because everyone is only a worker like everyone else; but it tacitly recognises the unequal individual endowment and thus productive capacity of the workers as natural privileges. *It is, therefore a right of inequality, in its content, like every right.* Right by its nature can exist only as the application of an equal standard; but unequal individuals (and they would not be different individuals if they were not unequal) are measurable by an equal standard only insofar as they are made subject to an equal criterion, are taken from a *certain* side only, for instance, in the present case, are regarded *only as workers* and nothing more is seen in them, everything else being ignored. (MECW 24:86–87)[10]

The concern here is entirely with *natural* differences between individuals with regard to "talent"—physical and mental. Nothing is said either of productivity differentials relating to learned skills or of the sort of consideration that Adam Smith and J. S. Mill take into account in their wage structure analyses, namely, the characteristics attached to various jobs and the attitudes toward them. The contrast is striking. For Smith and Mill the nonpecuniary characteristics explain how under

---

9. Marx's labor certificates would not circulate, and thus would not constitute *money.* They would be used solely to redeem consumer goods from the relevant producing authority, a cloakroom function only. On this matter, see also *Capital II:* "The producers may, for all it matters, receive paper vouchers entitling them to withdraw from the social supplies of consumer goods a quantity corresponding to their labour time. These vouchers are not money. They do not circulate" (MECW 36:356). Objections to Rodbertus and Dühring in this regard are discussed later in this chapter.

10. Marx adds: "Besides, one worker is married, another not; one has more children than another, etc., etc. Thus, given an equal amount of work done, and hence an equal share in the social consumption fund, one will in fact receive more than another, one will be richer than another, etc. To avoid all these defects, right would have to be unequal rather than equal" (ibid.).

competitive equilibrium conditions wage differentials exist despite *natural equality*. But Marx assumes *natural inequality* and would have had no reason to appeal to such differentials in the analysis of competitive conditions and a fortiori that of collective organization.

That natural inequality of labor had to be recognized in the "first phase" is represented as an inevitable "defect" in a communist society that has just emerged "after prolonged birth pangs from capitalist society. Right can never be higher than the economic structure of society and its cultural development which this determines" (MECW 24:87). This stage entails full-fledged common ownership and an absence of markets, a stage beyond the period of transition from capitalism discussed in the *Communist Manifesto* (see below). Marx's point is that in the first stage of communist society the original capitalist system nonetheless leaves its mark in sharp contrast, it is throughout implied, to the ultimate stage.

> Within the collective society based on common ownership of the means of production, the producers do not exchange their products; just as little does the labour employed on the products appear here *as the value* of these products, as a material quality possessed by them, since now, in contrast to capitalist society, individual labour no longer exists in an indirect fashion but directly as a component part of the total labour. The phrase "proceeds of labour," objectionable even today on account of its ambiguity, thus loses all meaning.
>
> What we are dealing with here is a communist society, not as it has *developed* on its own foundations, but on the contrary, just as it *emerges* from capitalist society, which is thus in every respect, economically, morally and intellectually, still stamped with the birth-marks of the old society from whose womb it emerges. Accordingly, the individual producer receives back from society—after the deductions have been made—exactly what he gives to it. What he has given to it is his individual quantum of labour. . . .
>
> Here obviously the same principle prevails as that which regulates the exchange of commodities, as far as this is the exchange of equal values. Content and form are changed, because under the altered circumstances no one can give anything except his labour, and because, on the other hand, nothing can pass to the ownership of individuals except individual means of consumption. But, as far as the distribution of the latter among the individual producers is concerned, the same principle prevails as in the exchange of commodity-equivalents; a given

> amount of labour in one form is exchanged for an equal amount of labour in another form.
>
> Hence, *equal right* here is still in principle—*bourgeois right,* although principle and practice are no longer at loggerheads, while the exchange of equivalents in commodity exchange only exists *on the average* and not in the individual case.
>
> In spite of this advance, this *equal right* is still constantly encumbered by a bourgeois limitation. The right of the producers is *proportional* to the labour they supply; the equality consists in the fact that measurement is made with an *equal standard,* labour. (85–86)[11]

And it is precisely at this point that Marx insists that the principle of distribution based on equal labor implies *inequality.*[12]

Engels on Dühring

The principle of historical materialism governs the critique by Engels of Eugen Dühring's *Revolution in Science*—the celebrated *Anti-Dühring* of 1878.[13] Distribution on this principle is the *dependent* variable.

> The materialist conception of history starts from the proposition that the production and, next to production, the exchange of things produced, is the basis of all social structure; that in every society that has appeared in history, the manner in which wealth is distributed and society divided into classes or estates is dependent upon what is produced, how it is produced, and how the products are exchanged. (MECW 25:254)

More specifically, characteristic of each historical stage is *growing inequality of distribution,* which signals "that the community is already beginning to break up"; this applies quite generally, although it is accompanied under capitalism by the emergence of sharp class differences

11. Again one notes the absence of markets and exchange, thus of money and "value"—the indirect measure of labor embodied—in Marx's perception of the first phase of communist society. This theme is much developed in the *Grundrisse* (MECW 28:92–96).

12. Marx also raises the objection to the party program that equal distribution to "all members of society" begs the question: "To those who do not work as well? What remains then of the 'undiminished proceeds of labour'? Only to those members of society who work? What remains then of 'the equal right' of all members of society?" (ibid., 84).

13. Marx read and approved of *Anti-Dühring* and in fact collaborated with Engels in various ways (see the editorial preface to MECW 25:xiii).

(MECW 25:136–37). The indication provided by inequality that "the community is already beginning to break up" reflects the necessitarian role played by inequality—that inequality is inevitable and incorrigible except by means of a transformation of the mode of production and exchange. As for the capitalist stage, the process had evolved with great rapidity: "modern capitalist production, which is hardly three hundred years old and has become predominant only since the introduction of modern industry, that is, only in the last hundred years, has in this short time brought about antitheses in distribution—concentration of capital in a few hands on the one side and concentration of the propertyless masses in the big towns on the other—which must of necessity bring about its downfall." In this sense, distribution was "not a merely passive result of production and exchange [but] in its turn reacts upon both of them" (137).

From all this there also emerges the irrelevance of any approach to inequality based on an appeal to morality and justice; in fact social abuses—"necessary consequences" of the existing mode of production—do not even appear as an injustice to the "exploited masses" until the appropriate historical moment (MECW 25:137–38). Accordingly, "The task of economic science"—"scientific socialism"—was "to show that the social abuses which have recently been developing are necessary consequences of the existing mode of production, but at the same time also indications of its approaching dissolution; and to reveal, within the already dissolving economic form of motion, the elements of the future new organisation of production and exchange which will put an end to those abuses" (138).

By contrast, the "new" (eighteenth-century) science of political economy presented the laws of production and exchange as "eternal laws of nature . . . deduced from the nature of man" not as an expression of the "conditions and requirements of their epoch." Engels had in mind here Smith and the physiocrats (MECW 25:139), but Dühring was in the same mold: he "could not offer us anything except a bad translation of Rousseau's theory of equality into the language of socialism, much as one has long been able to hear much more effectively rendered in any workers' tavern in Paris" (141). Engels himself does not hesitate to speak the language of "morality"; his point is the uselessness of all such appeals until the time is ripe (145). Thus, calls for "the abolition of class antagonisms and class distinctions . . . up to 1830 had left the working and suffering classes cold" (145). This was no longer the case; and Engels's summary explanation contains all the essentials of the Marxist position regarding the "crying contradiction" between the system of distribution based on the advanced capitalist mode of production and that mode itself—assuring the inevitable "revolution which will put an end to all class distinctions"—an account including (as usual) reference to both the downward absolute trend in real wages and cyclical instability (145–46).

Dühring's failure manifested itself precisely in his use of "force" to understand distributive patterns, and his appeal to a mutable standard of morality and law.

> Firstly, he saves himself the trouble of explaining the various forms of distribution which have hitherto existed, their differences and their causes; taken in the lump, they are simply of no account—they rest on oppression, on force. Secondly, he thereby transfers the whole theory of distribution from the sphere of economics to that of morality and law, that is, from the sphere of established material facts to that of more or less vacillating opinions and sentiments. He therefore no longer has any need to investigate or to prove things; he can go on declaiming to his heart's content and demand that the distribution of the products of labour should be regulated, not in accordance with its real causes, but in accordance with what seems ethical and just to him, Herr Dühring. But what seems just to Herr Dühring is not at all immutable, and hence very far from being a genuine truth. (MECW 25:144)

Marx, as we have seen, estimated that the redistribution envisaged in Proudhon's scheme "would certainly not assure a high degree of comfort for the individual participants" (above, 66–69). Engels, too, implies as much in *Anti-Dühring* by minimizing both the responsibility of "force" (including state intervention) in aggravating income inequality and its potential to reduce it.

Marx, as we know, insisted on wage differentials as a necessary feature even of the first stage of communism and a fortiori under capitalism. Now Dühring condemned Marx for adopting a typically *bourgeois* perspective, and Engels leaped to Marx's defense, insisting on wage-scale differentials under capitalism on the grounds that "[i]n a society of private producers, private individuals or their families pay the cost of training the qualified worker" (187). Moreover, understanding Dühring as denying that differential *values* emerged as a result of compound labor, he pointed out how fortunate it was for Dühring "that fate did not make him a manufacturer, and thus saved him from fixing the value of his commodities on the basis of this new rule [of treating all labor equally] and thereby running infallibly into the arms of bankruptcy"

(185). But the complaint is extended: Dühring applied his rule to his future commune "entailing the pure heavenly air of equality and justice." By contrast, under Engels's vision of socialism, the planners *would* ascribe "greater values" to productions of compound labor, *though pay differentials would not be recognized:* "In a socialistically organised society, these costs [of training] are borne by society, and to it therefore belong the fruits, the greater values produced by compound labour. The worker himself has no claim to extra pay. And from this, incidentally, follows the moral that at times there is a drawback to the popular demand of the workers for 'the full proceeds of labour.'"[14]

Here we seem to have pinned Engels down to a clear-cut statement regarding a crucial aspect of his position on distribution in his communist society. But in this case is there not a severe conflict with Marx, who insisted in 1875 on the recognition of "unequal individual endowment and thus productive capacity of the workers as natural privileges"? There is not if Marx intended specifically recognition of differentials reflecting "*natural*" characteristics, while Engels had in mind *acquired* characteristics involving training paid for by society as a whole. And this solution is the likely one since a primary purpose of *Anti-Dühring* was to refute the notion ascribed to Dühring of "*natural*" equality between individuals (88–99).[15] Engels did allow that the "idea of equality" still play[ed] an important agitational role in the socialist movement of almost every country" (95), but he insisted that the "real" or scientific content of the proletarian demand was *strictly limited* to "the abolition of classes" and went no further (99). Claims beyond that were an "absurdity," considering the enormous range of individual character differences. And Engels cites *Capital* to the effect that the idea of equality "already possesses the fixity of a popular prejudice."

We conclude then that Engels's own insistence on *equal* pay under communism must apply only to skills funded socially—in contrast to training funded privately under capitalism—and, as with Marx, not to *natural* differences. What, though, of the *ultimate* communist state? Workers—that is, all members of society—would be paid at that future time not in terms of equal pay per hour whether the work is that of a porter or an architect, as Dühring proposed—albeit presumptively at a "higher wage" than under capitalism—but on a completely different principle *since functional specialization would no longer exist* (186).

---

14. The term *value* is inappropriate (see my discussion of it in the following pages).

15. Engels maintained that Dühring himself, by introducing an entire range of character differences, undermined his own general notion of equality, as had already been done by Rousseau in *Discours sur l'origine et les fondemens de l'inégalité* (1754, published in 1755 [MECW 25:90–91]).

The Allocative Role of the Free Market versus Central Control

A keen appreciation of the allocative function of markets is apparent in a variety of contexts, one of which provides a potent example of Marx's insistence on the constraint imposed by the market system on income redistribution proposals. For Marx in *Poverty of Philosophy* (1847) rejected, on price-theoretic grounds and in terms of the dynamics of growth, the more specific proposals for state confiscation of rent by James Mill, Cherbuliez, and Hilditch, which he represented as "a frank expression of the hatred the industrial capitalist bears towards the landed proprietor" (MECW 6:203). Apart from the complexity that "rent" often included interest paid to the landowner on capital incorporated in the land, land valuation indexes ("cadastres")—on which any confiscation would have to be based—could not be taken as settled once and for all but were subject to continuous disturbance. Accordingly, "rent could not be the invariable index of the degree of fertility of the land, since every moment the modern application of chemistry is changing the nature of the soil and geological knowledge is just now in our days"—here referring to the English eastern counties—"beginning to revolutionize all the old estimates of relative fertility"; moreover, "fertility is not so natural a quality as might be thought [but] is closely bound up with the social relations of the time. A piece of land may be very fertile for corn growing, and yet the market price may induce the cultivators to turn it into an artificial pastureland and thus render it infertile" (203–4). And in rejecting Proudhon's view of land as "capital which never perishes" Marx points out, "Land as capital is fixed capital; but fixed capital gets used up just as much as circulating capital. Improvements to the land need reproduction and upkeep. . . . There are even instances when land as capital might disappear even though the improvements remain incorporated in the land"—such as the case when "rent proper is wiped out by the competition of new and more fertile soils" or when scarce improvements lose their value on becoming "universal owing to the development of agronomy" (205). All of this pointed away from the *static* conception of rent attributed to Proudhon—his notion (in Marx's terms) of an "invariable index of the degree of the fertility of the land" (203).

A striking instance of Marx's respect for the market is provided by a leading article in the *New York Daily Tribune* condemning Napoleon III's plan to regulate bread prices throughout France (13 December 1858, MECW 16:110–14). Marx's objection turns on the array of *further* interventions that would be required to enforce the controls, drawing on the experience of Paris, which had instituted them locally and where—at the end of the day—"the experiment proved a complete failure, the price of bread rising above the official maximum during the bad seasons, from 1855 to 1857" (111). His forecast regarding the extension to France as a whole—as it applied in practice to "good years" and the maintenance of a price floor—emphasizes the unthought of consequences of the proposed measure, including opportunities for "jobs and plunder" of all kinds.

> By the artificial demand to be created through the means of three months' reserve, Napoleon tries to enhance prices artificially, and thus stop the mouth to agricultural France. On the other hand, he proclaims himself a sort of socialist providence to the proletarians of the towns, although in a rather awkward way, since the first palpable effect of his decree must be to make them pay more for their loaf than before. The "savior of property" shows the middle class that not even the formal intervention of his own mock Legislatures, but a simple personal ukase on his part, is all that is wanted to make free with their purses, dispose of municipal property, trouble the course of trade, and subject their monetary dealings to his private cachets. Lastly, the question is still to be considered from the pure Bonapartist point of view. Immense buildings for public granaries will become necessary over the whole of France; and what a fresh field they will open for jobs and plunder. An unexpected turn is also given to the trade in breadstuffs. What profits to be pocketed by the Crédit Mobilier and the other gambling companions of his Imperial Majesty! At all events, we may be sure that the Imperial Socialist will prove no more successful in raising the price of bread than he has been in attempts to reduce it. (114)

Over and again in his *Poverty of Philosophy* of 1847, republished by Engels in the German edition of 1885, Marx insisted on the demand component: "The exchange value of a product depends upon its abundance or its scarcity, but always in relation to demand" (MECW 6:115); Proudhon "has simply forgotten about *demand,* and that a thing can be scarce and abundant insofar as it is in demand" (115); Proudhon's "abundance seems to be something spontaneous. He completely forgets that they are people who produce it, and that is in their interest never to lose sight of demand" (116). As for the long run, he forcefully rejected Proudhon's labor theory and also the labor-based prices proposed for a communist system.

> Products will in future be exchanged in the exact ratio of the labour time they have cost. Whatever may be the proportion of supply to demand, the exchange of commodities will always be made as if they had been produced proportionately to the demand. Let M. Proudhon take it upon himself to formulate and lay down such a law, and we shall relieve him of the necessity of giving proofs. If, on the other hand, he insists on justifying his theory, not as a legislator, but as an economist, he will have to prove that the *time* needed to create a commodity indicates exactly the degree of its *utility* and marks its proportional relation to the demand, and in consequence, to the total amount of wealth. In this case, if a product is sold at a price equal to its cost of production, supply and demand will always be evenly balanced; for the cost of production is supposed to express the true relation between supply and demand. . . .
>
> To return to M. Proudhon's thesis; since the labour time necessary for the production of an article is not the expression of its degree of utility, the exchange value of this same article, determined beforehand by the labour time embodied in it, can never regulate the correct relation of supply to demand, that is, the proportional relation in the sense M. Proudhon attributes to it at the moment. (132–34)

So much for the static level of conception. Capital movement between industries is dictated by alterations to demand-supply conditions.

It is not the sale of a given product at the price of its cost of production that constitutes the "proportional relation" of supply to demand, or the proportional quota of this product relatively to the sum total of production; it is the *variations in demand and supply* that show the producer what amount of a given commodity he must produce in order to receive at least the cost of production in exchange. And, as these variations are continually occurring, there is also a continual movement of withdrawal and application of capital in the different branches of industry.

It is historiographically significant that Marx should have cited, appreciatively, passages from Ricardo on the operation of the allocation mechanism in response to deviations of market from cost price.

> It is only in consequence of such variations, that capital is *apportioned* precisely, in the requisite abundance and no more, to the production of the different commodities which happen to be

in demand. With the rise or fall of price, profits are elevated above, or depressed below their general level, and capital is either encouraged to enter into, or is warned to depart from the particular employment in which the variation has taken place [Ricardo 1951–1973, 88, Marx's emphasis]. . . .

When we look to the markets of a large town, and observe how regularly they are supplied both with home and foreign commodities, in the quantity in which they are required, under all the circumstances of varying demand, arising from the caprice of taste, or a change in the amount of population, without often producing either the effects of a glut from a too abundant supply, or an enormously high price from the supply being unequal to the demand, we must confess that the principle which apportions capital to each trade *in the precise amount that is required,* is more active than is generally supposed [89–90] (MECW 6:134–35, Marx's emphasis in original)

These "neoclassical" themes are followed through with a vengeance by Engels. Appreciation of the allocative function of markets emerges strikingly in the preface to his 1885 edition, where he attacks Rodbertus's version of labor money precisely because of its *neglect of the competitive allocation mechanism.* Thus, whereas Marx's labor tickets fulfilled a cloakroom function only (see note 9), Rodbertus's labor tickets—according to Engels's account—allocated to workers in the various state industries, would circulate and be used freely to buy the commodities made available by the authority of the market at *given* labor-based prices, implying a degree of genuine consumer choice. Rodbertus maintained that all markets would clear on the basis of the planners' "calculation" relating to the number of labor tickets issued and the quantities of each type of good produced. It was to this scheme that Engels objected.

To desire, in a society of producers who exchange their commodities, to establish the determination of value by labour time, by forbidding competition to establish this determination of value through pressure on prices in the only way in which it can be established, is therefore merely to prove that, at least in this sphere, one has adopted the usual Utopian disdain of economic laws.

Secondly, competition, by bringing into operation the law of value of commodity production in a society of producers who exchange their commodities, precisely thereby brings about the

> only organization and arrangement of social production which is possible in the circumstances. *Only through the undervaluation or overvaluation of products is it forcibly brought home to the individual commodity producers what society requires or does not require and in what amounts.* But it is precisely this sole regulator that the Utopia advocated by Rodbertus among others wishes to abolish. And if we then ask what guarantee we have that [the] necessary quantity and not more of each product will be produced, that we shall not go hungry in regard to corn and meat while we are choked in beet sugar and drowned in potato spirit, that we shall not lack trousers to cover our nakedness while trouser buttons flood by the million—Rodbertus triumphantly shows us his famous calculation, according to which the correct certificate has been handed out for every superfluous pound of sugar, for every unsold barrel of spirit, for every unusable trouser button, a calculation which "works out" exactly, and according to which "all claims will be satisfied and the liquidation correctly brought about." And anyone who does not believe this can apply to the governmental chief revenue office accountant X in Pomerania, who has checked the calculation and found it correct, and who, as one who has never yet been caught lacking with the accounts, is thoroughly trustworthy. (MECW 26:287–88, emphasis added).

Hutchison is amazed that Engels would have condemned Rodbertus while neglecting to raise the same, or indeed any other, objection against communist organization, feeling no "intellectual or moral obligation to give some thought to the kind of economic organization which would, or could, follow" the demise of capitalism (1981, 14).[16] Hutchison is too harsh. Engels's complaint, as it emerges in the passage just quoted, is that Rodbertus *retained* significant features of a market system yet rejected the competitive pricing mechanism. A similar complaint is addressed against Dühring—that he wished *to retain elements of the market system* yet preclude its effective operation (MECW 25:275). This, to Engels, was an unacceptable halfway house. Like Marx, he perceived of a system *excluding markets,* one involving centralized decisions on in-

16. Sowell in his account sees no problem and writes simply: "Although it may be empirically true that different ideologies generally regard central planning in different ways, it is not ultimately in principle an ideological question. Marx and Engels were unsparing in their criticisms of their fellow socialists and fellow communists who wanted to replace price competition with central planning" (1980, 218). But I see a problem to be solved as Marx and Engels appreciated the competitive pricing mechanism but nonetheless supported central control.

vestment, output and pay, and—so it seems from the contrast with Rodbertus—consumer rationing.

Also in *Anti-Dühring* (1878)—a work approved of by Marx and to which he contributed (see note 13)—it emerges that in communist society, excluding money and markets, direct procedures suffice to arrive at labor embodiments. The indirect procedures of capitalism involving reference to money prices are avoided by "direct social production and direct distribution [which] preclude all exchange of commodities, therefore also the transformation of the products into commodities (at any rate within the community),[17] and consequently also their transformation into *values*" (MECW 25:294). The entire notion of *value* in fact becomes irrelevant.[18] All this is confirmed by further reference to such a society's *direct calculation* of the labor time required in the production of, say, "a steam-engine . . . or a hundred square yards of cloth of a certain quality" without reference to any "third product" acting as some sort of measure of value.

> From the moment when society enters into possession of the means of production and uses them in direct association for production, the labour of each individual, however varied its specifically useful character may be, becomes at the start and directly social labour. The quantity of social labour contained in a product need not then be established in a roundabout way; daily experience shows in a direct way how much of it is required on the average. Society can simply calculate how many hours of labour are contained in a steam-engine, a bushel of wheat of the last harvest, or a hundred square yards of cloth of a certain quality. It could therefore never occur to it still to express the quantities of labour put into the products, quantities which it will then know directly and in their absolute amounts, in a third product, in a measure which, besides, is only relative, fluctuating, inadequate, though formerly unavoidable for lack of a better one, rather than express them in their natural, adequate and absolute measure, *time*. . . . Hence, on the assumption that we made above, society will not assign values to products. It will not express the simple fact that the hundred square yards of cloth have required for their production, say, a thousand hours

17. This opens up a range of issues related to foreign trade.

18. This is true also of ancient Indian communities and the family communities of the southern Slavs, whose "members are directly associated for production; the work is distributed according to tradition and requirements, and likewise the products to the extent that they are destined for consumption" (MECW 25:294).

> of labour in the oblique and meaningless way, stating that they have the *value* of a thousand hours of labour (MECW 25:294).[19]

Fully to appreciate the position in *Anti-Dühring* we must keep in mind a concern that to permit money to circulate would inevitably lead to a reemergence of capitalist organization. For example, Dühring's money did not act as "a mere labour certificate" but fulfilled a genuine "monetary" function as far as concerns private saving with potentially devastating consequences.

> Herr Dühring gives everyone a right to "quantitatively equal consumption" [268], but he cannot compel anyone to exercise it. On the contrary, he is proud that in the world he has created everyone can do what he likes with his money. He therefore cannot prevent some from setting aside a small money hoard, while others are unable to make ends meet on the wage paid to them. He even makes this inevitable by explicitly recognising in the right of inheritance that family property should be owned in common; whence comes also the obligation of the parents to maintain their children. But this makes a wide breach in quantitatively equal consumption. The bachelor lives like a lord, happy and content with his eight or twelve marks a day, while the widower with eight minor children finds it very difficulty to manage on this sum. On the other hand, by accepting money in payment without any question, the commune leaves open the door to the possibility that this money may have been obtained otherwise than by the individual's own labour. . . . The commune does not know where it comes from. But in this way all conditions are created permitting metallic money, which hitherto played the role of a mere labour certificate, to exercise its real money function. Both the opportunity and the motive are present, on the one hand to form a hoard, and on the other to run into debt. The needy individual borrows from the individual who builds up a hoard. The borrowed money, accepted by the commune in payment for means of subsistence, once more becomes what it is in present-day society, the social incarnation of human labour, the real measure of labour, the general medium of circulation. All the "laws and administrative regulations" [323] in the world are just as powerless against it as they

19. The opening reference to variations in the "specifically useful character" of labor indicates the *first* not the *mature* stage of communism.

> are against the multiplication table or the chemical composition of water. And as the builder of the hoard is in a position to extort interest from people in need, usury is restored along with metallic money functioning as money. (MECW 25:289–90)

The retention of money as means of purchase and payment in *international trade* aggravated the private motive to accumulate and, with it, the demise of the entire commune system:

> Up to this point we have only considered the effects of a retention of metallic money within the field of operation of the Dühring economic commune. But outside this field the rest of the world, the profligate world, meanwhile carries on contentedly in the old accustomed way. On the world market gold and silver remain *world money,* a general means of purchase and payment, the absolute social embodiment of wealth. And this property of the precious metal gives the individual members of the economic communes a new motive to accumulate a hoard, get rich, exact usury; the motive to manoeuvre freely and independently with regard to the commune and beyond its borders and to realize on the world market the private wealth which they have accumulated. The usurers are transformed into dealers in the medium of circulation, bankers, controllers of the medium of circulation and of world money and thus into controllers of the means of production, even though these may still for many years be registered nominally as the property of the economic and trading communes. And so the hoarders and usurers, transformed into bankers, become the masters also of the economic and trading communes themselves (MECW 25:290).

We turn now to proposals regarding consumer demand. Direct calculation—involving mainly but not only labor inputs, as we shall see—is fundamental to the planning process envisaged, *given* the *pattern of consumption.*

> It is true that even then it will still be necessary for society to know how much labour each article of consumption requires for its production. It will have to arrange its plan of production in accordance with its means of production, which include, in particular, its labour-powers. The useful effects of the various articles of consumption, compared with one another and with the

> quantities of labour required for their production, will in the end determine the plan. People will be able to manage everything very simply, without the intervention of much-vaunted "value." (MECW 25:294–5)[20]

Whence the assumed pattern of consumption? Since nothing more is said regarding consumer demand, one is invited to conclude that it, too, is decided on directly by the central planners. This in fact is my impression. It is unlikely that Engels had in mind freedom of consumer choice when, a little earlier in the text, he compared the "social anarchy of production," as it existed, with the "social regulation of production upon a definite plan according to the needs of the community *and of each individual,*" referring here to "direct social appropriation, as means to the maintenance and extension of production" (investment) and "*direct individual appropriation,* as means of subsistence and enjoyment" (consumption) (MECW 25:267, emphasis added). After all, he had been expatiating on the *anarchical* character of capitalist production due in part to ignorance of markets: "No one knows how much of his particular article is coming on the market, nor how much of it will be wanted. No one knows whether his individual product will meet an actual demand, whether he will be able to make good his costs of production or even to sell his commodity at all" (259). The solution to the enormous waste of resources under capitalism, with an eye to cyclical instability in particular, lay precisely in "the socialized appropriation of the means of production."

> This solution can only consist in the practical recognition of the social nature of the modern forces of production, and therefore in the harmonising of the modes of production, appropriation, and exchange with the socialised character of the means of production. And this can only come about by society openly and directly taking possession of the productive forces which have outgrown all control except that of society as a whole. The social character of the means of production and of the products today reacts against the producers, periodically disrupts all production and exchange, acts only like a law of nature working blindly forcibly, destructively. But with the taking over by society of the productive forces, the social character of the means of production and of the products will be utilised by the producers with a perfect understanding of its nature and instead of being a

20. Here Engels refers to a passage in his earlier *Outlines* of 1844.

> source of disturbance and periodical collapse, will become the most powerful lever of production itself. (MECW 25:266)

All this, one should note, repeats what appeared in Engels's *Outlines* of 1844 (reprinted in MECW, vol. 3), that ignorance of the pattern of consumption was the source of "periodic upheavals" under capitalism in contrast to the communist solution: "If the producers as such knew how much the consumers required, if they were to organise production, if they were to share it out amongst themselves, then the fluctuations of competition and its tendency to crisis would be impossible" (434). This link between 1878 and 1844 is significant since Engels himself refers readers back to the former work. "As long ago as 1844 I stated that the above-mentioned balancing of useful effects and expenditure of labour on making decisions concerning production was all that would be left, in a communist society, of the politico-economic concept of value" (MECW 25:295n).[21] And he seems to answer our question—*Whence the given pattern of consumption that is taken for granted*?—for the allusion here is apparently to *communal* decision making regarding production based on "*inherent utility*" rather than *personal* judgment.

> Value is the relation of production costs to utility. The first application of value is the decision as to whether a thing ought to be produced at all; i.e., as to whether utility counterbalances production costs. Only then can one talk of the application of value to exchange. The production costs of two objects being equal, the deciding factor determining their comparative value will be utility.
>
> This basis is the only just basis of exchange. But if one proceeds from this basis who is to decide the utility of the object? The mere opinion of the parties concerned? Then, in any event, *one* will be cheated. Or are we to assume a determination grounded in the inherent utility of the object independent of the parties concerned and not apparent to them? If so, the exchange can only be effected by *coercion*, and each party considers itself cheated. The contradiction between the real inherent utility of the thing and the determination of that utility, between the determination of utility and the freedom of those who exchange, cannot be superseded without superseding private property; and once this is superseded there can no longer be any question

21. He adds: "The scientific justification for this statement . . . was made possible only by Marx's *Capital*" (MECW 25:295n).

of exchange as it exists at present. The practical application of the concept of value will then be increasingly confined to the decision about production, and that is its proper sphere. (MECW 3:426).[22]

As mentioned, the position of *Anti-Dühring* was approved of by Marx. Marx himself, in scattered comments, implies communal decisions regarding the allocation of consumption goods. It is suggested by the formulation whereby the vouchers distributed to workers "entitl[ed] them to withdraw from the social supplies of consumer goods a quantity corresponding to their labour time" (see note 9). And in *Poverty of Philosophy* he asserts, "In a future society, in which class antagonism will have ceased, in which there will no longer be any classes, use will no longer be determined by the *minimum* time of production; but the time of production devoted to an article will be determined by the degree of its social utility" (MECW 6:134).[23]

If my interpretation is accurate, it becomes easier to understand how, in the absence of money and markets, the actual allocation of consumer goods was to be accomplished.[24] What was apparently envisaged is a sort of "war economy" entailing the production of goods selected by the planners and allocated according to workers' claims based on their labor contributions—perhaps rights to a *bundle* of goods is what was envisaged—with account taken of natural skill differentials (see also p. 93, below regarding autarky). The objections to Rodbertus's labor ticket scheme, discussed earlier, also point in this direction.

All this reduces the force of Hutchison's criticisms. Even so, there remains the naive belief that the planners were capable of making accu-

---

22. There is, however, a passage that might be read as allowing consumer freedom.

> The truth of the relation of competition is the relation of consumption to productivity. In a world worthy of mankind there will be no other competition than this. The community will have to calculate what it can produce with the means at its disposal; and in accordance with the relationship of this productive power to the mass of consumers it will determine how far it has to raise or lower production, how far it has to give way to, or curtail, luxury. But so that they may be able to pass a correct judgment on this relationship and on the increase in productive power to be expected from a rational state of affairs within the community, I invite my readers to consult the writings of the English Socialists, and partly also those of Fourier. (MECW 3:435)

23. In corrections in Marx's hand, "à un objet" (to an article) is replaced with "aux différents objets" and the qualifying "social" is inserted (editorial notes, MECW 6:134n).

24. The question of freedom of consumer choice was central to the Dobb-Lerner debate of the 1930s. See, in chronological order, Dobb 1933; Lerner 1934–35a; Dobb 1934–35; and Lerner 1934–35b.

rate estimates of the labor inputs required and the distribution of labor tickets according to the pay differentials permitted and corresponding consumption quotas—that all this could be achieved, as Engels thought, "very simply." In point of fact, the planning task envisaged is rather more complex than we have so far suggested for planners would have to make allowance in their cost calculations, as shadow or accounting returns, for *interest* and *rent* based on the productivity contribution of land and capital and not only for labor. Engels insisted on this as early as 1844.

> If . . . we abandon private property, rent is reduced to its truth, to the rational notion which essentially lies at its root. The value of the land divorced from it as rent then reverts to the land itself. *This value, to be measured by the productivity of equal areas of land subjected to equal applications of labour, is indeed taken into account as part of the production costs when determining the value of products;* and like rent, it is the relation of productivity to competition—but to true competition, such as will be developed when its time comes. (MECW 3:430, emphasis added)

> If we abandon private property, then all these unnatural divisions [attributed to capitalism] disappear. The difference between interest and profit disappears; capital is nothing without labour, without movement. *The significance of profit is reduced to the weight which capital carries in the determination of the costs of production;* and profit thus remains inherent in capital, in the same way as capital itself reverts to its original unity with labour. (431, emphasis added)[25]

25. Marx in this period (1845) emphasized the *time* constraint under all social arrangements (MECW 4:49–50), but Engels's more general perspective was acceptable to him (see Hollander 2000). We may, therefore, dispose of a standard objection typified by Wicksell, who wrote, "Even in a socialist state, rent and interest would play exactly the same role as they do now, in determining the reciprocal value of the products, the only difference being that land and capital would then have other owners. It is simply Utopian to imagine that any transformation in the conditions of ownership would give natural forces existing in limited quantities the character of free commodities" (cited Gårdland 1958, 119–20).

The second of Engels's formulations continues by extending the observation to *labor*. Under competition, "the product of labour as wages is separated from it, and is in its turn as usual determined by competition—there being, as we have seen. . . , no firm standard determining labour's share in production." But under communal arrangement, "this unnatural separation also disappears. Labour becomes its own reward, and the true significance of the wages of labour, hitherto alienated comes to light—namely the significance of labour for the determination of the production costs of a thing" (MECW 3:431). The problem I find here is that there *is* a firm standard under capitalism, namely, subsistence costs.

Indeed costs would include an allowance for "science": "But in a rational order which has gone beyond the division of interests as it is found with the economist, the mental element certainly belongs among the elements of production and will finds it place, too, in economics among the costs of production (428).

I have suggested that the system envisaged was in effect one of a war economy. And this is further indicated by a document, composed by Engels at about the same time as *Anti-Dühring,* entitled "American Food and the Land Question." Here he describes the American "revolution in farming, together with the revolutionised means of transport as invented by the Americans," who exported wheat to Europe "at such low prices that no European farmer can compete with it—at least not while he is expected to pay rent." This, together with the prospect of similar developments in Russia and the Argentine—"all lands equally fit for this modern system of giant farming and cheap production"—could be expected to undermine European agriculture (*Labour Standard,* 2 July 1881, reprinted in MECW 24:398–99). The "upshot of all this," he predicts, "will and must be that it will force upon us the nationalisation of the land and its cultivation by co-operative societies under national control. Then, and then alone, it will again pay both the cultivators and the nation to work it, whatever the price of American or any other corn and meat may be" (399). Engels thus envisaged an *autarkic* regime, with activity—at least agriculture—organized by "co-operatives" under "national control," *suggesting no intercooperative competition.*[26] All this does not imply a failure to appreciate the operation of the market system. It was understood only too well.

In evaluating further the validity of Hutchison's charges we must, of course, not forget the efficiency *losses* attributed to the market system, which are due particularly to the "anarchical" dimension elucidated earlier relating to cyclical instability that would be eliminated by "systematic definite organization" (MECW 25:270). And to this must be added other potential sources of increased efficiency under communism, which, for one thing, "sets free for the community at large a mass

26. In a later letter to August Bebel, Engels writes more generally of cooperative organization as only "transitionally" acceptable and subject to the same qualification regarding national control: "Nor have Marx and I ever doubted that, in the course of transition to a wholly communist economy, widespread use would have to be made of cooperative management as an intermediate stage. Only it will mean so organising things that society, i.e. initially the State, retains ownership of the means of production and thus prevents the particular interests of the cooperatives from taking precedence on those of society as a whole" (20–23 January 1886, reproduced in MECW 47:389). Since national control is insisted on, the question of the role of cooperatives is far less significant than in the case of J. S Mill; even cooperatives could be incorporated within the "social regulation of production upon a definite plan" (MECW 25:267). This, too, seems to have been Marx's position, as we have seen.

of means of production and of products, by doing away with the senseless extravagance of the ruling classes of today and their political representatives" (269). Engels and Marx put more weight on the gains to be expected from the abolition of markets than on the loss of a signaling device that would, they envisaged, be replaced by effective central direction.

Some Unexpected Parallels

The position of Marx and Engels on distribution turns out in significant respects to be akin to that of the "classical liberal" economists Hayek and Mises. Of course, Marx predicted the collapse of capitalism and championed arrangements involving inter alia the abolition of money. I am not obviously *identifying* Marx with Mises and Hayek, only pointing to certain specific parallels reflecting the common ground that the capitalist system should not be *tampered* with, albeit for very different reasons.[27]

Consider the incessant rejection by Engels and Marx of approaches to distribution under capitalism based on moral criteria relating to "fairness." Such criteria are represented as short-sighted prejudice—derived from the competitive experience—having no absolute justification (above, 4–6; also 22–3). This was Hayek's position, too, as expressed in *The Road to Serfdom* (1944).

> Most people find it difficult to admit that we do not possess moral standards which would enable us to settle these questions—if not perfectly, at least to greater general satisfaction than is done by the competitive system. Have we not all some idea of what is a "just price" or a "fair wage"? Can we not rely on the strong sense of fairness of the people? And even if we do not now agree fully on what is just or fair in a particular case, would popular ideas not soon consolidate into more definite standards if people were given an opportunity to see their ideals realized?

27. Other commentators have also hit upon "parallels" between Marx and Hayek, though, to my knowledge, not with respect to our specific topic. Thus, Lord Desai refers to a common concern "with *modelling* capitalism, its cyclical character, the importance of money and credit, its long-term profits. . . . Their analysis of the dynamics of capitalism is similar. . . . There is also much in common in capital theory" (1997:1). Also see Howard and King: "Peculiar as it may seem, Friedrich von Hayek and James Buchanan have both broken with much of traditional neoclassical theory, and in doing so have unwittingly reasserted basic themes of Marx's economics by recognising that capitalist systems are indeed 'organic unities'" (2001,795). For various parallels relating to business cycle theory in particular, see the references in Ebenstein 2001, 378–79.

> Unfortunately, there is little ground for such hopes. What standards we have are derived from the competitive regime we have known and would necessarily disappear soon after the disappearance of competition. What we mean by a just price, or a fair wage is either the customary price or wage, the return which past experience has made people expect, or the price or wage that would exist if there were no monopolistic exploitation. (110–11)[28]

Hayek goes on to consider the claim for wage payments according to "the 'full produce of . . . labour,' to which so much of socialist doctrine traces back," and he commends the general rejection by *contemporary* socialists of such a claim (111). But we have seen that this, too, was precisely the position adopted by Marx in his polemic against the program of the German Workers Party, and his own insistence on labor "inequality" under communism (see discussion above).

There are also parallels with Mises. Permanent improvement in the living standards of the masses required, Mises insisted, increased accumulation per capita—the standard "classical" position, of course. There were no shortcuts: "The only means to raise wage rates permanently for all those seeking jobs and eager to earn wages is to raise the productivity of the industrial effort by increasing the per-head quota of capital invested" (1980 [1950], 27–28). And, to the contrary, intervention in the price system to alter distribution in labor's favor could only harm national economic performance: "Minimum wage rates, whether decreed and enforced by the government or by labor union pressure and violence, result in mass unemployment prolonged year after year as soon as they try to raise wage rates above the height of the unhampered market" (27). On the matter of *direct* interference with the pattern of distribution he was very clear regarding the damage to productivity that would result.

---

28. The parallel would presumably be rejected by those who believe that Marx applied postcapitalist standards of morality as embedded in the experience and consciousness of the proletarian class of those who do not own property (see note 2).

We would do well to recall here our caution regarding the very different *intentions* of the parties. Baldly stated, Marx and Engels refused to analyze capitalism in ethical terms because they wished to see that system replaced and sought to focus attention on the main issue for them, that of "exploitation," an issue pertinent to the realm of *production* rather than *exchange,* including income distribution; hence their objection to the Proudhonian anarchists, Dühring, other social democratic reformers, and the earlier "Ricardian socialists" who threatened to divert attention to marginal concerns. Hayek's refusal stemmed from his wish to see the system conserved, fearing that an approach in terms of ethics would divert attention from his main issue—that social order results from human action rather than design.

> The philosophy underlying the system of progressive taxation is that the income and the wealth of the well-to-do classes can be freely tapped. What the advocates of these tax rates fail to realize is that the greater part of the incomes taxed away would not have been consumed but saved and invested. In fact, this fiscal policy does not only prevent the further accumulation of new capital. It brings about capital decumulation. (32)

That economic performance and distribution are intimately connected was, as I have shown, insisted on by Marx and Engels; for them, too, distribution problems could *not* be dealt with independent of production for precisely the same reasons as those offered by Mises.[29] This position clashes with the *formal* contrast drawn by J. S. Mill between the "immutable" laws of production and the "malleable" laws of distribution; if we take this contrast seriously there is more scope for income redistribution without endangering productive capacity in the Mill scheme of things. I doubt, though, that we should read Mill literally (Hollander 1985, 216–22); it is certainly the case that he, too, opposed progressive taxation of earned income on the grounds of incentive with particular reference to accumulation (859–60).

I turn now to the "binary" approach to systems that emerges both in Engels and Marx and in Mises—their insistence on "pure" communism and "pure" capitalism, respectively—the common position that there is no halfway house between full-fledged capitalism and central control.

As for Marx, an excellent instance of his concerns in this regard is provided by a letter of 1859 objecting to the "Proudhonist socialism now FASHIONABLE in France"—that it "wants to retain private production *while organising* the exchange of private products, to have *commodities* but not *money*— . . . Communism must above all rid itself of this 'false brother'" (Karl Marx to Joseph Weydemeyer, 1 February 1859, reprinted in MECW 40:377). And, as we have seen, Marx and Engels were fearful that to tolerate money and markets to any extent would inevitably undermine any communist social structure.[30] The position implicitly attri-

29. The view has been attributed to Hayek that to redistribute wealth from those who succeed to those who fail would not only be "unjust" but would threaten wealth creation since there are "unified laws of production and distribution . . . [and] one cannot modify distribution without disturbing production" (Tomass 1998, 288). This attribution is stated rather too strongly as we shall presently see. David Levy has suggested to me that a necessarily deleterious effect on growth stemming from redistribution in labor's favor characterize the positions of Feldstein and Lucas more than that of Hayek.

30. I surmise that their apparent rejection of free consumer choice under communism can also be attributed to such a concern.

butes to the capitalist system a *robustness* that seems to conflict with the confident predictions regarding its more or less immanent collapse. As for the toleration of a capitalist sector (and also the progressive income tax proposals) in the *Principles of Communism* and the *Communist Manifesto,* we must not forget the explicit assumption that firm communist political control—the police no less—would beat back any incipient degeneration.

My concern now is not Marxist consistency but the parallel with Mises, who in his famous 1950 address "Middle-of-the Road Policy Leads to Socialism" also rejected halfway houses.[31] Mises sets out by denying that the essential dispute between socialism and capitalism relates to the distribution of the national dividend between wage earners and capitalists ([1950] 1980, 19–20), a position he shared with Marx and Engels, who downplayed the distribution problem as we have seen. The antagonism between systems had a much deeper source.

> The antagonism between capitalism and socialism is not a dispute about the distribution of booty. It is a controversy about which of two schemes for society's economic organization, capitalism or socialism, is conducive to the better attainment of those ends which all people consider as the ultimate aim of activities commonly called economic, viz., the best possible supply of useful commodities and services. Capitalism wants to attain these ends by private enterprise and initiative, subject to the supremacy of the public's buying and abstention from buying on the market. The socialists want to substitute the unique plan of a central authority for the plans of the various individuals. They want to put in place of what Marx called the "anarchy of production" the exclusive monopoly of the government. The

31. For the same general argument, see also Mises 1947, chap. 2, in particular: "The Dictatorial, Anti-democratic and Socialist Character of Intervention" (23–34). An elaboration will be found in Mises 1963. Notwithstanding, at the close of his 1950 address, Mises insists that "the coming of socialism is not inevitable" and warns rather of the "defeatism" spread by many "self-styled non-Marxians"—the "middle-of-the-roaders who think they have been successful when they have delayed for some time an especially ruinous measure" ([1950] 1980, 33–34). Accordingly:

> What can prevent the coming of totalitarian socialism is only a thorough change in ideologies. What we need is neither anti-socialism nor anti-communism but an open positive endorsement of that system to which we owe all the wealth that distinguishes our age from the comparatively straightened conditions of ages gone by (35).

See also Hayek, *The Road to Serfdom* (1944), foreword to the American paperback edition, first inserted in 1956, (xivf), on the psychological alteration to the character of a people due to long-term extensive government control.

> antagonism does not refer to the mode of distributing a fixed amount of amenities. It refers to the mode of producing all those goods which people want to enjoy. (20)[32]

For Mises, "The conflict of the two principles is irreconcilable and does not allow for any compromise. Control is indivisible. Either the consumers' demand as manifested on the market decides for what purposes and how the factors of production should be employed, or the government takes care of these matters. There is nothing that could mitigate the opposition between these two contradictory principles. They preclude each other" ([1950] 1980, 20–21). "Interventionism" thus could not be considered "a permanent system of society's economic organization," one that "retain[s] private ownership of the means of production, entrepreneurship and market exchange" but subjects it to government regulation (21). Again, "The middle-of-the-road policy is not an economic system that can last. It is a method for the realization of socialism by installments" (32–33).[33] A classic instance of what Mises feared is provided by a price maximum imposed on the price of milk. To render such intervention effective would, runs the argument, ultimately require control of the prices of *all* consumers' goods and *all* factors of production: "But when this state of all-round control of business is attained, there can no longer be any question of a market economy. No longer do the citizens by their buying and abstention from buying determine what should be produced and how. The power to decide these matters has devolved upon the government. This is no longer capitalism; it is all-round planning by the government, it is socialism" (24). The formal retention of private ownership of productive means, prices, wages, interest rates, and profits is meaningless since they are determined by the authorities with the government, not consumers, directing production. In Mises's words, "It is the Zwangswirtschaft of Hitler's German Reich, and the planned economy of Great Britain" (24–25).[34] As the matter is summarized in the 1947 formulation:

32. The closing phrase implies that for Mises the socialist position recognized consumer sovereignty; but this is less clear in what follows.

33. See also: "Interventionism cannot be considered as an economic system destined to stay. It is a method for the transformation of capitalism into socialism by a series of successive steps. It is as such different from the endeavors of the communists to bring about socialism at one stroke. The difference does not refer to the ultimate end of the political movement; it refers mainly to the tactics to be resorted to for the attainment of an end that both groups are aiming at" (Mises [1950] 1980, 28).

34. Unlike Hayek, who warned of the prospective transition to communism by societies with extensive programs of nationalization (1944, 60–61), Mises rather played down the British nationalization program, writing, "Great Britain is to be called a socialist country not because certain enterprises have been formerly expropriated and nationalized, but because all the economic activities of all citizens are subject to full control of the government and its agencies" (ibid., 26).

> Men must choose between the market economy and socialism. The state can preserve the market economy in protecting life, health and private property against violent or fraudulent aggression; or it can itself control the conduct of all production activities. Some agency must determine what should be produced. If it is not the consumers by means of demand and supply on the market, it must be the government by compulsion. (Mises 1947, 34)

This denial of a *stable* middle solution between systems is held in common with Marx and Engels with this difference: Mises's concern was the *fragility of capitalism;* and that of Marx and Engels was the *fragility of communism.* Nonetheless, Marx's technical analysis of the control of bread prices (discussed earlier) is wholly in line with that of Mises.

Hayek, too, in his "Pricing versus Rationing" ([1939] 1997) takes a similar position.

> It will be sufficiently evident that rationing, if it is not to lead to grave waste, would involve little less than central planning of all production *in every detail.* Not only all the "scarce" resources but their substitutes as well would have to be planned and controlled by some central authority. If one thing has been definitely established with regard to a planned or socialist system, it is that to stop halfway will only destroy the efficiency of the competitive mechanism without realizing any of the supposed advantages of a planned system. (155)

Yet there is some evidence that he did not go quite as far as Mises regarding the "fragility" of the market system.[35] All in all, Hayek was concerned with "the process through which *certain kinds* of measures can destroy the bases of an economy based on the market and gradually smother the creative powers of a free civilization" (emphasis added) but insisted that his "was not . . . an exhortation to resistance against any improvement or experimentation" (1944, x). He here had in mind the test provided by the rule of law, the principle that "government in all its actions is bound by rules fixed and announced beforehand," thus reducing to a minimum "the discretion left to the executive organs yielding coercive power" and avoiding "stultifying individual efforts by *ad hoc* ac-

35. It has been pointed out to me that even Mises saw a role for government in policing and the courts.

tion" (72–73; see also Hayek 1960).[36] The parallels we have encountered seem to be more marked between Marx and Mises than between Marx and Hayek.

Of particular significance for our present theme relating to "unexpected parallels" is Engels's insistence on the coordination function of markets in his criticism of Rodbertus's labor money (discussed earlier) of which Hutchison has said without exaggeration that "Mises and Hayek could hardly have made the point more forcefully" (1981, 15). And, finally, note should also be taken of an important observation by Vaughn regarding Hayek's emphasis on the limits of human knowledge in his technical essays on socialist planning (1935, 1940).

> Hayek was challenging not only the economics of central planning, but a particular way of conceptualizing economic theory. Economic planning requires not only the centralization of knowledge, but also the ability to identify what knowledge is worth centralizing. Yet Hayek believed that most economically useful knowledge is local, detailed, implicit and changeable. What kind of political economy—indeed what kind of economic theory—is relevant when economic actors possess knowledge like that? (Vaughn 1998, 236)

36. Hayek did not deny the suffering by some from the operation of the market system and himself insisted that "in competition chance and good luck are often as important as skill and foresight in determining the fate of different people"; he allowed, too, that chances are unequal considering the restricted opportunities open to the poor, exacerbated by inheritance (1944, 101—-2). His case was based rather on the *greater* freedom even of the badly paid unskilled worker under a market than under a control system, even should material comforts be lower. For the outcome "depends at least partly on the ability and enterprise of the people concerned" and is above all subject to "the impersonal character of the process by which everybody has to take his chance and no person's view about what is right and desirable overrules that of others" (102). Nonetheless, provided the latter conditions are not compromised—and though we tend "to habitually overestimate the extent to which inequality of incomes is mainly caused by income derived from property"—Hayek conceded "a strong case for reducing . . . inequality of opportunity as far as congenital differences permit." Beyond this, he also made a strong case for a guaranteed *safety net,* for "in a society that has reached the general level of wealth which ours has attained there is no doubt that some minimum of food, shelter, and clothing, sufficient to preserve health and capacity to work, can be assured to everybody" (120). And he recognized a legitimate role for the state with respect, first, to social insurance ("[T]here is no reason why the state should not assist the individuals in providing for those common hazards of life against which, because of their uncertainty, few individuals can make adequate provision" [121]); and, second, to macroeconomic stability ("[T]hough its solution will require much planning in the good sense, it does not—or at least need not—require that special kind of planning which according to its advocates is to replace the market. . . . [T]he very necessary efforts to secure protection against these fluctuations do not lead to the kind of planning which constitutes such a threat to our freedom" [121–22]).

It is precisely this perspective on "local, detailed, implicit and changeable" knowledge that in part determined Marx's rejection of rent confiscation schemes—the state did not have such knowledge. We were obliged in responding to Hutchison's charges, it will be recalled, to seek to understand the support for central control considering the Engels-Marx appreciation of the competitive market process. The solution we proposed lies in their presumption that such a sophisticated allocative device would be unnecessary under the simplified regime envisaged.

An Overview: The Evolutionary Dimension

The necessitarian logic behind the concept of historical materialism has often been remarked on, with reference to growing immizeration, wealth and income inequality, cyclical instability, centralization, and so forth, leading to revolution (see the recent account in Baumol 2001). The general evolutionary theme is nicely stated by Marx in the *Economic Manuscripts* of 1861–63 with respect to the dissolution of capitalism.

> This is an essentially different conception from that of the bourgeois political economists, themselves imprisoned in capitalist preconceptions, who are admittedly able to see how production is carried on *within* the capital-relation, but not how this *relation* is itself produced, and how at the same time the material conditions for its dissolution are produced within it, thereby removing its *historical justification* as *a necessary form* of economic development, of the production of social wealth. (MECW 34:466)

Particularly important are specific observations in *Capital III,* composed in the 1860s, regarding the joint stock company—"the ultimate development of capitalist production" (MECW 37:434)—as a manifestation of the transition from private to social organization.

> The capital, which in itself rests on a social mode of production and presupposes a social concentration of means of production and labour power, is here directly endowed with the form of social capital (capital of directly associated individuals) as distinct from private capital, and its undertakings assume the form of social undertakings as distinct from private undertakings. It is the abolition of capital as private property within the framework of the capitalist mode of production itself. (434)

The part played by credit is much emphasized in this context and also with respect to the growth of cooperative factories.

> They show how a new mode of production naturally grows out of an old one, when the development of the material forces of production and of the corresponding forms of social production have reached a particular state. Without the factory system arising out of the capitalist mode of production there could have been no cooperative factories. Nor could these have developed without the credit system arising out of the same mode of production. The credit system is not only the principle basis for the gradual transformation of capitalist private enterprises into capitalist stock companies, but equally offers the means for the gradual extension of cooperative enterprises on a more or less national scale. The capitalist stock companies, as much as the cooperative factories, should be considered as transitional forms from the capitalist mode of production to the associated one, with the only distinction that the antagonism is resolved negatively in the one and positively in the other. (MECW 37:438)

This theme is rehearsed by Engels in *Anti-Dühring* in 1878 with a focus on the evolution from joint stock organization to prospective nationalization of industry and "direction of production" by the capitalist state.

> The fact that the socialised organisation of production within the factory has developed so far that it has become incompatible with the anarchy of production in society, which exists side by side with and dominates it, is brought home to the capitalists themselves by the violent concentration of capital that occurs during crises, through the ruin of many large, and a still greater number of small capitalists. . . . The period of industrial high pressure, with its unbounded inflation of credit, not less than the crash itself, by the collapse of great capitalist establishments, tends to bring about that form of the socialisation of great masses of means of production which we meet with in the different kinds of joint-stock companies. Many of these means of production and of communication are, from the outset, so colossal that, like the railways, they exclude all other forms of capitalistic exploitation. At a further stage of evolution this form also becomes insufficient: the official representative of capitalist society—the state—will ultimately have to undertake the direc-

> tion of production. This necessity for conversion into state property is felt first in the great institutions for intercourse and communication—the post office, the telegraphs, the railways. (MECW 25:264–65)[37]

Engels refers to the prospective extension of state control as a natural, not forced, matter arising from the logic of the situation, which explains his representation of Bismarckian forms of "state-ownership of industrial establishments" as "a kind of spurious socialism" (MECW 25:265n). And, although even "natural" extensions of state control occurred without disturbing "the capitalist relation" insofar as "the workers remain wage-workers," it is part of the process whereby the ultimate "solution" to class conflict would be achieved.

> But the transformation, either into joint-stock companies, or into state ownership, does not do away with the capitalistic nature of the productive forces. In the joint-stock companies this is obvious. And the modern state, again, is only the organisation that bourgeois society takes on in order to support the general external conditions of the capitalist mode of production against the encroachments as well of the workers as of individual capitalists. The modern state, no matter what its form, is essentially a capitalist machine, the state of the capitalists, the ideal personification of the total national capital. The more it proceeds to the taking over of productive forces, the more does it actually become the national capitalist, the more citizens does it exploit. The workers remain wage-workers—proletarians. The capitalist relation is not done away with. It is rather brought to a head. But, brought to a head, it topples over. State ownership of the productive forces is not the solution of the conflict, but concealed within it are the technical conditions that form the elements of that solution. (265–66)

By "the elements of the solution" provided by nationalization of industry on the part of the *capitalist* state is intended, partly, that the *proletarians*—once they seize power—will have been "shown the way" to proceed with a well-established exemplar at hand.

> Whilst the capitalist mode of production more and more completely transforms the great majority of the population into pro-

37. See also Engels, *Socialism: Utopian and Scientific* (1880), in MECW 24:318.

> letarians, it creates the power which, under penalty of its own destruction, is forced to accomplish this revolution. Whilst it forces on more and more the transformation of the vast means of production, already socialised, into state property, it shows itself the way to accomplishing this revolution. *The proletariat seizes political power and turns the means of production in the first instance into state property.* (MECW 25:267)

Here we have a splendid illustration of Engels's belief that the tasks of scientific socialism included its revelation of "the elements [within capitalism] of the future new organisation of production and exchange which will put an end to . . . abuses" (above, 77).

The evolutionary dimension extends much farther. The very term *communist revolution* is misleading except insofar as it relates to the acquisition and maintenance of *political* power by the proletariat. Thus we have Marx's "political transition period in which the State can be nothing but *the revolutionary dictatorship of the proletariat*" (MECW 24:95; see also note 7), Engels's legitimization of "terror" by the revolutionary party against the "reactionaries" ("On Authority" [1874], reprinted in MECW 23:425), and the role he accorded the proletarian state in "keeping down its enemies" (Frederick Engels to August Bebel, March 1875, reprinted in MECW 24:71).[38] The notion of revolution must be strictly qualified if applied to economics. It is true that much of Engels's *Principles of Communism* (1847) implies that the foundations of a social transformation, manifested in enormous productive capacity, were *actually in place,* allowing communist society "to increase these productive forces in a short time to an infinite extent" (MECW 6:348ff.). Yet he answers question 17—"Will it be possible to abolish private property at one stroke?"—firmly in the negative.

> No, such a thing would be just as impossible as at *one* stroke to increase the existing productive forces to the degree necessary for instituting community of property. Hence, the proletarian revolution, which in all probability is impending, will transform existing society only gradually, and be able to abolish private property only when the necessary quantity of the means of production has been created. (350)

38. For all that, an allowance was made for the achievement of proletarian power via the ballot box at least in the British case; see, for example, *Principles of Communism* (MECW 6:350). On the role allowed coercion during the transition period to communism, see Popper [1945] 1983, 328n6; and Duncan 1973, 180–81.

It is an extraordinary concession to insist on the retention of private property institutions *after the achievement of proletarian political rule* in order to assure that degree of expansion of productive capacity required for the successful implementation of full-fledged communism. This position is confirmed by Engels's insistence on the "*gradual* expropriation of landed proprietors, factory owners, railway and shipping magnates" with the further remarkable qualification that it be done "partly through *competition* on the part of state industry and partly through *compensation* in assignations" (emphasis added).[39] In Marx's version, too, in the *Communist Manifesto,* "the proletariat will use its political supremacy to wrest, *by degrees,* all capital from the bourgeoisie" (MECW 6:504, emphasis added). The "radical onslaught upon private ownership," as Engels put it, is much less radical than one is initially led to believe.

It would, of course, entail fine judgment to specify the rate at which the capitalist sector might be safely dismantled by the communist regime. The same applies to the progressive taxation and related proposals whose specific purpose was to whittle away capitalism after the communist takeover.[40] Marx and Engels evidently relied on the ability of the new rulers not to compromise the hoped-for performance by the residual capitalist sector in creating the capacity required to assure the successful implementation of full-fledged communism.

Also relevant to the evolutionary theme are the further developments envisaged once the private property system had been entirely eliminated. I refer again to Marx's "first phase" and "higher phase" of communism. We have thus seen that in the first phase—as the system has emerged out of capitalism—wage *inequality* is to be recognized. Only in the later phase would the egalitarian principle apply: "From each according to his abilities to each according to his needs." And there is Engels's express statement that his and Marx's support for "cooperatives" applied only to a transitional arrangement (see note 26).

I have at last arrived at my conclusion—that violent transition between economic systems and within systems is rejected by Marx and En-

39. Much later, in discussing expropriation of big landed proprietors once "our Party is in possession of political power," Engels recalled, "We by no means consider compensation as impermissible in any event; Marx told me (and how many times!) that in his opinion we would get off cheapest if we could buy out the whole lot of them" (Engels [1894] 1958, 2:438).

40. There is a contrast between Engels and Marx on the matter of inheritance. Marx in the *Communist Manifesto* goes so far as to call for the "abolition of all right to inheritance" (MECW 6:505). Engels in the *Principles of Communism* did not (then at least) go so far, recommending a "high inheritance tax, abolition of inheritance by collateral lines (brothers, nephews, etc.)" and "[e]qual rights of inheritance to be enjoyed by illegitimate and legitimate children" (responses to questions 1 and 11, in MECW 6:350–51).

gels in favor of caution. It is an impressive insight to have emphasized transitional problems, one that might have served as a red flag for our modern day advisers and their clients who have rushed to dismantle control systems with the inevitable outcome—already clear to Smith and Ricardo when they, in their day, evaluated proposals to abandon various forms of contemporary control.[41]

Bibliography

Baumol, William J. 2001. "Priceless Value: Misunderstood Concerns (or Almost So) of Marx and Ricardo." In *Reflecting on the Classical Canon in Economics,* edited by Evelyn L. Forget and Sandra J. Peart, 224–40. London: Routledge.

Desai, Meghnad. 1997. "Hayek, Marx and Keynes." In *Hayek: Economist and Social Philosopher, a Critical Retrospect,* edited by Stephen F. Frowen, 1–8. London: Macmillan.

Dobb, Maurice. 1933. "Economic Theory and the Problems of a Socialist Economy." *Economic Journal* 43:588–98.

Dobb, Maurice. 1934–35. "Economic Theory and Socialist Economy: A Reply." *Review of Economic Studies* 2:144–51.

Duncan, Graeme. 1973. *Marx and Mill: Two Views of Social Conflict and Social Harmony.* Cambridge: Cambridge University Press.

Ebenstein, Alan. 2001 *Friedrich Hayek: A Biography.* London: Palgrave.

Engels, Frederick. [1894] 1958. *The Peasant Question in France and Germany.* In *Karl Marx and Frederick Engels: Selected Works,* 2:420–40. Moscow: Foreign Languages Publishing House.

Gårdland, Torsten. 1958. *The Life of Knut Wicksell.* Stockholm: Almquist and Wicksell.

Hayek, Friedrich A. [1939] 1997. "Pricing versus Rationing." In *Hayek: Economist and Philosopher, A Critical Retrospect,* edited by Stephen F. Frowen. London: Macmillan; New York: St. Martin's.

Hayek, Friedrich A. [1944] 1956. *The Road to Serfdom.* Chicago: University of Chicago Press.

Hayek, Friedrich A. 1960. *The Constitution of Liberty.* Chicago: University of Chicago Press.

Hayek, Friedrich A. 1997. *Socialism and War.* Vol. 10 of *Collected Works of F. A. Hayek,* edited by Bruce J. Caldwell. Chicago: University of Chicago Press.

Hollander, Samuel. 1985. *The Economics of John Stuart Mill.* Toronto: University of Toronto Press.

Hollander, Samuel. 2000. "The Marx-Engels Relation: On the Significance of Engels' *Outlines of Political Economy,* the Umrisse." Manuscript.

Howard, Michael C., and John E. King. 2001. "Where Marx Was Right: Towards a More Secure Foundation for Heterodox Economics." *Cambridge Journal of Economics* 25:785–807.

Husami, Ziyad. 1978. "Marx on Distributive Justice." *Philosophy and Public Affairs* 8:27–64.

41. On the role of Western advisers in the Russian economic disaster of the 1990s, see Klein and Pomer 2001.

Hutchison, Terrence W. 1981. *The Politics and Philosophy of Economics: Marxians, Keynesians, and Austrians.* Oxford: Blackwell.

Klein, Lawrence R., and Marshall Pomer, eds. 2001. *The New Russia: Transition Gone Astray.* Cambridge: Cambridge University Press.

Lerner, Abba. 1934–35a. "Economic Theory and Socialist Economy." *Review of Economic Studies* 2:51–61.

Lerner, Abba. 1934–35b. "A Rejoinder to Dobb." *Review of Economic Studies* 2:152–54.

Marx, Karl and Frederick Engels. 1975–2004. *Collected Works.* New York: International Publishers; London: Lawrence and Wishart.

Mises, Ludwig von. 1947. *Planned Chaos.* Irvington-on-Hudson, N.Y.: Foundation for Economic Education.

Mises, Ludwig von. [1950] 1980. *Planning for Freedom.* South Holland, Ill.: Libertarian Press.

Mises, Ludwig von. 1963. *Human Action: A Treatise on Economics.* 3rd rev. ed. New Haven: Yale University Press.

Popper, Karl R. [1945] 1983. "Marx's Theory of the State." In *A Pocket Popper,* edited by David Miller, 326–37. Oxford: Fontana.

Proudhon, P. J. [1840] 1841. *Qu'est-ce que la propriété? ou Recherches sur le principe du droit et du gouvernement.* Second edition. Paris: Prévot.

Service, Robert. 2000. *Lenin: A Biography.* London: Macmillan.

Sowell, Thomas. 1980. *Knowledge and Decision.* Princeton: Princeton University Press.

Tomass, M. 1998. "On the Relativist Fallacy." *Journal of the History of Economic Thought* 20:279–98.

Tucker, Robert. 1969. "Marx and Distributive Justice." In *The Marxian Revolutionary Idea.* New York: Norton, 37–53.

Vaughn, Karen. 1998. Review of *The Collected Works of F. A. Hayek. Journal of the History of Economic Thought* 20:235–37.

Wood, Alan. 1972. "The Marxian Critique of Justice." *Philosophy and Public Affairs* 1:244–82.

5 • Robust Analytical Egalitarianism
Worst-Case Political Economy and the Socialist Calculation Debate

Eric Crampton and Andrew Farrant

[I]f the purpose is one of drawing the constitutional limits on the taxing power, would it not be meaningful to utilize a worst-case scenario and to see model governments, anywhere and everywhere, as revenue-maximizing? That is, given any revenue source, would it not be best to assume maximal exploitation?

—James M. Buchanan 1992, 105

You must only take care to remove all the vices. If you remove part, you may render the matter worse. . . . For whatever may be the consequences of such a miraculous transformation of mankind, as would endow them with every species of virtue, and free them from every species of vice; this concerns not the magistrate, who aims only at possibilities. He cannot cure every vice by substituting a virtue in its place. Very often he can only cure one vice by another; and in that case, he ought to prefer what is least pernicious to society.

—David Hume [1752] 1985b, 279–80.

Introduction

Worst-case theorizing about government has a lengthy history in political economy (Levy 2002; Toma and Toma 1984). David Hume provides the classic statement of worst-case theorizing about government in political economy: "Political writers have established it as a maxim, that, in contriving any system of government, and fixing the several checks and controuls of the constitution, every man ought to be supposed a *knave*, and to have no other end, in all his actions, than private interest" (Hume [1752] 1985a, 42–43). Hume's worst-case model of government has attained canonical status in the contemporary constitutional political economy literature (see, e.g., Levy 2002; Brennan and Buchanan 1980, 1985; Sutter 1998; and Faria 1999).

J. M. Buchanan—a founding father of constitutional political economy—is (perhaps) uniquely responsible for the revival of worst-case theorizing about government in modern political economy (see Levy 2002).[1] Worst-case theorizing about government à la Buchanan necessitates adherence to a principle of analytical homogeneity or motivational symmetry: private and public chooser alike are modeled as pursuing their private interest. Failure to model private and public choosers symmetrically will, of course, unduly bias one's analysis in favor of private or public choice per se (Buchanan 1987, 85, 89–90). Just as knavery (the workings of self-interest) may generate market failure in a private choice context (e.g., externalities, private provision of public goods, and monopoly), we have no reason to think that said knavery will not similarly generate government failure when operative in any public choice context (Buchanan 1962; 1979a, 77).[2]

Buchanan is perhaps the most important advocate in modern economics of what we might term analytical egalitarianism. Analytical egalitarianism requires that all—whether black or white, master or servant, planner or kulak—be modeled symmetrically, any differences in their observed behavior lying not in any supposedly intrinsic preferences or abilities (or their national character per se) but rather in their historically contingent budget sets.[3] Analytical egalitarianism thus lies at the core of worst-case thinking in political economy. A key lesson of Buchanan's worst-case philosophy of constitutional political economy is that one ought not judge the desirability of political institutions[4] simply on the basis of their performance under ideal—or best-case—conditions (see, e.g., Brennan and Hamlin 2000, 124–125; and Levy 2002) but,

1. "[The] Leviathan assumption appears to be at the heart of the classical conception of constitutional government" (Toma and Toma 1984, 93). Brennan and Buchanan view their Leviathan model of government as exemplifying "the [worst-case] spirit of the classical political economists" ([1980] 2000, 220). James Mill's 1820 model of government as slave driver writ large is remarkably similar to the Leviathan model of government provided by Brennan and Buchanan in the late 1970s. Indeed, the suggestion that one should model government as a slave driver was not unique to Mill: "Every Monarch is a Slave-holder upon the largest scale" (Bentham [1822] 1989, 171). Toma and Toma (1984, 93) suggest that the Brennan-Buchanan Leviathan model "seems to apply naturally to a monarchial form of government."

2. "[T]he economist who utilizes *homo economicus,* who can identify market failure . . . is under an obligation to identify government or political failure" (Buchanan 1979a, 77).

3. "From Adam Smith through John Stuart Mill, classical economists presumed that, for purposes of analysis, people are the same" (Levy, Peart, and Farrant 2005, 3).

4. This can be thought of as alternative sets of "rules of the game," to invoke Buchanan's favored term.

rather, that one ought to evaluate them in accordance with their performance under decidedly less than ideal—or worst-case—conditions (e.g., the prevalence of Hume's political knaves). Thus, a policy that might prima facie appear optimal if we suppose that policymakers are wholly public-spirited may prove decidedly less than optimal when policymakers are rather more self-interested than we earlier supposed.

In this chapter we revisit the socialist calculation debate of the 1930s and 1940s. Our reexamination of the debate is squarely grounded in the tradition of Buchanan and Hume's worst-case political economy. Traditional accounts of the calculation debate center around the knowledge or quality of information (or lack of such) characterizing the putative socialist planner's information set (see, e.g., Steele 1992). We view the interwar calculation debate as providing a rather useful framework, however, within which critically to scrutinize the coherence (or lack of such) associated with various approaches to worst-case and best-case theorizing in political economy, respectively. In particular, we argue that the Austrian "socialist calculation" argument (Mises [1920] 1935; Hayek 1945) is not a "best-case" or "worst-case" critique of socialist planning per se but rather that the desirability (or otherwise) of socialist calculation is not independent of the assumptions we make about the planner's objective function. Thus, rather than questioning the information or knowledge (Hayek 1945) available (or otherwise) to economic planners or other public choosers, we follow the worst-case political economy tradition in public choice theory (especially the work of, say, J. M. Buchanan or Gordon Tullock) by largely focusing on worst-case motivational suppositions: private and public chooser alike are Homo economicus always and everywhere.[5] By taking planner self-interest (or conversely, planner benevolence) seriously we provide a rather novel interpretation of the interwar calculation debate. In particular, we challenge a variety of important Austrian political economy conclusions.

Participants in the socialist calculation debate of the 1930s and 1940s—whether favorable to market socialism or otherwise—modeled public choosers as rather more akin to what Buchanan characterizes as *non–Homo economicus* than to Hume's knave. Thus Buchanan's rather pungent remark that the caricature of "socialist bureaucrat . . . [as] *non–Homo economicus* in the purest sense . . . [has been present] in much serious discussion of real world policy" ([1969] 1999, 88) provides a wholly apt characterization of the calculation debate. Consequently, we may view Mises and Hayek, along with their market socialist opponents, as having subscribed to a supposition of motivational

5. "The incompatibility of the incentive structure was not a central feature of the socialist calculation debate of the 1930's" (Buchanan 2001, 235).

asymmetry during the socialist calculation debate: public choosers (planners) were modeled as public-spirited while private choosers were supposed to be self-interested. Where worst-case theorists such as Buchanan and Hume model all in accordance with worst-case motivational assumptions, Hayek and Mises appear to suppose that planner and kulak have asymmetric motivations.

Austrian political economy has traditionally posed the question as to whether socialist planners can allocate resources to attain any semblance of first-best efficiency.[6] Here, however, we ask whether the assumption of low "calculative efficacy" might prove desirable.[7] Is high calculative efficacy desirable per se or is any such desirability rather a function of whatever planner type (whether benevolent or self-interested) we suppose, conjunct with the particular welfare metric we invoke? To illustrate our argument we contrast the Austrian and public choice critiques of socialist economic planning. The Austrian critique of planning faults public choice theory for its purported failure to accept the logic of the Austrian economic calculation argument (see, e.g., Lavoie 1985a, 102), Ludwig von Mises showing in 1920 that socialist planners (even the public-spirited variety) were logically precluded from rationally organizing production to attain any semblance of first-best efficiency whatsoever due to their inability to accurately calculate relative scarcities and opportunity costs without market prices for capital goods. Mises argues that the inability of planners to engage in rational socialist calculation guarantees pervasive economic inefficiency. The public choice critique of planning, however, emphasizes the perverse incentives that lead self-interested planners to generate pervasive artificial shortages given that planning seems akin to monopoly writ large. Shortages, of course, allow planners to systematically extract bribes and other perquisites (all akin to artificial scarcity rents) from goods-starved consumers (see, e.g., Levy 1990; and Shleifer and Vishny 1992).

The essay contrasts the Austrian and public choice critiques of socialist planning, drawing particular attention to the markedly divergent empirical predictions associated with Austrian and public choice critiques, respectively, regarding the operation of real world Soviet-type "planning." Perfect information *is* a worst-case assumption if we sup-

6. On Austrian political economy, see, for example, the contributions of Mises and Hayek during the socialist calculation debate.

7. *Calculative efficacy* refers to the degree to which the central planner is able to overcome the Mises-Hayek economic critique of socialist planning. If calculative efficacy is low, the Mises-Hayek critique significantly constrains the planner's ability to allocate resources efficiently; conversely, if calculative efficacy is high, the Austrian critique does not hinder the planner.

pose that planners are self-interested. Where planners are nonbenevolent, we suggest that imperfect information possesses second-best efficiency type properties. We draw on this analysis to provide a sketch of "robust" political economy, paying attention to the role that assumptions regarding planner type and "omniscience" play in the Austrian and public choice critiques of planning.

Taking the Worst Case Seriously in the Socialist Calculation Debate

Robust political economy and worst-case thinking enjoy a rich heritage in political economy, tracing back through Hume's dictum (cited earlier) to Mill's warning.

> Whether the institution to be defended is slavery, political absolutism, or the absolutism of the head of a family, we are always expected to judge of it from its best instances; and we are presented with pictures of loving exercise of authority on one side, loving submission to it on the other—superior wisdom ordering all things for the greatest good of the dependents, and surrounded by their smiles and benedictions. All this would be very much to the purpose if any one pretended that there are no such things as good men. Who doubts that there may be great goodness, and great happiness, and great affection, under the absolute government of a good man? Meanwhile, *laws and institutions require to be adapted, not to good men, but to bad.* (Mill [1869] 1984, 287, emphasis added)

Robustness considerations therefore necessitate that we take Hume and Mill very seriously and focus on how institutions perform under worst-case conditions (e.g., where the supposition of planner benevolence in market socialist models is seriously weakened).[8] Political systems that depend on idealized assumptions of disjoint incentives between planners and ordinary people may work well when the planners are truly idealized philosopher-kings but do not work so well when the planners rejoin the human race. A pessimistic analytical egalitarianism provides for robust foundations (see Levy 2002).

The Austrian "economic" critique of socialist planning—the "economic calculation argument" associated with Ludwig von Mises (Mises [1920] 1935)—argues that any socialist "price" vector (shadow or other-

8. Stiglitz (1994,106–7) states, "[W]e can ask, is the model robust? Do slight changes in the assumptions—particularly the assumptions about which we may have limited confidence—result in marked changes in the conclusions?"

wise), while grossly suboptimal from the perspective of social efficiency, will, however, be wholly *unbiased.* The calculation argument thus predicts *generalized* calculational chaos under socialist planning: some prices are set too low, while others are set too high relative to their market-clearing values. Thus, the Austrian prediction—namely, that *unbiased* but systematically erring planners will generate pervasive shortages and surpluses—contrasts starkly with the public choice prediction concerning the *bias* that is thought all too likely to typify any real world, "centrally planned" price vector (Levy 1990). Self-interested planners generate pervasive artificial shortages, which, as recognized by Rothbard (1976) generate rent-extracting opportunities for the planner-cum-price setter to exploit.[9] Interestingly, Rothbard's remarks echo those of Stigler (1975, x): whereas Austrians generally argue that the failures of socialist planning (e.g., pervasive shortages) are simply an instance of planner error, the public choice account suggests that planner error is largely a chimera and Austrian political economy has simply incorrectly specified the planner's objective function.

The Austrian critique of planner "omniscience" (Hayek's "knowledge problem") is clearly applicable to the characteristic 1930s market socialist assumption that planners could easily acquire the information requisite for the formulation of a first-best efficient plan whether through some Lange-type "trial and error" process or by solving a system of simultaneous equations ex ante. H. D. Dickinson is representative in supposing that planners have sufficient information to ensure first-best efficiency.

> On the basis of its experience with changing prices and quantities the statistical service of every sales agency would be able to draw up a demand schedule for each type of good sold. . . . Under capitalism, demand schedules are apt to exist in the realm of faith rather than in that of works, but with the greater publicity and fuller statistics of the socialistic economy they would become much easier to draw up. (1939, 63)

Dickinson, of course, presupposes planner benevolence,[10] and with said benevolence full or high calculative efficacy is clearly a boon irre-

9. "[H]ow could Mises know that some advocates of price control do not *want* shortages? They may, for example, be socialists, anxious to use the controls as a step towards full collectivism. . . . Still others may favor price control, *even after learning of the shortages, because they or their political allies will enjoy well-paying jobs or power in a price-control bureaucracy*" (Rothbard 1976, 102, emphasis added).

10. See also Kornai: "Lange's model is based on erroneous assumptions concerning the nature of the 'planners.' The people at his Central Planning Board are reincarnations of Plato's philosophers, embodiments of unity, unselfishness, and wisdom. They are satisfied with doing nothing else but strictly enforcing the 'Rule,' adjusting prices to excess demand. *Such an unworldly bureaucracy never existed in the past and will never exist in the future*" (1986, 726, emphasis added).

spective of our welfare metric. Where planners are not wholly public-spirited, however, matters are not so simple. Public choice theory, while vigorously contesting the supposition of planner benevolence, suggests that low calculative efficacy may possess second-best efficiency properties. Interestingly, Dickinson's joint "best-case" supposition—planner benevolence conjunct with omniscience—raises the following, rather intriguing public choice speculation. Suppose the planning authority has perfect information concerning consumer reservation prices (Dickinson 1939, 63, 191). Why would planners of the self-interested rather than public-spirited variety not simply engage in perfect price discrimination (as would their self-interested private-choosing counterparts were they in a similarly monopolistic position), thereby extracting all the surplus from hapless consumers?

Intriguingly, Mises argues that planner type is utterly irrelevant to the socialist calculation debate (see also Hayek 1935, 2–3; and [1944] 1986, 44).

> [T]he socialist economy is impracticable not because men are morally too base, but because the problems that a socialist order would have to solve present insuperable intellectual difficulties. The impracticability of Socialism is the result of intellectual, not moral, incapacity. . . . Even angels, if they were endowed only with human reason, could not form a socialistic community. If a socialist community were capable of economic calculation, it could be set up without any change in men's moral character. (Mises [1932] 1981, 407, emphasis added)

Mises, however, neglects to explain why planners of the self-interested rather than benevolent variety have any interest in attaining first-best efficiency per se.[11]

Taking Benevolence Seriously?

Lavoie (1985b) suggests that the "knowledge" problem and the "totalitarian" problem (the Austrian "economic" and "political" critique of socialist planning and government intervention) are complementary arguments against planning. He (1985b, 20) notes:

---

11. "What is there in public choice theory that also gives the lie to the planning advocates? We need only return to the ancient Roman query: Who is to guard the guardians? Planners are also utility-maximizing individuals, and who could predict that planning decisions will be made contrary to the interests of those who make them?" (Buchanan 1979b, 272).

> Of the contemporary advocates of planning who consider the issue of past failures, most blame them on a lack of attention to democratic values, on the fact that the wrong personnel have been in charge, on a lack of statistical data, or on the supposition that its principles were not carried far enough. These rationalizations are not supported by the factual record and the primary arguments raised against national economic planning—which I will designate the "totalitarian problem" and the "knowledge problem"—are more fundamental and are almost completely unaddressed in contemporary planning proposals.

Nowhere, however, does Lavoie ask whether the Austrian political critique of planning is truly congruent with the Austrian economic critique of planning. Does the strength (or relevance) of any one Austrian argument (political or economic) simply serve to weaken whatever strength (or cogency) the other might have?

We suggest that the Austrian political critique of socialism (the totalitarian problem) and the Austrian economic critique of socialism (the knowledge problem) are rather incongruent with one another. If the totalitarian problem is the relevant worry, the knowledge problem is largely immaterial—or simply serves to attenuate the rapacity (surplus-extracting proclivities) of the planners. By contrast, were we to follow Mises and Hayek in assuming public-spirited planners and holding that the knowledge problem is the relevant concern, those planners, quickly recognizing the strength of the Mises critique, would eagerly retreat from the debacle of planning and institute a program of economic liberalization. Indeed, no Western democracy actually implemented a policy of wholesale planning during the twentieth century. Democratic constraints (the selection effects for both policy and officeholders alike, which are intrinsic to democratic "political markets") apparently worked to dramatically attenuate—and ultimately block—any move toward such planning (see, e.g., Wiles 1967, 18). By contrast, any examples of twentieth-century experiments in wholesale planning are provided by countries akin to the Soviet Union, where nonbenevolent agents both initiated the said experiments with planning and, because economic liberalization endangered their rents, vehemently resisted economic reform.

Of course, Austrian critics of planning such as Hayek ([1944] 1986), Lavoie (1985b), and Boettke (2001) argue that the adverse selection mechanisms supposedly intrinsic to political markets (their workings being decidedly exacerbated in the case of wholesale economic planning) will operate to guarantee that any initial set of planners—benevolent by supposition, responsible for setting up the planning machinery, and wholly willing to reverse course if planning is socially inefficient—are replaced by a set of rather more malign planners (see, e.g., chapter 10 of Hayek's *The Road to Serfdom*) and the "worst" will rise to the top of the planning bureaucracy. Lavoie's remarks are representative.

> The totalitarian problem of planning, which its critics [e.g., Hayek] have raised, was never claimed to be a consequence of the evil intentions of planning advocates, but rather of the kinds of institutions planning puts into place and the *inherent dynamics* of these institutions. . . . [Because] national economic planning involves *by its very nature* the concentration of immense political and economic power in a single agency . . . [this] concentration [of power] will naturally lend itself to abuse by those hungry for power and eminently competent in its exercise. *It does not matter who initially is put in charge or how much that person and his or her employees emphasize or love democracy.* (1985b, 20–21, emphasis added)

Lavoie's logic, however, appears rather lacking in empirical veracity. We remind the reader that Hayek's argument that the worst would arise to the top in a planned economy was not intended as a purely abstract argument: The argument Hayek provided in *The Road to Serfdom* was supposed to apply to the post-1945 Labour government in Britain ([1956] 1994, xxxvii–xxxviii). Toye is apposite: "[Stafford] Cripps himself admitted, *the* [1945 Labour] *government's determination not to violate its own democratic precepts* meant that it could not take the measures necessary to guarantee the execution of its own plans" (2004, 227, emphasis added). One may reformulate Lavoie's "intrinsic dynamics" argument to argue that benevolent planners lack sufficient ideological flexibility to retreat from planning even once its failure becomes readily apparent (see, e.g., Boettke 2005). Any such argument, however, would need to adequately explain how the selection effects intrinsic to democratic politics work to get the relevant "single-minded idealists" (Hayek [1986] 1994, 61) wholly lacking in ideological flexibility into the initial candidate pool (let alone into office). Democratic constraints selecting for those particular public choosers who actually get to vote for or against the implementation of any policy of wholesale planning are surely of the utmost importance. Thus, the extent to which such agents "love democracy" will determine their marginal willingness to trade off the constraints of democratic politics for an ever more rigorous plan.

Lavoie, of course, simply presupposes that a central planning authority is already in place. We suggest, however, that Austrian opponents of planning simply fail to provide anything akin to an adequate explanation as to why benevolent agents initially adopt central planning let alone why such agents would more vigorously pursue any such policy once the pervasive economic chaos supposedly inherent to planning rears its head. These points aside for the moment, however, we suggest that Lavoie's logic—assuming for the sake of argument that the Austrian "adverse selection" mechanism is accurate—suggests that the "knowledge problem" is a rather irrelevant critique of planning.[12] The dynamics supposedly intrinsic to planning generate a Stalinist-type or worst-case equilibrium whenever wholesale economic planning is attempted, irrespective of whether or not the said attempt is made by benevolent planners who, in Lavoie's words, "love democracy."[13] Thus, it appears that from the perspective of Austrian political economists it is the totalitarian argument against planning that provides a far stronger critique of planning than the knowledge problem irrespective of planner type. Calculative efficacy may prove to be low, with wholesale economic planning thereby generating pervasive deadweight losses, but any retreat from said planning is simply not possible (irrespective of whether planner type is public-spirited or self-interested). The institutional dynamics to which Lavoie makes reference supposedly militate against any possible retreat in the case of benevolent planners (who are replaced by Hayek's "worst") while nonbenevolent planners, by contrast, having no desire to retreat from planning anyhow, also have no desire to implement a socially efficient plan. Thus, any claim that the planners have low calculative efficacy is immaterial as the benevolent planners inevitably give way to planners who are rather less benevolent (or downright malign) and have no desire to attain a first-best efficient outcome in any case. Inability to calculate simply appears neither here nor there as regards the unfolding of the Austrian "planning leads to totalitarianism" mechanism.

An alternate interpretation of the "dynamics" inherent to planning is that the dynamics are *contingent* on planners having low calculative efficacy per se (Hayek's knowledge problem): without the failure of planning (pervasive calculational chaos), the conditions will never be ripe for the rise of the demagogue (see, e.g., Boettke 2001, 52). This interpretation, however, leaves much to be desired. Let us assume perfect calcu-

12. "Hayek's argument is an application of comparative advantage to the selection of leaders within the system" (Boettke 2001, 52).

13. Cullenberg (1992) refers to this worst-case equilibrium as "hideous communism."

lative efficacy and initial planner benevolence. The potential rents to be won by anyone capable of capturing the planning apparatus in such a case are huge. Consequently, a nonbenevolent would-be planner will be willing to bid up to the full value of those potential rents in order to secure the position. In order to maintain his position at the top of the apparatus, the benevolent planner will need to extract enough rents to defend his or her position (Crampton and Farrant 2006). More to the point, if we find the Boettke-Hayek-Lavoie mechanism sketched earlier at all persuasive, we would expect to see at least one data point where a benevolent planner, after having initially established the planning apparatus, was supplanted by a planner of the Stalinist type. To the best of our knowledge, such a case does not exist.[14] Where planning was initiated by the benevolent planner, a retreat from planning followed; where it was initiated by the nonbenevolent planner, however, there was no retreat until the ultimate collapse. The knowledge problem once again simply appears to take second stage to the totalitarian problem.

Intriguingly, F. A. Hayek apparently agrees with our point that the economic calculation argument takes a role of secondary importance relative to the public choice (incentives) critique of planning for the purpose of comparative institutional analysis. Anticipating Demsetz's Nirvana critique (1969), Hayek insists that one cannot compare institutions (or sets of rules of the game) as they would operate under ideal conditions (e.g., planner benevolence) with relatively imperfect existing institutions. Thus, Hayek suggests that in comparing markets and planning:

> If the comparison is to be of any value . . . it has to be made on the assumption that either system is realized in the form which is most rational under the given conditions of human nature [planner type] and external circumstances which must of course be accepted. (1935, 38)

If planner type ("human nature") provides an important constraint on which of various potential equilibria are more likely empirically, public choice theory clearly takes precedence over Austrian political economy as a critique of planning. Thus, we suggest that Austrian theory (particularly Hayekian strictures concerning imperfect information) has relatively little to add to the existing corpus of worst-case theorizing (public choice theory and constitutional political economy). Indeed,

14. Wiles is apposite: "[T]he war economies of Western Europe . . . have completely disappeared. Even mere social democracy has taken a bad beating in Western Europe since the war, and retains a toehold in power only at the price of total Revisionism. Hayek rightly diagnosed the nature of the game, but he grossly misjudged the strengths of the players" (Wiles 1967, 18).

given the primacy of the self-interested planner type, as we will argue, we ought to be thankful that self-interested planners cannot engage in rational economic calculation. Perfect information (ability to calculate) conjunct with planner self-interest generates the *worst-case* outcome: the perfectly extracting socialist Leviathan. Given Hayek's acceptance that analysis must proceed on the acceptance of a *given* planner type, it simply becomes immaterial whether would-be socialist planners can actually engage in rational economic calculation. Irrespective of the possibility—or otherwise—of economic calculation under socialism, Hayek appears to cede that the principal relevant consideration is the fact that socialist planners lack any incentive to allocate resources so as to maximize social welfare per se. Indeed, given the worst-case assumption of Homo economicus—or the "given conditions of human nature" (the absence of non–Homo economicus) as Hayek put it—quite the contrary is the case: planners will allocate resources to maximize their personal well-being irrespective of any deadweight losses that the resultant pattern of production and distribution might entail.

The Worst Worst-Case?

As we have suggested, given self-interested planners, the supposition of perfect information provides a worst-case assumption in public choice analysis. Welfare increases as we relax the worst-case supposition that planners have an unhindered ability to formulate and implement economic planning. By welfare, we mean some measure of the utility enjoyed by the model citizen; our results are robust to several alternative welfare measures. A median welfare standard suffices (the level of utility enjoyed by the median citizen). So, too, does any mean welfare standard (total societal utility divided by the number of people) that incorporates any nontrivial diminishing marginal utility of income—simply the idea that the marginal dollar appropriated by the central planner generates less utility for him or her than it would have provided to the citizen from whom it was taken. Imperfect information conjunct with agency problems (cooperative inefficacy) and imperfect monitoring may improve outcomes.

Our argument provides the "economic calculation" complement to Cowen and Sutter's (1999) agent-type critique of standard public goods theory. Cowen and Sutter suggest that any increase in what they term "cooperative efficacy" (161) will generate welfare gains *and* losses. When private or public choosers find it easier to engage in the degree of cooperation that is requisite if optimal (or near optimal) private or public provision of public goods is to prove feasible, they can also more easily cooperate with one another to produce a variety of public bads (163). We suggest that any increase in planner ability to calculate may similarly prove to be a public bad when planners are self-interested. Whereas Cowen and Sutter (161) refer to cooperative efficacy, we refer to the supposition of perfect information as calculative efficacy. Indeed, Cowen and Sutter's account complements the general thrust of our argument. Any posited increase in cooperative efficacy (given the "worst-case" planner type) will necessarily facilitate greater collusion among upstream and downstream monopolist planners (reducing the potential "defection" inherent to any agency relationship), thereby facilitating more efficient joint bargaining over the distribution of the surplus extracted from consumers (Shleifer and Vishny 1992). We suggest that worst-case political economy ought to posit maximum cooperative efficacy along with perfect information (calculative efficacy) and planner self-interest (table 5.1).

The public choice critique of planning traditionally posits that lower-level planners (industry managers) efficiently collude with one another to extract surplus (bribes) from consumers (see, e.g., Shleifer and Vishny 1992). Although such an assumption makes for analytical tractability (downplaying the importance of the "upstream-downstream" monopolists problem familiar from intermediate industrial organization texts), we find it somewhat ad hoc. Why do the "lower-level" planners not readily engage in equally efficient collusion with "higher-level" planners (e.g., the state treasury)? Such collusion would require that socialist industry managers maximize their rents by simply charging the "monopoly" monetary price (extracting their rents like any standard monopolist) rather than, as traditional public choice models of planning suppose, setting a price below that at which the market clears and inefficiently extracting their rents in the form of bribes. Thus, pub-

Table 5.1. A Taxonomy of Incentives and Efficacy

	Calculative Efficacy	Cooperative Efficacy
Benevolent Planners	Desirable. Allows for the formulation of the SWF-maximizing plan.	Desirable. Allows for the implementation of the SWF-maximizing plan.
Self-Interested Planners	Undesirable. Allows for the calculation of maximal surplus extraction; output is maximized but is entirely expropriated.	Undesirable. Prevents individuals from colluding with lower levels of government for protection from higher levels; allows perfect price discrimination result to obtain.

Note: SWF = Social welfare function.

lic choice models apparently presuppose some degree of cooperative inefficacy.

Less than full cooperative efficacy, however, possesses second-best efficiency properties. Full cooperative efficacy simply failed to obtain in the Soviet Union and fortunately so. Under the full worst-case scenario, planners at all levels would collude successfully and bargain efficiently. Perfect information, conjunct with maximum cooperative efficacy and a self-interested planner type ensures maximal surplus extraction—the worst *worst-case* scenario thereby obtaining. We suggest that the traditional public choice critique of planning provides a less than truly worst-case account on the grounds that, although total income is lower (as a result of inefficient rent extraction and the prevalence of upstream-downstream monopoly problems), citizen welfare is still somewhat greater than is the case in our suggested *worst worst-case* scenario.[15] Indeed, as Cowen and Sutter (1999, 166) note, "the optimal level of cooperative efficacy is higher when leaders are altruistic rather than self-seeking." Similarly, the optimal degree of calculative efficacy is higher when the planner type is "benevolent."

From the perspective of total output maximization, planner type is irrelevant where full cooperative and calculative efficiency obtains: the distribution of surplus is irrelevant to any welfare ranking based only on total output. Where full calculative efficacy obtains, self-interested planners select the socially optimal set of production projects, simply appropriating all resultant surpluses for their own use. With less than full calculative efficacy, however, planners select self-enriching projects irrespective of any divergence between the private and social costs of any such policy choice. Either way, it is planner type (planner self-interest), rather than calculative inefficacy per se, that is driving the story (table 5.2).

The self-interested planner—conjunct with calculative efficacy—will always provide the first-best efficient resource allocation since doing so allows for greater levels of surplus extraction. Output is maximized while welfare reduces to epsilon. From an output-based standard, a perfectly price-discriminating Leviathan is no worse than perfect competition. Where citizen welfare provides the relevant standard, however, the perfectly price-discriminating socialist Leviathan is the *worst* outcome.

15. We assume away the possibility of free entry into the "industry" of rent extraction. Shleifer and Vishny (1993) suggest that mean and median income will (within the limit) converge on zero where entry into the "corruption" or "bribe extraction" industry is totally free. In the Shleifer and Vishny case, as *N* increases, deadweight losses increase concomitantly. Alternatively, assume that maximal cooperative efficacy holds regardless of entry and that the joint maximal level of extraction obtains regardless of *N*.

Where government agents are self-interested, we suggest that calculative inefficacy may possess second-best efficiency properties. Thus, from a welfare perspective the socially optimal level of calculative efficacy will decline if selection effects induce knavish agents (Hume) to pursue positions in the planning bureaucracy. Hayek ([1944] 1986) argues that the "worst get on top" because the planners cannot calculate (see Boettke 1995). We argue that the worst are far more likely to get on top when calculative efficacy obtains.[16] Why select into the planning bureaucracy if opportunities for self-enrichment are few and far between?

To illustrate our point concerning cooperative and calculative efficacy, consider the case of two levels of government, each with surplus extraction authority over an individual. Under assumptions of full cooperative and calculative efficacy, the two levels of government efficiently bargain between themselves over a division of extracted total surplus. Calculative efficacy implies that each level of government can perfectly observe the individual's full demand schedules and reservation utility levels and cooperative efficacy implies that the levels of gov-

Table 5.2. Calculation and Cooperation with Benevolent Planners

	Calculative Efficiency	Calculative Inefficiency
Cooperative Efficacy	Maximal mean and median welfare. The efficient plan obtains.	Planners grope towards SWF improvements. Shortages are met with price and production increases; surpluses are met with price reductions and production cutbacks. Shortages and surpluses are equally likely. Plan is always updated to account for previous-period results. Equilibrium occurs by trial and error.
Cooperative Inefficacy	Central planner knows the overall SWF-maximizing plan, but local agents implement local SWF-maximizing plans instead. Efficiencies of larger-scope planning are lost.	Worst case. Even the suboptimal plan cannot be implemented. Pervasive economic irrationality and large deadweight losses result. Benevolent planners will retreat from planning.

Note: SWF = social welfare function.

16. A "realistic supposition is that governments pursue their own interests rather than the public interest. . . . It is not obvious that we wish to increase cooperative efficacy in governments of this kind" (Cowen and Sutter 1999, 168–69). Moreover, increasing "cooperative [calculative] efficacy for selfish governments may bring very high costs and also induce knavish politicians to pursue power" (169). Thus, we argue that Hayek's worst are more likely to reach the top where full calculative efficacy obtains.

ernment work together toward full extraction. From a welfare perspective, this is the worst possible worst-case scenario. The individual is left with the bare subsistence level of consumption.

Now let us relax the assumption of calculative efficacy while retaining that of full cooperative efficacy. Both levels of government will cooperate in the attempt to extract the fullest possible amount of surplus from the individual. Failing full calculative efficacy, however, the government cannot restrict itself to taxing only inframarginal gains: deadweight losses result as individual behavior responds to the tax rates. Although the total amount extracted will be lower than in the first case, the individual will be slightly better off.[17] From a welfare perspective, reductions in the amount of information available to the planning agency appear desirable despite the decline in total output.

Relaxing now also the assumption of cooperative efficacy along with the supposition of full calculative efficacy, each of the two different levels of government attempts to maximize its own taxation revenue. The local and regional levels of government attempt to extract quantities of surplus L and R from the individual; because they cannot restrict themselves to taxing inframarginal rents, however, they extract an amount equal to $L + R < T$, where T is the amount of extraction undertaken under conditions of full cooperative and calculative efficacy. We suppose that the local level of government offers the individual taxpayer assistance in helping to misinform the regional level of government as to the individual's available surplus. In that case, the individual faces surplus extraction of $L' + R' < L + R$, where $L' > L$ and $R' < R$. The individual is left better off by reductions in the ability of planning agents to calculate and coordinate their surplus extraction activities. When planning agents are self-interested, assumptions of full cooperative and calculative efficacy provide worst-case assumptions. Thus, where cooperative efficacy is less than perfect we should expect to see the center (seeking to maximize its share of the surplus) regularly rotating lower-level bureaucrats. Planner rotation weakens lower-level cooperative efficacy. Joseph Berliner (1952) notes the "relatively short tenure" in office of [Soviet] plant directors, arguing that such "fluidity of directors must impair the efficiency of management, and directors must lose a considerable amount of time in getting used to new plants." Rotation, however, generates "beneficial consequences for the [Soviet] State, such as the disruption of a smoothly operating system of 'mutual support' [lower-level

17. Olson (2000) provides an analysis of the Soviet Union under Stalin that complements our account. The Stalinist regime extracted surplus from the populace by taxing inframarginal wages very highly. Perfect information would have allowed the regime to engage in perfectly discriminatory taxation—thereby taxing away any surplus above that required for subsistence (125).

cooperative efficacy or collusion] among officials who have worked together a long time in the same plant" (362). Full cooperative efficacy is clearly a boon where planner type is benevolent and a liability where the planner type is selfish (table 5.3).[18]

Robust Political Economy?

Recently, Peter Boettke and various coauthors have provided a reading of Hayek's work—especially his contributions to the socialist calculation debate—which places Hayek squarely within the "worst-case" political economy tradition. Boettke et al. build on their worst-case reading of Hayek in advocating an approach to worst-case political economy that, while maintaining a Buchanan-Hume type of supposition of analytical egalitarianism regarding planner motivation—self-interest characterizes both private and public chooser alike—injects a decidedly Austrian flavor regarding information (see, e.g., Boettke 1999; Boettke and Lopez 2002; and Boettke and Leeson 2004). Elsewhere, Boettke suggests that a truly robust political economy "must explore both sides of the intellectual coin of comparative institutional analysis: incentives and information" (1999, xxx). Reiterating his earlier point, he states that a "robust political economy should work from a starting point which accepts neither benevolence nor omniscience. . . . There is a good case in

Table 5.3. Calculation and Cooperation with Self-Interested Planners

	Calculative Efficacy	Calculative Inefficacy
Cooperative Efficacy	Maximal ouput, minimal welfare. All surplus is efficiently extracted. Worst-case outcome from a welfare perspective.	Second-best efficiency in output. Planners grope toward maximal extraction. Deadweight losses result. Individuals keep some surplus as planners cannot calculate full extraction price levels.
Cooperative Inefficacy	Welfare is higher than in all but the lower-right-hand quadrant. An efficient extraction plan is devised by the central government, but lower levels subvert it, allowing consumers to keep some surplus in exchange for bribes.	Second-best citizen welfare.

18. "Low [cooperative-calculative] efficacy may have been preferable under the Soviet system, when the government did more good than bad" (Cowen and Sutter 1999, 171).

human affairs for striving to build institutions from *pessimistic assumptions* about *motivation* and *knowledge,* and thus guarding against the worst-case situations" (2001, 332, emphasis added).[19]

We argue here, however, that traditional worst-case theorizing à la Buchanan and Tullock is not necessarily incorrect in ignoring informational imperfections (Hayek's knowledge problem) and that the worst worst-case scenario is one where public choosers are both self-interested *and* have full information. While Hayek rightly argues that poor-quality information will plague any attempt by *benevolent* planners to rationally plan an economy, we argue that benevolent planners will (if we take benevolence seriously) surely retreat from planning once its failure becomes readily apparent. Alternatively, said would-be planners will never try a policy of wholesale command planning due to a variety of democratic constraints. Peter Wiles is rather apposite, writing, "It *is* difficult to reconcile parliamentary opposition and the rule of law with a command economy" (1967, 18).[20]

While a public choice reading of Hayek's *The Road to Serfdom* ([1944] 1986) might suggest that planners are self-interested and thus will not retreat from planning (see, e.g., Boettke 1995), we argue that the supposition of planner self-interest makes the Austrian economic critique of planning (the calculation or knowledge problem) either a largely irrelevant consideration—the planners are not seeking to attain first-best efficiency anyhow—or a constraint allowing for the second-best outcome with the knowledge problem attenuating the surplus-extracting venality that characterizes self-interested planners. When planners are not benevolent, irrespective of their putative information, first-best solutions simply cannot obtain in welfare space.[21] And in second-best worlds we cannot expect that moves toward optimality measured in first-best space are necessarily desirable. As Lipsey and Lancaster point out in their seminal article, if a constraint "prevents the attainment of one of the Paretian conditions, the other Paretian conditions, although still attainable, are, in general, no longer desirable" (1956, 11). We argue that similar strictures hold in the designation of best-case and worst-case assumptions. Specifically, if one of the underlying assumptions

19. Boettke and Leeson (2004) further reiterate the point.

20. Wiles intriguingly suggests that the trade unions may have acted as a veto player blocking any move toward Hayek's "serfdom" in postwar Britain. Government mandated wage freezes (surely an early step toward serfdom according to Hayekian logic) are not going to work "where trade unions are strong and it is held that law ought to rule . . . [for the policy provides] a tremendous historical affirmation that socialism excludes collective bargaining and socialist parties [e.g,, the Labour Party] must not be paid by trade unions. . . . [I]n a society such as ours . . . it is a complete non-starter" (Wiles 1976, 18–19).

21. Of course, under cooperative and calculative efficacy, first best output *can* obtain. The planner extracts all surplus.

that a political economy model makes concerning the state of the world fails to obtain, what serves as a worst-case assumption in the model can, in reality, prove to be something of a positive blessing.

In a first-best world of benevolent planners, full calculative and cooperative efficacies are highly desirable on either a welfare or an output metric. Thus, Boettke (2001, 332) and Boettke and Lopez (2002) argue that perfect information (calculative efficacy) is clearly a best-case assumption. We suggest, however, that they cannot relax assumptions of planner benevolence while simultaneously insisting that Austrian informational assumptions provide robust worst-case foundations.[22] Standalone assumptions of planner "benevolence" or "omniscience" cannot be designated as either worst-case or best-case suppositions per se (see, e.g., Boettke 1999, 2001; and Boettke and Leeson 2004). Whether any particular informational (or motivational) supposition provides a best-case or worst-case assumption is not independent of whatever complementary supposition the theorist makes regarding planner type (or omniscience). Where planners are self-interested, Austrian suppositions regarding imperfect information provide an inadequately "pessimistic" assumption about planner "knowledge" (*contra* Boettke 2001, 332; and Boettke and Leeson 2004). Calculative inefficacy may prove to be a boon where planners are wholly self-interested. In the second-best world of self-interested planners, neither full coordinative nor calculative efficacy is necessarily desirable. To assume full calculative and cooperative efficacies is to make a truly worst-case assumption.

Conclusion: Are Two Vices Preferable to One?

Robust political economy requires analytical egalitarianism as a starting point. This is, however, a necessary rather than a sufficient condition; while an assumption that all are alike in their omniscience, omnipotence, and beneficence satisfies analytical egalitarianism, such an assumption would not prove to be a solid grounding for robust political economy. We have shown that the best- or worst-case nature of particular assumptions regarding knowledge and incentives are entirely contingent on the joint assumptions made regarding their respective motivational or informational counterpart. While perfect calculative efficacy in our socialist calculation example might seem to be a very optimistic and best-case assumption, it is necessary when the Austrian assumption of benevolence is weakened. With less than perfect benevolence, perfect

22. Benson's remarks are particularly apposite: "[I]t may be that dropping the benevolence assumption does 'substantively' alter the conclusions of Austrian political economy" (2002, 253).

information hardly provides a best-case scenario. Consequently, while Boettke's relaxing of the benevolence assumption within Austrian political economy may yield important insights, it will not provide the robust foundations he seeks. A robust and analytically egalitarian political economy must apply Hume's dictum without recourse to Austrian informational considerations.

More to the point, relaxing the benevolence assumption within Austrian political economy helps us better to see the root of the Soviet system's undesirability. Mises and Hayek persuasively argued that even benevolent planners could not engage in the kind of economic calculation that would be necessary to create an efficient planned economy. However, they failed to provide any coherent explanation as to why a benevolent planner would inexorably set off down the road toward full-blown central planning, or to coherently explain the institutional dynamic preventing a benevolent planner from turning away from central planning, once the economic problems supposedly inherent in that system became apparent. Absent nonbenevolent agents, we can have little explanation as to why central planning would proceed beyond the first famines. Regardless of Stalin's ability to engage in rational economic calculation, one would not wish to be one of his subjects; the knowledge problem is at worst irrelevant and at best ameliorative when Stalin rules. We argue that a great deal will depend on the nature of the agent instituting central planning and on the institutional framework within which he or she operates. In no case has full central planning ever been initiated by benevolent agents who were supplanted by despots, as in Hayek's story; real world central planners were nonbenevolent ex ante. Contrarily, much of Western Europe started down the road to central planning in the years following the Second World War; but when problems emerged their governments turned away from planning and nationalization, preferring a welfare state to the totalitarian apparatus that would be necessary to implement full-scale planning.[23]

23. The Labour government "moved towards a final acceptance of a planning machine that had no executive power, and which has been compared with a mere 'think tank.' . . . This was partly because . . . there many direct obstacles to the creation of a planned economy in Britain. Equally, these institutional barriers were complemented and reinforced by the clear *inhibitions to comprehensive planning inherent in the ideology and structure of the Labour movement itself*" (Toye 2004, 236–37, emphasis added). "[I]t might well be argued . . . [that] the Atlee government's policy in the 1940's was merely interventionism under the barest veneer of planning" (4–5). "Herbert Morrison told the [1945] party conference, 'this document [the Labour party manifesto] *Let us Face the Future* may be described as Labour's Five Year Plan.' . . . [W]hen discussing the reconstruction of Britain, he [Morrison] was not afraid to refer to the Soviet example. . . . [The manifesto] had in practice about as much connection to a Russian plan as Churchill's four-year plan had to Goering's. There was no commitment to establish any form of supreme economic authority. Substantial 'constructive enterprise and private endeavour' would co-exist with publicly owned industries

Intriguingly, Lavoie remarks that it is "fundamentally misleading to view planning in practice only as a *failure* to achieve . . . progressive ideals. . . . [I]t can just as well be said that planning in practice has been a stunning *success* in achieving some entirely different goals . . . [and] the legacy of *practical* planning procedures traces to an unambiguously reactionary beginning" (1985b, 214). Thus Lavoie—thereby apparently undercutting his claim that the knowledge problem and totalitarian problem are complementary arguments against planning rather than substitutes—clearly recognizes what was so readily apparent to Frank Knight during the calculation debate: from the perspective of planner self-interest the "failure" of planning is no failure whatsoever. Lavoie is apposite: "Stalinism . . . is not an aberration or a betrayal of true planning or a failure of its designers to attain Marxist ideals but, rather, a *successful realization of reactionary ideals*" (215, emphasis added).[24] The totalitarian problem always outweighed the economic problem; consequently, the economic problem highlighted by Mises and Hayek proves to be something of a boon to those living under a socialist system. As robust political economy seeks to guard against the worst-case scenario, maintaining a narrow focus on the problem of governing the governors seems best.

Our essay began with Hume's warning concerning political knavery. In Hume's terms, the welfare losses attributable to one vice (or imperfection), namely, that of planner self-interest, are attenuated by that of low calculative efficacy.[25] Thus, to cure one vice (low calculative efficacy) without also replacing planner self-interest with planner benevolence would simply exacerbate welfare losses.

Bibliography

Benson, Bruce. 2002. "Regulatory Disequilibrium and Inefficiency: The Case of Interstate Trucking." *Review of Austrian Economics* 15, nos. 2–3: 229–55.

. . . [and] perhaps the strongest planning commitment, the national investment board, was abandoned by Labour in power" (154–55).

24. "The monopoly power of the Communist party and its government bureaucrats was successfully secured [by Stalin]; the economic system was brought to serve the interests of a New Class" (Lavoie 1985b, 229). Throughout the socialist calculation debate, Frank Knight argued that the technical issue of socialist calculation per se was not truly germane to the planning versus markets debate: "Theory and current experience warrant the gravest doubts as to whether the human group in command of a collectivist economy would make any serious effort to find for socio-economic problems [first-best] solutions of the form taken for granted by Professor Pigou and other liberals" (1938b, 243). Similarly, Knight argued that a "socialistic government would not try *intelligently to function in accord with economic principles in securing maximum satisfaction of the economic needs of the masses*" (1938a, 268, emphasis added).

25. See the epigraph that opens this chapter.

Bentham, Jeremy. [1822] 1989. *First Principles Preparatory to Constitutional Code.* Edited by P. Schofield. Oxford: Clarendon.

Berliner, Joseph S. 1952. "The Informal Organization of the Soviet Firm." *Quarterly Journal of Economics* 66, no. 3: 342–65.

Boettke, Peter J. 1995. "Hayek's *The Road to Serfdom* Revisited: Government Failure in the Argument against Socialism." *Eastern Economic Journal* 21, no. 1: 7–26.

Boettke, Peter J. 1999. "Introduction." In *The Legacy of Friedrich von Hayek,* edited by Peter J. Boettke, vol. 1. Northampton: Edward Elgar.

Boettke, Peter J. 2001. *Calculation and Coordination: Essays on Socialism and Transitional Political Economy.* London: Routledge.

Boettke, Peter J. 2005. "On Reading Hayek: Choice, Consequences, and *The Road to Serfdom.*" *European Journal of Political Economy* 21:1042–53.

Boettke, Peter J., and Peter T. Leeson. 2004. "Liberalism, Socialism, and Robust Political Economy." *Journal of Markets and Morality* 7, no. 1: 99–111.

Boettke, Peter J., and Edward Lopez. 2002. "Austrian Economics and Public Choice." *Review of Austrian Economics* 15, no. 2–3: 111–19.

Brennan, Geoffrey, and James M. Buchanan. [1980] 2000. *The Power to Tax.* Indianapolis: Liberty.

Brennan, Geoffrey, and James M. Buchanan. [1985] 2000. *The Reason of Rules.* Indianapolis: Liberty.

Brennan, Geoffrey, and Alan Hamlin. 2000. *Democratic Devices and Desires.* Cambridge: Cambridge University Press.

Buchanan, James M. 1962. "Politics, Policy, and Pigovian Margins." *Economica* 29 (February): 17–28.

Buchanan, James M. [1969] 1999. *Cost and Choice.* Indianapolis: Liberty.

Buchanan, James M. 1979a. "Professor Alchian on Economic Method." In *What Should Economists Do?* Indianapolis: Liberty.

Buchanan, James M. 1979b. "Public Choice and Ideology." In *What Should Economists Do?* Indianapolis: Liberty.

Buchanan, James M. 1987. *Economics: Between Predictive Science and Moral Philosophy.* College Station: Texas A&M University Press.

Buchanan, James M. 1992. *Better Than Plowing.* Chicago: University of Chicago Press.

Buchanan, James M. 2001. *Ideas, Persons, and Events.* Indianapolis: Liberty.

Cowen, Tyler, and Daniel Sutter. 1999. "The Costs of Cooperation." *Review of Austrian Economics* 12, no. 2: 161–73.

Crampton, Eric, and Andrew Farrant. 2006. "Relaxing Benevolence: Public Choice, Socialist Calculation, and Planner Self-Interest?" *Review of Austrian Economics* 19, no. 1: 81–93.

Cullenberg, Stephen. 1992. "Socialism's Burden: Toward a Thin Definition of Socialism." *Rethinking Marxism* 5, no. 2: 64–83.

Demsetz, Harold. 1969. "Information and Efficiency: Another Viewpoint." *Journal of Law and Economics* 12:1–22.

Dickinson, H. D. 1939. *Economics of Socialism.* Oxford: Oxford University Press.

Faria, J. R. 1999. "Is There an Optimal Constitution?" *Constitutional Political Economy* 10:177–84.

Hayek, F. A. 1935. *Collectivist Economic Planning.* London: George Routledge and Sons.

Hayek, F. A. [1944] 1986. *The Road to Serfdom.* London: Ark.

Hayek, F. A. 1945. "The Use of Knowledge in Society." *American Economic Review* 35, no. 4: 519–30.

Hayek, F. A. [1956] 1994. *The Road to Serfdom.* Chicago: University of Chicago Press.

Hume, David. [1752] 1985a. "Of the Independency of Parliament." In *Essays: Moral, Political, and Literary,* edited by Eugene F. Miller. Indianapolis: Liberty Classics.

Hume, David. [1752] 1985b. "Of Refinement in the Arts" In *Essays: Moral, Political, and Literary,* edited by Eugene F. Miller. Indianapolis: Liberty Classics.

Knight, F. H. 1938a. "Two Economists on Socialism." *Journal of Political Economy* 46:241–50.

Knight, F. H. 1938b. "Socialism: An Economic and Sociological Analysis." *Journal of Political Economy* 46:267–69.

Kornai, Janos. 1986. "The Hungarian Reform Process: Visions, Hopes, and Reality." *Journal of Economic Literature* 24, no. 4: 1687–1737.

Lavoie, Don. 1985a. *Rivalry and Central Planning.* Cambridge: Cambridge University Press.

Lavoie, Don. 1985b. *National Economic Planning: What Is Left?* Cambridge, Mass.: Ballinger.

Levy, David M. 1990. "The Bias in Centrally Planned Prices." *Public Choice* 67: 213–26.

Levy, David M. 2002. "Robust Institutions." *Review of Austrian Economics* 15, no. 2–3: 131–42.

Levy, David M., Sandra Peart, and Andrew Farrant. 2005. "The Spatial Politics of F. A. Hayek's *Road to Serfdom.*" *European Journal of Political Economy* 21: 982–99.

Lipsey, Richard, and Kelvin Lancaster. 1956. "The General Theory of Second Best." *Review of Economic Studies* 24, no. 1: 11–32.

Mill, John Stuart [1869]. 1984. *The Subjection of Women.* In *Essays on Equality, Law, and Education,* Vol. 21 of *Collected Works of John Stuart Mill,* edited by J. M. Robson. Toronto: University of Toronto Press.

Mises, L. von. [1920] 1935. "Economic Calculation in the Socialist Commonwealth." In *Collectivist Economic Planning,* edited by F. A. Hayek. London: George Routledge and Sons.

Mises, L. von. [1932] 1981. *Socialism: An Economic and Sociological Analysis.* Indianapolis: Liberty Classics.

Olson, Mancur. 2000. *Power and Prosperity.* New York: Basic Books.

Rothbard, Murray N. 1976. "Praxeology, Value Judgments, and Public Policy." In *The Foundations of Modern Austrian Economics,* edited by E. G. Dolan. Kansas City: Sheed and Ward.

Shleifer, Andrei, and Robert Vishny. 1992. "Pervasive Shortages under Socialism." *RAND Journal of Economics* 23, no. 2: 237–46.

Shleifer, Andrei, and Robert Vishny. 1993. "Corruption." *Quarterly Journal of Economics* 108, no. 3 (August): 599–617.

Steele, David R. 1992. *From Marx to Mises: Post-capitalist Society and the Challenge of Economic Calculation.* La Salle, IL: Open Court.

Stigler, G. 1975. *The Citizen and the State.* Chicago: University of Chicago Press.

Stiglitz, J. 1994. *Whither Socialism?* Cambridge: MIT Press.

Sutter, Daniel. 1998. "Leviathan at Bay: Constitutional versus Political Controls on Government." *Economic Inquiry* 34: 670–78.
Toma, E., and M. Toma. 1984. "Constitutional Tax Constraints within a Classical Model of Leviathan." *History of Political Economy* 16, no. 1: 89–105.
Toye, Richard. 2004. *The Labour Party and the Planned Economy, 1931–1951.* Woodbridge, U.K.: Royal Historical Society and Boydell Press.
Wiles, J. de la F. 1967. "The Political and Social Prerequisites for a Soviet-Type Economy." *Economica* 34, no. 133 (February): 1–19.

PART 2 • Smithian Themes

6 • Sacred Economics

Deirdre McCloskey

Part I. Wage Slavery

If you are simply *outraged* that I have not acknowledged that greed corrupts bourgeois life or that advertising dominates modern capitalism or that northern standards of consumption depend on imperialism over the South or that late capitalism is disastrous for the environment, stay for answers. I beg you to suppose for the time being that they might exist and that people of good will might sincerely and even wisely believe them.

On the side of production the capitalist system provides a field in which ordinary people can exercise their abilities harmlessly. Indeed, helpfully. Business can be, as Max Weber and Michael Novak put it, a "calling," a *Beruf,* a "vocation." "A career in business," writes Novak, "is not only a morally serious vocation but a morally noble one. Those who are called to it have reason to take pride in it and rejoice in it" (1996, 13). But of course that is not what the clerisy thinks. Quite the contrary: "If you actually made money yourself . . . maybe starting from nothing, you are given the subtle impression . . . such a career is rather sweaty, vulgar, and morally suspect" (5). When I started a course in business history at the business school at the University of Chicago in 1979 I started it with Mesopotamia, having the kids read business letters from 2000 BCE collected at the Oriental Institute, because I wanted them to know that they were embarking on an ancient and honorable profession, not, as the clerisy believes, a dirty modern aberration. As Novak says, to think of business as a calling—he and I have God in mind here—"would help tie [the young businesspeople] more profoundly to traditions going far back into the past" (37).

Making and selling steel or hamburgers is not the most prestigious field among intellectuals. Writing long books is. Or among artists installing artworks or making movies is. But running a fruit stall with energy and intelligence shares in the exhilaration of creativity.[1] Don't laugh. By doing so you exhibit a nasty snobbishness, oh you misled member of the Western clerisy. And you exhibit an undemocratic igno-

1. Thus James Norwood Corbett in Bowe, Bowe, and Streeter 2000, 250–54.

rance of the world's work to boot. Shame on you. Maimonides left no doubt that the clerisy's pretension is a mistake. "One who makes his mind up to study Torah and not to work but to live on charity profanes the name of God, brings the Torah into contempt, extinguishes the light of religion, brings evil upon himself, and deprives himself of the life hereafter."[2]

The psychologist Mihaly Csikszentmihalyi (CHICK-sent-me-high) calls the feeling of creativity "flow," those "flashes of intense living . . . when a person's skills are fully involved in overcoming a challenge that is just about manageable. . . . It is the full involvement of flow, rather than happiness, that makes for excellence in life" (1997, 30–32). By "happiness" here he means mere consumption, happiness according to the grossest sort of utilitarianism or Epicureanism *not* his Aristotle-derived ideal of the exercise of vital powers. As Martha Nussbaum notes, "Most Greeks would understand *eudaimonia* [often translated as "happiness" as a state of pleasure] to be something essentially active, of which praiseworthy activities are not just productive means, but actual constituent parts" (1986, 6n2). Csikszentmihalyi tells of Joe, who worked in the cacophony of a railcar factory.

> [Joe] had trained himself to understand and to fix every piece of equipment in the factory. He loved to take on machinery that didn't work, figure out what was wrong with it, and set it right again. . . . The hundred or so welders who worked at the same plant respected Joe, even though they couldn't quite make him out. . . . Many claimed that without Joe the factory might just as well close. . . . I have met many CEOs of major corporations . . . and several dozen Nobel Prize-winners—eminent people who in many ways led excellent lives, but none that was better than Joe's. (1997, 2–3)

In other words it is not merely through the piling up of goods that the market system succeeds. It is through the jobs themselves. Respect for work has been historically rare. Until the quickening of commerce in bourgeois societies, in fact, work except praying and fighting was despised. It was the rare stoic philosopher who viewed physical labor as anything but dishonoring. The historically more usual attitude may have been what prevented the classical Mediterranean civilization or medieval Chinese society from industrializing. Nowadays it is a problem for many poor societies. Women and slaves work. Real men smoke.

2. Maimonides, *Mishnah Torah,* ca. 1200 CE, quoted in Sachs 2002, 95.

Englishmen in the seventeenth century had no conception of dignity beyond what the sociologists call "ascription," that is, rank. The result, as the sociologist of science Steven Shapin has argued, is that seventeenth-century science used gentlemanly status as a warrant for believability. William Petty (1623–87), one of the founders of the English Royal Society, spoke of a gentleman as someone who had "such estate, real and personal, as whereby he is able to subsist without the practice of an mercenary employments" (Shapin 1994, 50). Only a gentleman could have *honor,* which was only gradually coming to mean our *honesty.* A gentleman was precisely someone without an occupation. The contemporary French phrase was *le honnête homme,* the "honorable" man being one who did not work. The early-twentieth-century irony about this convention is to call a bum a "gentleman of the road," as earlier the highwayman was a "gentleman of the highway." Such a man is very willing to fight but not to be seen to *work* even at that. Thus, the Prince Hal of *Henry IV* drinks and whores away the days and nights with Falstaff through Parts One and Two, and we are indulgently amused—though, Prince Hal explains, and Shakespeare in his protobourgeois way was recommending, that princes need this common touch.

Down to the nineteenth century, with fading echoes even now, the phrase "a gentleman of *business*" was considered an absurdity, a flat contradiction. The economist David Ricardo wrote in 1817 that a remission of rent to farmers from their landlords "would only enable some farmers [i.e., men of business in agriculture] to live like gentlemen [i.e., to have an income without working]" (1817, chap. 2, ¶15). But by the mid–nineteenth-century Charles Dickens represents a world turned upside down. As Northrop Frye noted, Dickens's "implicit social vision is . . . radical" despite his conservative nostalgia for a simpler time when the rich were charitable and the poor unspoiled, precisely in seeing gentlemen without occupations as parasites (1968, 230).

True, even the management of possessions provided by the work of others provided an opportunity for flow, as in the housewife's artful arrangement of her furniture or the collector's absorbed passion for his goods, heedless of capital gain. The curatorial art is aristocratic, as may be seen in the likes of Bernard Berensons and Kenneth Clarks (Clark studied as a young man with Berenson and ended life a baron), but capitalism permits the bourgeoisie to participate. And Berenson, at least, was a canny and some say unscrupulous businessman, as many an aristocrat has been in fact.

The piling up of goods, even in the pursuit of such a nasty thing as profit, has had the direct effect of giving billions of ordinary people the scope with which to pursue something other than subsistence. And on the nether side of subsistence, so to speak, the market has provided the billions with meaning in their lives through that very participation in the making of things for the market. Only an undemocratic snob, you might say, if you were inclined to speak frankly about one of the troubles with antibourgeois and antieconomic prejudices since 1848, denies dignity to anything but what priests or aristocrats do. As Frank Knight put it, "We are impelled to look for ends in the economic process itself, and to give thoughtful consideration to the possibilities of participation in economic activity as a sphere of self-expression and creative achievement" ([1923] 1997, 51).

Work in capitalism is nothing like alienating. Tzvetan Todorov quotes the protagonist of *Forever Flowing,* the posthumously published novel of Vasily Grossman (1905–64), who he says was the sole example of a successful Stalinist writer who converted wholly to anticommunism ("The slave in him died, and a free man arose").

> I used to think freedom was freedom of speech, freedom of the press, freedom of conscience. . . . Here is what it amounts to: you have to have the right to sow what you wish to, to make shoes or coats, to bake into bread the flour ground from the grain you have sown, and to sell it or not sell it as you wish; for the lathe-operator, the steelworker, and the artist it's a matter of being able to live as you wish and work as you wish and not as they order you. (Todorov [2000] 2003, 69–70).

If you are sure this is wrong, that workers are slaves under capitalism, as I tell you they are under socialism ("Under capitalism, man exploits man; under socialism, it's the other way around"), consider where you got the idea. If from your own actual experience at your life's employment or even from a blue- or pink-collar summer job or a few months as a journalist getting nickel-and-dimed in minimum wage jobs, you have at least the scientific spirit. You, me, and Barbara Ehrenreich can sit down and think through the balance of the evidence together. But if by any chance you got it straight from Marx, or from the many people influenced by Marx, I ask you to consider that Marx, like many of us aristocratic priests, never worked at anything but philosophy and journalism, never picked up a shovel for pay, never so much as set foot in a factory or farm. Marx—Engels was different—had not troubled to look at manual work much less try it out for himself. He preferred his angry theorizing in the Reading Room of the British Museum.

Studs Terkel, in *Working,* says that the job "is a search, too, for daily meaning as well as daily bread, for astonishment rather than torpor; in short, for a sort of life rather than a Monday through Friday sort of dying" (1974, xiii). It struck Marisa Bowe, while editing a follow-up to Terkel, that "very few of those we talked to"—and the interviewers seem to have talked to American workers pretty much at random—"hate their jobs, and even among the ones who do, almost none said 'not working' was their ultimate goal" (Bowe, Bowe, and Streeter 2000, xiii).

> You need not see what someone is doing
> To know it is his vocation,
>
> you have only to watch his eyes:
> a cook mixing his sauce, a surgeon
>
> making a primary incision,
> a clerk completing a bill of lading
>
> wear the same rapt expression,
> forgetting themselves in a function.[3]

A Cincinnati sewer worker interviewed on National Public Radio on 29 August 2002 joked that at first he viewed his job as a way of claiming credit with hippie girls that he was an "environmental" worker. But of course that's what he is. And he grew, he declared, to *love* his work, just *love* it, crawling around sewer mains. True, he earns $60,000 a year for his trouble, as the sandhogs digging tunnels for New York's water supply earn $150,000 a year. But *that* condition of a laboring vocation nowadays is made possible by the goods-piling-up machinery of capitalism.

A traveler from the (ideal, gentle) communist planet in Ursula LeGuin's *The Dispossessed* is startled by the prosperity of the "sturdy, self-respecting-looking people" in the (ideal but not so gentle) capitalist planet.

> It puzzled him. He had assumed that if you removed a human being's natural incentive to work—his initiative, his creative energy—and replaced it with external motivation . . . he would become a lazy and careless worker. But no careless workers kept those lovely farmlands, or made the superb cars and comfortable trains. The lure of *profit* was evidently a much more effective replacement of the natural initiative than he had been led to believe. (LeGuin, [1974] 2003, 82, emphasis in original)

3. W. H. Auden, "Horae Canonicae, Sext," in Auden 1976. When he wasn't being a poet, though, Auden had conventional attitudes about alienation.

LeGuin overlooks, though, the better case for capitalism, which is not that profit deftly replaces the instinct of workmanship. On the contrary, profit nourishes creative energy. Marx, Thorstein Veblen, Karl Polanyi, and others have been mistaken on the point. Good, well-paid workers are not alienated. Watch a team of trashmen working the public barrels from a truck along a Chicago street, working fast and accurately, skimming the empty plastic barrels back to their places, tipping them back into the cast iron holders, riding easily on the lip of the shoot, stormy, husky, brawling. I do not condescend. I've worked trash trucks in my day and know the feeling.

Charlie Chaplin's 1936 movie *Modern Times* or the opening scenes of Alan Sillitoe's angry-young-man novel *The Loneliness of the Long Distance Runner* (1959, movie 1962) say that many factory jobs are monotonous. Granted. I have *not* worked in a factory. But the monotony is, of course, pretty common in nonindustrial society, too. Planting rice is never fun. The idiocy of rural life is not always better for the soul than the idiocy of urban life. I *have* worked as a farm laborer. Ironically, only since romanticism and the rise of prosperous, healthy cities—London stopped killing more people than it bred by the end of the eighteenth century—have Europeans looked fondly back on their village roots. Poor people have moved in every country worldwide for centuries from the village to the city, freely if not joyously, even when the cities were killers. Witness the several hundreds of millions of Chinese peasants who moved in the 1990s and later to the cities of eastern China, the largest such migration in history. Living in a factory dorm room in the city of Changshu, north of Shanghai, and working seventy-seven hours a week for eleven months a year making intravenous drips for Western hospitals to bring home five hundred dollars in net pay, if she is very careful, seemed in 2004 better to the nineteen-year-old Bai Lin than staying in her home village of Two Dragons (Lev 2004). If you, as a city dweller and office worker, think that outdoor work must be *so* much nicer than being cooped up, it's a good bet you have never worked for more than a day or two in the out-of-doors, making hay in Wiltshire or making roads in Massachusetts, not to speak of planting rice in Two Dragons. There's a reason that most people, when given the choice, prefer to work under roofs and inside heated and air-conditioned offices and in the busy cities.

And a commercial society provides, on a scale unique since Adam delved and Eve span, opportunities for fully flowful jobs—which would not describe Bai Lin's eleven-hour days cutting rubber sheets but does describe her older brother Bai Li Peng's job as a foreman in a factory near Hong Kong. The skilled craftsperson of olden times was much admired by late romantics such as Morris and Ruskin. But sculpting masons and master builders were a tiny fraction of the medieval workforce and in their own day were *not* admired. No one who had to work with his or her hands, including artists, was admired. Most medievals were closer to the Monty Python vision of the groveling peasant than to the Pre-Raphaelite vision of free craftsman and noble saints of labor, admitting that both are fictions. Think of the clerkly professions in this way—being a college professor, for example. There are about a million of them today in the United States, 1 out of every 150 workers, more people, probably, than the cumulative total in all the centuries everywhere before, say, 1945. The great-great-grandparents of the average college teacher worked with their hands, often at jobs that provided less scope for flow. Like everyone else's, since that's what a nonmodern economy had on offer, mine were dirt farmers and lumberjacks and housewives—though my mother's mother took pride in her housewifery in an age of home canning and home sewing and homemaking of the sort Cheryl Mendelson talked about engagingly in *Home Comforts: The Art and Science of Keeping House* (2001), and I expect that some others of my ancestors and yours wielded a spade or spindle joyfully by God's grace.

But nonclerkly jobs in a market society provide more scope, too. The uncommon but by no means unheard of Chicago bus driver who works joyfully at making his passengers welcome and works conscientiously at arriving at each stop exactly on time, navigating the snowy streets of the South Side with brio, is living a flowful life on the job. The textbook salesman who pushes the envelope (he would say), venturing into new academic buildings to confront new curmudgeons in English or accounting armed only with his open and sunny personality and a giant catalogue he has memorized of Macmillan books, is testing the limits of his skill.

Of course, you can *refuse* to live flowfully, even in a rich, Western society. The tram drivers of Rotterdam are known for leaving just as the university student running to make the tram gets close to the door or speeding up to ram harder when the track is blocked by a careless auto driver. They get satisfaction, no doubt, in paying back the middle class. One wonders if they wouldn't do better to join it and make their trams into little sites of the bourgeois virtues.

Many college professors treat their unique jobs as though they were routine and become, as Adam Smith said of the effects of repetitive work, "as stupid and as ignorant as it is possible for a human creature to become." As they stroll between their few hours of classes a week they lament the appalling stress of their lives and form trade unions in a fantasy of proletarian status. True, the college administration encourages the fantasy by itself playing the role of The Suits, conspiring against common sense, staffing their executive suites with autobusy assistant and associate and vice thises and thats. But such college professors are refusing flow. Immanuel Kant lectured every morning all morning, including Saturdays, easily twice the average contact hours of a modern college professor, and was uncomplaining about it. As the son of a saddler he knew hard physical work. Yet in his spare time he managed to write—slowly, admittedly, by the frenetic standards of modern academic life—a few books that revolutionized Western philosophy.

"When the job presents clear goals," Csikszentmihalyi writes, "unambiguous feedback, a sense of control, challenges that match the worker's skills, and few distractions, the feelings it provides are not that different from what one experiences in a sport or an artistic performance."[4] And the pay matters. It is a thrill unique to a market society to find that people are willing to *pay* for one's product, to surrender by free will, as we put it, their hard-earned money. Remember your first paycheck and the feeling it gave of adulthood, of pulling your own weight. Remember when you last sold for a professional's price something *you* produced. In his play and novella *Home Truths* David Lodge imagines a conversation in a cottage in Sussex between two old friends, one a man who writes television plays and is on his way to Hollywood, the other a woman comfortably well off in retirement who makes pottery.

> He picked up a pottery vase. "This is nice. Did you make it?"
> "Yes."
> "Very nice . . . Is it for sale?"
> "Not to you, Sam. If you like it, have it as a present."
> "No way. Would a hundred be fair?"
> "Far too much."
> "I'll give you seventy-five." He took out his chequebook.
> "That's very generous. I *am* selling the odd piece now, actually. It's very satisfying." ([1999] 2000, 26–27).

It's satisfying especially to a married woman accustomed to giving care for no pay whose independence in a commercial society depends on a pay packet. As Peggy Seeger sang it (1971):

> I really wish that I could be a lady—
> I could do all the lovely things a lady's s'posed to do.
> I wouldn't even mind if they would pay me,
> And I could be a person too.

4. Csikszentmihalyi 1997, 38; cf. Knight [1923] 1997, 54.

. . . But now that times are harder and my Jimmy's got the sack
I went down to Vicker's, they were glad to have me back.
I'm a third-class citizen, my wages tell me that,
But I'm a first-class engineer.

Work in a capitalist society, or a noncapitalist society—though capitalism affords many more such jobs, and, I repeat, capitalistic pay is satisfying, too—can fulfill the Greek ideal of happiness reiterated to the boys at English private schools in the nineteenth century: "The exercise of vital powers along lines of excellence [*arête*] in a life affording them scope [i.e., pagan moral luck or Christian grace]." One can be an excellent mother in bringing up Connor and Lily to a full adult life or an excellent carpenter making a staircase with winding treads and housed stringers or an excellent clerk completing an intricate bill of lading or an excellent repairer of railcar-making machinery. (Schuttner 1998, 67ff). At least one can in a modern capitalist society.

Part 2: The Rich

Of course, the very rich are always with us. In the railcar factory Happy Joe had a boss, who grew rich "on" Joe's labor. Any discussion about the ethics of the market tends to devolve rapidly into a discussion of winners and losers, where losers are taken to be the workers. It's part of the zero-sum game that most noneconomists imagine is how the economy works.

Note at the outset, however, that the metaphor of profit and managerial incomes being "based on" the worker's labor is just that, a metaphor, more or less apt, whose aptness remains to be determined. It's not simply reality, as many noneconomists suppose. If you speak of the rich as parasites on real workers you are depending on a dichotomy of capital and labor devised before 1848, when workers were unspeakably poor, human capital was rare, local monopolies prevailed, and land was an important input, before capitalism had done its work. The labor theory of value, I report from economics, is simply mistaken, as almost everyone agrees who has studied the question.[5]

But what *about* those darn capitalists and their grotesquely high incomes? Do I believe in *good* capitalists?

My answer is like the old joke, "Do I *believe* in infant baptism?! Goodness, I've *seen* it!" Do I believe in good capitalists? Goodness, I've *seen* them, for example, Lionel Rothschild, Andrew Carnegie, J. P. Mor-

5. Nozick 1974, 156–62 contains an accessible demolition.

gan, and John D. Rockefeller. The first, third, and fourth, by the way, were pious followers of an Abrahamic religion, as Jew, Episcopalian, and Baptist. And Carnegie was raised among such people.

We have been told since the muckraking journalists of the early 1900s or, in another rich tradition, by the anti-Semites then and later, that these were just *terrible* men. I mean, how *else* did they get so rich? If you are inclined to think this way, I suggest gently that you may be working with a theory that the only way to get rich is by stealing. Zero sum: your gain is my loss. To Tillich and Wegener, each person in a capitalist society "is the enemy of the other, because his advantage is conditioned by the disadvantage or ruin of the other" (quoted by Sherman [1976, p. 168]). And to Comte-Sponville, "Western prosperity depends, directly or indirectly, on Third World poverty, which the West in some cases merely takes advantage of and in others actually causes"([1996] 2001, 89).

In the playroom it's true. Jip gets more toys—short of a subsidy from Mother—only by violence against Janneke. But such a theory is mistaken in a capitalist economy, in which food and toys and other goods and services are made fresh daily not merely reallocated from a God-given stock. And it is more mistaken the more quickly the goods-making skills of the economy are growing. Free market economies are positive sum.

Economies grow slowly—or not at all—when stealing or taxing becomes a simpler means to wealth than working or selling. Stealing and taxing discourage production, and so the outcome is worse even than zero sum. Such negative-sum alternatives to exchange have historically been the norm, which is one reason that sustained economic growth happened only once. According to Tacitus, the ancient German thought it "tame and spiritless to accumulate slowly by the sweat of his brow what can be gotten quickly by the loss of a little blood" ([98 CE] 1916, 114). In an aristocratic society, I have noted, work has little prestige. Along the Heroin Road from Afghanistan through Turkey to the streets of London easy money gotten quickly by the loss of a little blood corrupts the young. Why finish high school, why acquire skills on a building site, when you can earn a working man's income in a week of drug smuggling?

"Real wealth," in the economist's way of thinking, is not a pile of finished stuff merely to be allocated, as in the children's playroom. Nor does wealth consist of such beloved tokens of ownership as money in your pocket or stocks in your pension plan or profits from your drug deal. Wealth is the real ability in arm or brain or machine to produce *more* stuff, the "real" backing for the tokens. The recovery of Europe from the Second World War, I have said, did not come, as popular fable has it, from the United States of America and the Marshall Plan, gracious though the plan was. Recovery came chiefly from Europeans' arms and brains, from their real wealth. That the bricks had been toppled by bombs was only a temporary setback (Gordon and Walton 1982). The real wealth behind your pension is the ability in arm or brain or machine of employed labor or capital, that is, your kids' generation paying your Medicare bills. Who owns the stream of disposable income from the real wealth is a separate matter. If the government has plausibly promised to tax your kids to pay for your health care, you, in a sense, own that stream of income. But anyway the nation's real wealth is the productivity of the economy.

Private property and unfettered exchange—in a word, capitalism—is not the kingdom of heaven, Lord knows. But for allocating scarce goods, and especially for making more of them, and making them, well, capitalism is the worst form except for all the others that have been tried from time to time. It is better than Jip's violence in the playroom. It is better than the drug dealer's gun or the aristocrat's sword. It is better than beauty contests that depend on race, class, gender, creed, culture, region, age, education, politics, party membership, personal habits, or, as we saw 1917–89, central planning backed by a Cheka or a KGB. A nonmarket method of allocation gives the goods to the wrong people usually. And especially it doesn't encourage the production of more toys or food or onionskin Greek editions of the New Testament in the first place. Property and trade do, tempting producers into working to get your attention and your offers. If Brave Sir Botany appropriates the barley of peasants, the peasants have less incentive to use their arms and brains to grow more.

Unlike stealing or taxing or highhandedly appropriating, exchange is a positive- not a zero- or negative-sum game. If Sir Botany must tempt the peasants with offers of educational services or consultation on interior decorating in order to get the barley, both he and the peasants are better off. If he just grabs it, only he is better off and they are worse off. If I buy low and sell high, I am doing both of the people with whom I deal a favor. That's three favors done—to the seller, the buyer, and me in the middle and no one hurt except by envy's sting. The seller and buyer didn't have to enter the deal, and by their willingness they show they are made better off. One can say it stronger. *Only* such deals are just. As Robert Nozick puts it, "No one has a right to something whose realization requires certain uses of things and activities that other people have rights and entitlements to" (1974, 238). I do not have the right to use your house, even when you are on vacation. I do not have the right to make you work for me unless we have entered into a deal to that effect. I do not have a right to be equal to you in beauty, education, income, or health. The envious, jealous, spiteful, or begrudging person will want to bring in the state and its monopoly of violence to achieve such rights for himself. The charitable and sympathetic person will want to achieve the right to use your house or education or food on behalf of the poor. That is a good impulse, to help the poor. But it sets up the state as the Brave Sir Botany. State compulsion is not the voluntary cooperation that capitalism and our wealth are built on. The envious or poor man, Nozick says, "must put together, with the cooperation of others, a feasible package" (238). He must deal not steal.

Now, of course, if the market deal I offer is phony, then my victim is *not* benefited. But it's mainly outsiders to the business world, not insiders, who think that a lot of money is to be made by cheating. P. T. Barnum, John Mueller points out, did *not* say, ever, that a "Sucker is born every minute." Nothing like it. On the contrary, Mueller explains, Barnum and the Ringling Brothers rescued the circus industry from extinction by offering a novelty—cheap, *honest* entertainment. They patrolled their grounds with detectives, for example, instead of encouraging pickpockets to strip the rubes. They hired interesting acts instead of "Monday men" to rob the customers' houses when they were at the circus. Mueller quotes George Ade on the nineteenth-century circus kings: they "found the business in the hands of vagabonds and put it into the hands of gentlemen" (Mueller 1999, 24f). Well, they were gentlemen by an American, nineteenth-century, bourgeois definition. Profit is seldom a con game. Not in a bourgeois society.

True, if I buy low and sell high I get the profit. At any rate I get it until more low buyers turn up and spoil my game, turning the former profit into a gain to consumers from our competition in a proliferation of Home Depots and Costcos and T. J. Maxxes or of Microsofts and Yahoos and Googles. But I earn the profit because of a scarce virtue I have, my "alertness," as the economist and rabbi Israel Kirzner puts it (1994). One could also call it "judgment" (*gnomē*), as Aristotle did, and ally it with *phronesis,* "practical wisdom." It is a virtue that is good for *me* to be sure. But it is also good for other people. We want to encourage such alertness/judgment/*phronesis*/enterprise for the same reason we want to encourage Thomas Edisons and Albert Einsteins. I alertly *notice* what, for its best use, should be moved, that is, moved to its highest-valued use, from one person to another. Profit comes from noticing that people might want to buy the works of the reformed graffiti sprayer Keith Haring. It doesn't come from routine deals simply because by that time the competitors have entered. Barnum noticed that people wanted what was described as a "Sunday school" approach to circuses, and so he provided it, moving resources from pickpocketing to high-wire acts. What's the beef?

The beef was well expressed on the eve of the new bourgeois ideology by Louis Thomassin, a French theologian of the late seventeenth century, "a plain man of stupendous erudition" who, among other tasks in his posthumous multivolume *Traités historiques et dogmatiques* of 1697, attacked profit making (quoted in Muller 2002, 3). He criticizes, in a figure of argument going back to Aristotle, "those who accumulate possessions *without end and without measure.*" The Greek word (*Politics* 1257b35), *apeiros,* "without limit," finds echo in modern characterizations of capitalism from the Left, that "myth of *Kapitalismus*"—an allegedly new propensity to accumulate for accumulation's sake without limit. The Greek *to apeiron,* "unlimited (greed)," is the very meaning of *capitalism* in Marx and others, such as R. H. Tawney, among Marx's followers.

Thomassin instances "those who hoard huge quantities of wheat in order to sell at what to them is the opportune moment." They foolishly think "they are doing nothing . . . against divine law, because, as they imagine, they do no harm." By contrast, he wrote, "If no one acquired . . . more than he needed for his maintenance [i.e., did not hoard wheat] . . . there would be no destitute in the world at all" (quoted in Miller 2002, 40). That is, as Father Maurin said, "[P]eople would become better / if they stopped trying to be better off" (1936, 72). Plato and Aristotle, incidentally, were not especially interested in the causes of poverty, of course, since that was of concern to slaves not aristocrats. The Thomassin-Maurin argument is especially Christian, arising from a vision of poverty as a result of greed in a world of post-lapsarian limits. It finds expression in the late-nineteenth-century writings of the Protestant social gospel movement and in the parallel doubts about free market capitalism among Roman Catholics.

But a modern economist notes that buying wheat at a low price to sell it at a high price is *helpful* to those who buy at the high price, as Thomassin, who, after all, lived in an increasingly commercial age, admitted. It would "benefit those who would otherwise fall into great necessity," that is, those who would have *no* wheat at all in a famine if the capitalist granary had not stored it "in huge quantities." Nonetheless, he claims that it is "this urge to acquire more and more which brings so many poor people to penury." The assertion, though mistaken, has, as I say, become fixed Catholic doctrine by now, expressed in numerous pa-

pal encyclicals and bishops' letters. It is part of the leftist dogma that Western prosperity depends, directly or indirectly, on Third World poverty, which the West in some cases merely takes advantage of and in others actually causes. The pursuit of wealth, it is claimed, makes people poor. To which economics replies no, it makes the poor *better* off. If you understand "wealth" correctly you understand that to pursue it is to "pursue"; it is to build roads or make more shoes or notice that wheat wasted in a year of abundance can be moved to a year of dearth to the benefit of all. The wheat is allocated better across time as a result of the speculator's enterprise. And the pursuit of profit, I repeat, produces *more* wheat in the first place. The larger riches for the businessman, his "quasi rent" earned before competitors learn from his alertness, results in more, not less, wealth for his customers and employees.

The supposedly *apeiros* (unlimited) profit that makes the system produce so much more is in fact surprisingly small. Most people who have not looked into the matter greatly overestimate how much profit is earned under capitalism. Profit margins in American department stores are approximately 3 or 4 percent of sales. Profit margins in American grocery stores are approximately . . . But wait, let's see if you really do understand American capitalism. Go ahead, take a guess right now at the profit margin on groceries, the cents per dollar of your expenditure at the store going to the owners of the store. What d'you think? No peeking. No gamesmanship. Ten cents on the dollar? Twenty percent? Thirty?

A different concept, all profit as a share of all incomes in the United States, is about 14 percent. Social accounting can show that such a figure would imply a much lower one at the industry level, in which the margin is on all costs, including services and materials purchased from other companies, not just on labor and machinery and buildings and land used directly. It would be perhaps a high single-digit percentage of your next purchase of clothing or auto repair. The 14 percent of national income is composed of those evil corporate profits after taxes of 5.4 percent plus 8.6 percent from proprietors' income—for example, farms, mom-and-pop stores, your mechanic, your hairdresser. Whoever earns it, the national product goes up as a result of making deals, and deals are alertly noticed because of the profit. That's one way in which capitalism works.

On the 1 percent profit margin of American grocery stores.

Allocation of goods to the use of the highest value is one result of profit. The other is invention, which in a larger view is just another form of alertness in buying (ideas) low and selling high. The American economy in the late nineteenth century was a deal-making, inventive place, with secure private property, reasonably honest courts in which deals could be enforced when things went wrong, and a society that accorded work very high prestige. And so the national product per head went up smartly between 1870 and 1900—slower than it did in the 1990s, for example, but very respectably for the time. If you look into the way Carnegie and Rockefeller actually got their fortunes it turns out that it was mainly by making steel and transporting oil cheaper than their competitors did. They did *not* get it by hurting consumers with monopolies. Nor did they get it by hurting workers by paying less than other people did.[6]

Yes, I understand. You are *indignant* that I should make such a *crazy* assertion. Everyone *knows* that the Robber Barons were, well, robbers. But consider in the bowels of Christ that you may be mistaken. Consider it possible that our image of the barons of the Gilded Age has less to do with historical facts and permanent ethico-political values and more to do with, for instance, the careers of cartoonists and other journalists when cheap paper and steam presses and full color printing were being perfected.[7] Consider that it might possibly be that indignation about new methods of finance reflected less an alleged evil of "stock watering" and more the ancient hostility to middlemen, soon to be given official state sanction in American populism and European anti-Semitism. Consider that the muckrakers and other Progressives were disproportionately the children of Protestant clergymen reacting with guilt, as the clerisy did, to new prosperity and with envy to the businessmen among the parishioners who were even more prosperous. Consider that hostility to the visible hand of corporate capitalism in the United States in 1865–1914 may have had less to do with robbery by the trusts and more to do with the back projections of socialism triumphant.

Steel rails sold for about $100.00 a hundredweight around 1870 and about $25.00 a hundredweight around 1900. Crude petroleum sold for about $3.50 a barrel around 1870 and about $0.90 a barrel around 1900. Some robbery. As Michael Novak put the point, "Carnegie's staggering wealth . . . owed nothing to an 'original distribution' [which is to say that Andrew started out poor]. Neither had he robbed banks or otherwise gained his fortune immorally or illegally. He invented whole new ways of making iron, and later steel, and above all wholly new ways of organizing and administering a business" (1996, 59).

In 1870 the average American produced and consumed goods and

6. See Nevins 1940, cited to this effect in Mueller 1999, 37. Cf. McGee 1958.
7. McGee 1980.

services worth $2,460 in 1990 prices, roughly what the average Latin American produced and consumed in 1950.[8] By 1900, with Carnegie's fortune already made and Rockefeller's almost made, the figure was $4,100. That's a rise of $1,640, or 66 percent, in thirty years. Latin America in the thirty years after 1950 did better, with a rise of about 100 percent. In America in 1870–1900, to put it another way, the entire flow of goods and services—the average multiplied by the number of people—increased by $214,000 millions.

Now, the $300 million Carnegie made when he sold out to J. P. Morgan and his consortium in 1901 made him the richest man in the world, a Croesus, a veritable Bill Gates. *But it was only one and a half one-thousandths of the rise in production he helped deliver.* To put it another way, the richest man in the capitalist world possessed on the order of $1 out of every $20,800 of American human and physical capital, taking annual personal income as a return of 5 percent on human or physical capital. Some Croesus.

Carnegie himself is said to have made the same point in another way. A socialist came to his office and argued that the wealthy should redistribute their wealth to the poor of the earth. Carnegie immediately ordered an assistant to get him a rough estimate of his current wealth and the population of the earth. The assistant returned shortly with the figures, and, according to the anecdote, Carnegie performed a calculation, then turned to the assistant and said, "Give this gentleman sixteen cents. That's his share of the wealth."[9]

And then he gave every dime of his wealth away in accord with his Gospel of Wealth. Another businesslike Scot, Adam Smith, also gave away his considerable fortune, though, unlike Carnegie, he did not sound a trumpet before him when he did it. (Muller 2002, 54). Carnegie viewed the rich, as many did in the first age of Darwin, as men who had by the very fact of their richness proven themselves the best stewards of the world's wealth. But he viewed himself, by a doctrine parallel to the Jewish one of *tzedakah,* as the good steward only for life and only if he spent his wealth in good works: "The man who dies thus rich dies disgraced. Such, in my opinion, is the true gospel concerning wealth, obedience to which is destined some day to solve the problem of the rich and the poor" (Carnegie 1901, 19). It did not solve the problem and could not. The problem is solved by the education of the workers and

8. Maddison 1995, 196. He made some slight adjustments to these figures in Maddison 2001.

9. I say "is said" and "according to the anecdote" because the story is attested, as far as I know, only by Edmund Fuller in his *Thesaurus of Anecdotes* (1942), later retitled *2500 Anecdotes for All Occasions*). This is the attribution offered in Fadiman and Bernard 1985. It bears checking.

the entrepreneurship of the bosses, many of them, like Carnegie, former workers. That is, it is solved by the accumulation of real capital not by the reallocation of sixteen cents' worth of paper wealth.

But Carnegie carried through on his gospel. He gave to Carnegie Hall in New York, the Peace Palace at The Hague, the Carnegie Endowment for International Peace, and that library in Wakefield, Massachusetts, where I first read the anticapitalist classics. "Has Andhrew Carnaygie given ye a libry yet?" asked Mr. Dooley. "Not that I know iv," said Mr. Hennessy. "He will," said Mr. Dooley. "Ye'll not escape him" (Dunne 1906, 177). Notice that you have *not* heard of a Carnegie line of millionaires. It vanished with the millions. So, of course, did the British Rothschild give some of his fortune away, though less proportionately than did Carnegie. You *have* heard of a Rothschild line. You've also heard of Carnegie-*Mellon* University. The other half is from Andrew Mellon, another of those wretched Robber Barons, who gave his art collection to and the first building for the National Gallery in Washington and part of the rest of his fortune to the Mellon Foundation. Collis Huntington of Central and Southern Pacific Railroad fame gave millions to the Tuskegee and Hampton Institutes and his art collection to the Metropolitan Museum of Art. His nephew and heir, the interurban king Henry Huntington, gave his rare book collections to the Huntington Library. J. P. Morgan gave freely to the Metropolitan Museum and other causes during his life and in his will. In the words of Jean Strouse, a recent biographer, "[H]e was essentially in business importing financial capital to fuel the growing American economy [e.g., Edison's light] and in his off-hours he was importing cultural capital, basically stocking America's libraries and museums with the great treasures of the past" (Strouse 2000). Carnegie's henchman, Henry Frick—whose last message to his former boss was "Tell Mr. Carnegie I'll see him in hell, where we both are going"—gave away the Frick Collection in New York and most of the rest of his $50 million fortune.

Old John D. Rockefeller gave gobs and gobs of money away, as a devout Baptist who raised his son and by proxy his five grandsons to a gospel of public service. He gave away $500 million, many billions in present dollars. But it was not every dime he had, for he needed to keep some to distribute to waifs, and, unlike Carnegie, he did give large sums to those grandsons and a granddaughter in whom the gospel of wealth did not shine. George Soros, who in 2002 was worth $6 billion, plans to give it all away by 2010. The Gates Foundation gives away about as much as Soros's entire fortune every year. In 2004 Gates gave to his foundation all of the $3 billion he collected from Microsoft's first payment of dividends.

You'll want to reply, if you remain in thrall to the anticapitalist opinions of the Progressives, "Yeah, but they stole it in the first place." No, dear, they did not. Please try to listen more carefully. "The genius and labors of the so-called robber barons," writes Michael Novak, "transformed social possibilities . . . and set the lives of millions on an upward path" (1996, 76), including Novak's Slovak American ancestors, who were working in Carnegie's and Morgan's steel mills. Admittedly, they corrupted politics. But when have the rich not done *that?* Yon Cassius hath a lean and hungry look. And, as the Barons said in extenuation, weren't the politicians themselves at fault? We're just playing the game. Mark Twain remarked in 1897, in *Pudd'nhead Wilson's New Calendar,* that it could "probably be shown by facts and figures that there is no distinctly native American criminal class except Congress."[10] As Collis Huntington wrote in 1877, "If you have to pay money [to a politician] to have the right thing done, it is only just and fair to do it. . . . If a [politician] has the power to do great evil and won't do right unless he is bribed to do it, I think . . . it is a man's duty to go up and bribe."[11] Honest graft.

Seriously, now, these men were not saints of Love or Justice in their work. But they were not pirates, either. Their Pinkertons broke up labor unions, true. And people like Marshall Field and George Pullman in Chicago conspired to sic the police on law-abiding anarchists. Yet many other business leaders in Chicago in the Gilded Age, such as Montgomery Ward, looked forward even in the 1880s to a capitalism-enriched world in which workers like you and me would have to be *enticed* to come to work, paid $60,000 to work in Milwaukee's sewers, for example. Even Pullman looked forward to such a future, at least when he was allowed to boss people around in his lovely little town for the workers south of Chicago and to resist the unionization of his Pullman porters.

Carnegie, who before the Homestead strike had expended a good deal of wind preaching cooperation between labor and capital, was in fact appalled by the outcome—though he had left orders for Frick to break the unions and himself hid out on his estate in Scotland, corresponding with Pittsburgh and approving the steps taken. Later he never would admit that he had had a hand in it. These are serious ethical failures and sound reasons to think less of Huntington and Pullman and

10. Twain 1897, 99. Cf. Nozick 1974, 14: "Is there really anyone who, searching for a group of wise and sensitive persons to regulate him for his own good, would choose that group of people who constitute the membership of both houses of Congress?"

11. DeLong 1998. I do not mean to say that Untermyer, who was, over his long career, a prominent trustbuster and community figure, was motivated entirely by spite, only partly.

Carnegie. Novak says of the Robber Barons that "they sinned gravely" and of Carnegie that he "certainly was a moral coward" (1996, 61–62). But such failures, sins, cowardice are not peculiar to capitalism. They are human and political and can be found everywhere in any era. That businesspeople buy low and sell high in a particularly alert and advantageous way does not make them bad unless all trading is bad, unless when you yourself shop prudently you are bad, unless any tall poppy needs to be cut down, unless we wish to run our ethical lives on the sin of envy.

The clerisy is sure of its ground but hasn't much considered that it may be mistaken. The late Robert Heilbroner's *The Worldly Philosophers* (1953 and six later editions) propelled me, among many others, to major in economics. Although we disagreed about Marxism, I honor Bob. But in his chapter on his hero, Thorstein Veblen, he gives a "head-spinning example" of why the Robber Barons were bad. ([1953] 1999, 216–17). William Rockefeller—John D.'s younger brother—and Henry Rogers bought Anaconda Copper in 1899 for $39 million, which they did not have in their bank accounts. They quickly covered the check by getting a loan from a banker friend and then sold the company to the stock market for $75 million and paid back the banker. Result? A $36 million profit in a trice without risking a dime of their own money.

Bad? No. The Anaconda deal simply outraged the muckrakers, and Heilbroner joins in the general condemnation. "This free-for-all involved staggering dishonesty," he claims. It appears that the deal became notorious as an instance of Bad Barons chiefly because Samuel Untermyer, a lawyer for Rockefeller and Rogers who felt he had not received enough out of the deal, became counsel to a House committee in 1912–13 that was investigating the money trust (DeLong 1998).

What exactly is the beef? Rockefeller and Rogers had noticed that Anaconda was undervalued—that its old owners were willing to sell it for less than what the stock market, they reckoned, would value it at. There is no evidence put forward in the tale that Rockefeller and Rogers *fooled* the stock market. The new company did not fall in value when they cleared out, and in fact they did not clear out entirely (as Heilbroner implies). They sold only half the stock and would therefore have had no interest in allowing its market value to fall. The company was now correctly valued, the Barons getting their profit from alertness.

They bought it without having the money in the bank and persuaded the seller to wait to cash the check. So what? There's nothing unusual about this in capitalism or out. True, Rockefeller and Rogers were condemned at the time by the financial community. But it's hard to see anything but envy as a basis for the condemnation: why didn't *we* think of that? On the seller's side it was an open-eyed deal. The seller was extending credit to Rockefeller and Rogers, credit they deserved to have. They had shown themselves to be smart cookies and anyway had Standard Oil to back them. If the seller thought that Anaconda was worth only $39 million, there's no reason why he shouldn't accommodate the buyers by holding the check uncashed for a while if he knew them to be reliable chaps, as he did. Indeed, they quickly showed they were both smart and reliable by covering the check and then promptly repaying the bank loan that had covered it.

The Anaconda deal was utterly routine, the same kind you enter into when you buy any business—say, a house on spec—and finance the purchase with a loan. If you have been correct in your assessment that the market will value the business at more than the price you paid for it, then you can cash in your capital gain right away by reselling the business and paying off the loan. Rockefeller and Rogers were correct and did cash in. That's not bad. That's good. Companies should be correctly valued or else their real assets will be poorly employed. In the matter of Anaconda, William Rockefeller and Henry Rogers were good barons not robbers.

The American experience with capitalist fortunes has been odd, intertwined with the peculiarly devout American attitude toward God. It was well said in the 1980s that the two most religious countries in the world were the Islamic Republic of Iran . . . and the United States of America. Or alternatively, that India is the most religious country and Sweden the least, and the United States is . . . an India whose ruling class is Swedish. In France or Britain a fortune starts a dynasty, as the Rothschilds show. In America—and especially generously in America and Japan—rich people endow colleges, finance hospitals, support the opera. It's a civic impulse, often tied to a religious impulse, as in the many hundreds of private colleges. Rockefeller's University of Chicago was a Baptist institution. So was Denison University in Ohio. The new University of Chicago got money from that devout Baptist, John D. Rockefeller, though not as much as one might think. He gave to Chicago instead of adding to his earlier and generous gifts to Denison in part because the administration at Denison didn't take his advice seriously. A big mistake. If they had taken his advice the great private research university of the Midwest would be in Granville, Ohio, not in Chicago, Illinois.

Wesleyan University is not called so idly. Harvard, of course, was Congregational, founded for the purpose of training up a literate ministry, "First flower of their wilderness / Star of their night." And so on across the country to Pepperdine in far Malibu (Church of Christ). A

French millionaire assumes correctly, *au contraire,* that *l'État* will provide. He is more interested in buying that chateau in the Loire Valley or that vineyard outside Bordeaux, playing at aristocracy, like Carnegie on his Scottish estate, than "giving back to the community," as American millionaires are always putting it. To repeat, though, they didn't *take* it in the first place. They made deals. Rich people in America have more often than elsewhere showed a townsperson's public spirit, bourgeois virtues.

Any society, religious or not, has a sacred sphere and a profane, *S* and *P,* a sphere in which love and justice largely determine who gets what as against a sphere in which prudence and courage largely do so. But "largely" is not "exclusively." Life in a market is not exclusively a matter of the profane. Buyers and sellers show their sacred qualities, too. The economy is, as the sociologists like to put it, "embedded," which is to say that the economy is not a sphere of "prudence only" independent of other ethical considerations. Or, as we Episcopalians say, "Almighty God, whose Son Jesus Christ in his earthly life shared our toil and hallowed our labor; Be present with your people when they work."[12] And when they trade. And when they are devout and virtuous bourgeois withal.

Bibliography

Auden, W. H. 1976. *Auden: Collected Poems,* edited by E. Mendelson. New York: Random House.

Book of Common Prayer and Administration of the Sacraments and Other Rites and Ceremonies of the Church. 1979.

Bowe, John, Marisa Bowe, and Sabin Streeter, eds. 2000. *Gig: Americans Talk about Their Jobs at the Turn of the Millennium.* New York: Random House, 2001.

Carnegie, Andrew. 1901. *The Gospel of Wealth and Other Timely Essays.* New York: Century.

Comte-Sponville, André. [1996] 2001. *A Small Treatise on the Great Virtues: The Uses of Philosophy in Everyday Life.* Translated by Catherine Temerson. New York: Holt and Metropolitan/Owl Books.

Csikszsentmihalyi, Mihaly. 1997. *Finding Flow: The Psychology of Engagement with Everyday Life.* New York: Basic Books.

DeLong, J. Bradford. 1998. "The Robber Barons." Berkeley: University of California Press and National Bureau of Economic Research.

Dunne, Finley Peter. 1906. *Dissertations by Mr. Dooley.* New York: Harper and Brothers.

Fadiman, Clifton, and André Bernard. [1985] 2000. *Bartlett's Book of Anecdotes.* Rev. ed. New York: Little, Brown.

Frye, Northrop. [1968]. 1970. "Dickens and the Comedy of Humours." *The*

12. *Book of Common Prayer,* "Prayer for Industry and Commerce" (1979).

Stubborn Structure: Essays on Criticism and Society, 218–240. Ithaca: Cornell University Press.

Fuller, Edmund. 1942. *Thesaurus of Anecdotes.* New York: Crown Publishers.

Gordon, Donald F., and Gary M. Walton. 1982. "A Theory of Regenerative Growth and the Experience of Post–World War II West Germany." In *Explorations in the New Economic History: Essays in Honor of Douglass C. North,* edited by R. Ransom, R. Sutch, and G. Walton. New York: Academic Press.

Heilbroner, Robert. [1953] 1999. *The Worldly Philosophers: The Lives, Times, and Ideas of the Great Economic Thinkers.* 7th ed. New York: Simon and Schuster.

Kirzner, Israel. 1979. *Perception, Opportunity, and Profit.* Chicago: University of Chicago Press.

Kirzner, Israel. 1989. *Discovery, Capitalism, and Distributive Justice.* Oxford: Basil Blackwell.

Kirzner, Israel. 1994. "The Nature of Profits: Some Economic Insights and Their Ethical Implications." In *Profits and Morality,* edited by Robin Cowan and Mario J. Rizzo. Chicago: University of Chicago Press.

Knight, Frank H. [1923] 1997. "The Ethics of Competition." In *The Ethics of Competition,* new introduction by Richard Boyd. New Brunswick, N.J.: Transaction.

LeGuin, Ursula K. [1974] 2003. *The Dispossessed.* New York: Harper Collins.

Lev, Michael A. 2004. "The Great Migration of China." *Chicago Tribune,* 27–29 December.

Lodge, David. [1999] 2000. *Home Truths: A Novella.* London: Penguin.

McGee, John S. 1958. "Predatory Price Cutting: The Standard Oil (N.J.) Case." *Journal of Law and Economics* 1 (October): 137–69.

McGee, John S. 1980. "Predatory Pricing Revisited." *Journal of Law and Economics* 23 (October): 289–330.

Maddison, Angus. 1995. *Monitoring the World Economy, 1820–1992.* Paris: Organization for Economic Cooperation and Development.

Maddison, Angus. 2001. *The World Economy: A Millennial Perspective.* Paris: Organization for Economic Cooperation and Development.

Maurin, Peter. 1936. *Easy Essays.* New York: Sheed and Ward.

Mendelson, Cheryl. 2001. *Home Comforts: The Art and Science of Keeping House.* Cassell.

Mueller, John. 1999. *Capitalism, Democracy, and Ralph's Pretty Good Grocery.* Princeton: Princeton University Press.

Muller, Jerry. 2002. *The Mind and the Market: Capitalism in Modern European Thought.* New York: Knopf.

Nevins, Allan. 1940. *John D. Rockefeller: The Heroic Age of American Enterprise.* New York: C. Scribner's Sons.

Novak, Michael. 1996. *Business as a Calling: Work and the Examined Life.* New York: Free Press.

Nozick, Robert. 1974. *Anarchy, State, and Utopia.* New York: Basic Books.

Nussbaum, Martha. 1986. *The Fragility of Goodness: Luck and Ethics in Greek Tragedy and Philosophy.* Cambridge: Cambridge University Press.

Ricardo, David. [1817] 1951. *On the Principles of Political Economy and Taxation,* edited by Piero Sraffa. Cambridge: Cambridge University Press.

Sachs, Jonathan. 2002. *The Dignity of Difference: How to Avoid the Clash of Civilizations.* London and New York: Continuum.

Schuttner, Scott. 1998. *Basic Stairbuilding.* Newtown, Conn.: Taunton.

Seeger, Peggy. 1971. "I'm Gonna be an Engineer." ©1976, 1979 by Stormking Music, Inc.

Shapin, Stephen. 1994. *A Social History of Truth: Civility and Science in Seventeenth-Century England.* Chicago: University of Chicago Press.

Sherman, Franklin. 1976. "Tillich's Social Thought: New Perspectives." *Christian Century* 93, no. 6: 168–72.

Strouse, Jean. 2000. *Morgan: American Financier.* New York: Random House.

Tacitus, Cornelius. [98 CE] 1916. *Germania.* Edited by D. R. Stuart. New York: Macmillan.

Tacitus, Cornelius. [98 CE, 1948] 1970. *The Agricola and the Germania.* Translated by H. Mattingly and S. A. Handford. Harmondsworth: Penguin.

Terkel, Studs. 1974. *Working: People Talk about What They Do All Day and How They Feel about What They Do.* New York: Pantheon.

Todorov, Tzvetan. [2000] 2003. *Hope and Memory: Lessons from the Twentieth Century.* Translated by David Bellos. Princeton: Princeton University Press.

Twain, Mark [Samuel Clemens]. 1897. *Following the Equator.* Hartford, Conn.: American Publishing Company.

7 • The Origins of Das Adam Smith Problem and Our Understanding of Sympathy

Leonidas Montes

Introduction

The famous Das Adam Smith Problem, which questions the consistency issue between *The Theory of Moral Sentiments* (TMS) and *An Inquiry into the Nature and Causes of the Wealth of Nations* (WN) is still relevant for anyone attracted to Smith scholarship. Although there is agreement that both works are consistent and, furthermore, parts of an incomplete system, it seems that the Problem continues to attract interest not only for its historical and philosophical appeal but also, perhaps, for its implications for the current economics and ethics debates. However, within the vast energies dedicated to the Problem, what has gone relatively unnoticed is the historical and intellectual context that gave rise to it in the last half of the nineteenth century and its implications for our understanding of sympathy.

In this chapter it is argued that, well before the formation of the German Historical School, the economic hegemony of Great Britain may have played an important role in shaping the reception of Smith in Germany as the founder of the school of self-interest and laissez-faire. Then, after uncovering some sources and a possible reason for the emergence of Das Adam Smith Problem, a brief assessment of the current debate on the Problem follows. After Jacob Viner's seminal paper "Adam Smith and Laissez Faire" (1927), the Problem remained dormant for a while, but it soon became the subject of academic discussion. Finally, Smith's concept of sympathy will be reassessed within what I would call the sympathetic process.

The German context and Das Adam Smith Problem

The famous "Adam Smith Problem,"[1] put forward by the German Historical School, is still a subject of controversy. The Problem as such

---

This is an abridged and slightly improved version of Montes 2003. It is dedicated with gratitude to the memory of my friend and colleague Wiebke Krauss.

1. For a brief historical account of Das Adam Smith Problem, see TMS, intro., 20–25; and Raphael 1985, 87–90. Other basic sources are Oncken 1897, [1898] 2000; Morrow [1923] 1969, 1927); Nieli 1986, 612–16; and Otteson 2000, 134–36). On the emergence of the Problem, see Tribe and Mizuta 2002, 137–48; and Peters-Fransen 2001.

states that there is an irreconcilable difference or inconsistency between TMS, with its sympathy-based concept of human nature, and WN, which is founded on an egoistic theory of self-interest. It is true that self-interest is an important motive in both works, and it is also true that self-interest is not always egoistic behavior, but it is intriguing that nowhere in WN does Smith refer to sympathy. Moreover, in WN mention of his four principal virtues (prudence, justice, benevolence, and self-command) is scant. One could simply explain that one book is about ethics and the other about political economy, but this does not dissipate the Problem. Yet, if this and other puzzles add to the relevance of the Problem, its nature must be combined with an interpretation of *why* and *how* it actually emerged.

Although the German context during the first half of the nineteenth century is extremely complex in its political and social dimensions, I will try to show that the shaping of the Smith Problem can also be seen as the result of an intellectual context hostile to the British laissez-faire doctrine, which influenced not only some important predecessors of the German Historical School but also its foremost representatives.

A year after the publication of WN in English, and a few months after the publication of the first volume of Johann Friedrich Schiller's German translation,[2] the reviewer Johann Georg Heinrich Feder (1740–1821), who taught at Göttingen, wrote in the *Göttingische gelehrte Anzeigen* (10 March 1777) that "Many of his propositions cannot be accepted as principles of universal policy; they are adapted only to a particular stage of industry, wealth, and civilization" (quoted in Cohn [1873] 2000, 64). This early assessment of WN reflects a view that was basically carried forward, with a few exceptions, for more than a hundred years.

The Germans, whose nation was defined by its culture (*Kulturnation*) but not a state, had been seeking their own identity since well before unification in 1871. For example, the philosopher Johann Gottlieb Fichte's (1762–1814) *Reden an die deutsche Nation* (Addresses to the German Nation, [1808] 1968), an important influence on the final unification of Germany, represents a clear indication of the cultural tension between German nationalism and "foreignness." This nationalistic spirit was, for example, clearly reflected in the fraternity of university students (*Burschenschaften*) founded in Jena in 1815. Furthermore, historical evidence suggests that this search for identity was combined with

2. Books I, II and III of WN were translated into German the same year as the original publication. The second volume (books IV and V) of Schiller's translation appeared in 1778.

a strong German nationalism that was sometimes closer to chauvinism with racist overtones. In this nationalistic setting, Great Britain, in spite of its common history opposing Napoleon, was no exception. In addition, the achievement of a unified and centralized German empire occurred within an economic environment in which Great Britain had attained clear dominance in world manufacturing and trade. Under these circumstances, the industrializing process in Germany developed its own distinctive character (Milward and Saul 1977, 49–50), which was quite cautious compared to the more liberal British policies.

Initially, Smith entered Germany through the universities, and of course the University of Göttingen, in Hanover, which was established in the English king's territories, was the place to study Smith and the breeding ground for followers of his ideas. Considering that the cameralists–who taught *Cameralwissenschaft,* named in allusion to the *Kammer,* in which the administrative political power of the states deliberated economic and political issues—held a nationalistic and protective viewpoint, it is not overly bold to assume that the dissemination of Smith's liberal views was generally seen by traditional academics and politicians as a threat to the status quo. Yet, if Smith's doctrines, aside from Göttingen, remained rather dormant in Germany just after WN's first German translation, Christian Garve's popular translation, published in two parts in 1792 and 1794, definitely revived an interest in Smith.

August Ferdinand Lueder and Georg Sartorius both studied and taught at Göttingen, and were quite effective in spreading Smith's views. Lueder was not only influenced by Smith, but also by the ideas of the French Revolution.[3] Therefore, it is not surprising that later authors such as Bruno Hildebrand, as we will soon see, conflated the ideals of the French Revolution with Smith's legacy. But Sartorius did not follow Smith's liberal views on commerce, as he was aware of the limits and dangers of laissez-faire, proposing the intervention of the state in different situations, a theme that pervaded a complex intellectual process that would reach some important exponents of the German Historical School.

If in western Germany the influential University of Göttingen was

3. Georg Sartorius (1765–1828), a lecturer at Göttingen's Faculty of Philosophy since 1792, was one of the most influential of those who advocated Smith's political economy in Germany, especially through his *Handbuch der Staatswirthschaft zum Gebrauche bey akademischen Vorlesungen, nach Adam Smith's Grundsätzen ausgearbeitet* (Handbook of Political Economy for the Use in Academic Lectures according to the Basics of Adam Smith, 1796), although in 1806 he "returned to this work in a more critical frame of mind" (Tribe and Mizuta 2002, 131). August Ferdinand Lueder (1760–1819) analyzes Smith's WN from a universal-historical perspective (Tribe 1988, 168) in his bulky, three-volume *Ueber Nationalindustrie und Staatswirthschaft. Nach Adam Smith bearbeitet* (On National Industry and Political Economy. According to Adam Smith, 1800–1804).

crucial in the dissemination of Smith's doctrines, in the east it was the task of Christian Jacob Kraus,[4] a fervent admirer of Smith who had spent a year at Göttingen and studied and later taught at the University of Königsberg. He referred to WN, declaring that "certainly since the times of the New Testament no writing has had more beneficial results than this will have" (quoted in Hasek [1925] 2002, 87).

In addition, Adam Heinrich Müller (1779–1829), though acknowledging Smith as a most learned economist, saw him as a "one-sided" (*einseitig*) representative of English economic interests.[5] Another earlier source of the tradition leading to the German Historical School's hostility toward British political economy is Fichte, who in his *Der Geschlossene Handelstaat: Ein Philosophischer Entwurf als Anhang zur Rechtslehre* (The Closed Commercial State: A Philosophical Outline as an Appendix to Law, 1800), argued against laissez-faire policies. For this influential philosopher it was the duty of government not only to restrict and regulate foreign commerce but also to prohibit it. When Friedrich List (1789–1846) published his *Das Nationale System der politischen Ökonomie* (The National System of Political Economy) in 1841, both arguments were synthesized in a serious critique of what was later called *Smithianismus*. But one important underlying cause that motivated the latter is explicitly stated.

> It is a very common clever device that when anyone has attained the summit of greatness, he kicks away the ladder by which he has climbed up, in order to deprive others of the means of climbing up after him. In this lies the secret of the cosmopolitical doctrine of Adam Smith . . . and all his successors. (List [1841] 1904, 295)

Not surprisingly, in this setting Smith became known as the founder of the materialistic Manchester School, which preached the gospel of individual interest and free competition, in clear opposition to the older,

4. Christian Jacob Krauss (1753–1807), the student and later colleague and friend of Immanuel Kant at Königsberg, was the most influential academic figure who introduced and lectured on Smith's economic thought in Germany. Although he published little, his works in political economy were published posthumously as *Die Staatswirtschaft von Christian Jacob Kraus. Nach dessen Tode herausgegeben von Hans von Auerswald* (The Political Economy of Christian Jakob Kraus. Edited after his death by Hans von Auerswald, 5 vols., 1808–11).

5. Müller's works include *Die Elemente der Staatskunst* (Elements of the Art of State, a Set of Lectures Presented in Dresden during the Winter of 1808–9), *Theorie des Geldes* (Theory of Money, 1816), and *Von der Nothwendigkeit einer theologischen Grundlage der gesammten Staatswissenschaften und der Staatswirthschaft insbesondere* (Of the Necessity of a Theological Basis of the Entire Sciences of State and Political Economy in Particular, 1819).

cameralistic tradition, which assumed that society and its members needed guidance.

List considered that laissez-faire would benefit Great Britain but not the then developing economies, for which he proposed protective tariffs and an infant industry promotion strategy. His argument is quite explicit: "In order to attain freedom of trade to operate naturally, the less advanced nations must first be raised by artificial measures to that stage of cultivation to which the English nation has been artificially elevated" ([1841] 1904, 107). Accusing Smith, "the founder of the prevailing economic school" (108), and his successors of *Kosmopolitismus* might have been in part a consequence of the fact that the German states lagged far behind the spectacular economic achievements of Great Britain. List, as an influential precursor of the German Historical School's emphasis on the context of each country, argued that every man belongs to a nation, which has its own circumstances that cannot be ignored. But List's famous and pervasive comment about development, which is also a heated subject of contemporary debate, has a long intellectual pedigree that is inherited from the twilight of Cameralism while it was giving rise to *Nationalökonomie.*

Although it has been generally accepted that Wilhelm Roscher's (1817–94) *Grundriß zu Vorlesungen über die Staatswirthschaft: Nach geschichtlicher Methode* (Outline for Lectures on Political Economy: According to the Historical Method, 1843) at least marks the programmatic foundation of the German Historical School,[6] its formation, as has been briefly suggested, was the result of a long intellectual process. In this, we cannot ignore the complex social, political, and economic developments that followed the appearance of WN. Years of war, riots, famine, and radical social and political reforms witnessed and bred the formation of the German Historical School.

In Germany, Smith's reception—as the natural father of classical political economy—might appear rather peculiar to a modern scholar. Indeed, the familiar charge that he was the prophet of self-interest and free competition was combined with some odd claims. He was seen as a philosopher of the French Revolution and at the same time as a theorist who tried to create

6. For Joseph Schumpeter, Friedrich List was not only "a national hero" ([1954] 1994, 504) but also a "forerunner of the historical school of economics" (505). Geoff Hodgson argues that the inception of the school coincides with List's publication of *Das Nationale System der politischen Ökonomie* (List [1841] 1904) (2001, 58), but Karl Pribram considers that List "does not belong to it [the German Historical School]" (1983, 213) and for Mark Perlman and Charles McCann "the actual foundation of the German Historical School can be traced to the publication in 1843 of *Grundriß*" (1998, 416).

> a Political Economy for the world and humanity (*Welt und Menschheitsökonomie*) by deducing general axioms from the specific circumstances of single nations and stages of development. (Hildebrand 1848, 27)

Although there was a long-standing tradition in Germany of Adam Smith as the antihero of *Nationalökonomie,* which might also relate to Göttingen's peculiar situation in Hanover, it was certainly Bruno Hildebrand (1812–78) in his *Die Nationalökonomie der Gegenwart und Zukunft* (The National Economy of the Present and the Future, 1848),[7] published the same year as Marx and Engels's *The Communist Manifesto,* who successfully relaunched the attacks on Smith. Following Müller and List, Hildebrand also complained about Smith's "one-sidedness" (*einseitigkeit*) and his "abstract cosmopolitanism" (*Abstrakter Kosmopolitismus*), concluding that "the problem of the Adam Smith School is that it tries to monopolise manufacturing for England" (328).[8] But his project was more ambitious, as he attempted to overcome the "rationalistic Enlightenment" of which Adam Smith (like Rousseau according to Hildebrand) was a representative, restoring political economy as a historical discipline. Hildebrand not only pointed out the materialism of the *Smithsche Schule* (Smith School), with its emphasis on the atomistic nature of human beings, but he also criticized egoism as the central feature of Smith's economic system. According to Hildebrand, Smith and his followers wished to "transform political economy into a mere natural history of egoism" (275; also quoted in Gide and Rist [1915] 2000, 394). And for Hildebrand, as a representative of the German Historical School, the "deification of private egoism" (1848, 275) had serious consequences for political economy as a social science that is essentially ethical.

A little later, Karl Knies (1821–98), who considered Smith an "outstanding thinker" (1853, 21), criticized his "theoretical absolutism" (22) and attacked the classical notion of self-interest in his *Die politische Ökonomie vom Standpunkte der geschichtlichen Methode* (The Political Economy from the Point of View of Historical Method, 1853).[9] But he

7. Bruno Hildebrand projected a second volume about the future that never appeared.

8. Regarding the English economic hegemony, Hildebrand, like List, was aware that "a system of prohibitions was introduced by the government under which the English industry could grow" (1848, 4). But he defended, under certain circumstances, free trade policies.

9. In 1883 Karl Knies republished this book, with some minor additions, under the new title *Die politische Ökonomie vom geschichtlichen Standpunkte* (*The Political Economy from the Historical Point of View*). In the new preface he not only complains about the book's poor reception, it having been ignored even by Roscher, to whom it had been dedicated, but also spends some paragraphs explaining why the new title is better than the previous one.

also cunningly suggested that "it does not seem like an accident that between the publication of his *Theory of Moral Sentiments* and his economic *Inquiry* occurred his stay in France" (180). He is the originator of the so-called French connection theory (Nieli 1986, 612) that Smith's mental shift between TMS and WN was a consequence of his acquaintance with the French materialists.

If Karl Knies, as a representative of the "older school," set up the so-called *Umschwungstheorie* as the source of Das Adam Smith Problem, it was the task of the "younger school" not only to defend and develop this intuition but also to undermine Smith's reputation further.[10] Lujo Brentano (1844–1931), in *Das Arbeitsverhältniss gemäss dem heutigen Recht: Geschlichtliche und ökonomische Studien* (The Relation of Labor to the Law of Today: Historical and Economic Studies, 1877), was the next German economist to tackle the Problem. Brentano again criticizes Smith's individualism and explicitly argues that his acquaintance in France with Helvétius and his circle "can be seen in the revolution (*Umschwung*) that it exerted upon his basic ideas,"[11] since in WN "he adopts completely the views of Helvétius concerning the nature of men and selfishness as the only motivating force in human action" (61).

Only a year later, Witold von Skarzyński (1850–1910), a Polish nobleman who failed in his academic career at Breslau University, published *Adam Smith als Moralphilosoph und Schöpfer der Nationalökonomie: Ein Beitrag zur Geschichte der Nationalökonomie* (Adam Smith as a Moral Philosopher and Creator of National Economy: A Contribution to the History of National Economy, 1878). He was definitely Smith's fiercest critic. In more than 450 pages on Smith, Skarzyński attempted to prove that he was neither an original philosopher nor the creator of political economy but simply "a vain teacher and an honest man" (xvii), concluding that the physiocrats "are the founders of political economy" (201). His thesis, calling Smith a "subject of idolatry (*Abgötterei*)" (vii), was that neither TMS nor WN came from the mind of an original thinker. Both works were the result of external influences, that of Hume in TMS and of Smith's acquaintance with the physiocrats in France in WN. Incidentally, Skarzyński, following List and Hildebrand in their attacks on England, complained "how far is the English economic policy from the practical application of that basic idea, that high wages are a blessing for a nation, since that country has been trying without pause, to be the merchant and manufacturer of the whole

10. In 1898 August Oncken justly complained about the "low estimation of Adam Smith, particularly in Germany" ([1898] 2000, 85).

11. A better translation of *Umschwung* would be "drastic shift" or "radical change."

world" (126). He also referred, as Müller did, to the "one-sidedness (*einseitigkeit*) of the Smithian School" (27). But regarding Das Adam Smith Problem, Skaŕzyński put forward the idea that Smith's acquaintance with Helvétius motivated him to adopt the principle of self-love (189).[12] This intuition was finally expressed as follows.

> Smith was an Idealist, as long as he lived in England under the influence of Hutcheson and Hume. After living in France for three years and coming into close contact with the Materialism that prevailed there, he returned to England a Materialist. This is the simple explanation of the contrast between his *Theory* (1759), written before his journey to France, and his *Wealth of Nations* (1776), written after his return. (183)

The *Umschwungstheorie,* perceived by Knies (1853), suggested by Brentano (1877), and finally expanded on by Skaŕzyński (1878) did not accept the reliability of Dugald Stewart's *Account of the Life and Writings of Adam Smith* in two respects. First, it contained John Millar's report on Smith's lectures, in which the part labeled "expediency," which we know to be the source of his political economy, "contained the substance" of WN (EPS, 275). Second, Stewart wrote about, and quoted some sentences from, a 1755 manuscript by Smith (EPS, 321).[13] In this document Smith allegedly asserted the originality of his opinions "without any considerable variation" (EPS, 322) from a lecture delivered some six years earlier, that is, back in his days at Edinburgh in 1749. According to Stewart, in this manuscript "many of the most important opinions in *The Wealth of Nations* are there detailed" (EPS, 322). For Skaŕzyński, as for his predecessors, neither report denying French influence could be accepted as concrete evidence.[14]

At the turn of the century there were some references to the Problem (see Montes 2003, 73–78), but it was Viner's classic and seminal "Adam Smith and Laissez Faire" that not only challenged the traditional view of

12. Luigi Cossa (1831–96) considered Skaŕzyński "too ready to depreciate Adam Smith in comparison with the Physiocrats" (1880, 163). Indeed, Skaŕzyński not only argued that the physiocrats were the founders of political economy and Smith simply a compiler but that Smith's *Wealth of Nations* was full of contradictions.

13. Unfortunately, this manuscript did not survive. The editors of *Essays on Philosophical Subjects* (EPS) suggest that the original manuscript may have been "destroyed with Stewart's own papers by his son when suffering paranoia" (EPS, 266).

14. Another generally ignored early source in the literature, corroborating the fact that WN was part of Smith's lectures, is *The Early Life of Samuel Rogers,* in which the writer Henry Mackenzie, in 1791, is reported as sustaining this thesis (see Clayden 1887, 167). Cossa rightly suggested, regarding the idea of WN as part of Smith's lectures, that "it is much to be wished that some critic should consult the manuscripts of his lectures . . . so as to discover what truth there is in this assertion" (1880, 164).

Smith as a precursor of economic laissez-faire but also revived the inherent discrepancies between TMS and WN. Viner complains that the extensive revisions and additions to TMS did not diminish "in any particular the points of conflict between the two books," even allowing that "he was elderly and unwell" (1927, 217) when he revised it. Although this point is worth considering, since in part 6 of TMS, "Of the Character of Virtue," newly added to the sixth edition, Smith's memory fails him when he refers to some classical anecdotes (see TMS, especially 251–54), in my opinion this should not be taken as a serious reason to disregard his last additions. On the contrary, the additions are very relevant to understanding Smith's mature views on virtue, for example. But Viner's main point regarding the conflict between both works is that

> there are divergences between them which are impossible of reconciliation. (201)

But if the controversy was rich in content, for almost the next fifty years Das Adam Smith Problem remained relatively dormant until its revival after the bicentenary of the publication of WN.[15] Today, although clearly the formal Smith Problem has been surmounted, the content of the Problem is a subject that continues to generate further discussion, and so it is worth analyzing some current positions.

A Brief Review of the Current Debate

The publication of the Glasgow edition of TMS, which categorically dismissed the Problem as "a pseudo-problem based on ignorance and misunderstanding" (TMS intro., p. 20), created a period of condescension. Terence Hutchison considered the problem of consistency "as exaggerated or even imaginary" (1976, 482). Among others, one of the editors of WN, Andrew Skinner, also supported the point of view that the Smith Problem is based on a "misunderstanding of sympathy and self-interest" (1976, 112). This generally accepted position was clearly reflected in the review in the *Journal of Economic Literature* celebrating WN's bicentenary. It briefly stated that "it is now conventional wisdom that the so-called 'Adam Smith Problem' . . . is *passé*" (Recktenwald 1978, 66).

15. For example, regarding the consistency issue, Joseph Schumpeter thought that "both the *Moral Sentiments* and the *Wealth of Nations* are blocks cut out from a larger systematic whole" ([1954] 1994, 141). Alec Macfie, in his "Adam Smith's *Moral Sentiments* as Foundation for His *Wealth of Nations*" (1967), and Lamb (1974) persuasively defended the consistency of both works. One exception, to my knowledge, is Anspach, who thought, like Viner, that "the controversy aroused by the two conflicting images of Smith has however been by no means resolved" (1972, 176).

Winch's view coincides with "what most scholars accept, that there is no Adam Smith problem" (1978, 10),[16] and Haakonssen, taking the same position, deems it "futile to take any more rides on that old hobby-horse 'sympathy v. self-interest' in Smith" (1981, 197n19). Thus, suddenly scholars' attention to the Problem seems to have dwindled, as was reflected in Heilbroner's reference to the "once-heated, now largely quiescent problem" (1982, 427). In general, all these accounts represent the first stage of the debate, considering the Smith Problem to have been basically surmounted. The message was very clear: there was no need to delve into a meaningless controversy.

The second stage in the debate, which also defends the consistency position, argues that the Problem must not be overlooked. For example, Richard Teichgraeber attempts to draw attention to the Problem's humanistic normative assumptions in order to understand TMS, and consequently the Smith Problem, as "a document in the history of early modern humanist thought" (1981, 122). Laurence Dickey, challenging the view that the sixth edition of TMS is basically an extension of the first, considers that the problem "is still very much alive today" (1986, 609). Soon after, successive approaches acknowledged some kind of a solution and therefore presupposed, explicitly or implicitly, the importance of the Problem as a subject of research. (e.g., Nieli 1986; Evensky 1987; Griswold 1999; Dupuy 1993; Werhane 1991; Witzum 1998; and Brown 1994, among others)

Within a third stage, Spencer Pack (1997), analyzing the role of justice and prudence, shows that TMS presents an ethical defense of the acquisitive commercial society but concludes that this approach constitutes only a partial resolution of the Das Adam Smith Problem. He even suggests that Smith might not have wanted to complete his promised system, and in his view "the Adam Smith Problem will always remain, or rather it can be only partially resolved" (137–38). James Otteson contends that there is a real Adam Smith Problem and tries to show that the few attempts to solve it have been "unsatisfactory" (2000, 53), concluding that "there is a problem worth addressing, and that much of the current scholarly consensus rests on insufficient grounds" (70). This position deserves consideration, as we shall see in the next part of this chapter.

Das Adam Smith Problem has not been completely overcome and probably never will be. It seems that, "unlike old soldiers, old Adam Smith problems neither die nor fade away" but also that the Problem re-

16. It is noteworthy that later Winch was more skeptical, briefly referring to the Smith Problem as "the problem of establishing consonance, *if it exists*" (1996, 35, emphasis added).

mains "a worthy enterprise" (Young 1997, 203). The common view of TMS as foundational in relation to WN, that is, a moral basis grounding Smith's political economy, still pervades the debate on the Smith Problem, but, even if sympathy is not dealt with in WN, Smith's political economy, as it is widely acknowledged, is not devoid of moral content. Not only does TMS precede WN, but the title of the former begins with a definite article (*The Theory of Moral Sentiments*), and the latter simply begins with an indefinite one (*An Inquiry into the Nature and Causes of the Wealth of Nations*). This simple detail, together with Smith's dedication during his last years to the corrections and additions to "the" TMS, could be a sign of what he was thinking while he wrote his two books and what he might have thought during his last years. My contention is only a seedbed for further speculation, but with this fascinating and distinctively Smithian unintended consequence (i.e., the debate about the consistency between TMS and WN) Smith not only left us with a puzzling question but also with another elusive conundrum. Any attempt to defend the concordance of TMS and WN will finally depend on a broader understanding of sympathy and an appropriate one of self-interest.

Sympathetic Process and Moral Approbation

The editors of TMS have strongly defended the thesis that TMS and WN complement each other. But after dismissing the Smith Problem as "a pseudo-problem based on ignorance and misunderstanding" (TMS intro., p. 20), they argue that "Sympathy is the core of Smith's explanation of moral *judgement.* The motive to action is an entirely different matter" (21–22, emphasis in original).

Later David Raphael not only maintains but also develops this position by stating that "the role of sympathy in his book [TMS] is to explain the origin and the nature of moral judgement, of approval and disapproval" (1985, 29). My argument is that Smith's sympathy viewed as the broader sympathetic process not only explains "the origin and nature of moral judgement" but also explains the origin and the nature of morality itself. As, in my view, Elias Khalil has rightly argued, confining sympathy to a criterion of approbation and not a motive for conduct is like "throwing out the baby with the bathwater" (1990, 255). In my opinion it is a mistake to confine the broader sense of Smithian sympathy to moral judgment alone.

The first, and very well known sentence in TMS, "How selfish soever man may be supposed, there are evidently some principles in his nature, which interest him in the fortune of others, and render their happiness necessary to him, though he derives nothing from it except the pleasure of seeing it" (TMS, I.i.1.1, p. 9), already defines sympathy as an inner principle in human nature. Smith is aware that common language might mislead readers as to what he actually means by *sympathy.*

> Pity and compassion are words appropriated to signify our fellow-feeling with the sorrows of others. Sympathy, though its meaning was, perhaps, originally the same, may now, however, without much impropriety, be made use of to denote our fellow-feeling with any passion whatever. (I.i.I.5, p. 10)

This passage is interesting not only for its significance regarding how to interpret Smith's concept of sympathy but also because it provides a clue by clarifying what he did not mean by it. After stating that sympathy is not simply fellow feeling related to pity, as it pertains to "any passion whatever," Smith reiterates that it has to do with "joy and grief."[17] The Greek word *sumpátheia* was very important to the stoics.[18] For them, *sumpátheia* had a clear cosmic significance that also entailed social overtones, and, though it was a fundamental word in the stoic tradition, it had already been used by Plato, Aristotle, and Epicurus. The Greek prefix *sun,* which means "together" or "with" (as *symposium* means "drinking with"), is joined to *páthos,* and therefore there is an obvious and literal resemblance with the Latin *compassion* (the Latin prefix *cum* is the equivalent of the Greek *sun*), as Smith duly recognized in the passage just quoted. The etymological origin of the word *sumpátheia* would simply imply feeling with, or together with, merely sharing a fellow feeling. But Smith does not mean this kind of sympathy, so it is wrong to conflate sympathy with fellow feeling as has been sometimes done.

Smith stresses the importance of the causes of the passions, concluding, "Sympathy, therefore, does not arise so much from the view of the passion, as from that of the situation which excites it" (TMS I.i.1.10, p. 12). Therefore, sympathy is different from fellow feeling, or from its

17. After the first edition of TMS was published, Hume wrote a letter to Smith arguing, "I wish you had more particularly and fully prov'd, that all kinds of Sympathy are necessarily Agreeable. This is the Hinge of your System. . . . Now it would appear that there is a disagreeable Sympathy, as well as an agreeable. . . . An Hospital woud be a more entertaining Place than a Ball" (Smith 1987, 43).

18. Gloria Vivenza, argues, "An immediate point to make is that despite the similarity of terminology Smith's 'sympatheia' has little in common with classical *sumpatheia* apart from the basic sense of taking the part of, or 'suffering together with,' another person" (2001, 41). In fact, Cicero refers to the Greek *sumpátheia,* especially in his *De Divinatione,* and translates the Greek word first as "consensus" and then as a "natural connextion."

literal etymological sense, as it not only implies being in a person's shoes but also requires knowing where those shoes are standing. Of course, I will have fellow feeling with any passion, but I cannot sympathize "till informed of its cause" (I.i.1.8, p. 11). Etymologically, I could sympathize with you if you start crying, regardless the cause, but according to Smith I could not sympathize with you if you start crying bitterly because you cannot not find a pencil with which to underline this passage. In other words, I can feel and share your passion, but that does not necessarily mean I can sympathize with it.

The most important concept for Smith in the process of explaining sympathy is the role of imagination. The faculty of imagination enables the process, and it is by the "very illusion of the imagination" and "the idea of those circumstances" that this broad concept of sympathy takes place. No wonder we can even feel "the dread of death" (TMS I.i.1.13, p. 13). In sum, it is the role of imagination in combination with a circumstantial deliberative process that finally allows the agent to sympathize. The nature of the sympathetic process is finally determined by "the imaginary change of situations from which it arises" (I.i.4.1, p. 19). Strictly speaking, Smith's sympathy would be a special kind of *empátheia,* as the Greek prefix *en* means "in," "into," "toward," or "within," reflecting a change of places.

The actual sentiments of the person principally concerned become feelings of the spectator through an imaginative changing of places. But the way in which this change of situations takes place is not trivial. We face the problem of *how* the imaginary change is performed and what may be termed the identity problem. Certainly the sympathizer feels with the sympathizee, in what *sympathy* means, but some commentators have found a problem as there is a clear difference between what one would feel if one were in the other's shoes and what it actually implies to imagine oneself as the other person. The latter applies to Smith's sympathy, and, anticipating an answer to Thomas Reid's criticism that his sympathy was simply a refinement of a selfish system, he clearly states, contra Hobbes, in this long proleptic passage, that sympathy

> *cannot, in any sense, be regarded as a selfish principle.* When I sympathize with your sorrow or your indignation, it may be pretended, indeed, that my emotion is founded in self-love, because it arises from bringing your case home to myself, from putting myself in your situation, and thence conceiving what I should feel in the like circumstances. But though sympathy is very properly said to arise from an imaginary change of situations with the person principally concerned, yet *this imaginary*

> *change is not supposed to happen to me in my own person and character, but in that of the person with whom I sympathize.* When I condole with you for the loss of your only son, in order to enter into your grief I do not consider what I, a person of such a character and profession, should suffer, if I had a son, and if that son was unfortunately to die: but I consider what I should suffer if I was really you, and I not only change circumstances with you, but I change persons and characters. My grief, therefore, is entirely upon your account, and not in the least upon my own. It is not, therefore, in the least selfish. How can that be regarded as a selfish passion, which does not arise even from the imagination of any thing that has befallen, or that relates to myself, in my own proper person and character, but which is entirely occupied about what relates to you? *A man may sympathize with a woman in child-bed; though it is impossible that he should conceive himself as suffering her pains in her own proper person and character.* (TMS VII.iii.1.4, p. 317, emphasis added)[19]

The change of situation implies a change of person, as I may sympathize with a pregnant woman, though I have never experienced that particular situation nor will I. If Hume considered sympathy a means of communication related to contagion or infection, as an impression that becomes an idea, Smith transcends Hume by demanding, in addition, a change of person. Moreover, as Levy and Peart (2004) have convincingly argued, Smith's sympathy is more egalitarian than Hume's. In this sense Hume's account of sympathy would be more Hobbesian, as it depends on the sympathizer. Fontaine (1997) has explored the nature of sympathy, investigating what modern economists understand by it. According to him we should distinguish between "empathetic identification" and "partial empathetic identification." The former, which represents Smith's understanding of sympathy, implies an imaginary change of circumstances and personhood while the latter implies only a change of circumstances.

19. Confusion could arise in interpreting the following passage: "By the imagination we place ourselves in his situation, we conceive ourselves enduring all the same torments, we enter as it were into his body, and become in some measure the same person with him, and thence form some idea of his sensations, and even feel something which, though weaker in degree, is not altogether unlike them" (TMS I.i.1.2, p. 9). Otteson interprets it as meaning that "we imagine—contrary to what might have thought—not what our brother feels, but rather what we would feel in his situation; we then assume our brother is feeling what we would feel" (2000, 19–20), as we have no experience of the other. I believe the latter is fundamental, as sympathy for Smith necessarily involves a rational process in assessing the other's situation. What the person considered actually feels is only part of the process, as we must check what we should feel if we were in his or her situation.

The circumstances surrounding any passion are a necessary condition to attaining Smith's sympathy, but they are by no means always sufficient.

Although it is clear that sympathy entails moral approbation, as "[t]o approve of the passions of another, therefore, as suitable to their objects, is the same thing as to observe that we entirely sympathize with them" (TMS I.i.3.1, p. 16), the "suitableness to their objects" is fundamental to understanding the situational character of sympathy. This point demands the fundamental distinction between "the cause which excites it [the sentiment of affection of the heart from which any action proceeds], or the motive which gives occasion to it" and "the end which it proposes, or the effect which it tends to produce" (I.i.3.5, p. 18; cf. II.i.intro.2, p. 67).[20]

Sympathy, as a situational capacity, deals with causes and effects, with the proportioned nature of what triggers a passion and the manifestation of that passion. And for the purpose of assessing any situation the only possibility is for us to bring the case "to our own breast" (TMS I.i.3.9, p. 18). This would apparently contradict sympathy as a change of situation and person, leaving Smith's sympathy only as a "partial empathetic identification," but Smith is here thinking in terms of moral approbation, with sympathy as a canon for approval. The introduction of the impartial spectator, and then the supposed impartial spectator that represents our inner conscience, poses the question on how moral assessment should be carried out. According to Smith, "Every faculty in one man is the measure by which he judges of the like faculty in another. I judge of your sight by my sight, of your ear by my ear, of your reason by my reason, of your resentment by my resentment, of your love by my love. I neither have, nor can have, any other way of judging about them" (I.i.3.10, p. 19). But if the spectator is blind, deaf, a clinical idiot, or pathologically insensitive it does not necessarily mean that mutual sympathy cannot be attained or that Smith is presupposing an ideal society of perfect beings. It only confirms that he assumes the importance of social experience, which is closely related to the faculty of sympathy.

An understanding of sympathy only in terms of moral judgment implicitly assumes a consequentialist view of the sympathetic process in terms of mutual sympathy. Moral approval requires actions or situations

20. Smith immediately defines cause and effect, regarding the former "[i]n the suitableness or unsuitableness, in the proportion or disproportion which the affection seems to bear to the cause or object which excites it, consists the propriety or impropriety, the decency or ungracefulness of the consequent action" (TMS I.i.3.6, p. 18), and regarding the latter "[i]n the beneficial or hurtful nature of the effects which the affection aims at, or tends to produce, consists the merit or demerit of the action, the qualities by which it is entitled to reward, or is deserving of punishment" (TMS I.i.3.7, p. 18).

already exercised to be judged, and sympathy, if it were only restricted to the realm of moral approval, would play no part in the generating process per se. But sympathy as a principle in human nature is not only a capacity but also a disposition, and therefore it pertains to both the origin of moral judgment and to the process of attaining it. It is this process that grants moral autonomy, a fundamental theme in Smith's ethics (see Montes 2004, especially chap. 4) Indeed, the instrumental feature of the sympathetic process, as directed toward a concordance of sentiments, does not tell the whole story as a final cause to which all efficient causes tend. The fact that there is a natural tendency toward mutual sympathy does not necessarily mean that the sympathetic process will only take place when one is considering the future pleasure that the concordance of sentiments will produce. For Smith, human beings would exercise sympathy not only when foreseeing pleasure, or any outcome (to avoid a utilitarian or hedonistic connotation). The final cause of the sympathetic process could be seen as a telos but one that is understood in the Aristotelian sense, not as a simple attainment of an end but also as "contributing to it" for its own sake. It is in this grand sense that the sympathetic process is actually teleological and not simply consequentialist.

In fact, I believe that it is not correct to restrict sympathy as a concept of means to ends as the process is not merely instrumentally related to the concordance (or nonconcordance) of sentiments and therefore cannot be simply reducible to moral approval (or disapproval). Sympathy, understood as the sympathetic process, also entails a motivational force that is shaped by a continuous process of transformation inherent in human interaction, and a pleasurable end does not exclusively determine it. In can be argued that Smith, in terms of agency and structure, combines notions of Weber (voluntarism) and Durkheim (determinism), anticipating a kind of structuration theory.

To assume that sympathy is not related to moral motivation invalidates the sympathetic process in its broad sense. Sympathy narrowly understood as the exercise of moral judgment would in practice render the individual devoid of moral autonomy. For Smith, moral judgment is socially embedded since moral codes emerge from social interaction, but the ethical role of moral autonomy, represented by the "supposed impartial spectator," is fundamental to Smith's ethical system. Not only does TMS concentrate on the consequences of our behavior that allow moral judgment, but it also, and more importantly in my view, concentrates on the motives that trigger our conduct. Propriety, in contrast to merit, morally works as a motive for action (see TMS I.i.3.5, p. 18; and II.i.intro.2, p. 67). For Smith, in a proto-Kantian insight, morality also evolves at an ad intra level of consciousness. The Smithian distinctive metavirtue of self-command, which "is not only a great virtue, but from it all the other virtues seem to derive their principal lustre" (VI.iii.11, p. 241), is the paradigmatic example of propriety in this sense. Indeed, self-command is related to propriety since "the effects are too often but too little regarded" (VI. concl. 7, p. 264). The philosophical meaning of propriety, underpinned by the virtue of self-command, and the role of conscience introduced by the supposed impartial spectator, situates the sympathetic process within a philosophical tradition that seems closer to Kant than to utilitarianism. Indeed, for Smith moral actions are not simply determined as such by their outcomes but also by the motives for which they were undertaken. In this sense, sympathy grants moral autonomy to the individual.

The sympathetic process precedes and directs our behavior, relying not only on its consequences or effects but also on the antecedent causes that trigger our conduct. Fleischacker (1999) has greatly contributed to this debate, and I believe that Smith's ethical account also implies a deontological stance in which conscience plays a leading role.[21] The fact that this view has been practically ignored is, ironically, a consequence of Das Adam Smith Problem, as I have attempted to argue. Its major implication is that the role of moral autonomy in Smith's TMS has been relatively neglected.

Conclusions

Das Adam Smith Problem continues to be a source of debate. Ironically its history and the variety of interpretations shed light not only on an issue that is still pervasive but also on our understanding of sympathy. The traditional interpretation of the Problem as a misunderstanding of the meanings of *self-interest* and *sympathy* has led some scholars to consider the latter not as a motive for action but simply as entailing moral judgment. After an analysis of the sources and the debate, it has been argued that this instrumental position narrows Smith's concept of sympathy: sympathy understood within the sympathetic process is a richer and more complex phenomenon. Sympathy, in TMS, is presupposed as a principle in human nature that fosters a continuous relation-

21. To avoid confusion, let me explain what I understand here by deontology. Based on the Greek *to deon,* that which is binding, right, and even needful, implying not only a sense of moral obligation, but also one of being in want, Bentham coined the word *deontology* in 1814. Moreover, he wrote his *Deontology* between that year and 1831. However, Bentham's deontology is based on duties toward an end, as act consequentialism. But in the case of Smith's deontology it would be agent relative. It implies duty not determined by the consequences but motivated within the agent by the supposed impartial spectator, who is also influenced by the impartial spectator.

ship between spectators and agents, a natural interdependence among social beings. Sympathy, for Smith, not only accounts for moral judgment, but, more important perhaps, it influences human behavior ex ante. The emphasis on propriety, on what is "praiseworthy," distances Smith from his successors, especially those in the utilitarian tradition. His moral system also involves a process of self-transformation within the praxis of interaction through the moral autonomy of the "supposed impartial spectator."

However, the process of sympathizing is also part of a complex social phenomenon in which human beings take part in a continuous reciprocal interplay. In this natural process of human beings within society, the individual is even led to form "certain general rules concerning what is fit and proper either to be done or to be avoided" (TMS III.4.7, p. 159). Morality depends on social experience, as TMS "looks upon the individual not as an absolute and irreducible entity existing prior to social experience, but as a product of his social environment" (Morrow 1927, 179).[22] Propriety for Smith, in contrast with the effects or consequences of merit, not only entails an innate human faculty, but it is also the result of social psychology. Smith's ethical view of human beings' nature is mainly social and may be expressed by paraphrasing Kant's celebrated metaphor, "[S]ociety without agents is empty, but agency without society is blind" ([1787] 1990, 93).

Bibliography

Anspach, R. 1972. "The Implications of the *Theory of Moral Sentiments* for Adam Smith's Economic Thought." *History of Political Economy* 4, no. 1: 176–206.

Brentano, Lujo. 1877. *Das Arbeitsverhältniss gemäss dem heutigen Recht: Geschichtliche und ökonomische Studien.* Leipzig: Verlag von Duncker and Humbolt.

Brown, Vivienne. 1994. *Adam Smith's Discourse: Canonicity, Commerce, and Conscience.* London: Routledge.

Clayden, Peter W. 1887. *The Early Life of Samuel Rogers.* London: Smith, Elder.

Cohn, G. [1873] 2000. "The History and Present State of Political Economy in Germany." Reprinted in *Adam Smith: Critical Responses,* edited by H. Mizuta, vol. 1, pp. 63–64. London: Routledge.

Cossa, Luigi. 1880. *Guide to the Study of Political Economy.* London: Macmillan.

Dickey, Laurence. 1986. "Historicizing the 'Adam Smith Problem': Concep-

22. Glenn Morrow was probably the first to notice an agency-structure dichotomy in Smith. He suggests that in TMS society determines the ethical man but in WN it is the individual's self-interest that determines the economic structure (1927, 335–36).

tual, Historiographical, and Textual Issues." *Journal of Modern History* 58, no. 3: 579–609.

Dupuy, Jean-Pierre. 1993. "A Reconsideration of *Das Adam Smith Problem*." *Stanford French Review* 17, no. 1: 45–57.

Evensky, Jerry. 1987. "The Two Voices of Adam Smith: Moral Philosopher and Social Critic." *History of Political Economy* 19, no. 3: 447–68.

Fichte, Johann G. 1800. *Der geschlossene Handelsstaat: Ein philosophischer Entwurf als Anhang zur Rechtslehre und künftig zu liefernden Politik.* Tübingen: J. G. Cotta.

Fichte, Johann G. [1808] 1968. *Addresses to the German Nation.* New York: Harper Torchbooks,

Fleischacker, Samuel. 1999. *A Third Concept of Liberty: Judgment and Freedom in Kant and Adam Smith.* Princeton: Princeton University Press.

Fontaine, Phillip. 1997. "Identification and Economic Behavior: Sympathy and Empathy in Historical Perspective." *Economics and Philosophy* 13, no 2: 261–80.

Fontaine, Phillip. 2000. "Making Use of the Past: Theorists and Historians on the Economics of Altruism." *European Journal of the History of Economic Thought* 7, no. 3: 407–22.

Fontaine, Phillip. 2001. "The Changing Place of Empathy in Welfare Economics." *History of Political Economy* 33, no. 3: 387–409.

Gide, Charles, and Charles Rist. [1915] 2000. *A History of Economic Doctrines: From the Time of the Physiocrats to the Present Day.* In *Early Histories of Economic Thought, 1824–1914,* edited by Roger E. Backhouse, vol. 8. London: Routledge.

Griswold, Charles L. 1999. *Adam Smith and the Virtues of Enlightenment.* Cambridge: Cambridge University Press.

Haakonssen, Knud. 1981. *The Science of a Legislator: The Natural Jurisprudence of David Hume and Adam Smith.* Cambridge: Cambridge University Press.

Hasek, C. W. [1925] 2002. *The Introduction of Adam Smith's Doctrine in Germany.* Honolulu: University Press of the Pacific.

Heilbroner, Robert L. 1982. "The Socialization of the Individual in Adam Smith." *History of Political Economy* 14, no. 3: 427–39.

Hildebrand, Bruno. 1848. *Die Nationalökonomie der Gegenwart und Zukunft.* Frankfurt: J. Rütten.

Hodgson, Geoffrey M. 2001. *How Economics Forgot History—The Problem of Historical Specificity in Social Science.* London: Routledge.

Hutchison, Terence W. 1976. "The Bicentenary of Adam Smith." *Economic Journal* 86, no. 3: 481–92.

Kant, Immanuel. [1787] 1990. *Critique of Pure Reason.* Edited and translated by Norton Kemp Smith. Hong Kong: Macmillan.

Khalil, Elias L. 1990. "Beyond Self-Interest and Altruism: A Reconstruction of Adam Smith's Theory of Human Conduct." *Economics and Philosophy* 6, no. 2: 255–73.

Knies, Karl. 1853. *Die politische Ökonomic vom Standpunkte der geschichtliche Methode.* Braunschweig: C. A. Schwetschke und Sohn (M. Bruhn).

Lamb, Robert B. 1974. "Adam Smith's System: Sympathy Not Self-Interest." *Journal of the History of Ideas* 35, no. 4: 671–82.

Levy, David, and Sandra Peart. 2004. Sympathy and Approbation in Hume and Smith: A Solution to the Other Rational Species Problem. *Economics and Philosophy* 20, no. 2: 331–50.

List, Friedrich. [1841] 1904. *The National System of Political Economy.* London: Longmans, Green.

Macfie, A. L. 1967. "Adam Smith's Sentiments as foundation for His *Wealth of Nations.*" In *The Individual in Society: Papers on Adam Smith,* 59–81. London: George Allen and Unwin.

Milward, Alan S., and Samuel B. Saul. 1977. *The Development of the Economies of Continental Europe, 1850–1940.* London: George Allen and Unwin.

Montes, Leonidas. 2003. "Das Adam Smith Problem: Its Origins, the Stages of the Current Debate, and One Implication for Our Understanding of Sympathy." *Journal of the History of Economic Thought* 25, no. 1: 63–90.

Montes, Leonidas. 2004. *Adam Smith in Context: A Critical Reassessment of Some Central Components of His Thought.* London: Palgrave-Macmillan.

Morrow, Glenn R. [1923] 1969. *The Ethical and Economic Theories of Adam Smith.* New York: Augustus M. Kelley.

Morrow, Glenn R. 1927. "Adam Smith: Moralist and Philosopher." *Journal of Political Economy* 35, no. 3: 321–42.

Nieli, Russell. 1986. "Spheres of Intimacy and the Adam Smith Problem." *Journal of the History of Ideas* 47, no. 4: 611–24.

Oncken, August. 1897. "The Consistency of Adam Smith." *Economic Journal* 7:443–50.

Oncken, August. [1898] 2000. "The Adam Smith Problem." In *Adam Smith: Critical Responses,* edited by Hiroshi Mizuta. London: Routledge.

Otteson, James R. 2000. "The Recurring 'Adam Smith Problem.'" *History of Philosophy Quarterly* 17, no. 1: 51–74.

Otteson, James R. 2002. *Adam Smith's Marketplace of Life.* Cambridge: Cambridge University Press.

Pack, Spencer J. 1997. "Adam Smith on the Virtues: A Partial Resolution of the Adam Smith Problem." *Journal of the History of Economic Thought* 19, no. 1: 127–40.

Perlman, Mark, and Charles R. McCann Jr. 1998. *The Pillars of Economic Understanding: Ideas and Traditions.* Ann Arbor: University of Michigan Press.

Peters-Fransen, I. 2001. "The Canon in the History of the Adam Smith Problem." In *Reflections on the Classical Canon of Economics: Essays in Honour of Samuel Hollander,* edited by E. L. Forget and S. Peart. London: Routledge.

Pribram, Karl. 1983. *A History of Economic Reasoning.* Baltimore: John Hopkins University Press.

Raphael, David D. 1985. *Adam Smith.* Oxford: Oxford University Press.

Recktenwald, Horst C. 1978. "An Adam Smith Renaissance *anno* 1976? The Bicentenary Output—a Reappraisal of His Scholarship." *Journal of Economic Literature* 16, no. 1: 56–83.

Schumpeter, Joseph A. [1954] 1994. *History of Economic Analysis.* Routledge: London.

Skarżyński, Witold von. 1878. *Adam Smith als Moralphilosophie und Schöpfer der Nationalökonomie: Ein Beitrag zur Geschichte der Nationalökonomie.* Berlin: Verlag und Theobald Grieben.

Skinner, Andrew S. 1976. "Adam Smith: The Development of a System." *Scottish Journal of Political Economy* 23, no. 2: 111–32.

Smith, Adam. [1759] 1984. *The Theory of Moral Sentiments.* Edited by David D. Raphael and Alec L. Macfie, Indianapolis: Liberty Fund.

Smith, Adam. [1776] 1981. *An Inquiry into the Nature and Causes of the Wealth of Nations.* Edited by Roy H. Campbell and Andrew S. Skinner, Indianapolis: Liberty Fund.

Smith, Adam. 1982. *Essays on Philosophical Subjects.* Edited by William P. D. Wightman and James C. Bryce. Indianapolis: Liberty Fund.

Smith, Adam. 1987. *Correspondence of Adam Smith.* Edited by Ernest C. Mossner and Ian S. Ross. Indianapolis: Liberty Fund.

Teichgraeber, Richard F., III. 1981. "Rethinking Das Adam Smith Problem." *Journal of British Studies* 20, no. 2: 106–23.

Tribe, Keith. 1988. *Governing Economy: The Reformation of German Economic Discourse, 1750–1840.* Cambridge: Cambridge University Press.

Tribe, Keith, and H. Mizuta. 2002. *A Critical Bibliography of Adam Smith,* London: Pickering and Chatto.

Viner, Jacob. 1927. "Adam Smith and Laissez Faire." *Journal of Political Economy* 35, no. 2: 198–232.

Viner, Jacob. 1972. *The Role of Providence in the Social Order: An Essay in Intellectual History.* Philadelphia: American Philosophical Society.

Vivenza, Gloria. 2001. *Adam Smith and the Classics: The Classical Heritage in Adam Smith's Thought.* Oxford: Oxford University Press.

Werhane, Patricia H. 1991. *Adam Smith and His Legacy for Modern Capitalism.* Oxford: Oxford University Press.

Winch, Donald. 1978. *Adam Smith's Politics: An Essay in Historiographic Revision.* Cambridge: Cambridge University Press.

Winch, Donald. 1996. *Riches and Poverty: An Intellectual History of Political Economy in Britain, 1750–1834.* Cambridge: Cambridge University Press.

Witzum, Amos. 1998. "A Study into Smith's Conception of the Human Character: Das Adam Smith Problem Revisited." *History of Political Economy* 30, no. 3: 489–513.

Young, Jeffrey T. 1997. *Economics as a Moral Science: The Political Economy of Adam Smith.* Cheltenham: Edward Elgar.

8 • Adam Smith's Invisible Hand

Warren J. Samuels

Wednesday, 28 July 2004

SJP	Sandra J. Peart	MPP	Maria Pia Paganelli
WJS	Warren J. Samuels	SF	Samuel Fleischacker
DML	David M. Levy	YY	Yong Yoon
JMB	James M. Buchanan	Q	Questioner

SJP: We've all benefited this week already from having Warren in our midst. And today he's going to give the first of three talks. . . . It's one that will fit in very nicely with the theme of today, and he's going to talk about his "invisible hand" project.

WJS: Thank you. When I was invited to come here, the focus that I had was that this a student-oriented workshop. It seems like a typical workshop, typical session, and academic meeting,

[Laughter.]

so it was my intention to do three things: one was to tell you about my findings on the invisible hand, the second was to tell you something about how I work, and the third was to try make clear where I'm coming from. Since there are these two further sessions, particularly the "conversation" with Jim [reproduced in chapter 2 of this volume], I think we'll let it be on that, and there's also this book review that I refer to. People are taken, not by what I said, but by what Abba Lerner is quoted as saying. At any rate, the author of this book review gets me right, so you can learn a little bit about me from that . . . and, hopefully, from the conversation with Jim.

In the early 1980s, I made a decision to concentrate on the history of economic thought and, to some extent, methodology rather than law and economics. (That doesn't mean exclusively history of economic thought but to *concentrate* on it.) And I made a list of the projects that I had in mind, and they were in some sense related; at least they all were generated out of the literature of economics in the last century or century and a half. So I had this list of topics, and I decided that I would research all of them at the same time. And if I needed to, or wanted to, I would interrupt and work on something else (which I've done a lot of).

The kinds of topics that I was going to work on, and have been working on, are historiographical topics, for example, the filtration mechanism (what filters theories in and out of the system), methodological individualism and methodological collectivism (that's what I'll call the theory of precursors in economics), the problem of truth versus tools, the questions of epistemology and the philosophy of science . . . those and other questions under the heading of historiographical issues.

But the main topic that I was going to deal with was the origins of twentieth-century economics. How to explain how economics got from just before [Alfred] Marshall to where it was, say, in the 1980s. I was interested in economists's motivations, in the role of universities, in the meaning of schools of thought, the significance of formalism and its consequences, but basically what is it that explained the choices that economists made as to what they were going to do.

The third major topic was the different approaches within neoclassicism to the economic role of government. And then it occurred to me, as I was working this out and also doing reading, that I'd come across some odd statements. Not that the statements were in themselves odd, but they seemed odd to me in that I couldn't put them together in a meaningful sort of way. And these statements had to do with the invisible hand. So I thought, "Well, I'll look into that, too."

So what I have concentrated on is this very large project, but increasingly I have focused on the use of the concept of the invisible hand in economics. Now, you have to understand what I'm interested in and what I'm not interested in. I am not interested in "what Smith really meant"; I am not interested in "what is the invisible hand *really?*" or questions like that. I'm asking: here is all this data on all this usage, what of it? What are we to make of it?

Now the short description is multiplicity—on everything there are multiple positions. There's nothing that I have looked at that doesn't have multiplicity. I'm also interested in *Smith,* and not just the uses made by others of Smith, so I look at Smith and the uses made by others, and I learn from various and sundry people that one has to deal with the Scottish Enlightenment and, therefore, with the Enlightenment. And I look at the literature, and I find that the Enlightenment means different things to different people. Not only is [it] *weighed* differently by different people, and *valued* differently, but *defined* differently. And I see that Smith had his feet planted in a number of different paradigms and therefore one can interpret his work differently because you stress one paradigm or another. So we have this multiplicity at the beginning, and the conclusion, in one word, is "inconclusiveness." Okay?

Many years ago, in the early seventies, I wrote and published a paper on [the] history of economic thought as intellectual history, and one of the things that I proposed there was what I called the matrix approach to the study of the history of economic thought [Samuels 1974]. Kirk Johnson here, I think, is the only person here who's been my student, and he will attest to the fact—I hope he perceives it—that I was using this model in class but not calling attention to it every day because that would get terribly trite and boring.

What is the matrix approach? You have a question, and you have five or six different views on that question—say, five different schools of thought. And within each school of thought you have several different subsidiary views, branches, as it were. So you have *A, B, C, D,* and *E* and within each of them you have, say, *C*1, 2, and 3. So what is the object *X*? Is the object *X* to be understood by *A* or by *B* or by *C,* or *A*1 or *A*3 or *D*3? It seems to me that, even if I were to believe that *E*3 is the correct one, that if I look at the world, what's really going on out there, without putting myself in an *E*3 at the top of a pyramid, it's a *matrix* of positions, and that there must be something to be learned from the matrix formed by all these positions. I treat mercantilism that way, and I try to treat other things that way without making it so obvious that it becomes repetitious.

So, how do I address the question of the invisible hand? As I said, I'm not interested in what Smith really meant or whether there is an invisible hand or not and, if so, what is it? I'm interested in making *sense,* understanding what it is that's going on in all these uses. That's all. And the approach I'm taking is somewhat like the professor who was an agnostic who was teaching a course in comparative religion. It doesn't make any difference to him that these people believe in God and that he doesn't, but he wants to know what different religions have to do with God, what their theologies are, and, if there's no God, what substitutes for God, etc. . . . And also the nature of God and so on. He's not interested in rebutting all these things. They're there. He wants to understand what we might call the sacerdotal imperative or something like that, and in economics we have an invisible hand imperative. We use it all the time. Literally, we use it all the time. I have not counted, but I must have twenty thousand different citations or references that are pertinent to this discussion. Think of the literature written by [Friedrich] Hayek, or dealing with Hayek, on spontaneous order and unintended and unforseen consequences. That in itself is enough for a lifetime.

My problem is to make sense of this; my problem is not to solve the problems that these people are dealing with. . . . And somehow my problem is to learn what I've told numerous graduate students, that you gotta have a publication out of this sooner or later so that you can get a job. [Laughter.]

Now I don't have to get a job, but if I follow my wife's advice, and the advice of numerous colleagues, I'd better draw a line somewhere so I can finish the thing while I'm still alive. It's very hard to do that. I can't say, "Well, as of September first, no more additions to my reference list because somebody's bound to come out with something, Sam's [Fleischacker's] book, [which] I haven't read yet and a lot of other things that I have to reread and go back into.

I'll also tell you the procedure that I use. Everything that comes to my mind I put on a 5 × 8 card, and everything I read I outline and index with regard to all of these projects and on the computer I put the material with regard to the invisible hand. So that gives me right there at least *two* runs through the material, and then, since it's all indexed, every aspect of the invisible hand project is indexed when I go through it with regard to each item: I get another cut at this. And then, of course, when I'm writing it that's the real test.

But it's a tremendous chore on every point to pool all this material together. I don't advise you to do it at an early age, and, if you do it, you should do it—start it—before you're fifty. [Laughter.] That's what I was when I started it.

One area that I'm interested in, as I'm sure many of you are, has to do with what Smith really believed about God and religion. And I have no personal preconception here. I'm amassing views of other people; I'm amassing insights that I gathered from them and from reading Smith and also from what is not there.

Years ago, with Nicholas Mercuro I wrote a couple of articles on the Fifth Amendment taking clause (Samuels and Mercuro 1979, 1980), and I interviewed people with Michigan state government about—let's call it externalities and takings. And one type of question I asked was what was being done about this? When did it become an issue? And then I would broach the question of when *wasn't* it an issue, that these things are happening. And the same thing . . . is true here. If Smith doesn't take up certain material, why *doesn't* he take up certain material? Other people did; he didn't. And then I have the experience of [Francis] Hutcheson and [David] Hume and [Dennis] Robertson and others. At any rate, that's something I have a completely open mind on; I want to see where the balance of evidence may come out. I am familiar with much of the work in this area, and I can't tell you in advance where I'm going to come out.

Okay. It occurs to me that there are several questions that have to be asked and answered. One of them is, "What *is* the invisible hand?" The second question that has to be answered [is] "Where does it come from?" The third question: "What does it do?" The fourth question: "What are the conceptual ramifications and complexities?" And . . . the next one: "What are the substantive complications or ramifications?"

As you, I think, all know, the invisible hand comes up in three points in Smith. One, he is describing other peoples's uses where the invisible hand is the invisible hand of Jupiter in the "History of Astronomy," and the invisible hand deals with irregular events. There's a lot of interesting literature on *that;* there's a lot of interesting *history* on that. It was amazing to me years ago, before I ever got involved with the invisible hand, to read in Merle Curti's book on the history of American thought [Curti 1943] that in Boston, around the time of the adoption of the Constitution, there was an eclipse. And this was given a religious interpretation . . . as it has . . . ever since in some places. Any rate, that is the Jupiter use, which is not Smith himself. He's just reporting on this.

In the *Moral Sentiments,* you will recall, the invisible hand is alluded to or invoked because the capacity of human beings to consume is limited, and when rich people spend money they do it in such a way as to provide income for poor people, and the distribution of consumption will equal the distribution of wealth and income. So they're spending as if by an invisible hand—*no, by* an invisible hand. . . . I'm going to come to that; it leads to that effect.

Then, of course, in *The Wealth of Nations,* it is oddly situated, and people for many, many years, until relatively recently, have neglected the fact that it is situated here—it's situated in the discussion of foreign investment, and businessmen invest abroad, but they will be less inclined to invest abroad if there is greater security at home. We could factor that in and determine the mathematics of that, and there are several different ways you could go with it, but the *effect* that Smith has brought about by the invisible hand is greater investment in employment at home and even greater military strength at home. . . .

One of the more fascinating aspects of this study has to do with the proliferation of uses: you have the slippery hand, you have the slapping hand, and an unbelievable number of uses by journalists and by economists. But the most interesting twist in the economics literature and elsewhere is that about half of it refers to Smith saying "as if by" an invisible hand. He doesn't say that—he said "is led" by an invisible hand.

. . . Is that a figure of speech? Maybe there is an invisible hand—*no* figure of speech. I don't know the answer to that. Half the literature says "as if by"; half says "led by." Half I haven't weighed these and counted, but it's roughly that.

[Deirdre] McCloskey says that the market is a metaphor. One of the leading candidates for the identity of the invisible hand is the market. Now, if the invisible hand is a metaphor, to define the metaphor by the market is to define one metaphor using another metaphor. Though [William] Grampp, in his article in the JPE [*Journal of Political Economy*] a couple of years ago, says it's not a metaphor, it's a simile. It's been fascinating to try make sense of metaphor and simile—I am *not* convinced that there's a difference despite the use of the word *like* in discussions of simile. But there's more to it than that.

Then you have the idea [that suggests] "No, there's no invisible hand, but there's an invisible hand process." [Robert] Nozick, [Edna] Ullman-Margalit, and others. . . . A lot of things are invisible hand processes. I'm not sure . . . why one would distinguish them as this. Two football teams come together. They produce a result. There's going to be a result; it's within rules. What happens is a function of the rules, the quality of the players, how well they perform as their fatigue wears on, the roles assigned to them, but there's an interaction here and an aggregation, which is essentially the Hayekian solution. That's a *process.* I'm not sure one would dignify it as an invisible hand, but it certainly is an invisible hand *process.* Why not just call it a *process of interaction?* . . .

Q: Maybe one use of the invisible hand happens only when there is a result? You think it could have been intended independent of the process and then the process seems to go to that result without any . . .

WJS: Well, certainly it's the result [that] was intended by one team as opposed to the other. Hayek wants unforseen and unintended as well. I'm just trying to relay to you what's going on out there and the problems. I don't pretend to have an interest in solving them. So if I sound like I do, please discount what I'm saying. I have to move along.

So the question now is, "What is the invisible hand?" What is the invisible hand to the people that take a position on "what is the invisible hand"?

I have come out with close to four dozen answers that I found in the literature. There's a set of those that are the most common, and you know it better than I do—the market, the price system, the price mechanism, the competitive mechanism, the competitive market/price mechanism, competition—let's just start with those.

Q: Is the index that you're building of this, is it also categorically marked so that we could possibly see trends . . .

WJS: Okay, that's a common question. I do not see trends except in two regards: with the influence of Hayek, more recent emphasis on unintended consequences and spontaneous order. But that may be in my mind because I have all this Hayek material. It's certainly not the case outside the Hayek material, so this may just be artifactual. But the one that I'm fairly confident of is that in the nineteenth century—the idea was very neglected [and] you have to read very, very much to find very, very few sources of material here—it was not made a big thing of. It was not invoked, as it were.

Q: And what about at the end of the eighteenth century? Was it more prevalent . . .

WJS: No. No. The literature that we would call the "reception literature" doesn't make a big deal out of this.

Now, that literature *may* be interpreted as making a big deal of it, insofar as you divide it into certain sections: the theological and the non-theological. But even there, as I hope to have time to point out, the question is, "What if the invisible hand is God, [then] what is the role of God?" Is it [the] God that takes an active, personal role in this world or is it the God like the night watchman who sets up the system and then sits back and smiles as he's watching these foolish people? As far as I can see, there really is almost no discussion of the invisible hand, as such, in either case, but you can intuit it with regard to God. But one man's intuition is another man's blindness. . . . And, I'm not into that.

Now, when it comes to the market, what are we talking about here? Some people say the invisible hand *is* the market; some people say it is the *hand* of the market. I sense a subtle difference there. I also sense *more* than a subtle difference in the use that says, "the invisible hand moves the market.". . . So what I am telling you is that the formulations of "the invisible hand is the market" vary considerably. If you're at all sensitive to nuance and usage, these are big nuances.

Q: Just an addition [to] the nuance of metaphor versus simile: . . . in one case you employ *like* or *as* and in the other case you say the thing straight away (love is a rose, love is as if a rose) . . . [I]n the case of simile there's a self-consciousness to the figure that invites alternative comparisons, but in the case of metaphor the comparison is an attempt at streamlining so that it's easier to charge through the metaphor and not drag the questions whereas simile sort of invites alternative comparisons, and I know that maybe Smith doesn't have to be intent on one or the other. It seems as though people are misquoting, if I understood you correctly, but in general . . . it's not as though he can escape using figures. There's going to be a figure or trope one way or the other, but one says "I'm just trying to make a point" and the other sort of draws attention to that fact.

WJS: Well, the person who has paid closest attention to this is Sam's colleague, Bill Grampp in his JPE article. He comes out on the side of simile. A number of other people do, too. . . . I, myself, have no opinion on this. . . .

Q: I was just thinking in support of something that you said earlier here. The one thing that's important to hold onto is the thought that maybe it isn't a metaphor at all, maybe it's meant literally. Certainly if the invisible hand—I think this is wrong, but some people do say this—is supposed to be God then it needn't be a metaphor at all. It could be literally . . .

WJS: Well, that's the point I made earlier . . .

Q: . . . but bearing that in mind I think there may be more stakes in the simile metaphor distinction for some of the people you are looking at . . .

WJS: Yeah, oh yes, that's true. . . . I've not found an elaborate discussion or very many things even approaching elaborate discussion of this kind of question. The "is led" versus "as if led" is noted. The best on this is Bill Grampp, and I'm still not convinced that he is necessarily right. . . . And the reason I'm not convinced is because there [are] other alternatives that are, to me, in the sympathy analysis sense, persuasive. But I can't say one more than the other. . . .

But there's more to it than this with regard to market. Are we dealing with purely conceptual markets, "the market," or are we dealing with *actual* markets? There's a big difference here. Some people treat the market as an institution; other people treat it as a mechanism. How does that bear on this? The market is their answer as to what the invisible hand is, but what they *mean* by the market [are] different things.

Sometimes authors will talk about the market in some sense, per se, and other times they will stipulate that the market, as they're using it, is conditioned upon some structural feature or some other feature.

What about markets as a selection process? (That's what the invisible hand is doing presumably.) But what about markets as a *result* of a selection process? . . . I have in mind here [Ronald] Coase's theory and [Gardiner] Means's theory of the firm with regard to the formation of markets.

Okay—I could go on with regard to the market, and I can't cover all of these, but that's, I think, the leading candidate. People have asked me, "If you were asked by the man on the street what's meant by the invisible hand" [what would you say]? I'd say "the market" and then just move on because they don't want to hear my three-hour lecture.

Q: Warren, there are many interesting differences between use in the *Moral Sentiments* and *The Wealth of Nations,* but one that recently caught my eye, and Sam Hollander years ago mentioned this to me but I'd forgotten that I'd read it, is [that] in the *Moral Sentiments* there's a counterfactual relationship that the invisible hand sort of captures in a way that *The Wealth of Nation*'s version doesn't. So even if it *is* meant to be the market, it's a very interesting kind of market because it's captured something that would have been the case, some things left being equal or not. And in *The Wealth of Nations* that sort of perceptual-logical structure is not quite present the way it is in the *Moral Sentiments,* so he might have meant different things, you know.

WJS: If I were to do a hermeneutic analysis of this, I would argue that neither the *Moral Sentiments'* nor *The Wealth of Nations'* uses comport very well with the idea of the market.

Q: Well, you're not supposed to do that. I agree.

WJS: Okay, so we have the price system; we have competition. I don't believe that I need to tell you that there are half a dozen, at least, significant, different definitions of what competition is. So if the market is, excuse me, if the invisible hand is *competition,* what form of competition, what definition of competition? Competition by one definition yields implications that counter the definition elsewhere. . . . Hayekian competition and Smithian structural competition are what I have in mind.

Self-interest is also frequently given as the invisible hand, but I'm going to come back to that. That opens up a whole host of major issues.

The first one being whether the invisible hand *is* competition, excuse me, *is* self-interest, or whether the invisible hand is the *check* on self-interest. Because that is, after all, what markets do. . . .

The profit motive, private enterprise, free enterprise has been given, private property has been given as the invisible hand. The problem here is whether you're dealing with the *institution* of property or particular *rights* of property . . . and, further, whether you're dealing with rights that cannot be changed or rights that are subject to change, which basically begs the question to which an invisible hand analysis is usually applied.

Then we have the entrepreneur. That is another widely used example of the answer to the question, "What is the invisible hand?" There are some fascinating questions that arise under this heading: Is the entrepreneur a *person,* so you can identify a group of people, or is it a *function* performed by *all* economic actors? And, if so, what is the function? Maybe it's a group of people who we call entrepreneurs or maybe it's an aspect of the behavior of all actors, but we don't call them all entrepreneurs.

So what is it that makes the entrepreneur an entrepreneur or makes the entrepreneur an entrepreneurial function? Some writers emphasize finding a *niche,* others *making* a niche—two very different views. Some have the entrepreneur as *very* adventurous; some people have him adventurous but not *very* adventurous. The entrepreneur is not going to be able to be passive. . . . But this raises many, many other serious questions as well.

The economic system has been called the invisible hand; the system of natural liberty has been called the invisible hand. But what do they mean? Several people, not Hayekians, talk about an interactive system or an adjustment process. Some people talk about a specifically informational system. And then, of course, there's Hayek's spontaneous order. . . .

Then we have, just reading this list, natural selection; intersubjectivity; conditioned bettering; status emulation; the deception in the *Moral Sentiments;* sympathy; the division of labor; the propensity to truck, barter, and exchange; labor; exchange; consumer sovereignty; credit system; the Walrasian auctioneer (which I think is the one that brings a smile to one's face since the Walrasian auctioneer is a pseudo-central planner) . . .

[Laughter.]

capital accumulation; [and] technology with historical process. There is one person who has called the invisible hand positive externalities—Kregel, Jan Kregel. When I first read that, I also smiled, but the more I think about it the more I think that that's what Hayek is all about, and a lot of these other things, positive externalities. But that itself raises the question, "What causes negative externalities?" Do we have an alter ego? What's going on here? . . .

WJS: Final causes: nature, God, God as the machine. And then the one that brings the biggest smile to one's face is institutions, including government, which is what Robbins says the invisible hand is. And the reason why that brings a smile to one's face is because the usual use of the invisible hand invocation is to denigrate government vis-à-vis the invisible hand. But if the invisible hand is government—this is *Robbins*—this is not any number of left wingers.

How about the following? Covert power at a distance. (I just had to put this down for you.) "The CIA has been the invisible hand of American power for half a century." . . . There are sources on the Web where you can get newspaper uses of the invisible hand. I must have two dozen uses in which a president or premier or prime minister is saying, "Those rebels are led by a cabal, an invisible hand behind the scene." . . . And then, of course, there are the people who say the international organizations are the invisible hand. So, we just reduce this to covert power at a distance.

Now, there are some things to my knowledge that have never been called the invisible hand except perhaps by implication. I'm not sure, but I don't think anybody has said technology is the invisible hand, but I may be wrong on that. The interest rate, the marginal efficiency of capital, the multiplier accelerator—I don't think any of these things were called the invisible hand by Keynesians or anti-Keynesians, which may tell you something about the linguistic dimension of all of this. . . .

DML: He didn't say it, of course, but that would be a not unfair characterization of Stigler, that for Stigler everything's in Smith . . .

WJS: Also the Weblen-Ayresians . . .

DML: . . . so that would not be an unfair . . .

WJS: . . . I don't doubt that, but I have to limit myself, not to intuit it but to see if they're going to use it. They may very well be; I just haven't rescued it from my accumulation of materials. . . .

What does the invisible hand do? Let me skip to that. If you remember *The Wealth of Nations* use, it is sometimes but not always. Well, what is it that governs when the invisible hand does do what it does do?

Is it always? No. Is it sometimes? Is it conditional? Is it problematic? Are there what we would call limits to it? Is this a structural phenomenon? Is the invisible hand taking place in production? Distribution? Exchange? I think 90 percent or more is in the exchange context, very little in the distribution, and even less in production. But in the context of exchange are we dealing with allocative considerations or distributional considerations?

So what are these functions? Well, there are about a dozen or so, but they are so worded that you have many subtle nuances within what we'll call category. One category is order. The invisible hand produces order. The problem with that is that order is a subjective matter. It may involve the projection of some antecedent sense of order. At any rate, there are a variety of conceptions of what the order is.

Automatic self-regulation and adjustment—that's another common answer. Coordination is a common one, particularly among Hayekians. . . . But here you have some questions. What does coordination mean? When things are coordinated, what is coordinating? I remember when I was teaching principles of economics all the teachers would get together and coordinate what they were doing. I never figured out quite what that meant. . . . What is the meaning of coordination in relation to equilibrium? And self-regulation? And harmony? Is coordination a condition or is it a process?

Then we come to equilibrium You've heard a little bit about that at these sessions. Equilibrium is defined in different ways. Is equilibrium a definition of reality? Or is it a process? Is it something that we intuit and apply . . . in order to make sense of reality? Does it ever exist? Is it a tool? And what are these invisible hands that generate equilibrium?

See, one of the interesting things here is the combinations. You have all these identifications of the invisible hand, but then you have all these functions. Not all of the identifications lead to each of these functions. What's the difference with regard, say, to equilibrium or coordination when the invisible hand is the market or the price mechanism or the auctioneer or institutions? I don't have to rely just on Robbins. I can go to [Frank] Hahn. . . . Hahn defines this in terms of institutions.

And what about this equilibrium? Is this equilibrium a distortion? Is it a characteristic of the process of equilibration? Or is this equilibrium something we need not talk about? "All prices are equilibrium prices."

Then, another candidate for what the invisible hand does is what I'll call "general harmony and beneficence." Harmony in the sense of Bastiat; beneficence in the sense of just about everybody. But is all this apparent? Created? Real? Approximated? What is this harmony? Robbins, for example, . . . in his book on classical theory of economic policy [Robbins 1952] says that what harmony exists is a very rough harmony. But why is it a rough harmony? Why rough? It may be for the same reason that Smith says "sometimes."

Then we come to another interesting problem here. What does Smith say is done by the invisible hand? *It transmutes self-interest into social interest, social welfare.* That's the language of *The Wealth of Nations.* Is that the same thing as Pareto optimality? No. Or not necessarily. Some people say the invisible hand brings about harmony among self-interest. So the Buchanan Pareto optimality model has exhaustion of gains from trade as we end up with harmony among self-interest. Two different views of what harmony means in this context: harmony among or of self-interest [and] harmony of self-interest with the social welfare or the social interest. And if you think in terms of Pareto optimality and given that there you have an equilibrium with regard to the no gain without loss, exhausting gains from trade, what is . . . going on here? What is the *meaning* of this? Is it unanimity? Is it consent? Is it volition? Is it voluntarism? Is it freedom? Is this consensus? Jim is the expert on this, but there are a lot of other people who've written on that as well.

Well, if we're going to talk about harmony of self-interest with the social interest or the general welfare, social welfare, which is Smith's—this is the theme of Smith—what is it that we're dealing with here? Is there something called social welfare that you can identify? Is society an independent entity in any respect whatsoever? What is the directional flow of meaning? Does meaning flow from the harmony of self-interest to the general interest or does the meaning flow from the general interest to self-interest? Is the social interest the sum of private interest? (I don't know what that means, but it's a concept that's used.) Is there something about the social interest that is given or that has to be worked out? And so on and so forth.

Then we come to economic performance—the invisible hand generates economic performance—and that can be specified in many, many different ways, which I will not go into.

Then one of the things that the invisible hand does is natural selection, but that conflates. One of the identities in the invisible hand is natural selection, so is natural selection doing natural selection? But nobody says that, nobody's that naive.

Then, of course, you have the unforseen consequences principle and spontaneous order principle. . . . You have diverse combinations of functions, diverse combinations of what the invisible hand is and functions, and you have these very serious questions.

Now the question arises—I'll come to this next—where does the invisible hand come from? Are we talking about reality? A definition of reality? A system of belief? Language? A mode of discourse? What are we dealing with here? I will come back to that question.

But, as I intimated earlier, Smith is located, or Smith's feet, shall we say, are located, in a number of different paradigms: supernaturalism; naturalism; pragmatism or utilitarianism, which I would equate for this purpose; empiricism; historicism; secularism; materialism; individualism. If one is going to talk about the identity, in general, of the invisible hand in the sense of where it comes from, it can come from many, if not all, of those different paradigms.

And, as I intimated earlier, the question of the Enlightenment enters here. Is there a difference between the French and the Scottish Enlightenment that bears on this, and to what extent is there this difference, to what extent does it bear on that? And what does one mean by *Enlightenment?*

One concept that runs through all of this is naturalism. Naturalism is . . . the paradigm of the eighteenth century. Is it a definition of reality on an ontological level? Is it merely a system of belief in comparison? Or is it simply a Wittgensteinian mode of discourse? One thing you must appreciate, and I'm sure you do, is that *nature* and *natural* have been given many, many different meanings. There's literature on this in our literature and the literature of philosophers and others. Then you have the distinction between natural and artificial—one man's natural is another man's artificial. When is nature compelling on mankind? When is man in control of nature? What is the relationship of man and nature? Is man "good" and nature "bad" or vice versa? Is man a part of nature or differentiable from nature? What are the attitudes that may be taken with regard to nature? Alienation, compliance, aggression, you name it. Or is simply nature a resource? Or a potential resource?

Then we come to supernaturalism. The issues concerning Smith's theology are: whether he believes in God or not [and] the relationship of God and nature (and he has a lot of different linguistic expressions here). And then we come to the question of deism. Many people think that deism is a less stringent, less demanding, more amorphous version of theism for Christians, okay? (If you prefer to put it a little differently, I won't quibble with you.) In the eighteenth century, to be a deist meant to be an agnostic trying to cover your behind. . . because *deism* was a bad word. For one thing, it was associated with Hume. But it was more; it was broader than that.

Then with Smith you have the question, in part raised by the essay "The History of Astronomy," [of] whether the reference to the benign author, the divine author of nature, or providence, is a *fact* or a *belief* or simply a *term* used to sell an argument. What is the final cause, assuming there's a final cause, we'll call it God. . . . I once heard a Harvard divinity school professor, that was many years ago, I think it was Hans Hoffman, say that if the ordinary man in the street knew what theologians meant by God, they would think they were a bunch of atheists because the ordinary man on the street has a picture of God as an old man in a robe with a white beard. . . . That's not what theologians mean by God. So the question, then, [is] "If it's God, what is God?"

And then the question is what is his attitude toward organized religion? Smith doesn't have a good word to say about superstition, but I have talked with people who think the invisible hand is God who say, "Oh, no. Smith means, by superstition, the beliefs of the Roman Catholics, not the people that he associated with in Scotland." . . . Anthony Waterman, for example, believes that we're not talking about traditional religion; we're talking simply about a theodicy, meaning that the only question is that of the problem of Job. Why are there negative externalities?

. . . I'm certainly not the only [one] who believes this, or thinks it. I think Smith was one of the first sociologists of religion. Think about the *Moral Sentiments.* He is trying, in part, to answer the question, "Where do moral rules come from?" They're either given by God, which is not his answer, I think (and I'm giving you my own personal view here, okay?), nor, well, period. They're not given by God. But God, working through nature, implanted in man the principles of approbation. This approbation, plus the desire to look well in other peoples's eyes and in one's own eyes, and, therefore, through this process come moral rules, okay? It is in that sense that I think Smith is a sociologist of religion not a theologian of religion.

Q: I just wanted to say that one can read those two things together which I . . .

WJS: Which two things?

Q: Well, the idea that one can say that because God has given us the capacities that lead us to make moral rules . . . in that sense the moral rules come from God. And that would be a way in which Smith might well say that moral rules come *from* God but *through* nature. So the sociological, the naturalistic explanation and the, sort of, theological explanation are not necessarily incompatible. They're not given in the sense that . . .

WJS: I think I would agree with that, but there is this, what I consider [a] barrier question: why does he spend so much time on the process of working them out? Because if they were given why weren't they given ab initio. But the answer is very simple: man wasn't created perfect ab initio either. God has his ways of doing things. So, I understand that. Which is why I think it's not conclusive. . . . But I do think. . . there is an issue here; now that's what I'm trying to underscore here. Giving you my own view was to support the idea that he was a sociologist of religion. And if you go back and read what he has to say here, it is that. . . .

DML: There is also a good, almost contemporary (a little bit later) account of renown, and that's [William] Wilberforce. . . .Wilberforce reads Smith as a sociologist in *Practical Christianity,* and how come the religion of the rich folk is different from the religion of the poor folk. And Wilberforce signs on to that. Given Wilberforce's stature as a theologian in the evangelical tradition, that becomes really important for the kind of stuff we're doing. So it's a good reading. It puts your interpretation pretty close to Smith.

WJS: Well, I'm really not interested in supporting my interpretation. . . . But that point, though, is a terribly important point. Why? Because on every point that I'm dealing with, every one of these topics, there is a vast literature. So I've read [William] Paley; I've read plenty of these people. I just can't deal with all that. . . . I have to deal with the literature directly bearing on it because if I were to do that it would be a more impossible task than it is now. . . .

Q: I wanted to make the point that *The Wealth of Nations* does seem to have what we would call sociology and religion at some level?

WJS: Yeah, oh yeah, it's clear. . . . But I'm applying it more basically.

Now there's one other topic which I haven't talked about, and that's natural religion and natural theology, which I have done a lot of work on. It means a lot of things to different people. What its significance is for Smith relative to all these other questions, different people I think have different attitudes toward, although very few people in general have dealt with it.

Let me take up the question of language. . . . Clearly the invisible hand is a linguistic tradition in economics. There's no question about it. Is it a metaphor? Is it a simile? Is it an allegory? There is a domain of literature which, as I interpret it, is concerned with an interesting problem of invisibility. There are a couple of books and movies: *The Invisible Man.* [Another] one has to do with not seeing blacks—the whole idea of invisibility. The problem of things unseen, the Duke of Argyle's book, the significance of the realm of the invisible. That all bears on this. But you *do* have a linguistic tradition; you *do* have an allegorical tradition; you have a preoccupation of some people with invisibility. Is it a trope? Is it a set of significations? A set of stylistic, maybe psychological, maybe substantive effects created by the choice of words. Is it a sign, a signification? Is there a difference between trope and allegory? Is there a difference between myth, symbol, trope, and allegory? I've already talked enough about metaphor and simile; there's also analogy, euphemism, synecdoche. There are so many possibilities here as a figure of speech when *it may not even be a figure of speech*—if it's literal. . . .

Let's see. I haven't gone into social mythology or social symbolic systems, but let me just give you—well, you have the material that I distributed. The end result, I think, here is that you're dealing with a fundamental, a foundational concept in economics, but, like most foundational concepts in any discipline, they have differences in meaning, the meaning that is attributed to them. Whether they are taken to define reality or a system of belief or a tool, the key characteristic is multiplicity, and—maybe I'm influenced by my agnosticism in this—I think the end result is inconclusiveness. I think it's just an interesting term. It is, not just, it *is* an interesting term that people use to try to bait a hook to get other people interested in what they have to say. Aha! *X*—it's the invisible hand! Now since you know it's the invisible hand, it's a *foundational* concept, you better read what I have to say about *this* foundational concept.

Willie Henderson, just before I left home for this meeting, sent me a little piece where he interprets Smith in terms of irony and the invisible hand in terms of irony. As some of you know, Emma Rothschild thinks it's . . . a joke. I think you have to look at Smith in the light of the history of astronomy, of telling a story that seems complete and sets one's mind at rest. He would like to be able to tell the correct story, the true story, but he doesn't know, and maybe he's not willing to commit himself because . . . when his friend David [Hume] committed himself in public he caught a hell of a lot of trouble. Hume was risk assumptive, and I think Smith was risk averse. Now you say, "Aha, Samuels is not only the literary historian of thought, but he's a psychoanalyst, and he has Smith, the invisible Smith, on his couch!"

Q: I'd like to ask you, do you think that economists could do without the invisible hand concept? You've studied so much how they use it, . . . is this like a sort of professional reformation that they use this concept?

WJS: I don't have particular preference on that. I think they could. If it serves as a device to attract saliency, if it creates saliency, then maybe there would be less saliency and less opportunity to innovate. Maybe it provides a disciplinary, psychic balm. . . .

Q: I've got a couple of things. One is, under different definitions of what the invisible hand is, I think you put it, in the catalogue, it should be that not all definitions are equal and that some of them might be, even though they state a singular definition of this is what the invisible hand is, they might do that in ironic awareness of what the previous definitions are, and so . . .

WJS: Yes, I am aware . . . yes, that's correct.

Q: . . . you're not trying to say that this is all that is?

WJS: I think there is a lot of that. Certainly when people talk about the kicking hand or the slapping hand, they are doing it with ironic intentions, in fact, nastier intentions.

Q: Right. And even if somebody else says that the invisible hand is natural selection or something like that . . . it's not as . . . a journalist's sort of . . . in your face kind of definition, but it's a more scholarly attempt. . . .

Another thing would be, I know Hayek writes about the artificial-natural distinction and that because of it there's multivariant meanings for each of those words that you can do a little two-step where you can talk about the market or be looking at it as being artificial or natural, however it suits you, and you can either say, well, something that men do is artificial or you can say it's an outcome that men didn't intend and therefore it's natural. . . .

WJS: But that's only if you define *natural* that way.

Q: Well, I think it is because those means are available . . . [and] people just pick the one that suits the context. . . . And I think in large part that's why the discussion gets you to being supernatural, you know, man and nature . . .

WJS: The point you're making applies to more than to just that distinction. It's a very good point.

Q: And then the last thing would be I really don't think that there's a very fruitful position [from which] to talk about "well, what if it's just literal?" I think that sort of language by its very nature is figurative. When you say it's literal I understand that it's supposed to be a shared and noncontroversial meaning, but I don't think it's . . .

WJS: Well, I think it *is* a controversial meaning. All I'm saying is that there *is* a difference, no matter what else one feels about this, between "as if led by" and "led by." If I say to you that someone is a disciple of XXX that is different than saying he's acting *as if* he were a disciple of XXX.

Q: Right. But I would think that what you're meaning there is somewhat different, like measures of intent, measures of intensity, like you're still not somehow getting down to the matter of things in a way.

WJS: Oh, I agree. You know, the bottom line is I wish that Smith had had an editor. He published it himself. Just as Alfred Marshall published himself. It is only you and me that have to go through editors who say, "Samuels what the hell do you mean by that?" He didn't. I don't think he [Smith] had David Hume reading this stuff. I don't think he had his friends reading; he may have, but he did not have an editor. And I must say there are a hundred places, at least, where, if I were his editor, I would say what do you mean by this "truck, barter, and exchange" being one of them and the invisible hand, and also, on the page two pages before the invisible hand in *The Wealth of Nations* and then again at the end of that chapter, he says "necessarily." Well, Mr. Smith, oh, Dr. Smith, how can you say "necessarily" here but suddenly "sometimes," "frequently," [and] "but not always" there? And then he'd have to scratch his head and come up with better wording. . . .

JMB: Throughout this whole discussion I've been sitting here asking myself the question how I would start out writing, if I had to write an assignment, a paper, a book on the invisible hand, and I think I would come at it quite differently from the way you are going at it. Namely, in the following sense, I think I would . . . elevate Smith to a much more important position of the recognition of the self-organizing aspect of the system, that is, [the] spontaneous order aspect. And it seems to me that what happened then, you've got Smith and his eighteenth-century peers really understanding some of these elements of interaction. And then you've got . . . this whole mechanical sense of [the] neoclassical and everything is a sort of a mechanism, and then [comes] game theory. And game theory here is critically important. Only since game theory has come in this century, in the last century, and now, have you got this sort of more general understanding of self-organizing systems, which is all throughout the physical as well as social sciences. And so in a sense all this is validating Smith's genius and his insight into this possibility that you have again spontaneous order emerging from people. . . .

WJS: I understand that. . . . I would . . . not only expect it, I've seen you do it. Now . . . I've put on the shoes of Lionel Robbins, and Robbins would say, "Dear Jim, . . . The invisible hand, to Smith, is a process—maybe—as you call it. But you need to have moral rules and legal rules withdrawn from the opportunity set of individual choices—those choices that are going to muck things up *really bad,* and *then* you can have that. Do you agree?"

JMB: I agree. I agree.

WJS: You heard it!

MPP: I have two questions. One, whether you found how ideology plays into the use of invisible hand from Smith's [use of] laissez-faire and do you find that the use of invisible hand is only by laissez-faire economists and, if not, how other or non-laissez-faire economists use it?

WJS: That's not literally true. They don't . . . the non-laissez-faire economists don't "swear by the invisible hand" like Jim, but they use it as a term of a program, etc., etc., etc.

MPP: And the second one. In the literature that you reviewed, I'm interested [in knowing whether] . . . all the writers or authors are American or British . . .

WJS: Yeah, it's overwhelmingly English language, but I do have some foreign-language ones.

Q: . . . because it's not easy considering that you cannot define, quite, in one way or the other. I wonder about the problem of translating this concept into another languages for economics use . . .

WJS: I just can't answer that when you use the term laissez-faire, a very important term in this context.

I've written a paper, a short version and a longer version, relating to the HOPE [*History of Political Economy*] Conference . . . on the history of economic thought and the economic role of government, and at every turn, when you discuss that topic, the words *laissez-faire* pop up. And I argue that you need to have some minimum understanding of what *laissez-faire* means in order to make sense, to communicate, because otherwise these are just primitive, undefined terms. And I try to do that in that paper.

SF: One thing quickly. First, if you want German literature, Emma's [Rothschild's] new project is on the history of Smithian [thought] . . . so you may want to get in touch with her. . . .I also think, by the way, just looking at the Hegelian determinism and the coming of reason is actually like a child or grandchild of the invisible hand.

WJS: . . . John Davis, has an article that says that. Yeah, I agree.

SF: The other question I want to ask is this: I love this project and . . . I love the multiple nature of it, the way of looking at all these things. As a philosopher, maybe I have a hierarchical inclination, and so I want to see what it should mean as well as what it does mean, at least what it shouldn't mean in Smith's context. But . . . I'd suggest that . . .

WJS: . . . but you see, you're asking what he really meant by it . . .

SF: No, I'm not . . .

WJS: He has a position, what he really meant by it, but so does Robbins.

SF: Right. But. the way in which I think the question becomes acute, and anyone can shunt the question aside for economic purposes, is in the context *not* of economics but of *politics*. And it *is* important . . . that we agree on this, that the invisible hand comes up in book IV, late in the book—*not* in the beginning, *not* as a foundational principle. It comes up also in a very polemical context. One of the most polemical books . . .

WJS: Antimercantilism.

SF: Exactly. And right . . .

WJS: . . . but in a very narrow thing.

SF: Right, at that point. But then he does to some extent generalize it to say in this and in many other cases, basically, the government isn't impatient (whatever Robbins may say on this, and I think the institutional point is right). In the context, Smith's point is that not having government involved is better than having government involved, at least in this and many other cases, and I think here is where you get to the point where, at least in politics—forget economics here as a science—people want some answer as to, well, is it *true* that getting the government *out* is better, and if you believe the social order of whatever kind . . .

WJS: Okay, let me respond to that. I just finished my half of a chapter for Jeff Young's *Companion to Smith* on Smith's economic role of government, and one of the points I make in that is that, not withstanding the book V three tasks of the sovereign, you have to bring in the lectures in jurisprudence and you find out that law is, and therefore government is, very, very important—much more fundamentally important to Smith than the usual laissez-faire, and even anti-laissez-faire, people make it out to be. And the reason you have this problem . . . [is] you have Smith, who says (and Skinner has developed this) you have a tripartite model of society: the moral rules or morality domain, the market domain, the law and government domain. And what he does is basically to deal with each of them on their own terms. He needs to talk a little bit about nature and God and the wealth of nations (mainly nature, etc., etc., etc.), but you can't omit the lectures in jurisprudence because he covers this enormous domain of what is important and how it is important and how it works out in a manner comparable to the moral rules story without saying that it comes from God. . . .

YY: Okay. I think I'm totally confused with what to talk about Adam Smith because I have a simple understanding of Adam Smith. Especially you mention about deism, and the way I understand how you interpret Smith, deism, the way I understand it . . . my interpretation is . . . human beings have certain makeups. . . . Smith thinks it's inevitable for human beings to make progress if human beings behave in [a] certain way within this limitation. Is this . . . [what] Smith had in mind with deism?

WJS: I don't know; I just can't make my mind [up] on that. What I do think I have a good sense for is that the people in the eighteenth century, like people today, if they were to be denied their Jesus, as a personal God, that would be the core of theology or religion as they understand it, and, therefore, it would be an atheistic position. I mean there's no question that people reacted that way to deism, just as there are some "religions" today that mainstream churches react that way to. Now, remember this is only with regard to Western civilization, episcopacy, presbyterianism, the papacy—it has nothing to do with these other religions. Now, if we were to say, with Smith, let's reduce this to an equation and here are the possible variables, we put in some of these variables and ask him, "Do you want to include it or not?" That would be akin to saying to him, "Okay, here you have this discussion about investment and invisible hand and people not having enough security. Why isn't that an ordinary variable? Let's have an equation—comparative costs, all of the developments of the 1930s, which you don't know about, that enter into determining foreign trade, *and then* differential security." It's an element. Presumably, the invisible hand, whatever it is, would affect all of that process. There's no need to single that out. But for some reason he needed to single that out. So I guess if I were his editor I'd say, "Why are you singling that out? Does the rate of return have to be *higher*? Or are we dealing with an equilibrium situation in which you have a given rate of return and you carry it out to the certain point? Is there a premium for at risk because of insecurity? What do you mean to be saying here?" He'd probably scratch his head and say, "You know, I haven't thought about that," and I'd say, "Well, you gotta think about that because your reader wants to know—and, certainly, I want to know." Now, I might have let him get by with that, but I would much rather have got him on a few other things, like the invisible hand, and the difference between *necessary* and *sometimes.*

SJP: Thank you, Warren.

Bibliography

Curti, Merle, 1943. *The Growth of American Thought.* New York and London: Harper and Brothers.

Grampp, William D. 2000. "What Did Smith Mean by the Invisible Hand?" *Journal of Political Economy* 108, no. 3: 441–65.

Robbins, Lionel C. 1952. *The Theory of Economic Policy in English Classical Political Economy.* London: Macmillan.

Samuels, Warren J. 1974. "The History of Economic Thought as Intellectual History." *History of Political Economy* 6, no. 3: 305–23.

Samuels, Warren J., and Nicholas Mercuro. 1979. "Role and Resolution of the Compensation Principle in Society." *Research in Law and Economics* 1:157–94.

Samuels, Warren J., and Nicholas Mercuro. 1980. "Role and Resolution of the Compensation Principle in Society." *Research in Law and Economics* 2:103–28.

9 • *In Medio Stat Virtus*
An Alternative View of Usury in Adam Smith's Thinking

Maria Pia Paganelli

Some specific positions of Adam Smith have been, and still are, sources of problems and debates. Generally, the controversies concern apparent contradictions in the Smithian theory. An example of these puzzling contradictions in Smith is his position on usury laws.

> In countries where interest is permitted, the law, in order to prevent the extortion of usury, generally fixes the highest rate which can be taken without incurring a penalty. This rate ought always to be somewhat above the lowest market price, or the price which is commonly paid for the use of money by those who can give the most undoubted security. (WN II.iv.14)

How could a believer in the beauty and power of the market favor usury laws?

Modern literature tries to answer this question in at least three fashions: a "nonsense" interpretation, a "Keynes-like" interpretation, and a "Stiglitz and Weiss–like" interpretation. I will argue that these interpretations of Smith on usury laws are unsatisfactory because they neglect Smith's contextual knowledge.[1] I will show how the key to understanding the consistency of Smith's position on usury can be found in the difference between his contextual knowledge and ours.[2]

In this article, references to *The Wealth of Nations* are given as WN followed by the book, chapter, section (when applicable), and paragraph numbers; references to *The Theory of Moral Sentiments* are given by TMS followed by the part, section, chapter, and paragraph numbers.

Correspondence may be addressed to Maria Pia Paganelli, Department of Economics, Yeshiva University, 500 W. 185th Street, New York, NY 10033; e-mail: maria_paganelli@yahoo.com. I thank Tyler Cowen for his inestimable help, advice, and support. I am grateful for the inspiration and encouragement received from David Levy and for the comments of two anonymous referees. The remaining mistakes are mine.

1. On the difference between a modern-looking "rational reconstruction" and a historical analysis more respectful of the original context of an author ("historical reconstruction"), see Blaug 2001. For recent works on Smith that take into account his historical and intellectual context, see Tribe 1999; Evensky 1998, 2001; and Young 1997.

2. My interest is strictly to analyze Smith's consistency as a thinker regardless of whether or not his theories are correct.

Unlike most modern economists, Smith is a moral philosopher. He has a well-developed classical and, I would argue, consistent view of the world. In general, for the classical Greeks and Romans, extremes are dangerous because they are too far away to be seen and known. A middle position is therefore preferred to an "extreme" position. Moreover, different from modern economics, which assumes that information is unbiased and behavior error free,[3] Smith's economics observes and analyzes systematic biased information that leads to systematic errors. By acknowledging systematic bias and preferring a middle position, it is possible to make sense of Smith's position on usury.

Evidence that understanding Smith's defense of usury laws requires the tools of moral philosophy and systematic biases can be found in the extensive use of these two instruments in *The Wealth of Nations* and *The Theory of Moral Sentiments,* as well as in the interaction between Smith and his most famous intellectual adversary on usury—Jeremy Bentham.

To show how usury laws make sense in Smith's world, but not in Smith's world seen through some modern lenses, I will consider the possibility of reaching Smith both "from the past" and "from the future." Reaching Smith's position on usury laws from the past is my present attempt. Reaching Smith from the future is what current literature on Smith and usury laws has unsuccessfully tried to do.

Reaching Smith's Position on Usury with the Instruments Available in His Day

Before becoming the father of economics, Adam Smith was a professor of moral philosophy. I will therefore look into the "toolbox" of moral philosophy to find interpretative instruments.

Smith lived during the transition from the ancien régime to modernity. The principles (economic and otherwise) to which Smith subscribed coincide with some principles that are still recognized today, but Smith's understanding of economics was informed by his knowledge of Greek and Roman literature (see Paganelli 2000; and Griswold 1999). So, while Smith rejects a theological justification of usury laws, which was proposed by many before him,[4] he also does not embrace a more amoral rationality, which some of his contemporaries of less clas-

3. A major attempt to recognize the existence of bias and incorporating biased behavior in economic analysis can be found in Kahneman and Tversky 1979; and Kahneman, Slovic, and Tversky 1982.

4. For an overview of the religious justification of usury laws, see Nelson 1969.

sical education more likely held.[5] As I will show, Smith's justification of usury laws was nonreligious (in contrast to most of his predecessors) but rested on a moral base (in contrast to most of his contemporaries and successors).

The Classical *Medietas*

In the eighteenth century, moral philosophy was still heavily based on the works of the ancient Greeks and Romans. Smith gives us evidence in all his works of his deep knowledge of the classics.

The Greeks taught Smith that the good, the virtuous, lies within bounded limits. The Greeks, for instance, lived in a bounded polis. They expanded by poleis only, creating brand new poleis rather than developing around existing ones. Outside the limits of the polis, Aristotle reminds us, there are only gods or beasts because what is not bounded is not human. Infinity, indeed, is nonhuman, dangerous, and paradoxical. Infinity is not good for humans because it is not bounded and therefore not knowable.[6] What is knowable is only what can be measured, and what can be measured has to be bounded. As a consequence, the "sin" of hubris was the most nefarious and infamous act a person could commit. Hubris meant challenging the gods; it meant going outside the limits. The sailors who tried to cross the pillars of Hercules, which were the borders of the world, died throwing up green bile. What did all this mean? It meant that extremes were dangerous, that extremes were to be avoided. It meant that being in the "middle" was the good thing to do. Greek ethics is a reflection of this.

The Greeks were not unique. The Romans developed a similar ethical system: avoid the extremes and stay in the middle. Virtue is the middle point between two extremes. It is the balance between opposites. It is moderation. Choosing to moderate all passions leads one to the "just middle." In other words, the way to moral excellence is *medietas* or *mediocritas* (being in the middle).[7] It follows that the virtuous man is the prudent man, the man who has reached an internal balance within himself, who has his "soul in its just and proper order." And the social nature of human beings implied that the virtuous behavior of the indi-

5. See, for example, Jeremy Bentham's "Defence of Usury" ([1787] 1952).

6. See, for example, Plato's considerations of the lack of order associated with infinity in *Philebus* (24a–26d), Aristotle's analysis of the many problems deriving from the idea of infinity in *Physics* (III, 5, 204a and following), or the more popular paradox of Zeno's tortoise, in which a slow-moving tortoise wins a race against the swift-footed Achilles.

7. *Medietas* and *mediocritas* are equivalent and will be used interchangeably. I will use the Latin term since its translation into "mediocrity" would add a negative connotation that was absent in the ancient word.

vidual is possible thanks to conscious choice and his interrelations with the other individuals in the orderly society.

This concept of *medietas* (in modern statistical terminology, "the median") was the pivot around which revolved not just the classical world but also the medieval world and the world of the ancien régime.[8] Not by chance, Cicero's *De Officiis* was a major textbook until the nineteenth century. And during the ancien régime, as well as during the classical age, individual virtue and social virtue were strictly related. Virtuous individuals would create a virtuous society, and a society with virtuous moral rules would give individuals incentives to become virtuous. This interdependence between the *medietas* of the individual and the virtues of the society in which he lives is exemplified, among others, by *oeconomica*. Economics, indeed, not as a science in itself, as we know it today, but as an art, was presented by Aristotle, and by the literature of the ancien régime, as the discipline that involves a "just" government of the house (see Continisio 1994). It was part of moral philosophy. The governance of the house was different from the governance of the city or kingdom (*civitas*) because their domains of action were different, and both were well circumscribed. But both required the same practical virtue and ability in order to achieve the just, virtuous, and *mediocres* order. Indeed, the father of the family, as the "prince" of his family, was required to be virtuous, to have "economic prudence": "The practical character of economics. . . , following the traditional Aristotelian canons, puts it among the 'operative' disciplines that, unlike the 'contemplative' disciplines, which address the knowledge of things that are necessary, natural, and independent from human will, address the 'contingent' things, which are subject to human will, in order to guide action toward the just end. The art of good governance of the house 'is subjected to prudence, and it is domestic prudence itself'" (Frigo 1995, 36; my translation).

The Influence of *Medietas* on Adam Smith

With this in mind, read Smith's "advertisement" of the last edition of *The Theory of Moral Sentiments,* which he edited after writing *The Wealth of Nations.*

> In the last paragraph of the first Edition of the present work, I said, that I should in another discourse endeavour to give ac-

8. See, for example, Bishop Berkeley's (1975) mathematics and theory of vision, which, read as a scientific work or as metaphors, express the same distrust for infinity and extremes. See Levy 1992.

> count of the general principles of law and government, and of the different revolutions which they had undergone in the different ages and periods of society; not only in what concerns justice, but in what concerns police, revenue, and arms, and whatever else is the object of law. In the *Enquiry concerning the Nature and Causes of the Wealth of Nations,* I have partly executed this promise; at least so far as concerns police, revenue, and arms.

Smith, therefore, regarded *The Wealth of Nations* as continuing the sequence of thoughts set out in *The Theory of Moral Sentiments.* It seems that for Smith, the starting point in understanding *The Wealth of Nations* is *The Theory of Moral Sentiments.*[9]

In *The Theory of Moral Sentiments,* Smith shows man in all his dimensions, as the classics did. Individuals are characterized by a plurality of different feelings, both toward themselves and toward others, ranging from selfishness to benevolence. It is explicitly in part 7 of *The Theory of Moral Sentiments* where, dealing with moral philosophy as a system, Smith criticizes some then modern interpretations of ethics as presenting human behavior as motivated by only one thing, and he leaves little doubt about his borrowing from classical thought the idea of virtue as *medietas* between opposing extremes. And it is not by chance that Smith focuses on a variety of different passions, contrasting himself with some of his contemporaries, teachers, and friends. Indeed, if there were just one motivation for our behavior, where would virtue be? If there were just one extreme, where would the "just middle" of opposed passions be? To have a point in the middle, at least two extremes, and not just one, have to exist. Indeed, at the practical and individual level, a completed and developed human being, with the help of the impartial spectator, has to balance all his feelings and by achieving such a balance will be virtuous. At the abstract, and in a sense aggregate, level, a completed and developed moral system has to include all feelings, too, and virtue will consist in the proper, just, balanced combination of them.

Remember that from what Smith told us in the advertisement of his last edition of *The Theory of Moral Sentiments* his project was a large one. With *The Theory of Moral Sentiments,* he built a moral structure for human beings. With *The Wealth of Nations,* he analyzed how the same person, full of different passions, would set in a "police, revenue, and arms" context. The same individual passions can be amplified or re-

9. For a recent survey of Das Adam Smith Problem, see Peters-Fransen 2001.

strained in different proportions by different sets of political and economic institutions. The "prudent man" described in *The Theory of Moral Sentiments* is essentially the same person assumed to be at work in the commercial society described in *The Wealth of Nations.* Indeed, if it is true that in *The Wealth of Nations* the predominant presence is self-love, it is also true that it is never the only one (Bittermann 1940a, 1940b).

Smith was conscious, though, that virtue is not easy to achieve, that people are imperfect and not perfectible. At the same time, Smith was conscious that absolute principles may not always be appropriate and that a contextual analysis may offer a more appropriate basis for judgment. So, for example, sympathy is good but not always strong, self-interest is good but not on all occasions, and a limited presence of government is also good but not necessarily all the time.

More specifically, self-interest tends to prevail over sympathy in the context of market transactions. First of all, we do not get our dinner "from the benevolence of the butcher"; instead, self-interest prevails. Moreover, sympathy, which usually can constrain self-interest, tends to decrease the less we know about another person. But when dealing with strangers competition and repeated dealings offer "natural" restraints to an otherwise prevalent selfishness, and trade is able to channel in a positive manner one's self-interest (WN I.ii.2). The market, here, is able to bound human passions, keeping them balanced, preventing them from falling into vicious extremes. The presence of self-interest is seen, in this context, in a positive light—and as maintaining social harmony. When, instead, we are faced with an institutional context in which self-interest is left unbounded, self-interest assumes a negative connotation. Unbounded self-interest can become "rapacity" according to Smith. It is indeed self-interest that, breaking its bounds, flatters government in order to achieve monopolistic privileges, abandoning free trade. Engaging in unbounded selfish possibilities and acquiring an "artificially" predominant role through government-granted monopolies break the natural harmony of society by damaging the whole in favor of a small part (I.xi). Virtue is *medietas;* if one extreme prevails and the just middle is abandoned, the consequences cannot be positive. The dominance of self-interest, sustained by the force of government, not only moves the individual away from virtue but also moves society away from harmony.

Similarly, Smith is ready to accept the goodness of both the absence and the presence of government in society, depending on the specific context. If sympathy is weak, if the impartial spectator makes a mistake, if man cannot perceive well, a free market is preferred. But when, for whatever reasons, the free market fails, government intervention can do good.[10] An example of this positive role for government intervention is Smith's controversial position on public schools (controversial only if seen out of context). Smith noted that if specialization, as self-interest, is present in the "proper quantity," if it is balanced with other individuals' activities in the proper proportion (that depends on the specific institutional and historical context), its role is positive. Specialization can do wonders at the individual and societal levels. But if disproportional with respect to the "proper level," the consequences are negative, both at the individual and the societal levels (WN V.i.f.50). How to maintain specialization in the "proper measure"? Smith provided us with an antidote. Education and religion are indeed the instruments that, if promoted among the workers, can keep alive their minds and rebalance their selves (V.i.f). And if the market fails to provide schools, government is welcome to intervene, so that the just and good *medietas* can be maintained both at the individual level and the social level.

This being the case, Henry Bittermann (1940a, 516) is correct in saying, "Paradoxical as it may seem, the theory of ethics was less directly normative than the scientific work on economics. The moral theory was in the main descriptive; the economic theory neatly wove prescriptive elements into its descriptive-predictive fabric."

It follows, also, that David Levy (1987) is correct in saying that legal restraints in the economy (and not only there) work like a sort of moral code in Smith's framework.[11]

The Influence of Systematic Error on Adam Smith

How can sympathy be weak and the impartial spectator make a mistake? How can man not perceive well and the market fail? All of these problems can be related to systematic biases.

An example of weak sympathy is experienced the farther away (literally and figuratively) people are from each other. If this is the only problem, the market will usually take care of it. But more problems may come when accompanied by other defects.

Just as human beings have to learn how to perceive distances, human beings have to learn how to sympathize. Sympathy is the natural

10. On the active role of government in Smith, see Jacob Viner's 1927 essay "Adam Smith and Laissez-Faire," reprinted in Viner 1991.

11. "Smith's opinion that government officials have no role to play in the direction of private resources does not imply that law has no role. While Smith knew the notion of 'government failure' as well as modern public-choice theorists, legal restraints in Smith's work have an interesting similarity to moral codes. When people are not fully aware of the consequences of their action, both can provide benefits to the constrained individual. . . . In this case, where law can improve social well-being, Smith favors it" (Levy 1987, 399–400).

component of human beings that allows the existence of the impartial spectator. But the spectator who is in us since birth is "partial" (Levy 1995). This implies that the Smithian man is born with a strong egocentrism. By interacting with others, the individual realizes that he is not "the center of the universe," as he thought. Through his relationships with others, by imagining himself in somebody else's shoes, the individual grows morally and slowly transforms his internal spectator from partial to impartial.

The impartial spectator is therefore the fruit of a continuous interior work, helped by the presence of others, which leads the morality of the individual to maturity. The full maturity of the individual, his full morality, cannot be taken for granted. Virtue is a conquest not a given.

What about the possibility that human beings will make mistakes because of systematic bias? Smith opens both *The Theory of Moral Sentiments* and *The Wealth of Nations* by describing exactly this possibility.

The Theory of Moral Sentiments begins with descriptions of how we constantly make mistakes because we imagine ourselves in someone else's condition and keep reasoning with our own minds not theirs. So we feel sorry for the dead because they are alone and cold under the ground, while they, being dead, cannot feel anything. We feel sorry for the mentally insane, "but the poor wretch, who is in it, laughs and sings perhaps, and is altogether insensible of his own misery" (TMS I.i.11). And so on.

The Wealth of Nations opens with a famous misperception. The division of labor

> is commonly supposed to be carried furthest in some very trifling [manufacturing operations]. . . . In those great manufactures, on the contrary, . . . the work may really be divided into a much greater number of parts, than in those of a more trifling nature, [although] the division is not near so obvious, and has accordingly been much less observed. (WN I.i.2)

Systematic errors in perception turn out to be the norm. The implication is therefore that the starting point, the assumption (which in Smith's case is empirical observation) from which Smith starts to work, is perception errors that lead to systematic errors. And in the presence of systematic errors social harmony may have some troubles. One of these troubles is indeed with respect to the interest rate.

Even chapter 4 of book II, "On Stock Lent at Interest," opens with the description of a common error in perception. There are two kinds of borrowers, says Smith: the industrious borrower and the prodigal borrower. The industrious borrower will borrow capital to use it in a profitable way; he will be able to pay back the lender. The prodigal borrower will borrow for immediate consumption and "will soon be ruined, and he who lends to him will generally have occasion to repent of his folly" (WN II.iv.2). Many think that the proportion of the two kinds of borrowers is either equal or skewed toward the prodigal, but this cannot be the case. To verify that this is a biased perception, ask a rich lender. He will laugh at the idea of lending to the prodigal: "From the regard that all men have for their own interest, we may be assured, that it cannot happen [to lend to both the industrious and the prodigal] so very frequently as we are sometimes apt to imagine. Ask any rich man of common prudence, to which of the two sort of people he has lent the greater part of his stock, to those who, he thinks, will employ it profitably, or to those who will spend it idly, and he will laugh at you for proposing the question" (II.iv.2).

Making Sense of Smith on Usury

Now that we are equipped with Smith's analytical instruments—*medietas* and systematic perception error—we can try to understand why Smith favors usury laws.

Smith is saying that the interest rate should be regulated by law, and fixed "somewhat above the lowest market price" (WN II.iv.14). The other two rates he considers are no rates at all ("prohibition of interest" and "usury"). Note what we have: two extremes and a middle position. Prohibition is the lower extreme, usury is the upper extreme, and the legal rate is the middle point.

Smith as a moral philosopher teaches us that the extremes are dangerous and should be avoided. Smith as an economist says that both prohibition of interest and usury rates are deleterious and should be avoided.

Here is how Smith describes the consequences of prohibiting interest.

> In some countries the interest of money has been prohibited by law. But as something can every-where be made by the use of money, something ought every-where to be paid for the use of it. This regulation, instead of preventing, has been found from experience to increase the evil of usury; the debtor being obliged to pay, not only for the use of money, but for the risk which his creditor runs by accepting a compensation for that use. He is obliged, if one may say so, to insure his creditor from the penalties of usury. (WN II.iv.13)

> Indeed, "no law can reduce the common rate of interest below the lowest ordinary market rate at the time when that law is made. Notwithstanding the edict of 1766, by which the French king attempted to reduce the rate of interest from five to four per cent., money continued to be lent in France at five per cent., the law being evaded in several different ways." (II.iv.16)

And here is how he describes the consequences of usury.

> The legal rate, it is to be observed, though it ought to be somewhat above, ought not to be much above the lowest market rate. If the legal rate of interest in Great Britain, for example, was fixed so high as eight or ten per cent., the greater part of the money which was to be lent, would be lent to prodigals and projectors, who alone would be willing to give this high interest. Sober people, who will give for the use of money no more than a part of what they are likely to make by the use of it, would not venture into the competition. A great part of the capital of the country would thus be kept out of the hands which were most likely to make a profitable and advantageous use of it, and thrown into those which were most likely to waste and destroy it. (II.iv.15)

What Smith is describing in this passage is adverse selection. Given the presence of heterogeneous borrowers—prodigals and projectors as well as sober people—the higher the interest rate the riskier the projects (the ones by prodigals and projectors) that will be financed, leaving out more sober entrepreneurs.

Now consider Smith's analysis on risk premium: lending money gives the lender a higher return than investing in land, which is more stable. "The superior security of land, together with some other advantages which almost every-where attend upon this species of property, will generally dispose him to content himself with a smaller revenue from land, than what he might have by lending out his money at interest" (WN II.iv.17).

Indeed, high interest rates, as well as rates of profit, are present when there is high risk. And the riskier the project the higher the risk premium will be. Smith had already exposed this fact in book I of *The Wealth of Nations,* in chapter 10, part 1, titled "Inequalities Arising from the Nature of the Employments Themselves." In paragraph 33, he states:

> The ordinary rate of profit always rises more or less with the risk. It does not, however, seem to rise in proportion to it, or so

> as to compensate it completely. Bankruptcies are most frequent in the most hazardous trades. The most hazardous of all trades, that of a smuggler, though when the adventure succeeds it is likewise the most profitable, is the infallible road to bankruptcy. The presumptuous hope of success seems to act here as upon all other occasions, and to entice so many adventurers into those hazardous trades, that their competition reduces the profit below what is sufficient to compensate the risk. To compensate it completely, the common returns ought, over and above the ordinary profits of stock, not only to make up for all the occasional losses, but to afford a surplus profit to the adventurers of the same nature with the profit of insurers. But if the common returns were sufficient for all this, bankruptcies would not be more frequent in these than in other trades. (WN I.x.b.33)

Smith is therefore saying that prohibition of interest causes usury and usury rates are harmful to the individual and the economy because of the problems described earlier. A middle position is therefore preferred to the extreme positions. But why would interest rates rise to extreme levels? Why should the "just middle" be legally enforced?

Smith leads us to the answer when talking about the problems caused by high rates. People are attracted by the high profit potential of a risky project, but the more projectors the lower the profit will be. Many will be bankrupted. And so the question: if this is known, why do they not stay out of that activity? Why do they engage in such projects? Smith's answer: systematic bias. It is "the *presumptuous hope of success* [that] seems to act here as upon all other occasions" (WN I.x.b.33, emphasis added) that causes miscalculation of the probability of success. The projector, like the gambler, is facing a lottery-like situation. He is biased; he thinks he is "the center of the universe"; he thinks others will fail but not him. He will therefore overestimate the probability of his success and underestimate the probability of his failure.

> The over-weening conceit which the greater part of men have of their own abilities, is an ancient evil remarked by the philosophers and moralists of all ages. Their *absurd presumption in their own good fortune,* has been less taken notice of. It is, however, if possible, still more universal. There is no man living who, when in tolerable health and spirits, has not some share of it. The chance of gain is by every man more or less over-valued, and the chance of loss is by most men under-valued, and by

> scarce any man, who is in tolerable health and spirits, valued more than it is worth. (I.x.b.26, emphasis added)

Most of the time when we face a decision under uncertainty we are facing a maximization problem with "incorrect" data. The expected benefit, biased by the projector's/gambler's presumption, will exceed the expected cost of the project/bet. If the information used in his calculation were not biased, the expected cost would exceed the expected benefit and he would restrain himself from engaging in such a risky project. But the information is biased, so the project/bet will be undertaken.

Since people tend to systematically overestimate their probability of success, there is the tendency for interest rates to be higher than the market-clearing level. The overestimated interest rate leads to the problems of adverse selection, financing too many overly risky projects. A ceiling is therefore important to prevent the degenerative consequences of this process.

Confirmation of this reading of Smith comes from his adversary in the usury debate. Jeremy Bentham recognizes Smith's argument on systematic bias and turns it against Smith: if there is a bias on the borrower's side, there is also another bias, which goes in the opposite direction, as far as the lender is concerned. Even if the projector has a tendency to overestimate his probability of success, it is likely that the lender will underestimate it. The problem caused by the projector's bias is solved by the (opposite) lender's bias. These two opposite biases cancel each other out, making usury laws unnecessary.

> True it is, that in the jumble of occurrences, an over-sanguine projector may stumble upon a patron as over-sanguine as himself; and the wishes may bribe the judgment of the one, as they did of the other. The opposite case, however, you will allow, I think to be by much the more natural. Whatever a man's wishes may be for the success of an enterprize not yet his own, his fears are likely to be still stronger. That same pretty generally implanted principle of vanity and self-conceit, which disposes most of us to over-value each of us his own conceptions, disposes us, in a proportional degree, to under-value those of other men. (Bentham [1787] 1952, 181)

To further corroborate this reading of Smith, Bentham is explicit in the need to relate the usury problem to the lottery problem, where Smith openly presents his theory of systematic bias. And, while Bentham also recognizes the "lottery problem" in projects, he disagrees with Smith on the consequences. Bentham, unlike Smith, sees the "invention-lottery" not as what today we would call a negative externality but as, in today's words, a positive externality.

> Consider, Sir, that it is not with the invention-lottery (that great branch of the project-lottery, for the sake of which I am defending the whole, and must continue so to do until you or somebody else can shew me how to defend it on better terms). It is not I say with the invention-lottery, as with the mine lottery, the privateering-lottery, and so many other lotteries, which you speak of, and in no instance, I think, very much to their advantage. In these lines, success does not, as in this, arise out of embers of ill success, and thence propagate itself, by a happy contagion, perhaps to all eternity. ([1787] 1952, 182)

The problem of negative externality related to lotteries is picked up by David Levy (1987, 388), who, commenting on Smith's problem with gambling due to misperception, says, "So what? People, in the eyes of moralists of all parties, have always appeared foolish. If people are willing to pay for the pleasure of gambling or they fail to compute the correct odds of the gamble, aren't they bearing the consequences themselves? In Smith's account, this they are not. When investors gamble, they bet society's resources."

Actually, by betting society's resources, as Joseph Jadlow (1977) shows, they are also preventing others from making productive and safer investments. But while Jadlow and Levy claim different risk preferences, Smith claims that since we are not calculating with "true" values we can, without realizing it, create externalities because we may be maximizing our utility and at the same time turning our bill to someone else.

It is important to notice that Smith is aware of the difficulties of picking the "correct" legal ceiling. It is a difficult task for everybody, including government officials (WN II.iv.14).

Smith seems willing to impose an interest rate by law, incurring the risk that the interest imposed is not the correct one, because individual virtue and social virtue are interdependent. When individuals are virtuous, society, as a reflection, is virtuous as well. When society is governed by *mediocres* virtuous rules, individuals have more incentive to be virtuous. In other words, since laws are general rules, laws are required because the way to overcome systematic biases, at the individual as well as at the social level, is to rely on general (moral) rules.

To see the importance of general moral rules in dealing with systematic biases we have to rely, again, on the base of *The Wealth of Nations,* which is to say, on *The Theory of Moral Sentiments.*

This is what Smith has to say about "the nature of self-deceit, and of the origin and use of general rules" (TMS III.iv).

> There are two different occasions upon which we examine our own conduct, and endeavour to view it in the light in which the impartial spectator would view it: first, when we are about to act; and secondly, after we have acted. Our views are apt to be very partial in both cases; but they are apt to be most partial when it is of most importance that they should be otherwise. (III.iv.2)

Smith therefore claims that we judge our actions in a biased fashion, both before and after the action, since "every thing appears magnified and misrepresented by self-love" (TMS III.4.3). Indeed, "it is so disagreeable to think ill of ourselves, that we often purposely turn away our view from those circumstances which might render that judgment unfavourable" (III.4.4).

These biases have disastrous consequences, especially because they undermine social harmony. The way to maintain the "proper and just order," which is to say the way to maintain the virtuous order of society, is to follow "general rules." These general rules are moral and help the moral development of the individual as well as the orderly life of society.

> This self-deceit, this fatal weakness of mankind, is the source of half the disorders of human life. . . .
>
> Nature, however, has not left this weakness, which is of so much importance, altogether without a remedy; nor has she abandoned us entirely to the delusions of self-love. Our continual observations upon the conduct of others, insensibly lead us to form to ourselves certain general rules concerning what is fit and proper either to be done or to be avoided. . . .
>
> It is thus that the general rules of morality are formed. . . .
>
> Those general rules of conduct, when they have been fixed in our mind by habitual reection, are of great use in correcting the misrepresentations of self-love concerning what is fit and proper to be done in our particular situation. (TMS III.iv.6–8, 12)

As mentioned earlier, in the ancien régime the individual and society are strictly interrelated. The virtues or the vices of the individual are reflected in, and are a reflection of, the virtues and vices of his society.[12] The rules for individual virtue are the rules for a good social order. And *in medio stat virtus* ("virtue is in the middle," which is to say, *medietas*) is one of the most general rules to reach virtue and social harmony.

Smith's favor for usury laws and the free market are consistent with each other when we consider "stay in the just middle" as the most general rule to follow in order to achieve individual virtue as well as social harmony. Markets are, most of the time, able to achieve *medietas* without any external help. Interest rates instead are not able to achieve such results. Individuals are unfortunately but inevitably characterized by systematic perception biases. They systematically tend to overestimate the probability of winning in the "project-lottery." By leaving the situation unregulated, extremely high usury rates would arise. The traditional solution to this usury problem was extreme also: abolish the interest rate in toto. Therefore, we would fall in one of either two opposite extremes, both dangerous. One extreme would be usury, the deleterious effect of which would lead to adverse selection, as shown earlier. The second extreme would be the abolition of the interest rate, which brings consequences as deleterious as its opposite extreme.

Moral philosophy teaches us that the dangers of extremes can be overcome by following a general virtuous rule, which would lead to the "just and proper order": avoid the extremes, stay in the middle. In the case of the interest rate, the middle position would be a moderately positive rate of interest. Indeed, Smith proposes a legal maximum interest rate slightly above the market rate, which is more than zero and less than the usury levels. The rate should be "legal" because our systematic mistakes of perception would lead us to slide toward the upper extreme.

Reaching Smith's Position on Usury from Modern Mainstream Analysis

Part of modern economics is unable to reconcile Smith's justifications for usury laws with other positions held by him. This inability stems from the fact that modern economists insist on using their own instruments rather than Smith's. When modern economists attempt to see the consistency in Smith by analyzing his conclusions, they end up using faulty reasoning; when they attempt to see the consistency by focusing on his analysis, they fail to reach the same conclusion as Smith.

I view at least three major ways of analyzing the consistency of

12. Bernard Mandeville distances himself from this position in a revolutionary fashion by contrasting individual and social vices and virtues. Not by chance, Smith attacks and criticizes Mandeville openly and at length in TMS VII.ii.4.

Smith on usury laws in today's literature. One path of analysis, even if not necessarily following Smith's analysis, agrees with or justifies Smith's support for usury laws (what I call the Keynes-like interpretation). Another modern line of thought follows Smith's analysis closely but reaches opposite policy conclusions (what I call the Stiglitz and Weiss–like interpretation). In order to maintain my argument within tractable limits, I will present only a couple of scholars who can be located in each interpretative framework. The third line of analysis feeds on Das Adam Smith Problem and cannot make any sense of Smith's position on usury, accusing Smith of radical inconsistency or superficial analysis (see, e.g., Robbins 1968; and Stigler 1975). Given my interpretation of Smith, Das Adam Smith Problem does not arise. I will therefore dismiss this failed attempt to understand Smith, and, to avoid redundancy, I will not comment on it.

The Keynes-Like Interpretation

In what I call the Keynes-like interpretation, I bundle together scholars who are not necessarily Keynesian but who interpret Smith's support of usury laws in terms of growth, similar to Keynes. I consider three examples of analysis within this framework. In the first example, Smith's support for usury laws is seen as a way to encourage investment in low-risk sectors of the economy, stimulating growth. The second example answers Bentham's criticism that usury laws impede the financing of entrepreneurial activities, retarding innovation and growth. In the third example, usury laws are viewed as a weapon against rent seeking, which otherwise would bring a country to stagnation. For each of these examples, the modern argument is presented first, followed by some of the reasons why that argument fails to find consistency in Smith's thought.

I call this line of interpretation Keynes-like because Keynes aligns himself on Smith's side of the barricade, supporting usury laws.

Keynes ([1936] 1997, 351) wrote, "The rate of interest is not self-adjusting at a level best suited to the social advantage but constantly tends to rise too high, so that a wise Government is concerned to curb it by statute and custom and even by invoking the sanction of the moral law." Keynes favors usury laws because he thinks that they will stimulate economic growth by increasing investment. Income would increase as a consequence of the increased investment. But it has been noticed that Keynes does not offer any further specification (Blitz and Long 1965).

A first example of reasoning in the Keynes-like framework is by Levy (1987). Levy believes Smith favors usury laws because usury laws will discourage investment in risky sectors of the economy, like international trade, and will encourage investment in the safer sectors instead, such as agriculture. According to Levy, for Smith usury laws promote economic growth and therefore should be supported.[13] But Levy's reading raises at least three problems, the most serious of which is that Smith's support for free trade becomes an unexplainable counterexample.

First of all, although Levy interprets Smith as saying that agriculture is the key to growth and that agriculture should be preferred to foreign trade, he also sees Smith as putting strong limitations on this statement. Levy noted that Smith also said agriculture is only the first stage of economic development. Indeed, developed countries increasingly depend on industry, specialization, and trade. But if usury laws are useful because they support agriculture, and if agriculture is only the first stage of economic development, the implication would be that usury laws should be enforced only during the early stages of the economic development of a country. When a country reaches more advanced stages of economic development, the laws should be abolished. But this is not what Smith said. Second, in order to accept Levy's argument, it has to be proven that savings generated in the safe agricultural sector will move to the riskier foreign trade. If instead in rural society savings tend to be reinvested in agriculture (Blitz and Long 1965), usury laws would be useless because they would prevent a transfer of resources (from agriculture to foreign trade) that would never take place anyway. Finally, arguing that for Smith economic growth heavily depends on domestic agriculture would leave unexplained why Smith champions free trade. So, for instance, following Levy's reasoning, Smith's vigorous support of anti-corn laws, which favor international trade over domestic agriculture, would be left unexplained. A modern reading of Smith's support of usury laws such as Levy's, therefore, does not solve the puzzle of how Smith could support usury laws and the free market at the same time.

A second example of reading Smith on usury laws in the Keynes-like framework is Samuel Hollander (1999). Hollander explains why Bentham's criticisms of Smith's position on usury laws may be inappropriate, but he does not offer a solid explanation of why Smith favors such laws nor of why Smith proposes the specific maximum legal rate for England that he does.

Hollander's analysis of the debate (or the lack thereof) between Ben-

13. "Usury laws, in Smith's opinion, can benefit society by reducing the riskiness of society's investments. . . . By investing more in agriculture than in foreign trade, there is a net product which benefits society, but not necessarily the individual making the decision" (Levy 1987, 397). And: "The second determinant of growth is the composition of this productive labor: countries which employ more agricultural labor will grow most rapidly" (393).

tham and Smith is a defense of Smith against Bentham. Bentham worried that Smith, proposing usury laws, would strangle innovation, investment, and growth. But, explains Hollander, within-family lending and equity financing were the most common way of bankrolling "innovations" during Smith's time; therefore, in practice, usury laws would not deter investment, development, and growth, showing that Bentham's criticisms of Smith are inaccurate.[14] But were this the case we would be left without an explanation for why Smith proposes laws against usury since usury laws would block an interest rate for a loan that, in practice, is not requested. Moreover, Hollander himself recognizes that his reading of Smith faces another problem. If Smith's favor for usury laws is justified on practical grounds, the legal rate Smith picked as an example for England is inexplicable. Smith uses an interest rate that was below the market rate, rather than "slightly above," well before the last edition of *The Wealth of Nations.* Hollander cannot justify why Smith, having the time and the opportunity, did not revise the rate upward. On the other hand, when Smith's enterprise is analyzed in terms of a (moral) theoretical framework, rather than on a practical base, the attention is concentrated on the general principle: follow a general rule, legal when necessary, that keeps things in the "just middle" so that individual virtue and social harmony are achieved and preserved. The exact "practical" rate becomes, therefore, irrelevant.

Finally, let us analyze a third example of the Keynes-like interpretation of Smith's reasoning for supporting usury laws. In this reading, rent seeking is considered the key for interpreting Smith on usury laws.[15] Usury rates are viewed as the result of rent-seeking activities of the rich. But reading Smith as proposing usury laws against the deleterious rent-seeking self-interest "of the rich" raises at least three new problems. First, Smith seems to have forgotten the distinction he previously made between lenders (savers) and merchants; second, he would have made, simultaneously, opposite assumptions on the saving propensity of human beings; and, finally, he would have proposed policies difficult to sustain given his premises.

According to this view, Smith, like Keynes after him, believed that interest rates were kept artificially high by restrictions in the financial capital market and/or in its access. High interest rates are usually found in the absence of abundant capital, and, vice versa, low interest rates are present where there is abundant capital (WN I.ix.20, II.iv.8, among the

14. "Smith might, therefore, have defended himself against Bentham's charges by insisting that, *in practice,* his support of the usury laws did not imply that investment—innovatory or otherwise—would be starved of funding" (Hollander 1999, 537).

15. I am indebted to an anonymous referee for considering this point of view.

references). But market forces are not always free to work. Human intervention, via the power of legislation, can interfere and change the market results: "A defect in the law may sometimes raise the rate of interest considerably above what the condition of the country, as to wealth or poverty would require" (I.ix.16).

The law is "defective," it is argued, because it is molded by the selfish demands of the rich. The rich, owning capital, want to maximize their returns, and they achieve this goal by asking for government protection so that they can restrict the quantity of capital in the market and seek higher rents. China is mentioned as a country in which there are "laws and institutions . . . [that] establish the monopoly of the rich" and where, as a consequence, the interest rate is "large" (WN I.ix.15).

Furthermore, Smith aggressively attacks attempts to form cartels or monopolies, attempts that are motivated by the voracity for profits of "merchants," "master manufacturers," and "dealers."

> The interest of this third order [of those who live by profit], therefore, has not the same connection with the general interest of the society as that of the other two [of those who live by wages from labor and of those who live off of rent from land]. Merchants and master manufacturers are, in this order, the two classes of people who commonly employ the largest capitals. . . . [They know their interest very well.] The interest of the dealers . . . in any particular branch of trade or manufactures, is always in some respects different from, and even opposite to, that of the publick. (WN I.xi., p.10)

In this interpretative framework, Smith is claimed to propose usury laws to limit social abuses caused by these attempts at monopoly/cartel by those who live by profit.

The pillar of this line of argument is that lenders form a socially deleterious, rent-seeking interest group. But this interpretation cannot account for previous claims of Smith regarding the identity of the lenders and their role in society. Indeed, arguing that the achievement of the lenders' interest is in conflict with the social interest implies, as shown earlier, that lenders, owning capital, are among those people who live by profit, the target of Smith's attacks. But the group of people that Smith attacks is composed only of merchants, master manufacturers, and dealers, as Smith specifies. Lenders are not part of this potentially dangerous group. Lenders are indeed part of a different category of people—the "monied interest"—which differs from the "trading and manufacturing interest" since merchants, master manufacturers, and dealers do not lend their capital but rather they *employ their own capital.* "As such capitals are commonly lent out and paid back in money, they constitute what is called the *monied interest. It is distinct, not only from the landed, but from the trading and manufacturing interests,* as in these last the owners themselves employ their own capitals" (WN II.iv.5, emphasis added).

Indeed, according to Smith, lenders are savers (WN II.iii.4, 13), and savers of capital are a different group of people from the one that employs or consumes capital.[16] And Smith lauds the "frugal man" who saves (II.iii.19).[17] Lenders, being savers, are not an interest group that harms society. On the contrary, lenders benefit society.

A second set of difficulties occurs following this Keynes-like interpretation of Smith's usury laws. Reading lenders as able to control access to capital in the market, as proposed earlier, forming what today we call a cartel, fails to consider how lenders would hold their cartel in place over time. The rent-seeking cartel of lenders could stick together either through no capital growth or through preventing the increasing capital from affecting interest rates. But both of these solutions are implausible. In Smith's framework, indeed, the driving force of capital accumulation is saving.[18] The absence of capital growth, therefore, can be achieved by assuming that everybody is prodigal, that is, by assuming that there is no parsimony. If nobody saves, capital cannot grow. But Smith denies this option.[19] Alternatively, consider what happens when the assumption of a zero savings rate does not hold. Lenders, driven by their self-interest, lend to make money. Lenders therefore invest in profitable enterprises (WN II.iv.2). The profitable businesses will generate new capital. Part of the new capital will be reinvested in the same activity, and part will be saved and lent/invested in a different, new profitable activity (II.iii.4, II.iii.15). With parsimony, therefore, the total quantity of capital increases. By increasing the quantity of capital, interest rates will spontaneously decrease (e.g., II.iv.8). If there is downward pressure on interest rates due to the financing of successful enterprises and a positive savings rate, and if the lenders are a cartel, the cartel is

16. "What is annually saved is as regularly consumed as what is annually spent, and nearly in the same time too; but *it is consumed by a different set of people*"(WN II.iii.18, emphasis added).

17. Smith reproves instead the prodigal man who "tends not only to beggar himself, but to impoverish his country" (ibid., II.iii.20).

18. "Parsimony, and not industry, is the immediate cause of the increase of capital. Industry, indeed, provides the subject which parsimony accumulates. But whatever industry might acquire, if parsimony did not save and store up, the capital would never be the greater" (ibid., II.iii.16).

19. "But the principle which prompts to save, is the desire of bettering our condition, a desire which, though generally calm and dispassionate, comes with us from the womb, and never leaves us till we go into the grave" (ibid., II.iii.28).

subject to competitive pressures that may lead to its disintegration. But if lenders are self-interested rent seekers, as assumed earlier, they can ask for and achieve protective laws. The logical prediction derived from this reasoning would be that the lenders ask for a price floor to prevent the interest rate from decreasing. This, though, is unheard of.

Furthermore, granting some credit to the possibility of adverse selection as presented by Smith (WN II.iv.15), we face the problem of a group of lenders artificially holding up interest rates but only to finance risky projects with a low probability of being repaid. This seems to contradict the idea that the "third order" (those who live by profit) knows its interest (I.xi., p. 10).

Finally, the conclusion of this variant of the Keynes-like interpretation is that the source of the problem is "bad laws," as in China. The government, which gave in to the flattery "of the rich," is the source of the "bad laws" that generated usury rates. Were the "rent-seeking interpretation" of usury laws correct, the government would be left with no apparent good reason to accept the implementation of usury laws because the powerful rich would seek to maintain their protection rather than accept their dismantling. Moreover, assuming it were true that usury rates are caused by rent-seeking laws and ignoring the objection put forward earlier, Smith would have avoided many predictable problems by proposing to abolish those laws rather than adventuring into such muddy territory (as recognized by Smith himself in WN II.iv.14) as fixing interest rate ceilings. Were this "rent-seeking argument" correct, Smith would leave us with new problems regarding his consistency since the government would simultaneously and inexplicably be the source of the problem as well as its solution.

A reading with modern instruments is, once again, more problematic than a reading with old instruments.

The Stiglitz and Weiss-Like Interpretation

The other modern approach to Smith on usury is to try to follow him step-by-step in his analysis of the interest rate ceiling and restate it in more rigorous analytical terms. I call this approach the "Stiglitz and Weiss-like" interpretation because Joseph Stiglitz and Andrew Weiss (1981) were able to model credit rationing in markets with imperfect information in a way that is strikingly similar to Smith's analysis, as Hollander (1999) also recognizes. Stiglitz and Weiss, as well as Smith, show the existence of non-market-clearing equilibrium interest rates because of moral hazard and adverse selection. Moreover, four years before the publication of the renowned article by Stiglitz and Weiss, Joseph Jadlow

(1977) successfully modeled as an externalities problem the analysis that leads Smith to support usury laws.

The problem with this modern line of modeling Smith is that, independent of which model is used, the policy conclusions (of both Stiglitz-Weiss and Jadlow) are diametrically opposed to Smith's. While Smith concludes that there is a positive role for usury laws, the modern analyses lead us to consider usury laws as unnecessary.

Let us go back to Stiglitz and Weiss's analysis, at the base of which there is a market with imperfect information. Not surprisingly, Stiglitz and Weiss consider the problem of imperfect information in a principal-agent framework, where the problem of gathering all the information is a monitoring cost.[20] Stiglitz and Weiss, as modern economists, use modern tools, that is, they assume strict rationality that leads to "perfect" maximization. Stiglitz and Weiss proposed usury laws in the specific case in which the interest rate would be too low to finance a safe project, so banks would pick a higher interest rate, which would instead encourage riskier projects. But under normal conditions there is no need for usury laws because the profit-maximizing bank would never ask usury rates. If Stiglitz and Weiss are correct, their analysis presents two opportunities to reconcile Smith's dilemma. If, in practice, the market interest rate would always be "too low," the bank would be led to pick the too high "risky" rate, therefore making usury laws optimal. Or what is perceived as the maximizing interest rate in reality is not, opening again the door to usury laws.

George Stigler (1988) understood that Smith's answer was the second one; he saw one of the different analytical tools that Smith used but did not accept it. Smith built his system starting from the observation of human behavior and human errors. Stigler started from the assumption that systematic error is impossible. He accused Smith of considering lenders as "foolishly shortsighted." Smith started from the observation that systematic error exists. For Smith, lenders are in fact shortsighted. But being shortsighted does not mean being "foolishly" so. Adam Smith, as a classical moral philosopher, uses ancient tools, that is, he observes "irrational" misperceptions that lead to gross mistakes.

The difference in the possibility of systematic perception error is important. It is this difference that makes many modern economists unable to rationally explain gambling or voting behavior. Not surprisingly, Smith has no problem explaining these irrational behaviors (voting, ac-

20. The nature of the problem is important. Monitoring costs are costs related to vision, the fact that we simply cannot see with our own eyes everything relevant that is occurring. In Smith's framework, the ability to see (literally and figuratively) is generally biased, leading to systematic errors. See also Berkeley's *New Theory of Vision* in Berkeley 1975.

tually, was not explained because it was not an issue in his time). As mentioned earlier, Smith believes that people have systematic misperceptions. Therefore, Smith is not saying that individuals, in our case gamblers as well as borrowers and lenders, are irrational but that they are maximizing with "incorrect" data. If Smith's individual would have had perfect perception, I believe he would have acted exactly like Stiglitz and Weiss's individual, Smith would have reached precisely the same policy conclusions as Stiglitz and Weiss, and Stigler would have been happier with Smith.

In Stiglitz and Weiss's world, human beings perceive perfectly, so a ceiling will generally be self-imposed by the banks themselves. In Smith's world, human beings have biased perceptions, so the ceiling will not appear spontaneously but should be legally imposed in order to preserve social harmony.

A Possible Response by Smith to Modern Economists

The first modern economist who accused Smith of inconsistency because he favored the free market as he simultaneously favored usury laws was Jeremy Bentham ([1787] 1952). Bentham, in my reading, recognized one of the two instruments of analysis that Smith used—perception biases and the systematic errors that follow—but failed to recognize and understand the other—moral philosophy; therefore, his attack against Smith's position.

Siding with Bentham, at least as far as his modern positive (amoral) tools of analysis are concerned, modern literature tries, in vain, to rationalize the relationship (or lack thereof) between Smith and Bentham. Jacob Viner (1965, 18–19) can be considered a representative example:

> A friend of Bentham's, George Wilson, reported to Bentham in a letter of 4 December 1789 that Smith had in conversation with William Adam, another friend of Bentham, spoken respectfully of Bentham and his argument in *The Defense of Usury* and that Smith "seemed to admit that you were right." With only this to go on, Rae states that "Bentham won—what is rarer—his [i.e., Smith's] conversion from the doctrines impugned." Professor W. Stark has recently published the draft of a letter Bentham wrote to Smith either late in 1789 or early in 1790 in which Bentham reports that he has heard of an apparent acceptance by Smith of Bentham's position and asks for permission to make

> public Smith's conversion to Bentham's position. Smith died on 17 July 1790. Bentham received no reply to his letter, but there reached him at the same time as news of Smith's death "a present" from Smith in the form, according to Stark, of a presentation copy of *The Wealth of Nations.* [At this point Viner has a footnote: See W. Stark, *Jeremy Bentham's Economic Writings,* London, 1952, I, 26–27, 189–90.] It seems more likely that it was either a copy of *The Theory of Moral Sentiments* only, or copies of both *The Theory of Moral Sentiments* and *The Wealth of Nations,* which Smith sent to Bentham in 1790. A fifth edition of *The Wealth of Nations* was published in 1789. A sixth edition of *The Theory of Moral Sentiments* was published in 1790, shortly before Smith's death. Bonar reports that University College, London, has Bentham's presentation copy of the sixth edtion of *The Theory of Moral Sentiments.* (*A Catalogue of the Library of Adam Smith,* 2d ed., London, 1932, Introduction, p. xxxiii, and pp. 201–203). John Bowring, Bentham's editor, states that Bentham "received a copy of Smith's *works* which had been sent to him as a token of esteem." (*The Works of Jeremy Bentham,* John Bowring ed., Edinburgh, 1838 ff., III, 52, italics mine). From the information available all that can be safely inferred is that Smith bore Bentham no ill will for his criticism and possibly did not deny that it had some force.

Smith's 1790 silence is seen as a possible implicit acceptance of Bentham's position, notwithstanding that even in the 1789 edition of *The Wealth of Nations* Smith does not change his favorable attitude toward usury laws. Now, consider that on his deathbed Smith asked that all his unpublished manuscripts be burned, fearing that imprecisions would lead to misunderstanding of his thoughts (West 1976). But some modern readers claim that Smith believed he had erred with respect to usury laws and left that error in place, although he had three years in which to correct himself. According to modern analysis, Smith not only was inconsistent in his thought but reinforced his inconsistency by also acting inconsistently.

If we instead consider *The Theory of Moral Sentiments* as the key to understanding Smith's consistency, Smith answered Bentham (standing in for all the future economists who analyze Smith with modern tools) by sending him the last edition of his two volumes: *The Wealth of Nations* is unchanged on the usury laws regardless of many criticisms; read *The Theory of Moral Sentiments* to understand why.

Conclusion

Viewing Adam Smith as inconsistent because he promoted the free market and usury laws at the same time can be the result of analyzing his work with inappropriate instruments. Adam Smith's view of usury laws may represent the verbalization and systematization of centuries of experience and observation that some modern economists tend to forget. Indeed, inappropriate instruments of analysis leave behind an author's contextual knowledge and therefore the possibility of fully understanding his work. When, instead, Smith's contextual knowledge is taken into account, different interpretative instruments emerge. I propose to see Smith's political economy as Smith saw it, namely, as a branch of moral philosophy. If this is the case, two interpretative instruments—virtue in the form of *medietas* and systematic perception errors—expose the original logic of Smith's work and its consistency: the free market and legally controlled interest rates are both ways to follow the general moral rule *in medio stat virtus* and to maintain an orderly good society.

Bibliography

Aristotle. 1983. *Physics: Books III and IV.* New York: Oxford University Press.

Bentham, Jeremy. [1787] 1952. *Defence of Usury.* In *Jeremy Bentham's Economic Writings,* Vol. I, edited by W. Stark. George Allen and Unwin.

Berkeley, George. 1975. *Philosophical Works, Including the Works on Vision.* London: Dent.

Bittermann, Henry J. 1940a. "Adam Smith's Empiricism and the Law of Nature I." *Journal of Political Economy* 48, no. 4: 487–520.

Bittermann, Henry J. 1940b. "Adam Smith's Empiricism and the Law of Nature II." *Journal of Political Economy* 48, no. 5: 703–34.

Blaug, Mark. 2001. "No History of Ideas, Please, We're Economists." *Journal of Economic Perspectives* 15, no. 1:145–64.

Blitz, Rudolph, and Millard Long. 1965. "The Economics of Usury Regulation." *Journal of Political Economy* 73, no. 6: 608–19.

Bonar, James. 1932. *A Catalogue of the Library of Adam Smith.* 2d ed. London: Macmillan.

Continisio, Chiara. 1994. "La Politica Aristotelica: un Modello per la Convivenza Ordinata nella Trattatistica Politica Italiana dell'Antico Regime." *Cheiron, Saperi politici e forma del vivere nell'Europa d'Antico Regime* 22:149–65.

Evensky, Jerry. 1998. "Adam Smith's Moral Philosophy: The Role of Religion and Its Relationship to Philosophy and Ethics in the Evolution of Society." *History of Political Economy* 30, no. 1: 17–42.

Evensky, Jerry. 2001. "Adam Smith's Lost Legacy." *Southern Economic Journal* 67, no. 3: 497–517.

Frigo, Daniela. 1995. "Amministrazione Domestica e Prudenza 'Oeconomica': Alcune Riflessioni sul Sapere Politico di Antico Regime. *Annali di Storia Moderna e Contemporanea* 1:29–49.

Griswold, Charles. 1999. *Adam Smith and the Virtues of Enlightenment.* Cambridge: Cambridge University Press.

Hollander, Samuel. 1999. "Jeremy Bentham and Adam Smith on the Usury Laws: A 'Smithian' Reply to Bentham and a New Problem." *European Journal of the History of Economic Thought* 6, no. 4: 523–51.

Jadlow, Joseph. 1977. "Adam Smith on Usury Laws." *Journal of Finance* 32, no. 4: 1195–1200.

Kahneman, Daniel, Paul Slovic, and Amos Tversky. 1982. *Judgment under Uncertainty: Heuristics and Biases.* Cambridge: Cambridge University Press.

Kahneman, Daniel, and Amos Tversky. 1979. "Prospect Theory: An Analysis of Decision under Risk." *Econometrica* 47, no. 2: 263–91.

Keynes, John Maynard. [1936] 1997. *The General Theory of Employment, Interest, and Money.* New York: Prometheus.

Levy, David M. 1987. "Adam Smith's Case for Usury Laws." *History of Political Economy* 19, no. 3: 387–400.

Levy, David M. 1992. "Bishop Berkeley Exorcises the Infinite: Fuzzy Consequences of Strict Finitism." *Hume Studies* 18:511–36.

Levy, David M. 1995. "The Partial Spectator in the *Wealth of Nations:* A Robust Utilitarianism." *European Journal of the History of Economic Thought* 2, no. 2: 299–326.

Nelson, Benjamin. 1969. *The Idea of Usury: from Tribal Brotherhood to Universal Otherhood.* Chicago: University of Chicago Press.

Paganelli, Maria Pia. 2000. "Adam Smith: il Primo o l'Ultimo?" *Annali di Storia Moderna e Contemporanea* 6:421–34.

Peters-Fransen, Ingrid. 2001. "The Canon in the History of the Adam Smith Problem." In *Reflections on the Classical Canon in Economics,* edited by Evelyn L. Forget and Sandra Peart. London: Routledge.

Plato. 1972. *Philebus.* Cambridge: Cambridge University Press.

Robbins, Lionel. 1968. *The Theory of Economic Development in the History of Economic Thought.* London: Macmillan.

Smith, Adam. [1776] 1981. *An Inquiry into the Nature and Causes of the Wealth of Nations.* Indianapolis: Liberty Fund.

Smith, Adam. [1759] 1984. *The Theory of Moral Sentiments.* Indianapolis: Liberty Fund.

Stigler, George J. 1975. *The Citizen and the State: Essays on Regulation.* Chicago: University of Chicago Press.

Stigler, George J. 1988. *Memoirs of an Unregulated Economist.* New York: Basic Books.

Stiglitz, Joseph E., and Andrew Weiss. 1981. "Credit Rationing in Markets with Imperfect Information." *American Economic Review* 71, no. 3: 393–410.

Tribe, Keith. 1999. "Adam Smith: Critical Theorist?" *Journal of Economic Literature* 37, no. 2: 609–32.

Viner, Jacob. 1965. *Guide to John Rae's Life of Adam Smith.* New York: Kelley.

Viner, Jacob. 1991. *Essays on the Intellectual History of Economics.* Princeton: Princeton University Press.

West, Edwin. 1976. *Adam Smith: The Man and His Works.* Indianapolis: Liberty Press.

Young, Jeffrey T. 1997. *Economics as a Moral Science: The Political Economy of Adam Smith.* Lyme, N.H.: Edward Elgar.

10 • The Measure of Real Price

Adam Smith's Science of Equity

Eric Schliesser

THE professed object of Dr Adam Smith's inquiry is the nature and causes of the wealth of nations. There is another inquiry, however, perhaps still more interesting, which he occasionally mixes with it; I mean an inquiry into the causes which affect the happiness of nations or the happiness and comfort of the lower orders of society, which is the most numerous class in every nation.

—T. R. Malthus, *An Essay on the Principle of Population* (1798)

In this chapter I offer a new argument regarding the egalitarian nature of Adam's Smith's economics: even the analytic core of the *Wealth of Nations* (hereafter WN) shows that Adam Smith's book is aimed at aiding the large number of working poor.[1] It has been argued that Adam Smith introduced his technical notion, "real price" (WN I.v, especially, I.v.22, 56), to measure welfare. I build on this to show that this measure is especially appropriate to capture living standards of the working poor. This is revealed through a new analysis of Smith's measure of the measure. Along the way, some common confusion about real price is removed. The argument of this chapter thus offers important independent line of support for the interpretive positions developed in recent years by David Levy, Spencer Pack, Emma Rothschild, and Samuel Fleischacker.[2] As the epigraph that opens this chapter shows, this re-

David M. Levy called my attention to the remarks in the opening epigraph, Levy 1995. Cf. Rothschild 2001, 89: "There is a 'double nature' or 'twofold character' of Smith's work, [Beatrice] Webb wrote, in which he is both a theorist who seeks to discover (and put to practical use) the laws of production, and at the same time a 'reformer' of social abuses."

1. For more on nature of Smith's science, see Berry 2007; Montes 2004, chap. 5; or Schliesser 2005a and 2005b and Schliesser 2006a and 2006b.

2. Levy (1995) first made me take seriously my hunch that Smith was not interested in mere aggregate happiness. I must thank Mark Blaug for calling my attention to Pack 1991. Pack's book is curiously ignored in the scholarly literature on Adam Smith's politics (e.g., Rothschild 2001; and Fleischacker 1999, 2004) but deserves wider recognition. For an argument that Smith excluded redistribution, see Hont and

captures the original reception of Smith, which also includes the admiration for Smith by Mary Wollstonecraft and Sophie de Grouchy de Condorcet.

In his discussion of exchange value, Smith draws important distinctions: the difference between "natural" and nominal or market prices; and the difference between absolute, or "real," and nominal/market prices. (This list is not exhaustive.) Elsewhere I scrutinize the former distinction.[3] In what follows, I explore Smith's distinction between real and nominal prices.

Let me provide a simple modern example to illuminate what the distinction is driving at. When somebody's paycheck increases by 5 percent we call that a nominal increase. But we need the inflation number, say, 3 percent, before we can judge the real increase of the salary, which is a little under 2 percent. For Smith, the nominal price of the wage earner is the number on the check, or, as he says, "the quantity of money," whereas the real price is constituted by the "necessaries and conveniencies of life which are given [in return] for" this quantity of money (WN I.v.9, 51) or, to put it differently, the labor "commanded" or "purchased" (I.v.19, 55).

Two initial points need to be made here. First, the nominal price of things can only be measured at any given time: "[A]t the same time and place, therefore, money is the *exact measure* of the real exchangeable value of all commodities. It is so, however, at the same time and place only" (WN I.v.19, 55, emphasis added). There is, thus, no relevant distinction between real and nominal prices at a single location in time. That is, for most practical purposes—"the business of common life" (I.v.4)—and in the absence of hyperinflation, nominal prices are all that matter; the price mechanism provides merchants and laborers with the information they need (I.v.20, 55).

Second, in my wage earner example, I assume some familiarity with the notion of purchasing power. As Smith writes, "The power which that possession immediately and directly conveys to him, is the power of purchasing; a certain command over all the labour, or over all the produce of labour which is then in the market" (WN I.v.3, 48). The ability to command labor is not obviously the same as purchasing power; in contemporary thought this involves a weighted basket of goods. As others have shown, Smith introduces real prices in order to measure some-

Ignatieff 1983, 24; or Griswold 1998, 250. See Fleischacker 2004 (chap. 10) where these objections are refuted. For a recent, sophisticated interpretation of Smith that does not accept the revisionist approach, see Otteson 2002. I criticize Otteson in Schliesser 2003 and Schliesser 2006b.

3. See Schliesser 2005a.

thing akin to what we would call welfare.[4] Smith clearly feels that work, or labor, can be irksome and that everybody wants to save "toil and trouble" (I.v.2, 47) and command other people's labor (embodied in their products and services).[5] He goes on to claim that "Labour . . . never varying in its own value, is alone the ultimate and real standard by which the value of all commodities can at all times and places be estimated and compared" (I.v.7, 51). For present purposes, the importance of this quote is to illustrate why Smith *cares* about an ultimate and "real" standard. Before I get to that, I must note two issues. First, there is confusion stemming from this quote. The word *labor* can be (and is) interpreted in two ways: (1) as a number of man-hours; and (2) (to use modern terminology) as units of disutility, that is, the psychological and social cost of work to the individual, the "toil and trouble" mentioned before. If all work has the same character, that is, if man-hours and units of disutility are somehow related, then these two interpretations coincide (as Smith thinks they do in a hunting economy). Many commentators note that Smith switches between different types of economies in WN I.v.[6]

Moreover, the phrase "real price" has often served as encouragement to emphasize the ontological aspects of Smith's approach—labor as an ultimate and real standard of value. Many readers forget, however, that Smith *only* introduces a notion of a real price as a *measure* of "value in exchange" (WN I.iv.15, 15), which he distinguishes from "value in use" (I.iv.13–18, 44–46). Whatever else the distinction between "value in use" and "value in exchange" is supposed to do for Smith, there can be no doubt that he thinks *any* given commodity can have at least two kinds of values, use and exchange. Real prices measure only *one* kind of value: exchange. Moreover, Smith indicates not only that he knows quite well that some jobs are more enjoyable than others (even if they require the same amount of labor) but also that the value we put on the same job necessarily varies from one society to another or even within a society depending on one's social rank (e.g., I.x.b.2–3, 117–18). So, for

4. See Blaug [1954] 1986; and Hollander 1973. O'Donnell (1990, 64–65) claims it was effectively a measure of productivity. (But even a measure of productivity could be a proxy for measuring welfare). Baroni (2004) offers strong arguments against reading the language of modern subjective utility theory into Smith. For the purposes of my argument, I can remain agnostic as to what degree welfare is subjective or objective in Smith.

5. For Smith people naturally want to save labor, while in "Of Interest" Hume ([1777] 1985) thinks "there is no craving or demand of the human mind more constant and insatiable than that for exercize and employment" (200).

6. See O'Donnell 1990, 63ff. and 236n1, for further references.

Smith, a real price can never measure some most fundamental entity beyond exchange.[7]

Yet, even if we were to grant that Smith did want to call attention to some ontological element, a focus on ontology misses the purpose: Smith wants to be able to compare purchasing power in different times and places. As he writes, "*In such a work as this,* however, it may sometimes be of use to compare the different real values of a particular commodity at different times and places, or the different degrees of power over labour of other people which it may, upon different occasions, have given to those who possessed it" (I.v.22, 55, emphasis added). The idea of a real price seems to be absent from Smith's *Lectures on Jurisprudence.* It appears to be a conceptual innovation designed for WN.[8]

Here I have not done full justice to the intricacies of Smith's exposition.[9] But let us assume, for the sake of argument, that a criterion of welfare has been established. The question remains, whose welfare is to be measured?[10] To get a grip on that we need to analyze the method of measurement that Smith advocates; this reveals his purpose.

If one wants to compare the wealth of different locales at the same time or people's welfare at different times, one cannot simply compare the nominal (money) prices of goods. The value of gold and silver is not invariant across time and not even across place.[11] In a complex commercial society it is impossible to calculate real prices directly without solid data for "the current prices of labour at distant times and places can scarce ever be known with any degrees of exactness" (WN I.v.22, 55). The nominal wages of labor are uninformative if we do not know what they buy. Even if one thinks that one ought to measure the "toil and

7. Cf. Fleischacker 2004, 129. I am not using *ontological* in an anachronistic way. The *Oxford English Dictionary* lists Smith as one of the first to use *ontology* in English in the modern sense (the sense of science treating the qualities and attributes common to metaphysics and physics); see WN V.i.f.29, 771.

8. Fleischacker (ibid., 131) argues quite rightly that an important reason for Smith to wish to measure welfare is to rebut the mercantilist case regarding the relationship between the discovery of gold and silver and the growth of wealth in Europe.

9. See ibid., 123–31, for a useful introduction.

10. Of course, a fuller discussion must distinguish between a measure of (1) general purchasing power, (2) the purchasing power of individual commodities or incomes, and (3) a price index to measure welfare. But that is beyond the scope of the argument of this chapter. See O'Donnell 1990, 73ff., for criticism.

11. See also Turgot [1770] 1889, §XLVI. One would think, as Turgot claims, that in a global economy at any given time (at least in the long run) gold would have the same value everywhere. But Smith shows that the transportation costs of shipping gold and silver would have to be very low and there needs to be trade between the different areas for that to be true. In Smith's time there were, in effect, despite the existence of a single international currency (specie), different regional, relatively autonomous, monetary zones: Europe, the Americas, India, China, and the East Indies (WN I.v.20, 55; I.xi.g.25–28, 220–25).

trouble" of work, how does one go about doing this across many centuries? Smith chose the price of corn (the eighteenth-century word for edible seeds) as a second-best way of measuring the real price of things.[12]

> Those [prices] of corn, though they have in few places been regularly recorded are in general better known and have been more frequently taken notice of by historians and other writers. We must generally, therefore, content ourselves with them, not as being always exactly in the same proportion as the current prices of labour, but as being the nearest approximation which can commonly be had to that proportion. (I.v.22, 56)

Smith chose corn for four reasons. First, relatively reliable and long-running data were available to him (see the earlier quote), especially because rents were often paid in corn. Smith discusses the quality and sources of these data in WN I.xi.e.16–38, 200–210. Smith's long "Digression concerning the Variations in the Value of Silver during the Course of the Four Last Centuries" at the end of book I (pp. 195–267) exploits that possibility with a careful analysis of data covering more than five hundred years. Smith's data start in 1205, although he also uses ancient sources going back to Roman times. Second, although there are many short-term fluctuations in the price of corn (due to fluctuations in harvests and political conditions), its long-run prices are relatively stable due to near constant cost of production (I.xi.e.28, 206; I.v.16–17, 53–54).[13] There are many complications. For example, because the price of corn is tabulated in nominal prices Smith needs to figure out how to compare coinages of different periods. This is not an exact science, and Smith returns to it throughout WN (e.g., I.iv.9–10, 41–44; I.xi.e–i, 195–234). Also, when a society moves from one technological stage of development to another, the corn wage may change (I.v.15, 53). Third, Smith thought that "the desire of food is limited in every man by the narrow capacity of the human stomach." He probably thought that demand for bread would not increase very much with an increase in a standard of living. He specifically contrasts the limited demand for corn with demand for "the conveniences and ornaments of building, dress, equipage, and household furniture, seems to have no limit or certain boundary" (I.xi.c.7, 181).

---

12. See Hollander 1973, 129ff., n. 46.

13. This is emphasized by O'Donnell (1990, 67ff.). O'Donnell also points out that Smith had to assume that the corn wage of common labor is relatively constant across long periods of time (WN I.v.15, 53). Smith claims that "even equal quantities of corn will not do . . . exactly."

Fourth, it was a most useful yardstick given his interest in advancing the interests of the working poor in Europe. For, "Corn, besides, or whatever else is the common and favourite vegetable food of the people, constitutes in every civilized country, *the principal part of the subsistence of the labourer*" (WN I.xi.e.29, 206, emphasis added; cf. I.v.15, 53). The price of corn is *only* a useful measure of the purchasing power of the *poor* because it makes up most of their subsistence.[14] However, the price of corn is less significant as such a measure for rich folks for whom the part of the budget devoted to subsistence is insignificant, although Smith thinks that as a basic staple corn will "regulate" the price of all other things (I.xi.b.34–35, 175). Of course, corn is not the staple everywhere. In China, for example, the workers' staple is rice, and in other places it will be potatoes (I.xi.b.36–40, 175–77). Comparing the absolute prices in economies with different staples can only be a qualitative affair. By contrast, in economies with the same staple the price of that staple can be used to compare welfare across time.

In Smith's time, the working poor make up the vast majority of the people.

> Servants, labourers, and workmen of different kinds, make up the far greater part of every great political society. But what improves the circumstances of the greater part can never be regarded as an inconveniency to the whole. No society can surely be flourishing and happy, of which the far greater part of the members are poor and miserable. It is but equity, besides, that they who feed, clothe, and lodge the whole body of the people, should have such a share of the produce of their own labour as to be themselves tolerably well fed, clothed, and lodged. (WN I.viii.36, 96)

Smith's "science" is not value neutral;[15] it is driven by equity.[16] This is made further evident by his appeals to the readers' "humanity" and "reasonableness" (e.g., WN V.ii.e.6, 842; V.ii.e.19; 846; I.viii.36, 96; I.viii.44, 100) or his outrage at the "folly and injustice" of European

14. Thus, "[I]n Europe, corn is the principal produce of land which serves immediately for human food. Except in particular situations, therefore, the rent of corn land regulates in Europe that of all other cultivated land" (WN I.xi.b.35, 175). See also I.xi.l.12, 245; I.xi.b.9, 165; and I.xi.b.14, 16.

15. For a different argument with the same conclusion, see Berry 2006.

16. For a rich discussion of Smith's emphasis on "equity," see Rothschild 2001, 88ff. See Pack and Schliesser 2006 for an account of Smith's analysis of justice.

colonists (vii.b.59, 588).[17] Smith's measure will capture the welfare of most. He does not seem to be bothered that his measure may not capture total welfare. His choice of measure, then, is at once practical and equitable. The measure reveals the purpose behind the concept.

Bibliography

Baroni, Chiara. 2004. "The Road to Virtue: Adam Smith and the Economy of Happiness." Presented at "New Voices on Adam Smith." Fairfax, VA.

Berry, Christopher. 2006. "Smith and Science." In *The Cambridge Companion to Adam Smith,* edited by Knud Haakonssen. Cambridge: Cambridge University Press.

Blaug, Mark. [1954] 1986. "Welfare Indices in the Wealth of Nations." In *Economic History and the History of Economics.* Cheltenham, UK: Edward Elgar.

Fleischacker, Samuel. 1999. *A Third Concept of Liberty: Judgment and Freedom in Kant and Adam Smith.* Princeton: Princeton University Press.

Fleischacker, Samuel. 2004. *Adam Smith's Wealth of Nations: A Philosophical Companion.* Princeton: Princeton University Press.

Griswold, Charles L. 1998. *Adam Smith and the Virtues of Enlightenment.* Cambridge: Cambridge University Press.

Hollander, Samuel. 1973. *The Economics of Adam Smith.* Toronto: University of Toronto Press.

Hont, I., and M. Ignatieff, eds. 1983. *Wealth and Virtue: The Shaping of Political Economy in the Scottish Enlightenment.* Cambridge: Cambridge University Press.

Hume, David, [1777] 1985. *Essays, Moral, Political, and Literary.* Edited by Eugene F. Miller. Rev. ed. Indianapolis: Liberty Fund.

Levy, David M. 1995. "The Partial Spectator in the *Wealth of Nations:* A Robust Utilitarianism." *European Journal of the History of Economic Thought* 2, no. 2: 299–326.

Levy, David M., and Sandra J. Peart. 2004. "Sympathy and Approbation in Hume and Smith: A Solution to the Other Rational Species Problem." *Economics and Philosophy* 20:331–49.

Montes, Leonidas. 2004. *Adam Smith in Context: A Critical Reassessment of Some of Central Components of His Thought.* Houndmills, Basingstoke: Palgrave Macmillan.

O'Donnell, Rory. 1990. *Adam Smith's Theory of Value and Distribution: A Reappraisal.* New York: St. Martin's.

Otteson, James. 2002. *Adam Smith's Marketplace of Life.* Cambridge: Cambridge University Press.

Pack, Spencer J. 1991. *Capitalism as a Moral System: Adam Smith's Critique of the Free Market Economy.* Brookfield, Vt.: Edward Elgar.

Pack, Spencer J., and Eric Schliesser. 2006. "Smith's Human Criticism of Hume's Account of the Origin of Justice." *Journal of the History of Philosophy* 44:47–63.

Rothschild, Emma. 2001. *Economic Sentiments: Adam Smith, Condorcet, and the Enlightenment.* Cambridge: Harvard University Press.

17. On Smith's appeals to "humanity," see Levy and Peart 2004; Schliesser 2005b; and Schliesser 2006b.

Schliesser, Eric. 2003. Review of James Otteson's *Adam Smith's Marketplace of Life. Philosophy in Review* 23 (October): 364–66.

Schliesser, Eric. 2005a. "Some Principles of Adam Smith's 'Newtonian' Methods in the Wealth of Nations." *Research in the History of Economic Thought and Methodology* 23A:35–77.

Schliesser, Eric. 2005b. "Wonder in the Face of Scientific Revolutions: Adam Smith on Newton's 'Proof' of Copernicanism." *British Journal for the History and Philosophy of Science* 13:697–732.

Schliesser, Eric. 2006a. "Adam Smith's Endorsement of Deception," Forthcoming in *Adam Smith Review* 2:209–14.

Schliesser, Eric. 2006b. "Articulating Practices as Reasons: Adam Smith on the Conditions of Possibility of Property." *Adam Smith Review,* Vol. 2.

Smith, Adam. [1776] 1984. *An Inquiry into the Nature and Causes of the Wealth of Nations.* Edited by R. H. Campbell, A. S. Skinner, and W. B. Todd. Indianapolis: Liberty Classics.

Smith, Adam. 1978. *Lectures on Jurisprudence.* Edited by R. L. Meek, D. D. Raphael, and P. G. Stein. Indianapolis: Liberty Classics.

Turgot, A. R. J. [1770] 1889. *Reflections on the Formation and Distribution of Riches.* New York: Macmillan.

PART 3 • The Role of the Expert

11 • Attitudes toward Race, Hierarchy, and Transformation in the Nineteenth Century
The Role of the Expert

Sandra J. Peart and David M. Levy

Introduction

Using the debates between classical political economists and their critics as our lens, this chapter examines the role of the expert in the seemingly simple question of whether we're the same or different.[1] As we noted in chapter 1, at the beginning and throughout much of the nineteenth century, social scientists endorsed a hard form of what we have termed "analytical egalitarianism." Starting with Adam Smith, classical economics presumed that humans are the same in their capacity for language and trade; observed differences were then explained by incentives, luck, and history, and it is the "vanity of the philosopher" incorrectly to conclude that ordinary people are somehow different from the expert (Smith 1776, 1.2 §4). Such analytical egalitarianism was overthrown in the postclassical period sometime after 1850 when notions of race and hierarchy came to infect economic and social analysis as a result of attacks on homogeneity by the Victorian sages (including Thomas Carlyle and John Ruskin), in anthropology and biology (James Hunt and Charles Darwin), and among political economists themselves (W. R. Greg).[2] We sketch some disastrous consequences of the transition to hierarchical thinking, and we make the case that political economy in the classical tradition *rightly* presupposed human homogeneity and *rightly* rejected hierarchical presuppositions of any sort.

At issue between analytical egalitarians and their critics were two

1. This chapter draws heavily on material in our book, *The "Vanity of the Philosopher": From Equality to Hierarchy in Post-classical Economics* (Peart and Levy 2005a). We thank Masazumi Wakatabe for encouraging us to write this summary statement and for his patience with us throughout the process.

2. This list of characters is not exhaustive; see ibid. for details. We prefer *postclassical* to the more familiar *neoclassical* terminology. On the origin of the term *neoclassical*, see Colander 2001, 154ff. We find that the transition, entailing the rise of hierarchical thinking, the loss of sympathy, and the endorsement of eugenic remaking, infects a broad set of economists, not all of whom would be considered neoclassical. Traditions within and outside of neoclassical economics—the Austrian School scattered by the coming of the Hitler era, as well as the London School and Chicago—revived the presupposition of equal competence in the twentieth century (Peart and Levy 2005a).

questions: whether everyone's preferences count equally; and whether everyone is equally capable of making economic decisions. In Smith's account, all people, philosophers and subjects alike, are motivated by fame and fortune, and we are all equally capable of making decisions. The oppositional view held that some among us are different from others. Since "difference" implied "superiority" in the period we study, we call this doctrine analytical hierarchicalism.

Those who opposed the classical economists' presumption of homogeneity focused on two purported heterogeneities between the expert and his subject. First, the expert was presumed to be untainted by considerations of self-interest while his subject is motivated by self-interest. Second, perhaps because of superior self-control or some other inherent difference, the expert is supposed to be superior to or smarter than the subject he studies. It is important to note that this intellectual superiority is not merely a matter of better information: the expert with whom we are concerned is someone who simply doesn't trust all subjects, who holds that some will always be hopelessly prone to making persistent mistakes no matter how much we educate, train, and inculcate.[3]

The notion of the expert is deliberately left broad. The key feature of those *we* refer to as experts is that the he or she is someone who makes recommendations about how others might achieve human happiness. Depending on the specific context involved in what follows, experts may be social commentators, biologists, or political economists (see Peart and Levy 2005a).

It is precisely the supposition of superiority by the experts that Smith opposed as the "vanity of the philosopher." Such vanity implies that the subject is in need of guidance from the expert.[4] It also implies that the expert will be predisposed to disapprove of (and even disallow) the subject making unfettered choices in a marketplace or in the direction of his or her affections in the household and elsewhere. As long as the expert maintains that he or she possesses insight into the sorts of preferences people "should" possess—if they only knew better—he or

3. In Smith's account, people proceed from their understanding of the world as summarized by proverbial wisdom. Like Smith, Malthus recognized that the agents about whom he wrote have theories or beliefs of their own: people can *foresee* the misery attendant on an overly large family, and they take that into account when they decide to marry. In one remarkable passage Malthus explains that the foresight of ordinary people is an attempt to unwrap the regularities of nature. Because of these regularities, people are both able and willing to work and plan (1798, chap. XVIII, ¶10). For Malthus, at foundation there is no difference between the foresight of the ordinary person and the activity of the greatest of all natural philosophers, Newton. The ordinary person's wisdom takes proverbial form so that others might profit from it. For more on how Malthus fits into our account, see Peart and Levy 2005b.

4. In Peart and Levy 2005a we examine Smith on how proverbs might provide such guidance, and we develop a technical account of how ordinary people might obtain much of the advice they require from the experience of others.

she must also accept, and may perhaps even demand, responsibility for directing those preferences until the subjects gain the same sort of sophistication.[5] We suggest here that the "science" of eugenics operationalized this doctrine.[6] By contrast, the classical economists' egalitarian notion of homogeneity—motivational and otherwise—and choices unfettered by the direction of one's "betters." go hand in hand.

Racism as the Primitive

Notions of "race" and hierarchy are ill-defined, indeed unstable, in the mid-nineteenth and well into the twentieth century. Arguments about race and hierarchy frequently played out in terms of both the Irish and the former slaves in Jamaica (Curtis 1968, 1997). The "laboring classes" were also included in racially charged discussions of inherited incompetence, and hierarchy and competence were mapped to gender and religion as well.

This instability of race and hierarchy invites us to take what we shall call "racism" as primitive for our analysis and to consider what distinctions were made by those we study.[7] Taking racism as the foundation for our analysis is very much akin to what Bishop Berkeley proposed by taking perception as the foundation for his work on vision. One learns, Berkeley said, to perceive distance (Levy 2001). In line with classical economists such as John Stuart Mill, we suggest that people learn to perceive "similarity" or "difference." Part of the learning process involves images and stories that insist on human homogeneity as well as images and stories that imply that some people are closer to beasts than they are to people. Even as the perception of homogeneity widened to encompass people across the globe and sympathy extended to other races, the argument was put forward that some are more deserving of sympathy than others, that "charity begins at home." This slogan is central to nineteenth-century "paternalism" in that it recognizes that

5. The expert might also challenge consumer sovereignty. Twentieth-century examples in recent history include Maurice Dobb (1933) and J. K. Galbraith (1958). They were countered by Abba Lerner (1934) and F. A. Hayek (1961). But neither Dobb nor Galbraith challenged the doctrine of the stability of the agent's personal identity through choice.

6. Our focus in what follows is mainly on the theories of human nature, transformative or otherwise, rather than the technical investigations of eugenics-influenced economists and statisticians late in the nineteenth century. For those details, see Peart and Levy 2005a; and Levy and Peart 2004b.

7. We use the more familiar *racism* rather than the unwieldy *hierarchicalism* here to signify thinking in which groups are perceived as superior versus inferior. Glenn Loury's axiom "'Race' is a socially constructed mode of human categorization" (2002, 5) is much to the point. In Peart and Levy 2005a we focus on the microfoundations of such a construction while attempting (by using Mill's constructions) to use the machinery found within the period we study.

unregulated sympathy and choices can endanger hierarchy. Taking racism as primitive lets us deal with the question of the Jewish "race" with the same facility with which we deal with the Irish "race." A race is what people of the time perceive it to be.

To provide a thumbnail sketch of the debates on human hierarchy, we use an index of humanity—or human hierarchy—which we denote α for the Greek *anthrop,* the "human." We use this device to characterize two major positions in the period we study. We shall use α in what follows to *define* a race because we find that race is conflated in our period with religion, gender, and class. Political economy enters the argument because race is also conflated with *choice.* This conflation is perhaps best illustrated by a remarkable 1860 image by Charles Bennett, which conveys the message that a woman who exits the household to engage in market activity changes race (fig. 11.1). The image, entitled "Slavey," captures the malleability of race unforgettably.[8] A woman who exits hierarchy through markets—by entering the labor force—devolves into "an enslaved African type of humanity." She is now perceived as having chosen to be different, and she must be so.

The "progressive" doctrine that hierarchy humanizes, while exiting hierarchy to make self-directed choices causes racial devolution, is central to Charles Kingsley's influential children's tale *The Water-Babies* (1863), as well as to the *Punch* images we have studied (Peart-Levy 2005a). *Water-Babies* contains the story of the DoAsYouLikes—fond of playing a Jew's harp—whose devolution to apes and consequent extermination is a matter of no regret. As the last ape-man perishes at the hands of a European hunter, he tries to say that he was "man and a brother," but, having lost of the power of speech, he fails in the attempt. The collision with classical economics occurred by necessity because such transformations made no sense to those economists who see the expert as someone within the economic system.

Theories of Human Capability

What defines the human and measures human capability? By common consent it is "rationality." In our period, the concept of rationality had a social aspect because it presupposed both a common language and the

8. The accompanying text makes it clear that Bennett is on Carlyle's side in his debate with Mill over slavery: "It will be noticed that the eidolographic development of Miss Hipswidge is strikingly suggestive of the enslaved African type of humanity. The banjo, castanets, 'abundant pumpkin,' and other conventional solaces of that persecuted race are, however, wanting to make the resemblance perfect" (Bennett and Brough 1860, 33). The "abundant pumpkin" is a phrase from Carlyle's "Negro question" discussed in Levy 2001; and Levy and Peart 2001–2.

Fig. 11.1. "Slavey." Charles Bennett 1860.

capacity for individual choice. Adam Smith supposed a social foundation for political economy when he conjectured that humans trade because they reason and speak a common language (Smith [1776] 1904, I.ii. §2; Rubinstein 2000). Thus, in terms of our α, there will be a discontinuity of the relation between α and reason at the edge of the development of language.

Having attained the status of human, in the debates we study human capability is related to the ability to make economic and political choices, including the decision to marry and have children. For classical economists, there are two key aspects of this capability: the ability to sympathize, that is, to take into account other people in the self-interested calculus (Levy and Peart 2004a); and what contemporary economists call "time preference."[9]

The ability to reason involves the ability to abstract. Those who opposed classical economics held that such judgments were not to be trusted unless they were directed. Unregulated sympathetic judgments might yield resources to the undeserving. In the debates we have studied, positive time preference was also viewed as a failing.[10] As the case was made that some among us fail to make decisions optimally, perceptions of hierarchy and race entered economics: early British postclassical writers maintained that lack of patience was a particularly Irish characteristic (see Peart-Levy 2005a).

Here we are interested in different specifications of the relationship between humanity and economic ability (entailing sympathetic and intertemporal judgments) in the great debates over hierarchy.[11] We focus on two foundational views of the relationship: Adam Smith's and a "developmental" account.

Adam Smith

Smith considers all humans to be alike with the potential exception of those who are regarded by their fellows as heroic. These "imagined" types are objects of approval and emulation. All "real" individuals are equally human (fig. 11.2).

Developmental

Figure 11.3 presents two developmental views of human nature that are often confounded. First, there is the utilitarian developmental view associated with Mill and Herbert Spencer. Here there is a positive monotonic relationship between α and economic ability. Second, there is the biological developmental view associated with Greg and Galton. Here α attains a maximum at H^* and then bends downward. The downward-sloping portion reflects the biologists' criticism of utilitarians for paying

9. On the significance of sympathy, see Levy and Peart 2004a, Peart and Levy 2005. On the characterization of time preference late in the nineteenth century, see Peart 2000.

10. W. S. Jevons, for instance, argued that in matters of intertemporal decisions the laboring classes were inherently myopic and prone to making systematical mistakes. For a demonstration of such views in Jevons, Marshall, Pigou, and Fisher, see Peart 2000; on Pigou, see Collard 1996.

11. Since we are more interested in racism than race, there are many aspects of the debates on race that will concern us very little. For example, we consider the doctrine of separate creation, "polygenesis," only briefly in Levy and Peart 2004a, where we also examine differences between Hume's and Smith's views on human equality.

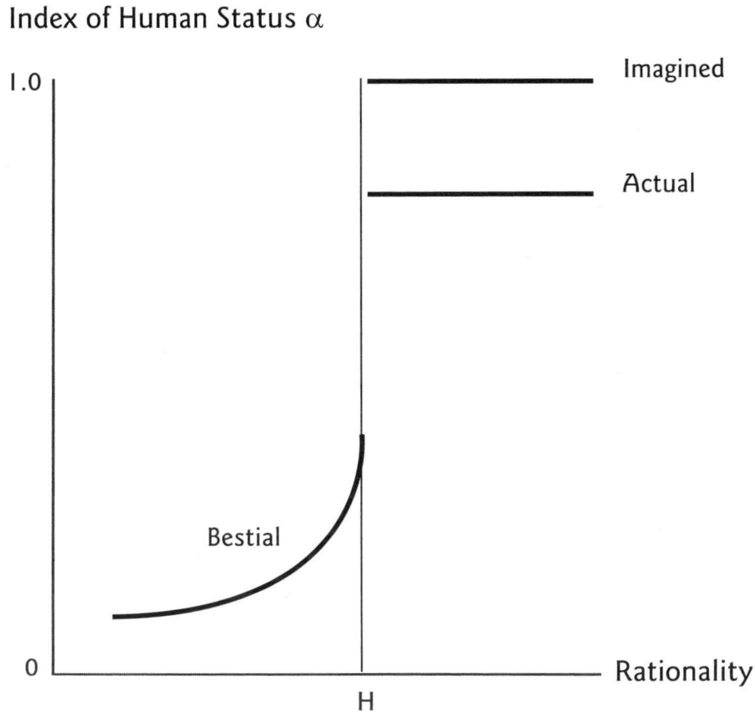

Fig. 11.2. Adam Smith's View of Human Status.

insufficient attention to the deleterious consequences of undirected sympathy and ethics.[12]

Consider the solid line, which represents the utilitarian developmental view. The simple curvature does not tell us what is the causal arrow. Do we become better humans as we gain ability to make sensible choices or do more developed people make more sensible choices? Not surprisingly, there were different views on the matter. For Mill, the improved ability to make choices, manifested in part as widened sympathy, improved one's human status. For Mill, the maximum was attained by Socrates and Jesus Christ, who revealed a willingness to die for strangers. And, although Mill was critical of crude American materialism, he believed that the highest national α was attained by Americans who were willing to die to abolish the slavery of their fellows (Peart and Levy 2003).

12. Is it possible to be "too" rational? Thomas Carlyle judged his adversary, John Stuart Mill, to be a "logic-chopping machine." At the beginning of Mill's attempt to bring justice to murdered and mutilated Jamaicans, he wrote that we must not let narrow self-interest distract us from the demands of impartial justice for our fellow creatures (Peart and Levy 2005a).

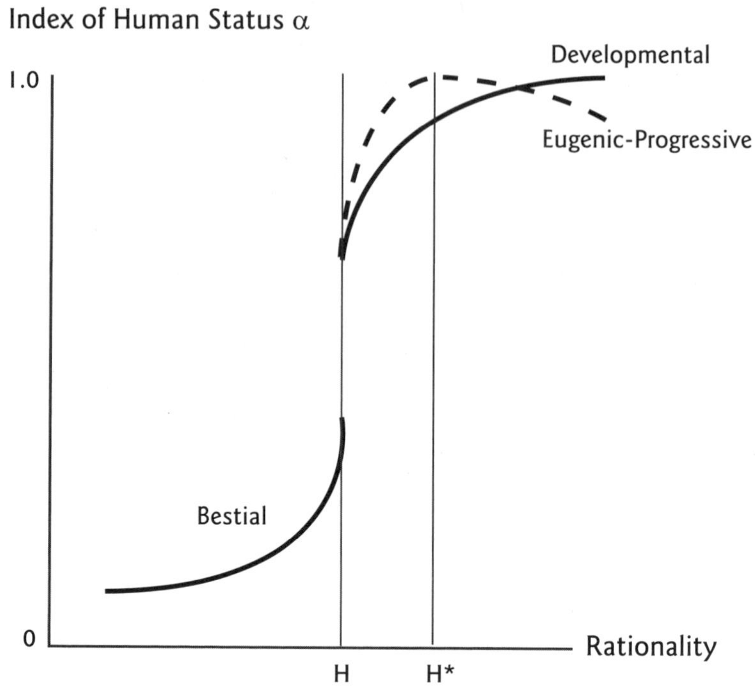

Fig. 11.3. The Developmental and Eugenic View of Human Status.

In the second half of the century, biologists called for a reduction, or at least a directing, of human sympathy and ethics—critical considerations in the developmental view. A. R. Wallace had argued in 1864 that the principle of natural selection does not operate with humans because people possess sympathy for their fellow humans: we do not let the mentally infirm and the physically unable perish (Wallace 1864). The founders of what became known as eugenics responded that if this survival of the unfit was the result of sympathy in humans sympathy should be suppressed.[13] Thus, without suppression (via eugenic policy), beyond a certain point—H*—an increase in ability entailing expanded sympathetic judgments, actually reduces α. Such thinking led to the eugenicists' program of biological remaking in order to prevent the biological decay that was said to follow the undirected acquisition of sympathetic tendencies in humans, in other words, to keep the human race from moving to the right of H*. The great divide on which we focus in what follows is between those for

13. Greg 1869. See Peart and Levy 2005a; and Levy and Peart 2004b for the texts and details.

whom the lives of some people are worth more than the lives of others and those for whom they are not.[14]

Transformation Theories

The critics of classical political economy held that human nature was malleable, and classical economists erred in supposing that people simply respond to incentives. So in their view the dotted-line version of human development in figure 11.3 pertained, and it was up to the so-called expert to prevent people from achieving the downward-bending portion of the curve. In other words, they predicted that without help from their betters many human beings were incapable of developing properly and they might instead simply devolve.[15] Human nature was malleable, and Mill and other political economists were incorrect to presume otherwise.[16]

The poet John Ruskin made this case most forcefully in 1860. He contrasted his "chemical" view of political economy with the "mathematical" view of classical political economists such as Mill. The mathematical approach supposed that the nature of man is fixed and people respond to incentives. By contrast, the chemical approach presupposes that people can be transformed (by experts or other social forces).[17]

> But the disturbing elements in the social problem are not of the same nature of the constant one: they alter the essence of the creature under examination the moment they are added: they

14. In opposition to Mill's equality proposition, Edgeworth responded, "Accordingly in the 'koomposh' of an unlimited pauper population, the most favourable disposition might seem to be (abstracted from practical considerations, and *if* the delineation of Wundt be verified within and beyond the region of sensation), might seem perhaps to be, that adhering *ex hypothesi* to the letter of the first problem, we should be guided by the spirit of the second problem, should wish to cut off the redundant numbers with an illusory portion, so as to transfer substantial (equal) portions to a few. There might be, as it were, a mulcting of many brothers to make a few eldest sons" (Edgeworth 1877, 61). We examine Edgeworth's position in Peart and Levy 2005a.

15. We focus here on the "character" transformation argument, leaving aside the "biological" devolution argument of the eugenicists outlined earlier.

16. Mill is clearly in opposition to Ruskin in this debate, but he takes a different position from that of Smith. For Mill, human improvement is possible: the human nature characterization is upward sloping. What separates him from Ruskin and other "progressives" of the time is that, for Mill, "improvement" was to be self- (rather than expert-) directed. Unlike Ruskin, human development occurs as individuals freely recognize their human potential in the context of discussion and trial and error. No expert is required to show people what to do or choose, and all are equally capable of human improvement. See Peart and Levy 2003.

17. Ruskin (and other critics of Mill's political economy) sometimes writes as though one individual can be transformed into another (better or worse) individual. At the same time, the case was also made that there are group variations: Irish or blacks as a whole need to be transformed.

> operate, not mathematically, but chemically, introducing conditions which render all our previous knowledge unavailable. (Ruskin 1905, 26)[18]

For those who subscribed to the chemical view, the problem with classical economics was that it failed to contemplate how to improve the subject.

Admirers of the transformative view often suppose that transformation works in the upward direction, for example, that exposure to the right sort of art "improves" people while exposure to market-generated culture cannot.[19] The nineteenth-century view of transformation *also* focused on the possibility of transformation downward. If direction and hierarchy improve the human, the question arises, what happens if this hierarchy is removed? In 1849, Thomas Carlyle asserted that the emancipation of the West Indian slaves had reduced them to subhuman status (1849; Levy 2001). But nineteenth-century arguments about institutions were longer lasting than the attempt to preserve slavery by Carlyle and his followers. Other, less extreme forms of hierarchy were offered up as transformative institutions that might improve not only the behavior but also the "essence" of individuals who operated within the hierarchy while renunciation of hierarchy was said to degrade that essence.

This transformational argument was made in both literary and visual forms—in the popular children's tale by Charles Kingsley, *Water-Babies,* and the caricatures of Irish Fenians published in the 1860s in *Punch.* In both its forms, the argument constituted an attack on classical political economy. In chemical political economy, the renunciation of hierarchy by those who need direction transforms a human into an ape-man. The Irish who chose to achieve self-rule, like the woman who left the home to work in the "Slavey" image (fig. 11.1), devolved into a lesser race.

To illustrate the nature of chemical political economy further, consider Ruskin's analysis of the impact of railroad travel on the lower orders in *Fors Clavigera.*[20] Here is a description of an English worker's transportation in the old days, quoted in a contemporary magazine article:

---

18. Classical political economy also failed because it supposed that the exchange of untransformed goods was profitable. For exchange to generate net benefits, Ruskin held, there must be a transformation (1905, 90–91).

19. Jevons's "Amusements of the People" relied on this distinction when he called for the "deliberate cultivation of public amusement" and "the well-conducted Concert-room versus the inane and vulgar Music-hall" ([1878] 1883, 7). The discussion within economics over the possibility of metapreferences (George 2001)—when an individual favors one set of preferences over another—assumes that to the extent that an individual is remade he or she is in charge of his or her own decisions. The problem of *adult* rehabituation as one moves from (say) slavery to markets was much on J. S. Mill's mind in his *Principles of Political Economy.* See Peart and Levy 2003.

20. We quote from the nineteenth-century republication in an American periodical to emphasize the contemporary importance. The extracts by Walter Levin in Ruskin (1893) are taken largely from *Fors Clavigera.*

> In old times, if a Coniston peasant had any business at Ulverstone, he walked to Ulverstone; spent nothing but shoe-leather on the road, drank at the streams, and if he spent a couple of batz when he got to Ulverstone, "it was the end of the world." Coan (1878, 61)

In the market economy, postindustrialization, the worker becomes "idle" and "stupid."

> But now he would never think of doing such a thing! He first walks three miles in a contrary direction to a railroad-station, and then travels by railroad twenty-four miles to Ulverstone, paying two shillings fare. During the twenty-four miles transit, he is idle, dusty, stupid, and either more hot or cold than is pleasant to him. In either case he drinks beer at two or three of the stations, passes his time between them with anybody he can find, in talking without having anything to talk of; and such talk always becomes vicious. He arrives at Ulverstone, jaded, half-drunk, and otherwise demoralized, and three shillings, at least, poorer than in the morning. Of that sum a shilling has gone for beer, threepence to a railway shareholder, threepence in coals, and eighteen pence has been spent in employing strong men in the vile mechanical work of making and driving a machine, instead of his own legs to carry the drunken lout. The results, absolute loss and demoralization to the poor on all sides, and iniquitous gain to the rich. Coan (1878, 61)

An English worker got on the train. But the train ride transformed him into a "jaded, half-drunk, and otherwise demoralized" barely human being. The worker is sorely in need of someone's guidance.

We have emphasized the importance of the egalitarian doctrine of abstract economic man in the opposition to racial accounts of political economy. In his 1848 *Principles,* Mill outlined the implication of such a method. He rejected racial "explanations" of outcomes, which he condemned specifically with reference to the Irish. Institutions, not "Irishness," explained the Irish problems.

> Is it not, then, a bitter satire on the mode in which opinions are formed on the most important problems of human nature and life, to find public instructors of the greatest pretensions, imputing the backwardness of Irish industry, and the want of en-

> ergy of the Irish people in improving their condition, to a peculiar indolence and *insouciance* in the Celtic race? Of all vulgar modes of escaping from the consideration of the effect of social and moral influences on the human mind, the most vulgar is that of attributing the diversities of conduct and character to inherent natural differences. ([1848] 1965, 319)

The doctrine of abstract economic man has always been contested, and in the Victorian period the criticism focused on abstraction from the "fact" of racial difference. As an important instance of this contestation, we quote from an article in the *Quarterly Review* written by the cofounder of eugenics, W. R. Greg.

> "Make them peasant-proprietors," says Mr. Mill. But Mr. Mill forgets that, till you change the character of the Irish cottier, peasant-proprietorship would work no miracles. He would fall behind the instalments of his purchase-money, and would be called upon to surrender his farm. He would often neglect it in idleness, ignorance, jollity and drink, get into debt, and have to sell his property to the newest owner of a great estate. . . . In two generations Ireland would again be England's difficulty, come back upon her in an aggravated form. Mr. Mill never deigns to consider that an Irishman is an Irishman, and not an average human being—an idiomatic and idiosyncratic, not an abstract, man. (1869, 78)[21]

An Englishman got on Ruskin's train; Greg's Irishman got off. Chemical political economy implies that humans are transformed or improved, changed from one race to another. Unfettered choices that occur with industrialization and economic development serve to reduce human status because the improving influence of the expert is renounced. On the other hand, guidance by the social commentator, embodied in paternalistic institutions, prevents a movement downward to a lower human status and may move the individual up in the hierarchy of human status.

Transformation by Obedience

If racial stereotypes form the molecules of chemical political economy, then we need to consider how Victorian perceptions of human hierarchy

21. Curtis (1968, 47–48), who does not know the author—the *Victorian Index* was not yet published—emphasizes the importance of this review for its paradigmatic character.

changed in the latter half of the nineteenth century.[22] Scholars have long made a distinction between literary racists (Thomas Carlyle in the forefront) and the scientific racists who clustered around James Hunt and his *Anthropological Review.* These groups had at least one member in common: Charles Kingsley.[23] Kingsley is known for many contributions. He seems to have contributed one of "facts" in Hunt's *The Negro's Place in Nature.*

> —"Many observers have noticed the fact that the Negro frequently uses the great toe as a thumb." (Hunt 1863b, 7)

The same claim appeared in Kingsley's *Water-Babies,* which was published in installments earlier that year in *Macmillan's Magazine.* Kingsley's Negroes

> laid of the branches with their great toes, as if they had been thumbs, just as a Hindoo tailor uses his toes to thread his needle. (1863, 217)

First published in book form in 1863 and never thereafter out of print, Kingsley's story for children was arguably the most successful and long-lived disseminator of the chemical thesis. *Water-Babies* had the distinction of being reviewed by both the *Times* and Hunt's *Anthropological Review.* One of Kingsley's explicit targets is the political economy of his contemporaries, which denies the possibility of transformation.[24]

One is transformed by following the recommendations of one's betters, the experts, and submitting to hierarchy. The telling episode in *Water-Babies* occurs in the tale of the now extinct DoAsYouLikes, who exit hierarchy.

---

22. We do not wish to imply that it is impossible to conceive of transformation possibilities independent of race. There may also be gender and religious transformations. There is a hint of simianization in a purely English context in a *Punch* cartoon of 4 August 1866, "No Rough-ianism" which carries the caption: "Working-Man: 'Look here, you vagabond! Right or wrong, we won't have *your* help!'" The *English* ruffian holds a rock and a broken branch.

23. Letters from Kingsley to Hunt have been published in Levy 2001, answering an open question about the Hunt-Kingsley connection. Andrew Farrant and Nicola Tynan are thanked for bringing the importance of Kingsley's *Water-Babies* to our attention.

24. The agents of transformation in *Water-Babies* are fairies: "Some people think that there are no fairies. . . . And Aunt Agitate, in her Arguments on political economy, says there are none. Well, perhaps there are none—in her political economy" (Kingsley, 1863, 60). Fairies also play a role in Kingsley's *Roman and Teuton* (1864), his Regis Lectures of Modern History at Cambridge.

> And in the next five hundred years they were all dead and gone, by bad food and wild beasts and hunters; all except one tremendous old fellow with jaws like a jack, who stood full seven feet high; and M. Du Chaillu came up to him, and shot him, as he stood roaring and thumping his breast. And he remembered that his ancestors had once been men, and tried to say, "Am I not a man and a brother?" but had forgotten how to use his tongue; and then he had tried to call for a doctor, but he had forgotten the word for one. So all he said was "Ubboboo!" and died. (Kingsley 1863, 247–48)

In the midst of the American Civil War, no one could miss the reference to the abolitionist question—"Am I not a man and a brother?"[25] And we have a loss of language that accompanies the devolution to the bestial.

In this episode about how the absence of compulsion causes racial devolution, Kingsley makes an Irish reference to the jaw as a marker of the primitive.

> "Why," said Tom, "they are growing no better than savages."
>
> "And look how ugly they are all getting," said Ellie.
>
> "Yes; when people live on poor vegetables instead of roast beef and plum-pudding, their jaws grow large, and their lips grow coarse, like the poor Paddies who eat potatoes." (1863, 244)[26]

The conjunction of Darwinian science, Carlyle, and the devolution thesis in Kingsley is explicated by the review of *Water-Babies* in the *Times* of London.

> And if we should never [have] heard of Tom and Ellie but for the development of Marine Zoology, we may add that Master Tom's education would have been impossible had not Mr. Darwin published his book on the Origin of Species. Mr. Kingsley trips up the Darwinian theory, and asks us how we like its application when inverted. If an ascent in the order of life be possible, must not a degradation of movement downwards be equally

25. This was commented on in the review in the *Anthropological Review* (Hunt 1863a, 472). The review adds to the information on the title page ("The Rev. Charles Kingsley") that the author is "Honorary Fellow of the Anthropological Society of London, and Professor of Modern History in the University of Cambridge" (1863a, 472).

26. Curtis remarks on "Charles Kingsley's description of the poor peasants he saw in County Mayo and Connemera in 1860 as 'white chimpanzees'" (1997, 100).

> possible? If beasts can be turned into men, must not men be liable to be turned into beasts? Here, indeed, Mr. Kingsley might have quoted the authority of one of his great masters, Mr. Carlyle, who long ago warned us of the fate of the dwellers by the Dead Sea who refused to listen to the preaching of Moses. They became apes, poor wretches, and having once had souls they lost them. (26 January 1864)

Those who renounce the advice of the experts devolve and exit humanity. This argument was also made visually in the cartoons of the Victorian magazine *Punch*. Consider the example in figure 11.4, in which the unruly Irish have devolved to apelike status. By contrast, those who choose to serve their British masters are viewed as fully human (fig. 11.5).

The message is one of "noblesse oblige": the expert takes on the much needed responsibility of ensuring that mankind avoids such terrible outcomes. The contrast with classical political economy is striking: Smith, Malthus, and Mill all trust individuals to make choices on their own, presupposing no special knowledge of what these choices should be.

Conclusion

This chapter has examined how the political economists' view of human nature—we're all the same, equally capable of making choices and self-improvement—was attacked on a number of fronts in the mid–nineteenth century. We have argued that the divide occurred in terms of *how* transformation might occur: by one's self (the view of Mill) or by one's "betters" (the view of Kingsley, Ruskin, and Carlyle).

We have been told more than once that our outrage at mid- to late-nineteenth-century notions of race and hierarchy is misplaced. Everyone, we have been told, "was a racist then."[27] It will now be clear that we reject this counterargument. We do so because we find it factually incorrect and analytically flawed. In point of fact, our research demonstrates that there was significant (though unsuccessful) resistance to hierarchy and race. Classical economists rejected racial explanations of observed behavior and were criticized for doing so. More than this, we believe the counterargument embodies a form of not so subtle hierarchical thinking:

27. We first encountered this criticism at a Christian A. Johnson conference that featured some of our research at Middlebury College in 2000. The conference proceedings contain a number of pieces that criticize our work as well as our response; see Colander, Prasch, and Sheth 2004.

Fig. 11.4. *Punch,* 16 December 1865.

PUNCH, OR THE LONDON CHARIVARI.—JANUARY 4, 1868.

A HINT TO THE LOYAL IRISH.

"AH, THIN, MISTHER BULL! GIVE US THE OATH AN' SOME O' THIM STICKS. SURE, THERE'S HUNDHREDS O' THE BOYS AS IS READY TO HELP YE, SOR."

Fig. 11.5. *Punch,* 4 January 1868.

the thought that we today are superior to those of the past and that we who are nonracist must excuse the racist writers of the past because they simply reflect their times.

The classical economists' explanation for observed heterogeneity was to appeal to the incentives associated with different institutions. So, for instance, classical economists such as John Stuart Mill argued that the Irish problem was largely a matter of institutions rather than inherent indolence.[28] Mill was strenuously opposed by those who claimed the Irishman was "idiosyncratic" and would never be the hardworking Scot. The policy conclusion followed: special measures were required to look after the Irishman, whose inherent difference meant he lacked the capacity to rule himself. Mill struggled with the problem of transition from one set of institutions to another, how new habits are formed as institutions change. Economists who have become accustomed to institution-free analysis fail to appreciate how much of classical economics is designed to deal precisely with the problem of self-motivated human development in the context of institutional change.

A second potential difficulty for our position is that, while Carlyle's attitudes on race and hierarchy were horrible, those of, say, a Kingsley were rather more "progressive" and less hateful. The sages' opposition to markets, it is claimed, may have been framed along lines that we haven't yet considered. By offering paternalism as an alternative to both markets and slavery, some of the sages might be salvaged as caring, progressive, social commentators, commentators who genuinely wished to see the lot of the working poor improved. Thus, there may have been some paternalists whose distrust of markets can be contrasted with our characterization of Ruskin and Carlyle (Levy and Peart 2001–2). Those paternalists, the argument continues, were not necessarily racists.

We have argued that, as a matter of fact, those paternalists *were* racists. Posing the problem as a choice among markets, slavery, and (somewhere in between) paternalism suggests why contemporary scholars might be prepared to defend the Victorian sages even today. Their analysis today, as in the nineteenth century, is a form of elitism that we find particularly objectionable: in defending Ruskin, Carlyle, and Kingsley, our critics are arguing, today, that the working classes of nineteenth-century England were in need of transformation by their "betters." We are much more comfortable with Mill's position that to the extent that transformation might occur it would be the result of self-discovery and

28. Senior also attributed outcomes to institutions rather than inherent differences: "Almost all the differences between the different races of men, differences so great that we sometimes nearly forget that they all belong to the same species, may be traced to the degree in which they enjoy the blessings of good government" [1836] 1936, 76.

choice rather than at the recommendation (and imposition) of experts.[29] We hold that the classical economists got it right: an analytical system in which everyone counts equally and is presumed equally capable of making decisions is the only system that seems morally defensible.[30] And, not surprisingly, we find analytical systems that presume hierarchy to be indefensible. This chapter has attempted to explain why. First, we find the history compelling—and awful. In all the instances we know of in which a group has been treated as "different," difference has turned into hierarchy, and hierarchy has sometimes led to terrible analytical and policy consequences.[31] As noted earlier, we also find that systems in which hierarchy is invoked are extraordinarily pliable. The "inferior" becomes any group that is out of favor with the analyst.

Most compelling for us, the analysis that presumes difference is terribly tempting to the analysts and policymakers. Once difference creeps into the analysis, the temptation is to presume that difference implies inferiority. It also seems often to imply that the writer, whether social commentator or scientist, somehow "knows better." And here we find that this is not simply a presumption that the analyst has better information. Instead, it extends to a presumption of inherent superiority. For whatever reason, the analyst presumes that the subjects' choices aren't to be trusted but instead require looking after. Somehow, the analyst is privy to knowledge about what decisions "should" be made and what preferences individuals "would" have if they only knew better. As a society and a community of academics, we have come to accept the proposition that the scientist is somehow superior to—better motivated or more able than—the individuals under investigation. We fail to trust those individuals to make reasonable choices. We find such a presumption of superiority on the part of the analyst to be the last, unrecognized, and resisted form of hierarchy in social science. It is, we argue, simply the "vanity of the philosopher."

Finally, James Buchanan has asked us: what if there are real differences among people? A look around us at any moment suggests that

29. To fully appreciate the importance of "progressives" such as Kingsley, one must consider how he came to endorse the biologists' goal of human "progress" at the expense of the economists' goal of human "happiness" and claimed that the doctrine of racial survival was the "natural theology of the future." This is the topic of Levy and Peart 2006.

30. This is not to say that we agree in all respects with all classical economists or that we always disagree with all of their opponents. We find analysis that presumes homogeneity compelling, and we object to treatments that entail hierarchy. We find that, on balance, the classical economists fall on the side of homogeneity, while (again on balance) their critics fall on the side of hierarchy.

31. Much of the material in our *The "Vanity of the Philosopher"* (Peart and Levy 2005a) has in fact been difficult for us to read. We reproduce it there, and examine the arguments made thereby, in order to set the record straight, to learn from the past, and to make our case in favor of analysis that presumes homogeneous competence.

people are, in fact, different; inherent physical differences, for instance, abound. (One of us is under 5 feet 2 inches tall, and the other is about 6 feet tall, and relative price changes are not likely to reduce this difference.) So our argument has much in common with that of Lionel Robbins, who in 1938 remembered the debates in economics over the differential capacity for happiness.

> I have always felt that, as a first approximation in handling questions relating to the lives and actions of large masses of people, the approach which counts each man as one, and, on that assumption, asks which way lies the greatest happiness, is less likely to lead one astray than any of the absolute systems. I do not believe, and I never have believed, that in fact men are necessarily equal or should always be judged as such. But I do believe that, in most cases, political calculations which do not treat them as if they were equal are morally revolting. (1938, 635)

The lesson we draw from history in our *The "Vanity of the Philosopher*" (Peart and Levy 2005a) is that a presumption of *group* difference—when the definition of the group is pliable and the analyst is presumed to be in the superior group—is dangerously tempting. Analytical egalitarianism is a defense against the temptation of the theorist.

Bibliography

Anonymous. 1864. "Mr. Kingsley's Water-Babies." *Times* 26 January 1864, p. 6.

Bennett, Charles H., and Robert B. Brough. 1860. *Shadow and Substance.* London: W. Kent.

[Carlyle, Thomas.] 1849. "Occasional Discourse on the Negro Question." *Fraser's Magazine for Town and Country* 40:670–79.

Coan, Titus M. (1878). "Ruskin's 'Fors Clavigera.'" *Appleton's Journal* 5 (July): 58–65.

Colander, David, 2001. *The Lost Art of Economics: Essays on Economics and the Economics Profession.* Cheltenham: Edward Elgar.

Colander, David, Robert E. Prasch, and Falguni A. Sheth, eds. 2004. *Race, Liberalism, and Economics.* Ann Arbor: University of Michigan Press.

Collard, David, 1996. "Pigou and Future Generations: A Cambridge Tradition." *Cambridge Journal of Economics* 20 (September): 585–97.

Curtis, L. P., Jr. 1968. *Anglo-Saxons and Celts.* Bridgeport: Conference on British Studies at the University of Bridgeport.

Curtis, L. P., Jr. 1997. *Apes and Angels: The Irishman in Victorian Caricature.* Rev. ed.. Washington, D.C.: Smithsonian Institution Press.

Dobb, Maurice. 1933. "Economic Theory and the Problems of a Socialist Economy." *Economic Journal* 43 (December): 588–98.

Edgeworth, F. Y. 1877. *New and Old Methods of Ethics; or "Physical Ethics" and "Methods of Ethics."* Oxford: James Parker.

Edgeworth, F. Y. 1881. *Mathematical Psychics.* London: C. Kegan Paul.

Galbraith, John Kenneth. 1958. *The Affluent Society.* Boston: Houghton Mifflin.

George, David. 2001. *Preference Pollution: How Markets Create the Desires We Dislike.* Ann Arbor: University of Michigan Press.

[Greg, W. R.] 1869. "Realities of Irish Life." *Quarterly Review* 126:61–80.

Hayek, F. A. 1961. "The Non-sequitur of the "Dependence Effect." *Southern Economic Journal* 27, no. 4: 346–48.

[Hunt, James.] 1863a. "Kingsley's *Water Babies.*" *Anthropological Review* 1, no. 3: 472–76.

Hunt, James. 1863b. *The Negro's Place in Nature: A Paper Read before the London Anthropological Society.* New York: Evrie, Horton, and Co., 1864.

Jevons, W. S. [1878, 1883] 1965. "Amusements of the People." In *Methods of Social Reform,* 1–27. New York: Augustus M. Kelley.

Kingsley, Charles. 1862–63. "The Water-Babies: A Faerie Tale for a Land-Baby." *Macmillan's* 6–7.

Kingsley, Charles. 1863. *The Water-Babies: A Fairy Tale for a Land-Baby.* London and Cambridge: Macmillan.

Kingsley, Charles. [1863] 1865. *The Water-Babies: A Fairy Tale for a Land-Baby.* Illustrated by Linley Sambourne. London: Macmillan.

Kingsley, Charles. 1864. *The Roman and the Teuton.* Cambridge and London: Macmillan.

Lerner, A. P. 1934. "Economic Theory and Socialist Economy." *Review of Economic Studies* 2 (October): 51–61.

Levy, David M. 2001. *How the Dismal Science Got Its Name: Classical Economics and the Ur-Text of Racial Politics.* Ann Arbor: University of Michigan Press.

Levy, David M., and Sandra J. Peart. 2001–2. "The Secret History of the Dismal Science." http://www.econlib.org/library/Columns/LevyPeartdismal.html.

Levy, David M., and Sandra J. Peart. 2004a. "Sympathy and Approbation in Hume and Smith: A Solution to the Other Rational Species Problem." *Economics and Philosophy* 20:331–49.

Levy, David M., and Sandra J. Peart. 2004b. "Statistical Prejudice: From Eugenics to Immigrants." *European Journal of Political Economy* 20 (March): 5–22.

Levy, David M., and Sandra J. Peart. 2006. "Charles Kingsley and the Theological Interpretation of Natural Selection." *Journal of Bioeconomics* 8:197–218.

Loury, Glenn C. 2002. *The Anatomy of Racial Inequality.* Cambridge: Harvard University Press.

Malthus, T. R. [1798] 1926. *First Essay on Population, 1798,* edited by James Bonar. London: Macmillan.

Mill, John Stuart. [1848] 1965. *The Principles of Political Economy with Some of Their Applications to Social Philosophy.* Volume 2 of *Collected Works of John Stuart Mill,* edited by J. M. Robson. Toronto: University of Toronto Press.

Packe, Michael St. John. 1954. *The Life of John Stuart Mill.* New York, Macmillan.

Peart, Sandra J. 2000. "Irrationality and Intertemporal Choice in Early Neoclassical Thought." *Canadian Journal of Economics* 33:175–88.

Peart, Sandra J., and David M. Levy. 2003. "Post-Ricardian British Economics, 1830–1870." In *The Blackwell Companion to the History of Economic Thought,* edited by Warren Samuels, Jeff Biddle, and John Davis, 130–47. Malden, Mass.: Blackwell.

Peart, Sandra J., and David M. Levy. 2005a. *The "Vanity of the Philosopher": From Equality to Hierarchy in Post-classical Economics.* Ann Arbor: University of Michigan Press.

Peart, Sandra J., and David M. Levy. 2005b. "Happiness, Progress, and the 'Vanity of the Philosopher.'" www.econlib.org/library/Columns/y2005/PeartLevymalthus.html.

Robbins, Lionel. 1938. "Interpersonal Comparisons of Utility: A Comment." *Economic Journal* 48 (December): 635–41.

Rubinstein, Ariel. 2000. *Economics and Language.* Cambridge: Cambridge University Press.

Ruskin, John. 1893. *Ruskin on Himself and Things in General.* Edited by William Lewin. Illustrated by J[ohn] W[allace]. Cope's Smoke-Room Booklets, no. 13. Liverpool: Cope's Tobacco Plant.

Ruskin, John. 1905. "Unto This Last." In *The Works of John Ruskin,* edited by E. T. Cook and Alexander Wedderburn, 17:1–114. London: G. Allen.

Senior, Nassau W. [1836] 1936. *An Outline of the Science of Political Economy.* London: Allen and Unwin.

Smith, A. [1776] 1904. *An Inquiry into the Nature and Causes of the Wealth of Nations.* Edited by Edwin Cannan. London: Methuen & Co.

Wallace, A. R. 1864. "The Origin of Human Races and the Antiquity of Man Deduced from the Theory of 'Natural Selection.'" *Journal of the Anthropology Society* 2: clviii–cixx.

12 • Frank Knight, Worst-Case Theorizing, and Economic Planning
Socialism as Monopoly Politics

Andrew Farrant

Introduction

Peter Boettke and Karen Vaughn (2002, 155–76) draw attention to the important differences characterizing the respective cases made against socialist planning by Frank H. Knight, Ludwig von Mises, and F. A. Hayek. Whereas Mises and Hayek asserted that the impossibility of socialist economic calculation precluded any possibility of efficient socialist planning (see, e.g., Lavoie 1985; and Steele 1992), Knight remained rather agnostic toward the Mises-Hayek claim (Knight 1938c, 867). Indeed, as Boettke and Vaughn (2002) correctly recognize, Knight thought pure economic theory per se—essentially the logic of choice—had little of any real consequence to say concerning the planning versus markets controversy (see, e.g., Knight 1936, 255; 1938b, 268; and [1940] 1982, 160). Knight insisted that the real problems of socialist planning lay in the political realm. Intriguingly, Boettke and Vaughn (2002, 166) suggest that it is altogether unclear as to precisely what Knight thought would constitute a "*good political argument*" (166, emphasis added) against planning. Moreover, they charge Knight with despising one particularly illustrious political argument (166): that provided in Hayek's infamous *The Road to Serfdom* ([1944] 1986).

I suggest here that Boettke and Vaughn rather misconstrue Knight's political critique of planning. In particular, they appear to inadequately appreciate the worst-case logic underlying Knight's political critique of planning. Indeed, the situational logic operative in Knight's critique of planning is rather more akin to Hayek's critique of socialism as represented by *The Road to Serfdom* than Boettke and Vaughn suggest (see, e.g., Knight 1938a, 868–69; and 1952, 414–15). Despite the apparent similarities in their respective analyses, it is Knight rather than Hayek who provides the logically more compelling political critique of wholesale economic planning. Indeed, whereas Knight's worst-case (nascent public choice) critique of planning makes immediate intuitive sense, the situational logic underlying the analysis provided in Hayek's *The Road to Serfdom* appears to be predicated on some rather unsatisfactory suppositions regarding planner type.[1]

Knight's Worst-Case Insight: Socialism as Monopoly Politics

Knight charged that socialists were entirely under the sway of best-case theorizing (roughly akin to the benevolent despot assumption so despised by public choice theory). Best-case theorizing is essentially the view that the state, "conceived in the abstract as a *benevolent and all-powerful agency—essentially as God rather than realistically as politicians*—could order economic affairs rightly without generating new evils or incurring serious social costs" (Knight [1940] 1982, 159, emphasis added; cf. Knight 1938a, 868; and 1938c, 244). Best-case theorizing regarding planner type was endemic during the socialist calculation controversy and was readily adopted by both the pro- and antiplanning sides of the debate (see, e.g., Levy 1990; and Buchanan [1969] 1999, 88). Despite ceding that planning was superior to markets given a posited lack of self-interest on the part of the planners (see, e.g., Knight [1940] 1982, 160), Knight was equally insistent that the attractions of socialist planning waned dramatically once the planners were allowed to rejoin the human race.[2]

Throughout the 1930s and 1940s, Knight had repeatedly warned that self-interested planners (Homo economicus) would clearly exploit the fact that socialist planning replaces the market economy (competitive or otherwise) with a giant monopoly (Knight 1935b, 205; [1944] 1982, 431). Knight's worst-case logic—planning as monopoly politics—provides a staple of the modern public choice literature on socialist price setting (see, e.g., Levy 1990; Shleifer and Vishny 1992; and Boettke and Anderson 1997). The argument, of course, is simply the application of Gordon Tullock's (1967) canonical rent-seeking insight into the economics of socialism. That Knight was aware of the situational logic driving the modern public choice critique of planning is clear.

1. A person may be one of two types: wholly public-spirited or wholly self-interested.

2. "It can in fact be shown that *if* human beings conformed to appropriate [best-case] specifications, and government likewise—*operated by the same or similar men, or by a special race of men, or by angels or Gods*—the ends could be even better accomplished under a system of centralized control, i.e., socialism or collectivism. . . . However, *there are very cogent reasons for believing that with men at all as they are—and with governments as they will be, if staffed by such men*—neither socialism nor anarchism in any approximation to the ideal pattern is a practical possibility" (Knight [1941] 1982b, 209, emphasis added). "The liberal will admit that much is to be said for an aristocratic constitution of society, including slavery, in an idealized form—*if* it could be assumed that there is any practicable way of having it in an ideal form. *This 'if' is enough by itself to give away the whole case*" (Knight [1946] 1982, 474).

> Socialists themselves generally assume that there will be very much more monopoly under socialism, even in particular industries, to say nothing of the fact that all production would in the nature of the case be one gigantic monopoly in the hands of the government—but of course all are *assumed to be managed in the public interest.* (Knight [1940] 1982, 170–71, emphasis added)

Intriguingly, Knight vehemently rejected any suggestion that such public-choice-type reasoning was in any way part of economic theory, steadfastly insisting that economic analysis per se (the pure logic of choice) necessarily precluded any "treatment of the essential issues" (Knight 1938c, 243) that were at stake in the planning versus markets controversy (see, e.g., Knight 1936, 255, 257).[3] The logic of choice per se, while clearly illuminating the "character of the economic problems with which socialism proposes to deal" (Knight [1940] 1982, 161), was necessarily mute when it came to saying anything about the thorny issue of planner type (benevolent or otherwise), and thus pure theory was unable to grapple with the "problem of how to get men of the utmost possible competence and good will into actual charge of the economic order" (Knight 1938c, 243).

Knight viewed economic theory (the pure logic of choice) as providing a set of a priori propositions that were necessarily true at all times and in all places (see, e.g., Knight [1939] 1982, 68–69; and [1940] 1982, 163–64). Thus, pure economic theory per se did not adopt any particular theoretical supposition concerning the fixity (or otherwise) of human nature. Indeed, any supposed fixity of human nature (benevolent or otherwise), while rather akin to a "relatively absolute absolute" (to invoke a favorite Knightian phrase) analytical constraint (Knight [1921] 1957, 335),[4] necessarily lacked the a priori character of the pure logic of choice (Knight [1940] 1982, 160). Thus, we can readily infer why Knight thought (contra Mises and Hayek) that any *economic* model of socialist failure was simply not possible.[5]

Indeed, economic theory, although true a priori, was decidedly irrelevant to any resolution (pro- or antiplanning) of the planning versus

3. For Knight, the problem was one of providing "concrete means for getting officials really to act *for the interests of society rather than in their own interests*" ([1939] 1982, 101–102, emphasis added). "What is there in public choice theory that also gives the lie to the planning advocates? We need only return to the ancient Roman query: Who is to guard the guardians? Planners are also utility-maximizing individuals, and who could predict that planning decisions will be made contrary to the interests of those who make them?" (Buchanan 1979, 272).

4. On the phrase, see Buchanan 1992, 78–79.

5. "Only within fairly narrow limits, and subject to *explicit hypothetical postulates,* can economic science make any pronouncement as to conditions as they would exist under socialism" (Knight [1940] 1982, 160).

markets debate. Knight the *economist* was insistent that the economic theorist must assume away any inkling of socialist monopoly (1936, 260), and thereby necessarily presupposing civic-minded planners, in order to make any prediction regarding the welfare properties of planning (see, e.g., 255, 259). Knight the *social philosopher,* however, was utterly skeptical toward the veracity of any such supposition. Indeed, Knight the social philosopher was insistent that planner type (at least for the present and foreseeable future) was emphatically *not* of the benevolent despot variety (see, e.g., Knight 1938a, 242; and 1946, 452–453).[6] Intriguingly, Knight's worst-case insight into the importance of planner type led him to suggest that the purely technical question of socialist calculation per se was simply not germane to the issue at hand; indeed, Knight suggested that the "real issues . . . namely the political issues,"[7] made those which were "economic [the possibility of socialist calculation] in any narrow sense pale into triviality" (1935a, 812). Planners of the Homo economicus variety simply lack any interest in socially efficient planning per se (Levy 1990). Thus, it was largely irrelevant that the Austrian critique of planning (positing the impossibility of socialist calculation) supposedly precluded efficient socialist planning.

> Theory and current experience warrant the gravest doubts as to whether the human group in command of a collectivist economy would make any serious effort to find for socio-economic problems solutions of the form taken for granted by Professor Pigou and other liberals, (Knight 1938c, 243)[8]

Knight's Political Critique: Planner Type and the Worst-Case Logic of Planning

Interestingly enough, Mises ([1932] 1981, 407) and Hayek (1935, 2–3) had initially suggested that questions concerning planner type were not

6. Knight charges that socialists posit an "explicit premise which eliminates in advance all rational discussion. To assume that the establishment of socialism will change 'human nature' is to destroy all possibility of predicting the future from the past, and one can establish any sort of subsequent social life desired or fancied by simply asserting the appropriate change in human nature" (1938a, 868). Knight's 1937 review of Keynes's *General Theory* is pungent: "Reformers seem characteristically to pass somewhat lightly over the fact that these are human problems [any suggested political substitute for the economic machinery of private property], essentially political problems, that there is no way which men will generally agree upon as valid to *call in God and the angels to make the decisions and carry out the policies*" (1937, 118, emphasis added).

7. Knight refers to the "danger that special interest groups may organize for the exercise of monopoly power" (1935a, 812).

8. "[A] socialistic government would not *try intelligently to function in accord with economic principles in securing maximum satisfaction of the economic needs of the masses. . . .* But such political prediction or prophecy is one thing, and reasoning in terms of economic principles is another" (Knight 1938b, 268, emphasis added).

pertinent to the socialist calculation debate.[9] It is rather fitting, therefore, that Hayek had to invoke some decidedly ad hoc assumptions regarding planner type in order to generate the "despotic" equilibrium posited in *The Road to Serfdom.* The similarities between Knight's critique of socialism and that provided by Hayek are readily apparent (see, e.g., Knight 1938a, 869–70; [1940] 1982, 166; [1941] 1982b, 242; and 1952, 414–15). Knight's critique, however, unlike that provided by Hayek, is mostly written in a worst-case vein. Thus, rather than despising Hayek's *The Road to Serfdom,* as Boettke and Vaughn suggest (Boettke and Vaughn 2002, 166), Knight (1946, 453) actually wrote, "I agree with his [Hayek's] general thesis, that general replacement of the free market organization by a predominance of centralized political control will mean the destruction of democracy and freedom and the establishment of a totalitarian social order. This seems as certain as any general political prediction can be, which of course, is not comparable to the status of established scientific laws, to say nothing of logical necessity."

The worst-case motivational suppositions underlying Knight's nascent public choice critique of socialist planning make logical sense. Hayek's critique, however, is predicated on some thoroughly ad hoc motivational suppositions, thereby apparently undercutting the allegedly noncontingent situational logic that Hayek attributes to planning in *The Road to Serfdom.* Knight considers his critique of planning entirely contingent and predicated on the assumption that planner type is not public-spirited. Hayek, however, while initially supposing benevolent planners,[10] invokes planner "wickedness" (emphatically *not* planner rent seeking) in chapter 10 of *The Road to Serfdom* (Hayek [1944] 1986, 100–101).[11] Hayek treats his own argument as a noncontingent account outlining the institutional dynamics intrinsic to socialist planning.

9. Durbin follows the Austrian lead: "All difficulties [e.g., incentives] which are not accountancy difficulties are not susceptible to theoretical dogmatism. 'The calculations will not be made.' . . . [Such objections] are not problems that the professor of economic theory is competent to discuss" (1936, 678).

10. "A proper understanding of the reasons which tend to incline so many of the intellectuals towards socialism is thus most important. . . . [I]t is neither selfish interests nor evil intentions but mostly honest convictions and good intentions which determine the intellectuals views" (Hayek [1949] 1978, 184).

11. Boettke (1995) attempts to provide a public choice reformulation of *The Road to Serfdom,* suggesting that Hayek takes a worst-case (rent-seeking) view. *The Road to Serfdom,* however, emphatically does not provide a rent-seeking critique of planning. Indeed, Hayek explicitly rejects any public choice type of suggestion that planners will readily exploit their monopoly position (Hayek [1944] 1986, 69–70). Hayek (1935, 222–29) similarly rejects the worst-case implications of the "planning equals monopoly writ large" insight. Remarkably, Levy (1990), Boettke (1995), and Caldwell (1997) pay no attention to these passages in *Collectivist Economic Planning* and *The Road to Serfdom.*

Keynes's remarks regarding *The Road to Serfdom* are apposite.[12] Why would planners of the public-spirited variety pursue planning all the way to serfdom despite its apparent failure? Knight would answer that we have misunderstood the "true" goals of planning, namely, to generate rents for a political elite. By *that* goal, planning is no failure whatsoever (see Stigler 1975, x). The planners were simply not public-spirited and had no interest in first-best efficiency. Hayek appears to have no satisfactory answer, however, to Keynes's pungent insight. One simply cannot plausibly generate the road to serfdom from truly public-spirited intentions (see, e.g., Durbin 1945, 361, 363). Error? Perhaps. Self-interest? Most certainly.[13] Public-spiritedness? Decidedly not.

Bibliography

Boettke, Peter J. 1995. "Hayek's *The Road to Serfdom Revisited:* Government Failure in the Argument against Socialism." *Eastern Economic Journal* 21, no. 1: 7–26.

Boettke, Peter, and Gary Anderson. 1997. "Soviet Venality: A Rent-Seeking Model of the Communist State." *Public Choice* 93:37–53.

Boettke, Peter, and Karen Vaughn. 2002. "Knight and the Austrians on Capital and the Problem of Socialism." *History of Political Economy* 34, no. 1: 155–76.

Buchanan, James M. [1969] 1999. *Cost and Choice.* Indianapolis: Liberty Press.

Buchanan, James M. 1979. "Public Choice and Ideology." In *What Should Economists Do?* Indianapolis: Liberty Press.

Buchanan, James M. 1992. *Better Than Plowing.* Chicago: University of Chicago Press.

Caldwell, Bruce. 1997. "Hayek and Socialism." *Journal of Economic Literature* 35 (December): 1856–90.

Durbin, E. F. M. 1936. "Economic Calculus in a Planned Economy." *Economic Journal* 46 (December): 676–90.

12. "You [Hayek] will not expect me to accept all the economic dicta in it [*The Road to Serfdom*]. But morally and philosophically I find myself in agreement with virtually the whole of it. . . . [W]hat we need is the restoration of right moral thinking—a return to proper moral values in our social philosophy. . . . I accuse you of perhaps confusing a little bit the moral and material issues. *Dangerous acts can be done safely in a community which thinks and feels rights, which would be the way to hell if they were executed by those who think and feel wrongly*" (Keynes [1944] 1980, 385–88, emphasis added).

13. "There is another aspect of socialism which is patent enough to any person of good sense (including economists) but which strangely enough is so generally overlooked that it may be mentioned. This is, *that in promoting socialism its devotees are seeking political power for themselves*" (Knight [1940] 1982, 162, emphasis added). "All political opposition to this programme [Marxism] is assumed as a matter of course to derive from the bourgeois class itself, either directly or through paid agents and dupes. (Non-Marxist economists are allowed to hover more or less between these two classifications, paid agent and dupe.) . . . [T]he allegation of selfish interest which is glibly pinned on the opposition applies even more obviously to the promoters of the class war themselves. They are *assumed to be free from any taint of self-interest*!" (Knight [1939] 1982, 117–18, emphasis added).

Durbin, E. F. M. 1945. "Professor Hayek on Economic Planning and Political Liberty." *Economic Journal* (December): 357–70.

Hayek, F. A. 1935. *Collectivist Economic Planning.* London: Routledge.

Hayek, F. A. [1944] 1986. *The Road to Serfdom.* London: Ark.

Hayek, F. A. [1949] 1978. "The Intellectuals and Socialism." In *Studies in Philosophy, Politics, and Economics.* London: Routledge.

Keynes, J. M. [1944] 1980. Letter to Hayek. In *The Collected Writings of John Maynard Keynes,* edited by Donald Moggridge, vol. 27. London: Macmillan.

Knight, Frank H. [1921] 1957. *Risk, Uncertainty, and Profit.* New York: Kelley and Millman.

Knight, Frank H. 1935a. "Barbara Wootton on Economic Planning." *Journal of Political Economy* 43 (December): 809–14.

Knight, Frank H. 1935b. "Intellectual Confusion on Morals and Economics." *International Journal of Ethics* 45, no. 2: 200–220.

Knight, Frank H. 1936. "The Place of Marginal Economics in a Collectivist System." *American Economic Review* 26, no. 1: 255–66.

Knight, Frank H. 1937. "Unemployment and Mr. Keynes's Revolution in Economic Theory." *Canadian Journal of Economics and Political Science* 3, no. 1: 100–123.

Knight, Frank H. 1938a. "Lippmann's *The Good Society.*" *Journal of Political Economy* 46 (December): 864–72.

Knight, Frank H. 1938b. "Socialism: An Economic and Sociological Analysis." *Journal of Political Economy* 46 (April): 267–69.

Knight, Frank H. 1938c. "Two Economists on Socialism." *Journal of Political Economy* 46 (April): 241–50.

Knight, Frank H. [1939] 1982. "Ethics and Economic Reform." In *Freedom and Reform: Essays in Economics and Social Philosophy.* Indianapolis: Liberty Press.

Knight, Frank H. [1940] 1982. "Socialism: The Nature of the Problem." In *Freedom and Reform: Essays in Economics and Social Philosophy.* Indianapolis: Liberty Press.

Knight, Frank H. [1941] 1982a. "The Meaning of Democracy: Its Politico-Economic Structure and Ideals." In *Freedom and Reform: Essays in Economics and Social Philosophy.* Indianapolis: Liberty Press.

Knight, Frank H. [1941] 1982b. "Religion and Ethics in Modern Civilization." In *Freedom and Reform: Essays in Economics and Social Philosophy.* Indianapolis: Liberty Press.

Knight, Frank H. [1944] 1982. "The Planful Act: The Possibilities and Limitations of Collective Rationality." In *Freedom and Reform: Essays in Economics and Social Philosophy.* Indianapolis: Liberty Press.

Knight, Frank H. [1946] 1982. "The Sickness of Liberal Society." In *Freedom and Reform: Essays in Economics and Social Philosophy.* Indianapolis: Liberty Press.

Knight, Frank H. 1946. "Freedom under Planning." *Journal of Political Economy* 54, no. 5: 451–54.

Knight, Frank H. 1952. "The Logic of Liberty." *Philosophical Review* 61, no. 3: 411–15.

Lavoie, Don. 1985. *Rivalry and Central Planning.* Cambridge: Cambridge University Press.

Levy, David M. 1990. "The Bias in Centrally Planned Prices." *Public Choice* 67:213–26.

Mises, Ludwig von. [1932] 1981. *Socialism: An Economic and Sociological Analysis.* Indianapolis: Liberty Press.

Shleifer, Andrei, and Robert Vishny. 1992. "Pervasive Shortages under Socialism." *RAND Journal of Economics* 23, no. 2: 237–46.

Steele, David Ramsay. 1992. *From Marx to Mises: Post-capitalist Society and the Challenge of Economic Calculation.* La Salle, IL: Open Court.

Stigler, George J. 1975. *The Citizen and the State.* Chicago: University of Chicago Press.

Tullock, Gordon. 1967. "The Welfare Costs of Tariffs, Monopolies, and Theft." *Western Economic Journal* 5 (June): 224–32.

13 • On Hayek's Road to Serfdom
Sixty Years Later

M. Ali Khan

. . . a book whose central message is timeless, applicable to a wide variety of concrete situations. In some ways it is even more relevant to the United States today than it was when it created a sensation.

—Milton Friedman 1994

. . . neither the provision of signposts on the road nor, in most circumstances, that of the roads themselves, can be paid for by every individual user.

—F. A. Hayek 1944

. . . if the state of affairs assumed by the theory of perfect competition ever existed, it would not only deprive of their scope all activities which the verb "to compete" describes but would make them virtually impossible.

—F. A. Hayek 1946

Introductory Comment

The three articles on which I have been invited to comment open three windows onto Hayek's "road to serfdom" and thereby into Hayek's oeuvre: Levy, Peart, and Farrant view it through the eyes of its contempora-

---

The opening epigraphs are drawn from Friedman's introduction to the fiftieth anniversary edition of *The Road to Serfdom* (Hayek [1944] 1994, 44); and Hayek 1948, 92. All quotations from Hayek in the balance of the text are from this edition of *The Road to Serfdom* with page numbers appended in parentheses.

My engagement with the ideas explored here began with my experience as a discussant at a session on Hayek at the Eastern Economic Association Meetings held in Washington, D.C., on 20–22 February 2004 at which an earlier version was presented. This version was presented at the Fifth Summer Institute for the Study of History of Economics at George Mason University, 26–29 July 2004. It benefited particularly from a conversation between James M. Buchanan and Warren J. Samuels, which led the session on "politics as exchange," reproduced in this volume. I am grateful to Jim Buchanan, Andrew Farrant, David Levy, Sandra Peart, Warren Samuels, and Warren Young for their (different) invitations and for stimulating conversation.

neous (and past) interlocutors, Rosser sees it as a testable prediction of where we are to be today, and McPhail relies on the lens of Belloc's servile state.[1] This brief comment responds to this tripartite perspective by opening additional windows and viewing it, and the "road" it surveys, from four, perhaps even complementary, perspectives: security versus freedom, impersonal forces and the market, rules and the rule of law, and education and language. These registers (angles, rest points, subspaces, and signposts at heart simply phrases) all go toward forming a composite of what we are to take from a text that Milton Friedman sees as "timeless."[2] This (my) commitment to the composite and the plurality it necessarily entails, to complementation rather than substitution, implies that there is no correct or singular view of the "road," certainly not a view that fails to properly recognize itself as a view, a view from nowhere, but rather one, not uniquely compelling or persuasive, that invites only an additional look and asks for further reading of passages whose meaning one had thought exhausted, stale, and spent, one that seeks to find and open other windows rather than closing all but one of the existing ones.[3]

On Security and Freedom

Hayek's ninth chapter and signpost on the road to serfdom concerns security and freedom and draws on the distinction, also used earlier by his cousin Wittgenstein and his cousin's friend Keynes,[4] between the *relative* and the *absolute:*

> It will be well to distinguish at the outset between the two kinds of security: the limited one, which can be achieved for all and is therefore no privilege but a legitimate object of desire; and absolute security, which in a free society cannot be achieved for all and ought not to be given as a privilege (132).

For Keynes it is absolute needs that are limited and attainable; if not now, then surely "within a hundred years." Man's "permanent problem—how to use his freedom from pressing economic cares" revolves

1. See Levy, Peart, and Farrant 2005; McPhail 2005; and Rosser 2005.

2. See note 34. Perhaps my own background leads me to blur the distinction between the "timelessness of the book" and the "timelessness of its central message." On the relevance of composite photography to theorizing, and to ethics, see Leys 1991; and Khan's discussion (2003b, 2004a) of Wittgenstein's "Lecture on Ethics," reprinted in Wittgenstein 1993.

3. These four sentences respond, in their own way, to a question posed to the author by Warren Samuels. For the methodological stance they convey, also see Žižek 2004, particularly the last paragraph of his opening section.

4. For Hayek's own view of the former relationship, see Hayek 1977; for the latter, see McGuiness and Wright 1995.

around relative needs, those that are "insatiable" and unlimited in the sense that "the higher the general level, the higher are they."[5] Keynes's employment of the distinction had already turned Wittgenstein's usage on its head: a relative meaning of a word was circumscribed by context and conditionality, by the purpose it served, whereas it was the absolute meaning that was transcendent, taking sense into non-sense. "To be safe essentially means that it is physically impossible that certain things should happen to me and therefore it is nonsense to say that I am safe whatever happens."[6]

But let me remain focused on Hayek. While noting the possible slippage in the contrast between a "legitimate object of desire" and an undefined privilege, a striving opposed to a granting, let me emphasize that Hayek is fully aware of the elusive nature of his distinction and underscores it by what can be seen as his signature statement concerning the law of unintended consequences.[7]

> There are difficult questions about the precise standard that should thus be assured. . . . An incautious handling of these questions might even cause serious and perhaps dangerous political problems. . . . Indeed, when security is understood in too absolute a sense, the general striving for it, far from increasing the chances for freedom, becomes the gravest threat to it. . . . [T]he more we try to provide full security by interfering with the market system, the greater the insecurity becomes; and, what is worse, the greater becomes the contrast between the security of those to whom it is granted as a privilege and the ever-increasing insecurity of the under-privileged. (133–43)

Even though the two basic linguistic parameters, the relative and the absolute, remain the same, a dynamic is introduced, one that opens up interesting possibilities for interrogation and reflection. How does an attempt to expand the space contract the space? Does an aspiration toward the unlimited only tighten the limits? Does going toward certainty increase the uncertainty? How does Hayek conceive of the distinction between "serious" and "dangerous"? And when he uses the term *gravest* am I to take him literally and think of some underlying notion of maxi-

---

5. Quoted from Keynes's 1930 essay on the economic possibilities for our grandchildren reprinted in Keynes [1932] 1963. See also section 6 of Khan 2004b for a reading.

6. Quoted from Wittgenstein's 1929 "Lecture on Ethics," reprinted in Wittgenstein 1993. See also Khan 2003b for a reading.

7. See Ullman-Margalit 1978. I would caution that Vanberg's (1986) quotation of her phrase "minding their own business" ought not to be read as necessarily indicating any passivity on the part of the agents."

mality (minimality to be "more" precise) rather than a simple metaphor that stands for "decreasing the chances for freedom"?

But perhaps these questions arise from a reading that, in its closeness and attention to detail, misses what Hayek takes to be the point of his text. I need to move back to get a better view, perhaps to work in terms of a distinction that is more singularly Hayekian, that between a "commercial and a military type of society" (140).

> This [unlimited] security is, however, inseparable from the restrictions on liberty and the hierarchical order of military life—it is the security of the barracks. . . . So long as only a part of society is organized on military lines, the unfreedom of the members of the military organization is mitigated by the fact that there is still a free sphere to which they can move if the restrictions become too irksome. (140–41)

Hayek's twelfth signpost concerns the socialist roots of nazism, returns to the commercial spirit, and falls on Sombart's denunciation of the "most infamous maxim that has ever been pronounced by a commercial mind." It is here that the distinction between individual striving and collective granting, and the limits that underlie both, comes to a head.

> [T]his old socialist welcomed the "German War" as the inevitable conflict between the commercial civilization of England and the heroic culture of Germany. His contempt for the "commercial" views of the English people, who had lost all warlike instincts, is unlimited. . . . Claims of the individual are always an outcome of the commercial spirit. (186)[8]

It is the commercial spirit that allows a move away from the heroic (zero-one, black-white, them-us) conception of security and sees it as a commodity that can be appropriated and allocated, a private divisible rather than an public indivisible good,[9] something that can be acquired and doled out in parts. It is not that society can be made secure or left insecure but that differing levels of security can be purchased for it:

8. One may perhaps pause here and ask, with Wittgenstein, whether Sombart's "contempt" is to be read in a relative or absolute sense.

9. For these technical terms in (neoclassical) economic theory—commodity, private good, public good—see the relevant entries in Eatwell et al. (1987), hereafter *Palgrave*.

> But the polities which are now followed everywhere, which hand out the privilege of security, now to this group and now to that, are nevertheless rapidly creating conditions in which the striving for security tends to become stronger than the love of freedom. If you guarantee to some a fixed part of a variable cake, the share left to the rest is bound to fluctuate proportionally more than the size of the whole. (141)

But perhaps I myself have been appropriating Hayek inappropriately, in giving meaning to the term that is more ours than his; in keeping with the tenor of the times, I may have read security in terms that are altogether too broad and encompassing. Hayek's narrower concern is with "the security of minimum income and the security of the particular income a person is thought to deserve (133)." However, before I find my footing and move from recruitment back to retrieval,[10] let me stay with what comes to mind when we hear the word *security,* at least here and now, and ask with Hayek whether security in this topical sense "can be provided for all outside of and supplementary to the market system [or] . . . provided only by controlling or abolishing the market" (133), whether the law of large numbers, of the central limit theorem and of unintended consequences, the regularity that renders Lyapunov's theorem a theorem, by itself guarantees security without the need for an explicit guarantor. Or are the risks so essentially correlated, the sets so unboundedly nonconvex, that an invocation to these conditional guideposts is in vain and a provider, however conceived and designed, is necessary?[11] And, if so, how is his solution to be preserved and not undercut by "free riding," security being provided only to those who are willing to make the necessary sacrifices for it (and then only in proportion to the payment)? Hayek is not one to duck these problems.

> [T]here is particularly the important question whether those who thus rely on the community should indefinitely enjoy all the same liberties as the rest. There are also serious problems of international relations which arise if mere citizenship of a country confers the right to a standard of living higher than elsewhere and which ought not to be dismissed too lightly. (133)

10. For my struggle with this binary, see Khan 1993a, in particular the concluding paragraph.

11. These two sentences are technical but not (therefore?) empty of conceptual meaning; see the relevant entries in *Palgrave.* In a famous 1945 essay, Hayek refers to such laws, arguing that the "number of elements with which we have to deal is not large enough for such accidental forces to produce stability" (1948, 83).

However, if the spontaneous order of the market is to be resorted to, if security is to be provided entirely through the domain of the economic, perhaps, as Tiebout was later to conceive it,[12] we need a robust and workable conception of the "economic," an understanding of the meaning that Hayek gives to the terms *market* and *competition.*[13]

On Impersonal Forces and Competition

Hayek's fourteenth chapter or signpost on the road to serfdom has a passage on ideal ends that could be regarded as a synecdoche for the entire work.

> The refusal to yield to forces which we neither understand nor can recognize as the conscious decisions of an intelligent being is a product of an incomplete and therefore erroneous rationalism. It is incomplete because it fails to comprehend that the coordination of the multifarious individual efforts in a complex society must take account of facts no individual can completely survey. And it fails to see that unless this complex society is to be destroyed, the only alternative to submission to the impersonal and seemingly irrational forces of the market is submission to an equally uncontrollable and therefore arbitrary power of other men (224).

There is one equality and at least two deductions, two *therefores,* in this remarkable passage: a view of error as a consequence of incompleteness and a view of arbitrariness as a consequence of the lack of control. And woven into these claims is *submission,* a crucial Hayekian term (as I am in the process of discovering), and the refusal and recalcitrance that are bound with it and to it give it shape and meaning. Indeed, Hayek uses *submission* as a lever to unlock and explain the *longue durée.*[14]

---

12. On the Tiebout hypothesis, see the relevant entries in *Palgrave,* as well as Buchanan 1965; Hamilton 1975, 1976; and their references. For the recent surge of interest initiated by Buchanan's 1965 essay, see Scotchmer 2005 and her references, particularly those to the writings of Birgit Grodal.

13. I resist the temptation to add the adjective *perfect* to *competition,* as in my *Palgrave* entry, in light of Hayek's imperative that "we should worry much less about whether competition in a given case is perfect and worry much more about whether there is competition at all" (1948, 105). The same goes for the adjective *free* in relation to the noun *market.*

14. Elsewhere in the book he contests Laski's view of "this mad competitive system which spells poverty for all peoples, and war as an outcome of that poverty" as a "curious reading of the last hundred and fifty years" (219).

> It was men's submission to the impersonal forces of the market that in the past has made possible the growth of a civilization which without this could not have developed; it is thus by submitting that we are everyday helping to build something that is greater than any of us can fully comprehend.

The question, of course, is: how does one submit to the impersonal forces of the market? Wherein lies the refusal to recognize the limits to one's individuality and independence? An answer to these questions is evident and available in Hayek's third pointer and signpost: the difference between individualism and collectivism and how this difference can be used to articulate the notion of "competition."[15]

> It is necessary in the first instance that the parties in the market should be free to sell and buy at any price at which they can find a partner to the transaction, and that anybody should be free to produce, sell and buy anything that may be produced or sold at all. And it is essential that the entry into the different trades should be open to all on equal terms and the law should not tolerate any attempts by individuals or groups to restrict this entry by open or concealed force. (42)[16]

It is worthy of emphasis that this view of competition is being put forward by a theorist whose theory is undergirded by a humility that subscribes to the incompleteness of any theory, to the fact that no phenomena can be "completely surveyed" or fully understood.[17] However, even in its openness and lack of precision Hayek is ruling out a canonical construction such as that of Debreu (1959) in which (1) free entry and "new" commodities are forbidden by fiat; (2) there is no room for divergences between private and social costs; and (3) parties, rather than searching out partners, all submit, passively, individually, and even rather blindly in the considered case of a finite number, to the dictates of

15. For modern theorizing, of this important and early interest of Hayek's, see Žižek 2004 and his references.

16. Also see Hayek's desiderata in his 1946 essay "The Meaning of Competition," reprinted in Hayek 1948, 95.

17. Hayek writes, "Individualism is thus an attitude of humility before this social process and of tolerance to other opinions and is the exact opposite of that intellectual hubris which is at the root of the demand for comprehensive direction of the social process" (182).

a ruling price system.[18] The Hayekian view of competition is richer and more nuanced.[19]

> To prohibit the use of certain poisonous substances or to require special precautions in their use, to limit working hours or to require certain sanitary arrangements is fully compatible with the preservation of competition. Nor is the preservation of competition incompatible with an extensive system of social services—so long as the organization of these services is not designed in such a way as to make competition ineffective over wide fields. (43)

This is a difficult and elusive passage. Hayek views "competition as a principle of social organization" (42) and allows its modification provided that its essential nature is kept unmodified: we can feed hormones to the chicken to the extent that the chicken remains a chicken, design measures to facilitate the operation of individual self-interest in such a way that these measures themselves do not fall prey to the exercise of self-interest, and in this feeding and designing we are constantly learning more about the nature of that whose essentiality is being presupposed. But more is true.

> The functioning of competition not only requires adequate organization of certain institutions like money, markets, and channels of information—some of which can never be adequately provided by private enterprise—but it depends, above all, on the existence of an appropriate legal system, a legal system designed both to preserve competition and to make it operate as beneficially as possible. (43)

And in these distinctions between open and concealed force, effective and ineffective competition, commodities that can, or can never, be provided by the market, Hayek is in his most dialectical mood, subtle and elusive at the same time. He wants to enlarge the domain of competition by not allowing it into certain domains, to use the ladder precisely to show that the ladder was not necessary, to design a system so that spon-

18. It is outside the scope of this brief essay to contrast McKenzie's (2002) conception of perfect competition with that of Debreu (1959), particularly as it differs on the importance of the differing assumptions regarding time and the aggregate technology available to a particular society at a "period" in time.

19. I leave it to future work to investigate Hayek's conception of competition in the comparative light of other views, particularly those of his precursors; see Morgan 1993 and her references.

taneous order is allowed its full play and spontaneity and the design, if not discarded, is redesigned and redirected into maintenance.

> The successful use of competition as a principle of social organization precludes certain types of coercive interference with economic life but it admits of others. (42)

Hayek tries to approach the notion through another route, by viewing by what it is in terms of what it is not, of what ought to be in terms of what ought not to be. Toward this end, he follows others in appropriating the term *planning* and fixing its meaning.[20]

> The meaning of this term becomes somewhat more definite if we make it clear that we mean that sort of planning which is necessary to realize any given distributive ideals. But, as the idea of central economic planning owes its appeal largely to the very vagueness of its meaning, it is essential that we should agree to its precise sense before we discuss its consequences. (39)

And this precise sense is captured in centralization, in the commonality of purpose, in a conception of a "rational utilization of our resources [that] requires central direction and organization of all our activities according to some consciously constructed 'blueprint'" (40–41). Whereas Hayek sees a monopoly negatively, he does not see its absence as a prerequisite for competition, does not rule out the possibility of "railways, road and air transport, or the supply of gas and electricity [being] inevitably monopolies"; the point is that they ought to "remain separate monopolies . . . [and not be] coordinated by a central control" (216). And these views are attested by the familiar signature and the familiar invocation of incompleteness.

> Very frequently even measures aimed against the monopolists in fact serve only to strengthen the power of monopoly. . . . Private monopoly is scarcely ever complete and even more rarely of long duration or able to disregard potential competition. (215–16)

20. At the outset, Hayek admits that an "economist, whose whole task is the study of how men actually do and how they might plan their affairs, is the last person who could object to planning in this general sense" (40). However he follows the practice of "socialists of all parties [who] have appropriated the word 'planning' for planning" (41). The contextually rich discussion of Levy, Peart, and Farrant (2005) can also be read as a focus on this fixture.

And the chapter closes around the "very necessary planning which is required to make competition as effective and beneficial as possible" (48) and around a basic nonconvexity, which privileges purification and pure strategies over mixed ones that involve fuzzy randomization and gray diversification.

> Both competition and central direction become poor and inefficient tools when they are incomplete . . . [and] planning and competition can be combined only by planning for competition but not by planning against competition. . . . [T]hey are alternative principles used to solve the same problem, and a mixture of the two means that neither will really work, and the result will be worse than if either system had been consistently relied upon. (48)

And now that I have a better understanding of the Hayekian conception of competition,[21] I can sharpen the question I asked in the previous section: can the market, by itself, finance and provide an "optimum" amount of security and thereby sustain itself and the society it supports? Surely this question must impinge on the legal, if not the ethical.

On Rules and the Rule of Law

Whereas the tension between control and discretion runs throughout the entire work,[22] it is in his sixth chapter and signpost on the road to serfdom that Hayek explicitly turns to rules, the rule of law, and the important but elusive distinction between formal and substantive rules.

> The difference between the two kinds of rules is the same as that between laying down a Rule of the Road, as in a Highway Code, and ordering people where to go; or better still, between providing signposts and commanding people which road to take. (82)

The thrust of the instrumental/substantive distinction lies in its subscription to anonymity, to its deliberate avoidance of the recognition of "types and particularities"; instrumental rules are to be "made in advance, in the shape of formal rules which do not aim at the wants and

21. Obviously my understanding is still incomplete. I return to this subject in Khan 2004c.

22. This tension in Hayek's thinking is critically brought out, for example, in the concluding section of Forsyth 1988.

needs of particular people" (81), which do not "set up distinctions of merit between the needs of different people" (82). Hayek refers to "typical situations into which anyone may get and in which the existence of such rules will be useful for a great variety of individual purposes" (83), and his target is distributive justice.

> [A]ny policy aiming at a substantive ideal of distributive justice must lead to the destruction of the Rule of Law. To produce the same result for different people, it is necessary to treat them differently. To give different people the same objective opportunities is not to give them the same subjective chance. . . . Thus the Rule of Law could clearly not be preserved in a democracy that undertook to decide every conflict of interests not according to rules previously laid down but "on its merits." (87–92)

The boundary between particularity and universality is itself elusive (after all, no rule is designed to apply to only one particular mother-in-law), but it is important that Hayek be understood at the precise level at which he makes his argument; his objection to "higher wages for nurses, . . . more extensive services for the sick, more milk for children, or better wages for agricultural workers, or . . . employment for the unemployed" is not based on the substance of these prescriptions, but on the law of unintended consequences: "[I]n our endeavor consciously to shape our future in accordance with high ideals, we should in fact unwittingly produce the very opposite of what we have been striving for" (7), and so an effort to "make reason supreme . . . ends by destroying reason" (181). The results of a policy cannot be completely surveyed or fully comprehended and are thereby never fully free of error.

But there is a conundrum here. As I have read Hayek so far, there are inevitable tradeoffs, necessary substitutions to be made on the margin between security and freedom, between submission and refusal, and now between substance and instrumentality, and the obvious question is how these are to be made. Even though *The Road to Serfdom* was not meant to be a scholarly work,[23] it inevitably leads to the (by now) clichd question as to the rules for the making of the rules, to the charting of the precise boundary between the relative and the absolute, maintenance and design, formality and substance.

23. The preface to Hayek 1948 warns "the reader that the present volume is not intended for popular consumption," the author having "published not long ago a more popular book on problems related to some of those discussed here" (v).

> The Rule of Law was consciously evolved only during the liberal age,[24] and is one of its greatest achievements not only as a safeguard but as a legal embodiment of freedom.[25] . . . This rule has little to do with the question whether all actions of government are legal in the juridical sense. They may well be and not conform to the Rule of Law. The fact that someone has full legal authority to act in the way that he does gives no answer to the question whether the law gives him power to act arbitrarily or whether the law prescribes unequivocally how he is to act. . . . By giving the government unlimited powers, the most arbitrary rule can be made legal; and in this way a democracy may set up the most complete despotism imaginable (90–91).

This is an important passage, and here Hayek may be more influenced by his cousin than he supposes. It is, of course, outside the scope of this brief comment to go into this influence in any detail, but I need at least to recall (in Kripke's reading of Wittgenstein's so-called private language argument) the terrifying moment when a teacher makes a judgment on whether the student is, or is not, to be admitted into the community and into what it deems to be its "forms of life."[26]

> Now, what do I mean when I say that the teacher judges that, for certain cases, the pupil must give the right answer? I mean that the child has given the same answer that he himself would give. Any individual who claims to have mastered the concept of addition will be judged by the community to have done so if his particular responses agree with those of the community in enough cases. . . . Those who deviate are corrected and told (usually as children) that they have not grasped the concept of addition. One who is an incorrigible deviant in enough respects simply cannot participate in the life of the community.[27]

---

24. This emphasis on evolution, conscious or spontaneous, based on the individual or on the group, and its own evolution in Hayek's subsequent thought is one of many strands that deserves more careful study; see, in particular, chapter 4, on the evolution of systems of rules of conduct, in Hayek (1977) and its reading by Vanberg (1986); Paul (1988); Gamble (1996); and Aimar, Bensaid, and Cubeddo in Birner et al. 2002.

25. Hayek inserts the qualification that "As a vague ideal it has, however, existed at least since Roman times, and during the last few centuries it has never been so seriously threatened as it is today" [1944] 1994, p. 90.

26. I wish to emphasize that this is one particular reading of Wittgenstein; for another, to me more compelling reading, the reader can see the second lecture in Cavell 1990.

27. These passages are quoted from Kripke 1982—the first two sentences from page 90, and the last two from pages 91–92.

The point is that arbitrariness and coercion are inevitable here. A rule is not self-sufficient, does not possess in it the resources needed to guide its own application. A language, a money, a culture can hardly be seen as an outcome of purposeful cost-benefit analysis; they must, at some level, be blindly and passively accepted, must be, can only be, understood as being rooted in loyalty, faith, and trust, and only such an understanding can serve as the passport for membership in a functional and surviving community.[28] Just putting up a signpost is not the end of the matter; it must draw on the way in which, tacit but fully imbibed, the pointer is to be seen, on the precise meaning that is to be given to its slant, in the clarity that such a slant is not theorized but arbitrarily imposed, and in this very imposition gives the theory all of the hues that will color it.

> I feel that the "poetic" element . . . gets lost in translation from one poetic convention to another. And most of it, I suggest, is not just irrelevant moral stuff, but is concerned with the slant that theory has on reality—with the completeness and incompleteness of the picture of the real world that the theory affords, with the perspective and "projection" and dimensions it is employing, with what it throws into relief as causally important and what it relegates to the shade.[29]

The question, then, is who is to decide who is or is not one of us, who is or is not playing the language game as it ought to be played, subscribes and furthers the culture in the way that it ought to be subscribed to and furthered, who rules that the exigencies of the situation demand that the checks and balances of the past now need to be bracketed and the exceptional no longer regarded as the exceptional. Put more succinctly, and more topically, who is the true patriot and who is the authority that is going to identify the patriot and hold him or her up as the exemplar of true patriotism, of how to add or to quadd?[30]

On Language and Education

Hayek apocalyptically titles his eleventh and thirteenth signposts on the road to serfdom "The End of Truth" and "The Totalitarians in our Midst" and uses them to turn his full attention to the dangers of fashioning a

28. See Khan 2002 for a more leisurely and sustained reflection on these issues.
29. This passage is from Dobb's 1941 letter to Joan Robinson, dated 31 January 1941; see Khan 2004b for a precise reference and further discussion.
30. For a meaning of these terms, see Kripke 1982.

common purpose, to optimization in the large, to global rather than local control of human conduct. The reader is offered another window into the difference between a commercial and a military form of organization through parameters that are by now familiar.

> Every activity must derive its justification from a conscious social purpose. There must be no spontaneous, unguided activity because it might produce results which cannot be foreseen and for which the plan does not provide. (178)

> Although those responsible for a decision may have been guided by no more than a prejudice, some guiding principle will have to be stated publicly if the community is not merely passively to submit but actively to support the measure. (171)

An interesting binary is now introduced between passive submission and active support, and Hayek is not to be deterred that this might run counter to his earlier imperatives, that passive acceptance might not be effective precisely because it is passive and, in thereby cutting into its own efficacy, may not be acceptance at all. However, the line between the active and the passive hinges on the distinction between training and education, propaganda and information, on both the limitations and potentialities of dispersed and diffused knowledge.

> Socialists . . . traditionally hope to solve this problem by education. But what does education mean in this respect? Surely we have learned that knowledge cannot create new ethical values, that no amount of learning will lead people to hold the same views on the moral issues which a conscious ordering of all social relations raises. (125)

> The interaction of individuals, possessing different knowledge and different views, is what constitutes the life of thought. The growth of reason is a social process based on the existence of such differences. It is of its essence that it results cannot be predicted. . . . The idea that the human mind ought consciously to control its own development confuses individual reason, which alone can consciously control anything, with the interpersonal process to which its growth is due. (181)

In describing a process by which "people [are made] to serve the validity of the values they are to serve" (172), in using public slogans and sound bites to whip the public into line, to do what Hayek is loath to do as exemplified by the way he presents "the road to the serfdom," he gives a fuller sketch of the nightmare that is inevitably to follow.

> And the most efficient technique to this end is to use the old words and change their meaning. Few traits . . . are . . . so characteristic of the whole intellectual climate as the complete perversion of language, the change of meaning of the words by which the ideals of the new regimes are expressed. . . . Gradually, as this process continues, the whole language becomes despoiled, and words become empty shells deprived of any definite meaning, as capable of denoting one thing as its opposite and used solely for the emotional associations which still adhere to them. (172–74)

The relevant question, of course, pertains to the nature of the agency that is to bring this about and how it fares with the law of unintended consequences. Does language become all the more uncontrollable if earnest and sustained attempts are made to control it, does society (or equivalently, for the purposes of this essay, an economy, polity, or community) become all the more unmanageable if attempts are made to manage it? Or is there a threshold to the distribution of power and opportunity, of access, with the problem arising only after that threshold is crossed? But let us read further and not interrupt one who is on a productive roll.

> It is not difficult to deprive the great majority of independent thought. But the minority who will retain an inclination to criticize must also be silenced. . . . Public criticism or even expressions of doubt must be suppressed because they tend to weaken public support. (174–75)

It is important to understand here, or so it seems to me, that forceful external coercion is not necessarily involved, that the engines for compliance and conformity are already internally and individually lodged and fueled by individual perceptions of what counts for and constitutes success and the path of least resistance that is to attain it. All that is needed for the ruling authority, be it a market or a bureaucracy or some hybrid, is the security that comes from individual striving governed only by self-interest, an interest curtailed and controlled by the rules and the choice variables that the authority, in representing the community over which it exercises its authority, has itself put into place.[31] It is in my self-interest to conform, to loudly declare my patriotism in the tones and colors that are now required for such a declaration. With this sense of purpose, ambiguity and ambivalence can be rooted out, and, insofar as human conduct can be captured and quantified through an optimization problem, it furnishes all the fetters that an authority can ask for and needs for the pursuit of its own (self-?) interest. And efficiency in the choice of technique translates into efficiency in the choice of curriculum.[32]

> [P]erhaps no other country provides a better illustration of the effects on a nation of a general and thorough shift of the greater part of its educational system from the "humanities" to the "realities" than Germany between 1840 and 1940. . . . I believe that it was the author of *Leviathan* who first suggested that the teaching of classics should be suppressed, because it instilled a dangerous spirit of liberty! (209)

And in describing the world as it is, giving a face to who "we" are and therefore who we aspire to be, good theorizing is separated from bad, error corrected, and truth sifted from falsehood.

> Facts and theories must become no less the object of an official doctrine than views about values. And the whole apparatus for spreading knowledge—the schools and the press, radio and motion picture—will be used exclusively to spread those views which, whether true or false, will strengthen the belief in the rightness of the decisions taken by the authority; and all information that might cause doubt or hesitation will be withheld. The probable effect on the people's loyalty to the system becomes the only criterion for deciding whether a particular piece of information is to be published or suppressed (175–76).

This is Hayek at his reflexive best. It is not the particular authority but fear of impediments to advancement that it instills and institutes; the monopolistic, concealed, but arbitrary power that it exercises are at issue. Hayek's achievement in *The Road to Serfdom*—the timelessness of his message, if one prefers—is to shift attention from the label that is given to an economic system and turn it to the distribution of power, of

31. On how a modern theorist can see as the indispensability of self-interest for successful theorizing, see Khan 2004b.

32. See Khan 1992, 1993b, for an emphasis on curriculum as opposed to "rates of return."

the way in which decisions of the margin, at the margin, are made in any society, be it "developed" or "less developed." The questions, then, with which I would like to conclude this section are these. Is there room in our conception of a process that renders everything commensurable, reduces all to the common denominator of the dollar, for a counterprocess that preserves the noncommensurable and the uniquely individual, fosters heterogeneity as part of the quest for homogeneity, and gives security and encouragement to idiosyncracy precisely when it is seeking a consensus? Are there forces endogenous to the market that prevent a monopoly in the market of ideas, keep a level playing field in a world where no field is level, and ensure that no particular point of view restricts (or, better still, silences) other points of view?

Concluding Comments

In conclusion, my four different registers merge into one on the importance of judgment and balance as to the "precise standard that should be assured"; labels by themselves do not suffice, and bald polarities have to be interrogated for the tradeoffs they conceal—between security and freedom, submission and supplementation, rules and discretion, training and education—all imbricated by the limitations of the language we are given to work with. On this count, I am also at one with the authors whose work stimulated this comment; rather than opening additional windows, perhaps I have been looking through ones they have already provided.[33] All interrogate the binaries that proxy similarity and difference and have attained a canonical conventionality in recent discussions of Hayek's book:[34] leftist and rightist socialists; planning (command or indicative) versus competition; democrats versus national, social, or closet social democrats; and many others.[35] If there is timelessness in Hayek's message, it is not so much for the verdict on one or the other as because an investigation of the terrain they circumscribe will always be with us.

However, there is one issue that none of my authors touch, and I should like to conclude with it. This concerns reparation and insurance,

33. Thus, Rosser (2005, 1018) explicitly considers the tradeoff between security and freedom, Levy, Peart, and Farrant (2005) can be read as emphasizing nonconvexities, and pure outcomes, in the space of economic systems, and McPhail (2005, 1001) argues that, insofar as Belloc is a precursor of Hayek, his argument is a criticism of capitalism and not socialism.

34. Indeed, this particular book has been laid aside as being too much a product of its time in a considered treatment of Hayek's work. Thus, in the third paragraph of his introduction, Rosser sees it "very much a book of its immediate time, World War II, often to an almost absurd degree" (2005, 1013).

35. See, for example, the opening sentence of McPhail 2005, the section headings in Rosser 2005, and the discussion of the Durbin-Hayek overlap in Levy, Peart, and Farrant 2005.

the fact that difficult judgments made in a context of incomplete information are bound to lead to errors, some false hypotheses inevitably accepted and true ones inevitably rejected, even surgical strikes causing grievous damage to collateral; the issue is rather the compensatory mechanisms to cope with and compensate for these errors after they are made and the very effect that the presence or the absence of these mechanisms has on the propensities of the risk-taking agents to take risks and the consequent probabilities of the errors that their actions then entail. In defense of one's way of life, perceived or real, relative or absolute, are these mechanisms to evolve spontaneously or be put in place consciously, ex ante or ex post. Are they to ask for an evaluation (valorization, condemnation, or perhaps neither but simply enlightened understanding) of the market not on account of its efficiency but for its ability to compensate for type I and type II errors and thereby on its robustness as a system over time? These seem to me to be the questions that come out of Hayek's project and one that, even after sixty years, has yet to be given the serious attention it deserves.[36]

Bibliography

Birner, Jack, Pierre Garrouste, and Thierry Aimar. 2002. *F. A. Hayek as a Political Economist.* London: Routledge.

Buchanan, James M. 1965. "An Economic Theory of Clubs." *Economica* 32:1–14.

Cavell, Stanley. 1990. *Conditions Handsome and Unhandsome.* Chicago: University of Chicago Press.

Debreu, Gerard. 1959. *Theory of Value.* New York: Wiley.

Eatwell, John, Murry Milgate, and Peter K. Newman, eds. 1987. *The New Palgrave.* London: Macmillan.

Forsyth, Murray. 1988. "Hayek's Bizarre Liberalism: A Critique." *Political Studies* 36:235–50.

Gamble, A. 1996. *Hayek: The Iron Cage of Liberty.* London: Polity.

Hayek, F. A. [1944] 1994. *The Road to Serfdom.* Chicago: University of Chicago Press.

Hayek, F. A. 1948. *Individualism and Economic Order.* Chicago: University of Chicago Press.

Hayek, F. A. 1952. *The Sensory Order: An Enquiry into the Foundations of Theoretical Psychology.* London: Routledge and Kegan Paul.

Hayek, F. A. 1967. *Studies in Philosophy, Politics, and Economics.* London; Routledge and Kegan Paul.

Hayek, F. A. 1977. "Remembering My Cousin Wittgenstein (1889–1951)." *Encounter* 36:20–22.

Hamilton, Bruce W. 1975. "Zoning and Property Taxation in a System of Local Governments." *Urban Studies* 12:205–11.

36. This paragraph draws on many discussions with Veena Das.

Hamilton, Bruce W. 1976. "Capitalization of Intrajurisdictional Differences in Local Tax Prices." *American Economic Review* 66:743–53.

Keynes, J. M. [1932] 1963. *Essays in Persuasion.* New York: Norton.

Khan, M. Ali. 1992. "Comments on Professor Summers." *Pakistan Development Review* 31:394–400.

Khan, M. Ali. 1993a. "On Economics and Language." *Journal of Economic Studies* 20:51–69.

Khan, M. Ali. 1993b. "On Education as a Commodity." *Pakistan Development Review* 32:541–79.

Khan, M. Ali. 2002. "Trust as a Commodity and on the Grammar of Trust." *Journal of Banking and Finance* 26:1719–66.

Khan, M. Ali. 2003a. Erratum to M. Ali Khan's "Trust as a Commodity and on the Grammar of Trust." *Journal of Banking and Finance* 27:773.

Khan, M. Ali. 2003b. "On the Ethics of (Economic) Theorizing." Paper presented at an American Statistical Association panel on ethics at the Joint Statistical Meetings, 3–7 August 2003, San Francisco.

Khan, M. Ali, 2004a. "Composite Photography and Statistical Prejudice: Levy, Peart, and Marshall on the Theorist and the Theorized." *European Journal of Political Economy* 20:23–30.

Khan, M. Ali, 2004b. "Self-Interest, Self-Deception, and the Ethics of Commerce." *Journal of Business Ethics* 20:23–30.

Khan, M. Ali. 2004c. "Sustainability, Structural Change, and the Ethics of Globalization." Mimeo.

Kripke, Saul. 1982. *Wittgenstein on Rules and Private Language.* Cambridge: Harvard University Press.

Levy, David M., Sandra J. Peart, and Andrew Farrant. 2005. "The Spatial Politics of Hayek's *Road to Serfdom.*" *European Journal of Political Economy* 21:982–99.

Leys, Ruth. 1991. "Types of One: Adolf Meyer's Life Chart and the Representation of Individuality." *Representations* 34:1–28.

McGuiness, B. and G. H. von Wright. 1995. *Cambridge Letters.* London: Blackwell.

McKenzie, Lionel W. 2002. *Classical General Equilibrium Theory.* Cambridge: MIT Press.

McPhail, Edward. 2005. "Does the Road to Serfdom Lead to the Servile State: An Assessment." *European Journal of Political Economy* 21: 1000–1011.

Morgan, Mary. 1993. "Competing Notions of 'Competition' in Late Nineteenth-Century American Economics." *History of Political Economy* 25:563–604.

Paul, Ellen F. 1988. "Liberalism, Unintended Orders, and Evolutionism." *Political Studies* 36:251–72.

Rosser, J. Barkley, Jr. 2005. "The Road to Serfdom and the World Economy: Sixty Years Later." *European Journal of Political Economy* 21:1012–25.

Scotchmer, Suzanne. 2005. "Consumption Externalities, Rental Markets and Purchase Clubs." *Economic Theory* 25:235–53.

Stigler, George J. 1957. "Perfect Competition, Historically Contemplated." *Journal of Political Economy* 65:1–17.

Tiebout, Charles. 1956. "A Pure Theory of Local Expenditures." *Journal of Political Economy* 64:416–24.

Ullman-Margalit, Edna. 1978. "Invisible Hand Explanations." *Synthese* 39:263–91.

Vanberg, Viktor. 1986. "Spontaneous Market Order and Social Rules." *Economics and Philosophy* 2:75–100.

Wittgenstein, Ludwig. 1993. *Philosophical Occasions, 1912–1951.* Edited by James Klagge and Alfred Nordmann. Indianapolis: Hackett.

Žižek, Slavoj. 2004. "From Purification to Subtraction: Badiou and the Real." In *Think Again,* edited by P. Hallward. London: Continuum.

14 • Hiring a Foreign Expert
Chile in the Nineteenth Century

Juan Pablo Couyoumdjian

Introduction

The standard literature on the political economy of foreign economic advisers recognizes that this is a problem that has important political dimensions (Drake 1994; see also Schneider 1998). In this framework, however, advisers are ordinarily viewed as agents who only attempt to serve the public good, albeit within the context of the political constraints they face. But, surely, experts are also ordinary people, just like the rest of us, in that they have preferences over different dimensions of their work. After all, the axioms of rational choice postulate that all economic agents are self-interested and will act accordingly given the constraints they confront.[1]

In this chapter I will focus on the problem of hiring a foreign expert when advice seekers have an imperfect knowledge about the field in which they want to acquire expertise. As can easily be imagined, in this situation making mistakes is not only easy but can also be very dangerous. As long as advice seekers are unable to determine adequately and screen the most relevant attributes of a potential expert, their decisions will involve nontrivial risks unless an adequate arrangement can be implemented to avoid these dangers. This was the predicament faced by advice seekers in nineteenth-century Chile, who in particular were searching for an adviser in the field of economics. In 1855 Chilean

---

Preliminary versions of this chapter were presented at the Summer Institute for the Preservation of the History of Economics at George Mason University (2002) and the History of Economics Society meetings at Duke University (2003). Comments from participants, especially Salim Rashid at the Summer Institute, and my discussant at the HES meetings, Steve Meardon, are greatly appreciated. I am also thankful to the staff at the Archivo Histórico del Ministerio de Relaciones Exteriores, and the Archivo Nacional, both in Santiago, Chile, for their assistance in working through their collections. At the same time, comments from an anonymous reader and conversations with and suggestions from Ricardo Couyoumdjian, Eugenio Guzmán, Philippe Nataf, and Carlos Scartascini are gratefully acknowledged. David Levy and Sandra Peart deserve a special mention for their invaluable editorial suggestions, for their encouragement, and for many helpful comments throughout this project. Of course, the usual caveat applies.

1. This is a point that has been addressed in some recent works on the economics of expertise. See, for example, Krishna and Morgan 2001; Morris 2001; and Ottaviani and Sørensen 2003. See also Levy 2001.

officials hired the French economist Jean Gustave Courcelle-Seneuil as a professor of political economy and economic adviser to the government, and he was to be highly influential in the country during his tenure there, as well as in the ensuing period (Fuentealba 1945; Villalobos and Sagredo 1987; Will 1960). Yet his legacy has, by and large, been considered strongly negative (Fuentealba 1945; Hirschman 1963; Pinto 1962; Urzúa 1884). As I shall explain more carefully in the following pages, these reactions are mainly based on a strong contempt for classical economics, which was the doctrine the French expert explicitly advocated. But does the way in which the foreign expert was selected also play a role in these arguments? Might the fact that Courcelle-Seneuil was perceived as being selected as the result of an ideological connivance be one of the reasons for this reaction against him? Here, then, I will carefully reexamine Jean Gustave Courcelle-Seneuil's hiring by the Chilean government as a way to shed some light on this issue. Since this is a project that was long overdue in the study of the history of economic ideas in Chile, I believe this study has a double significance.

By proceeding in this way, of course, I will not be able judge the real worth of the evaluations of Jean Gustave Courcelle-Seneuil's work that we find in the Chilean economic history literature. But this is not my purpose. What I propose to show, instead, is that hiring a foreign adviser under conditions of imperfect information on the part of the advice seekers may be a serious problem that deserves careful examination. Note, then, that here I will only focus on the problem from the point of view of an advice seeker who, we assume, is seeking scientifically unbiased advice. Given the motivational assumptions I have set forth, the problem for the expert is very easy: if and when he or she takes the job on being offered it, he will simply optimize given his preferences and the constraints he faces.

Jean Gustave Courcelle-Seneuil in Chile

Jean Gustave Courcelle-Seneuil (1813–92) was born in France and was a prominent member of the French school of economics. In this sense, Albert Hirschman termed him a "stalwart defender of free trade and laissez faire" principles (1987, 707), which, as is well known, are distinctive characteristics of the tenets of this school.[2] But such assessments are not unique to Hirschman. In his posthumous eulogy of Courcelle-Seneuil, published in the *Journal des Économistes,* Gustave de Molinari also observed that "for sixty years . . . Courcelle-Seneuil fought all false eco-

2. On the nineteenth-century French School of Political Economy, see, for example, Gide and Rist 1915; and Alcouffe 1989.

nomic theories; the protectionist ideas now so popular, as well as socialism which is now less favored. He was one of those rare men of principles and one of those even rarer men who remain faithful to their principles" (1892, 80). And, similarly, Clément Juglar also referred to Courcelle-Seneuil as a resolute liberal economist.[3] In any case, in his beginnings Jean Gustave Courcelle-Seneuil was more of an expository writer than what we would consider an academic economist. On the other hand, once his professional reputation was established it is fair to say that it was his work on banking theory, where he was a strong proponent of a free banking system, that led to this recognition. Of course, we should note that during his lifetime Courcelle-Seneuil not only published on this subject (on this, see his *Le crédit et la banque* [1840] and *Traité théorique et pratique des opérations de banque* [1853]); he also wrote a treatise on political economy, *Traité théorique et pratique d'économie politique* (1858),[4] and several works in law, accounting, politics, and philosophy. Thus, while he was a member of the section of political economy of the French Académie des Sciences Morales et Politiques, "Courcelle-Seneuil would have been entitled to be a member of any section. Philosopher, moralist, legislator, economist, historian, he would have been at home anywhere; his works and his research bear witness to this" (Juglar 1895, 850).[5]

But why did Jean Gustave Courcelle-Seneuil come to Chile? Or, to put it another way, why was he hired by Chilean officials? And what was expected of him in Chile? In an obituary of Courcelle-Seneuil originally published in the *Anales de la Universidad de Chile* in 1892, the historian Diego Barros Arana gives the following account in this respect.

---

3. "Liberal in politics, Courcelle-Seneuil was more so in economic matters, fighting the intervention of the state in all areas that could restrict social, political or industrial freedom" (Juglar 1895, 857). Courcelle-Seneuil's membership of the Société d'Economie Politique and his numerous original collaborations in the *Journal des Économistes* provide further support to our argument that he was an archetypal member of this school. As Gide has argued, Courcelle-Seneuil "was virtually the *pontifex maximus* of the classical school; the holy doctrines were entrusted to him and it was his vocation to denounce and exterminate the heretics. During many years he fulfilled this mission through book reviews in the *Journal des économistes* with priestly dignity. Argus-eyed, he knew how to detect the slightest deviations from the liberal school" (quoted by Hirschman 1987, 707).

I am responsible for translating the previous passages from the French. Unless otherwise noted, all the ensuing translations from works written in French or Spanish should be understood as being mine.

4. This work was well received in French circles when it was first published; see Passy 1859. At the same time, it also seems to have endured well throughout time (Gide and Rist 1915, 380).

5. What is more, W. S. Jevons placed Courcelle-Seneuil as a member of a "succession of great French Economists" (1965, xliv) that had made important contributions to economic theory. I am grateful to Sandra Peart for calling my attention to Jevons's references to Courcelle-Seneuil.

> Towards the end of 1854, the Chilean government had offered Mr. André Cochut, who had come to be well known in the country for his collaborations in *El Araucano,* the official newspaper of those years, the chair in political economy in the university. Mr. Cochut excused himself for family problems and suggested Mr. Courcelle-Seneuil as the most suitable candidate for that position in France. The contract was settled by General Blanco Encalada, then Chilean Minister in Paris. (Barros Arana 1914, 197)

In his *Courcelle-Seneuil en Chile* (1945), the most comprehensive study on Jean Gustave Courcelle-Seneuil's tenure in Chile, Leonardo Fuentealba provides further information regarding this process. In this sense, he explains that it was the desire to improve the instruction in political economy in the country that motivated the search for a foreign economist in the first place. Fuentealba also transcribes the agreement signed between Courcelle-Seneuil and the Chilean consul in France, which gives us some light as to the obligations the foreign adviser was taking upon himself and the remuneration he was to receive for his job. In this respect, the French economist's agreed-upon obligations were basically three: to teach political economy at the University of Chile, to work as an economic adviser at the Ministry of Finance, and to educate the public on relevant economic issues through the press. In exchange he was to receive a salary amounting to FF$18,000 per annum plus FF$5,000 for transportation and settlement expenses.

While seemingly informative, however, this expanded account is still incomplete in several ways. In particular, the important question as to why Jean Gustave Courcelle-Seneuil, or, as it turns out, André Cochut, was initially selected remains unanswered. That is, we do not know how Chilean officials first proceeded in their search for an expert such that they ended up hiring Courcelle-Seneuil. Moreover, we are not told what requirements, if any, were demanded from the candidate that would fill this new position. These are some of the questions I will attempt to answer in the following section, where we will reconstruct the narrative associated to the hiring of Jean Gustave Courcelle-Seneuil by the Chilean government.

Before we proceed to that problem, however, we must also ask ourselves why Jean Gustave Courcelle-Seneuil wanted to leave France or at least why he was willing to accept the Chilean government's offer. The fact that the political situation in France was uncertain at the time seems to be a prime reason in this sense; Louis-Napoleon Bonaparte's coup of December 1851 and the regime that followed were a blow to Courcelle-Seneuil's republicanism. At the same time, the pay offered seemed to be respectable, extending sufficient compensation for his opportunity cost and some considerations of equalizing differences in wages. In this sense, it is probable that the Chilean government's offer came at a very opportune time for him and, thus, he left France for what Luc Marco (1991, 142) calls a "voluntary exile" in Chile.

Whatever his reasons, Courcelle-Seneuil did come to Chile, where he lived between 1855 and 1863, and became the critical first mover for the classical-liberal school and its period of dominance in terms of Chilean economic policy discussions during the second half of the nineteenth century. In Chile he was to become a teacher to a whole generation of economists and policymakers. At the same time, as adviser to the Ministry of Finance he participated directly in many policy discussions and was the intellectual architect of several legislative proposals.[6] Thus, regarding the standing of economic thought in Chile during the second half of nineteenth century, the following quotations are very illustrative.

> The majority of our most distinguished public men, independent of their political affiliations . . . were imbued by these types of ideas [i.e., liberal economic principles], which were the only ones considered truly scientific. (Subercaseaux 1924, 113)

> [As opposed to those in the United States], we were dumbfounded by the doctrines of free trade. This doctrine of educated gentlemen: based on an opportunistic rhetoric, which had its own syllogisms and even its own logic. We were captured by the theories, the technicalities, and the abstractions. We prostrated [ourselves] under the feet of the new idol and preached its principles in our schools and universities. A school was born. Yet how could it not be so? Who would have dared to disobey Adam Smith, Say, Bastiat, or Courcelle-Seneuil? (Urzúa 1884, 11, paragraph break omitted)[7]

6. Now may be the appropriate time to explain that I have translated Courcelle-Seneuil's job description, which in Spanish is "Primer Jefe Auxiliar del Ministerio de Hacienda," as economic adviser to the Ministry of Finance. As bilingual readers will be able to tell, the transliteration is not perfect, but I believe this is, in modern parlance, the best way to characterize the work Courcelle-Seneuil was to undertake as an economist in the Chilean government.

7. To be sure, I should stress that these remarks should not be interpreted as suggesting that liberal economic principles were unknown in Chile until the mid–nineteenth century. Will (1964) provides evidence that classical economics was known since the early days of independence yet was disregarded. Policy pragmatism predominated both because a doctrinaire approach to economic policy did not seem appropriate at a time when severe problems had to be addressed (i.e., after independence) and because the knowledge and level of instruction in classical political economy in the country was very poor.

As the remarks of the Chilean lawyer Pedro N. Urzúa clearly suggest, it was due to the influence of the French expert that liberalism created a school in the country. So let us briefly review how influential Courcelle-Seneuil was in Chile, focusing both on his impact as a teacher and an economic adviser to the government.

As a professor of political economy in the School of Law of the university, Jean Gustave Courcelle-Seneuil was famous and respected; his classes were well known and his teachings highly valued. In this sense, Hirschman has even argued that "the principal influence exercised by Courcelle-Seneuil resided in his forceful teaching" (1987, 707).[8] Indeed, there seem to be good reasons for such an assessment.

> As a professor of political economy in Chile, he [Courcelle-Seneuil] was a virtual prophet of this science, not only because he was good at teaching it but, more important, because he was able to transmit its importance and awaken in his students an interest in the subject. (Rodríguez 1893, 199)[9]

When in 1860 the Consejo [Governing Board] of the Universidad de Chile approved a new syllabus for the course in political economy at the School of Law, it followed Courcelle-Seneuil's *Traité* very closely (Courcelle-Seneuil 1860). The Chilean government also financed a translation of this book into Spanish, and thus it was not only available in this language as of 1859 but it also seems to have been widely circulated (Subercaseaux 1924, 114).

At the same time, Courcelle-Seneuil was seen as the physical embodiment of the now famous liberal ideas Guillermo Subercaseaux referred to in the previous quotation. And this, in turn, led to the fact that the field of political economy became a more respectable discipline in Chile. But, more than that, Courcelle-Seneuil's mentoring implied the creation of a unique liberal tradition in the Chilean academy and underscored a period of liberal dominance in public policy.

8. For a similar evaluation, see the following quotation from Juglar 1895: "With the new professor, the teaching of political economy was revamped. . . . These five years of teaching had a great influence on the youth of Chile, who, imbued with the principles of this science, contributed to the propagation of the principles of industrial liberty, which is the source of the extraordinary development of the wealth of people" (856).

9. Further, "Mr. Courcelle-Seneuil taught political economy as an exact science, positive in its fundamental principles, positive in the manifestation of economic phenomena, and positive in terms of the consequences that were derived from it. His explanations, presented modestly, in familiar conferences, arranged so as to make them clear and comprehensible . . . were calculated to develop a spirit of observation among the young people, and to banish learning by rote, which was how most of their studies were taught" (Barros Arana [1892] 1914, 198).

> The fact that economic liberalism subsisted as the foundation of economic policy after 1863 must be credited to the small group of disciples that Courcelle-Seneuil left behind him, who continued imparting the teachings of classical economics as policy-makers and faculty at the Universidad de Chile. Moreover, the economic conditions in Chile after 1870 provided a favorable environment for the subsistence of the economic policy then in course. (Will 1960, 256–57)[10]

Regarding his influence on Chilean economic policy, given the importance of the subjects for contemporary Chileans, Jean Gustave Courcelle-Seneuil's participation in trade and banking policy discussions was particularly prominent and thus deserves to be examined more carefully. This is what I will do next.

On the first topic, early in 1856 Courcelle-Seneuil prepared a comparative analysis of trade policy in Chile, France, Great Britain, and the United States (Courcelle-Seneuil 1856). Here, to the surprise of many, the foreign adviser concluded that the Chilean legislation was superior to that of these other countries in terms of both the tariff structure and the greater freedom it gave to commerce. Yet, even though the French expert implicitly supported the existing system, it seems that he was not able to convince government officials on the uncalled for need for a new tariff regime, which he was called on to design. Thus, in 1859 he drafted a new tariff project, which, however, was only presented to Congress in 1861 and approved in 1864 after suffering various modifications in Congress. In the congressional debates on the enactment of this law, controversy centered between groups that opposed a uniform tariff rate, instead preferring a discriminatory system that protected the national industries, and those that preferred low overall tariffs. The end result was a compromise project that favored the uniformity criteria, thus forfeiting, at least to some extent, the protection of national industries.[11]

Regarding Chile's banking policy, the establishment of a formal banking system had long been a subject of contention in the country, yet for many years nothing had come out of these discussions. By the time Courcelle-Seneuil was in Chile, however, he not only took part in this debate (see, e.g., Courcelle-Seneuil 1857a) but it seems that the time was

10. In this sense, not only did Courcelle-Seneuil's disciples succeed him at the Universidad de Chile (for an account in this respect, see Rodríguez 1889), but they published their own treatises in political economy, which were strongly influenced by their French professor (Cruchaga 1870; Rodríguez 1894). Moreover, political economy issues were discussed more widely throughout the country; for more on these topics, see Fuentealba 1945; Villalobos and Sagredo 1987; and Will 1960.

11. This statute is reprinted in Anguita 1912–16. For a narrative on the legislative discussions on this ordinance, see Fuentealba 1945; and Zilci 1990.

ripe for policy actions and he directly influenced the final legislative outcome. As it is, a project inspired by Courcelle-Seneuil was presented to Congress in 1859 and enacted in 1860 after suffering some changes during its discussions (Fuentealba 1945; Subercaseaux 1922). In essence, the final legislation considered the establishment of a regime of free banking, though with some limits on the issue of negotiable bills in relation to the bank's capital. At the same time, the regulatory role of government included other provisions regarding the inspection of the banks' accounts and the determination of the value of the lowest denomination of notes to be issued by the private banks.

While my examination of these topics has been very brief, it is important to explain that these episodes constitute some of the main foundations on which the negative assessments of Courcelle-Seneuil's work in Chile are based.[12] Note, in particular, Hirschman's evaluation of his legacy.

> Poor Courcelle-Seneuil! His one-man technical assistance mission could hardly have been more successful, according to ordinary standards of performance. His advice was punctiliously followed, the laws he drafted were passed, his bust stands in the University of Chile and his influence as a teacher and publicist came to be widely felt. But just because of that, virtually every serious ill subsequently experienced by the Chilean economy, from inflation to monoexportation, has been traced to him. (1963, 166)

The banking and tariff laws inspired by Courcelle-Seneuil have been alleged to represent, at least to some extent, the causes of the monetary instability and dependence on the exports of natural resources referred to by Hirschman. Jean Gustave Courcelle-Seneuil's work in Chile has thus received a disparaging assessment. Such opinions were generally based on the fact that he represented the period of dominance of lib-

12. Another instance worth referring to is related to the management of the economic cycle in Chile. In particular, in the late 1850s, following an export boom to Australia and California, where the gold rushes had created a strong demand for agricultural products, Chileans were forced to face the consequences of their most recent intertemporal consumption decisions. In this sense, Chileans sadly found that while they had based their consumption decisions on an increase in income that they expected to be permanent such wealth effects turned out to be transitory. Confronted with this issue as an economic adviser of the government, Courcelle-Seneuil publicly argued that the problem was not monetary but real and clearly was not the government's fault (see, e.g., Courcelle-Seneuil 1857b). Thus, he advocated a hands-off approach to economic policy such that the automatic adjustment mechanism should be left to work its way and private economic agents should accept the costs of their misjudgments. Naturally, such a position led to heated debates in the country, as Fuentealba (1945) explains.

eral ideas in Chilean economic policy decisions. For one such example in this sense, see the following from Aníbal Pinto.

> The main representative of this [liberal] orientation was the French economist Courcelle-Seneuil, who worked in Chile between 1855 and 1863, advising the government and propagating his ideas at the university. Under his guidance the first generation of national economists, who exercised an almost overwhelming influence on public policy, were born. . . . This economic philosophy . . . was applied in Chile as a revealed truth, with the most nefarious consequences for our economic development. (1962, 34–35)[13]

As is apparent, these evaluations contain a great deal of negative ideological regard for liberal economics. And this, I strongly believe, has tainted the pure economic assessments of Courcelle-Seneuil's legacy. But these arguments also suggest that the foreign adviser advocated liberal policies out of the blue, so to speak, since no discussion as to the nature of the advice he was to give was ever brought about ex ante. As we shall see, this seems to be a fair allegation. In any case, I must emphasize that the broader issue of how the foreign expert was selected in the first place is also very important. As should be obvious, there exists a very close relation between the determination of the requirements for an expert's job and the process by which such an expert is selected.

Revisiting Courcelle-Seneuil's Hiring by the Chilean Government

As I have argued, the information available on the hiring of Jean Gustave Courcelle-Seneuil by the Chilean government is sorely incomplete. Here, then, I will attempt to revisit this history by examining the correspondence of the people who, we are told, participated in this selection process; in particular the correspondence between the Chilean minister in France and his superiors in the Ministry of Foreign Affairs and Ministry of Education in Santiago. This undertaking, long overdue in the study of the history of economic ideas in Chile, I have been able to conduct in Santiago. I should mention, however, that, as will soon become

13. See, also the following from Fuentealba 1945: "The influence of the French economist, considered from an economic point of view, was pernicious to Chile. With his admirable erudition he established the ascendancy of liberal doctrines. . . . And under the sway of such wise theories the Chilean oligarchy was able to hand over to foreign capitalists the main sources of the nation's wealth in exchange for political predominance" (108).

evident, the narrative of the process by which Courcelle-Seneuil was selected as a foreign expert by the Chilean government still suffers from some important gaps. This follows from the unfortunate fact that not all of the communications relevant to the process seem to have been preserved. In any case, I still believe that this account provides a clear picture of the process by which Jean Gustave Courcelle-Seneuil was eventually hired by the Chilean government. In turn, it should clear up some of the confusion and alleviate some of the cynicism that surrounds his hiring.

As a starting point, some brief remarks are in order concerning the desire to improve the knowledge of political economy in Chile, which, as we have seen, has been identified as the catalyst in the hiring of a foreign professor. In his *Memoria del Rector de la Universidad de Chile correspondiente al año 1852,* Andrés Bello addressed the issue of the teaching of this subject at the university, in particular the importance of improving the study of political economy in the country.[14]

> [T]he professor of Political Economy, who only imparts his classes every other year, and thus only receives a remuneration every other year, cannot but consider teaching as an accessory and inferior activity compared to more lucrative and permanent activities. Further, in these conditions it cannot be expected that he dedicates as much time and effort as necessary to teach a discipline that is not at all trivial and should be encouraged and extended. (Bello 1853 [1982], 85)
>
> I believe that it is not only necessary to keep [the studies of] Political Economy in the place they at present occupy but that three lectures a week, for a course of only one year are insufficient. . . . [Thus], daily lessons for a full academic year is the least we can assign to the instruction of a subject that is so important for the country. (id, 86–87)

To be sure, the problems with the poor state of teaching in political economy in Chile seem to have been known for many years. As early as 1850, the Chilean lawyer Cristóbal Valdés observed:

> The teaching of political economy at the Instituto Nacional is not only insufficient . . . but is also so boring that it provokes students lose their interest in the subject. (Valdés 1850 [1993], 229)

14. This is the result of debates within the Consejo of the university regarding this subject; on this, see the *Anales de la Universidad de Chile* for the year 1853.

At the same time, in his well-known remarks in the translator's preface to Courcelle-Seneuil 1859, Joaquín Bello likewise noted:

> Till very recently, the formal instruction of Political Economy in Chile was in the most deplorable state. . . . The studies in this subject were reduced to [the recitation of] a few chapters of Say's work, the least instructive, and which the teacher explained badly and his students learnt worse. (Courcelle-Seneuil 1859, v)

From the prestige of his position, Andrés Bello's explicit arguments in favor of promoting the study of political economy in the country represented a very important statement. And yet, at least given the information available, it seems that the government's interest in the hiring of a foreign professor of political economy antedates these official remarks by the president of the university.[15] In effect, in May of 1853 the Chilean consul in France, José Marcó del Pont, acknowledged a letter from the minister of education, dated 14 January, in which an advanced state of affairs with respect to the hiring of a foreign professor is implied. In particular, in his letter Marcó del Pont stated that he had been informed "that the President has requested that a Professor of Political Economy for the Instituto Nacional be hired in Europe, and that Mr. Félix Frías is in charge of this matter and has recommended Mr. A. Cauchut for this position."[16] Note, then, two important points that emerge from this letter. First, the communicating parties refer to the hiring of an expert for a professorship in political economy with the requirement that the candidate be engaged in Europe. At the same time, notice that the request was first directed to Félix Frías, who, although he seems to have made good contacts while he lived in Chile, was no expert on economic issues, at least as far as I can tell. Although there is no solid evidence as to why the president's request was handled through Frías, it seems likely that the lack of information on the part of Chilean policymakers may be have been the overriding factor. I will return to this issue in the following pages.

15. The relationship between the government and the university in Chile during these years was very straightforward for the Universidad de Chile was a public university, with all that that entails. See, for example, Jaksić and Serrano 1990.

16. Marcó del Pont to Ochagavía, 14 May 1853, Archivo Nacional (AN), *Fondo Ministerio de Educación,* Vol. 29, #70. Félix Frías (1816–81) was an Argentinean publicist and diplomat. After the internal civil wars of 1839–41 and the victory of J. M. Rosas, he left his country and lived as an exile in Bolivia (1841–43) and Chile (1843–48). In 1848 he left for France to work as a correspondent for the Chilean newspaper *El Mercurio.* He finally returned to Argentina in 1855, where he worked as a publicist, was elected a congressman, and, several years later, was named Argentinean minister to Chile. On this, see Cortés 1875; and Romero and Quezada 1995.

Next our account intersects with another story; that of finding a collaborator for the official newspaper, *El Araucano.* The Chilean minister in Paris, Manuel Blanco Encalada, had been asked by the minister of the interior to find a person for such a position, and so he did.[17] In April of 1854, however, Blanco Encalada wrote to Minister Varas, "I now find out that Minister Ochagavía [the minister of education], bypassing me, contacted a M. Acné, manufacturer of *necessaires,* who, without even informing me, has already hired M. Cochut." Thus, he claimed, "This is what motivated M. Cochut to not leave for Chile" (Blanco Encalada to Varas, 30 April 1854, in Varas 1919, #31). So from this dispatch we gather that the "Cauchut" referred to in the previous communication was André Cochut. And he declined the offer to go to Chile because he was named the collaborator of *El Araucano* instead. Indeed, he was duly hired for a monthly salary of FF$350 in exchange for writing two collaborations a month for this newspaper (Varas to Blanco Encalada, 30 May 1854; AH MINREL, *Fondo Histórico,* Vol. 11c, #53).[18]

But who was this André Cochut, whose name also came up in Barros Arana's narrative? Charles Coquelin and C. Guillaumin's *Dictionnaire de L'Economie Politique* (1864) indicates that Cochut (1812–90) was a collaborator of the *Revue des deux mondes* and a journalist at the *National* in France who also had a great interest in international affairs. In this sense, it would seem that his background was one of a publicist of economic ideas more than an economic theorist. Whatever the case may be, the fact that he worked at an influential French journal and seems to have been a learned man may explain why he was approached for a job in Chile.[19] In a country where knowledge about economic issues

17. As Luis Valencia Avaria (1986) has shown in his chronology of the Chilean executive, between 1850 and 1856 the Ministries of the Interior and of Foreign Affairs were headed by the same person, Antonio Varas. On the other hand, the correspondence of the Chilean minister in France during the 1850s shows the very wide range of requests he received from Chile; these included everything from buying paintings for public offices to buying books, journals, and uniforms for the military and obtaining the services of French nuns to come to Chile! On this, see, for example, Chile, AN, *Fondo Legación Chile—Francia y Gran Bretaña,* vols. 24, 26, 27, 30.

18. It is interesting to note, incidentally, that the story of the hiring of a collaborator for *El Araucano* also involves Félix Frías. It seems he was the first person Chilean officials thought of as a possible collaborator for the newspaper. However, he declined the offer. On this, see Varas to Blanco Encalada, 14 August 1853, Varas 1919, #3; and Blanco Encalada to Varas, 14 October 1853, Varas 1919, #8. On the other hand, it is probable that the "M. Acné" referred to by Blanco Encalada was the French litterateur Théodore Anné (1797–1869). On this, see *Le grande encyclopédie* (1886[?]–1902, vol. 3).

19. Note, for example, that he contributed an essay to Coquelin and Guillaumin's *Dictionnaire* (1864), on the topic of "Morale," and wrote a review of Courcelle-Seneuil's *Traité* in the *Revue des deux mondes* in 1859. We also know, by the way, that by the time of his death he was an honorary vice president of the Société d'Economie Politique (Letort 1890).

was very slight, anyone who even appeared to be well versed on the subject would seem fit to teach in this field. A cursory examination of the *El Araucano* for the second half of the 1850s, where we do indeed find contributions by Cochut, confirms that he was more of a news commentator or publicist than an economic theorist or philosopher. Thus, he wrote regularly for the international section of the newspaper, reporting on social, political, and economic events in Europe. At longer intervals, he also contributed some more substantive economic articles that had been originally published in the *Revue des deux mondes*.[20]

At any rate, and returning to our narrative, nothing seems to have happened regarding the professorship of political economy for some time. Then, in January of 1855, Minister Varas wrote the following to Blanco Encalada:

> For some time now the Chilean government has been looking for a professor of Political Economy in Europe. As you know, this work, which is being headed by Mr. Irarrázaval, led to a letter from Mr. Ochagavía to Mr. Cochut. He has replied, indicating two names, Mr. Molinari and Mr. Courcelle Seneuil. Either of them seems satisfactory given the recommendations they present. It is probable that Mr. Cochut has already contacted you, and I recommend that you pursue this matter very seriously. (Varas to Blanco Encalada, 14 January 1855, in Varas 1919, #46)

This is also the first communication in which we find that the job requirements for the foreign expert fully spelled out: "The person who is hired should: 1st. Teach Political Economy at the university; 2nd. Assist the Ministry of Finance in the capacity of adviser; 3rd. Inform and illustrate the public on economic issues according to the requirements of the government's agenda" (Varas 1919, #46). Whether working at the Ministry of Finance had been a requirement for the job all along or it was added as an enticement to attract candidates for the available position in Chile we do not know.[21] In any case, it is interesting to note that although he had presumably been working in *El Araucano* for only some

20. Of course, one could also argue that it was these types of contributions that were required of him by the editors of the Chilean newspaper. And for a salary of FF$350 for two articles a month he would probably write about whatever he was asked to!

21. Likewise, I have found no information regarding the involvement that Ramón Luis Irarrázaval, who by this time had only recently returned to Chile after a diplomatic mission in Rome (and was to leave for Peru soon after), had in this process. I am grateful to Ricardo Couyoumdjian for his help in identifying this "Mr. Irarrázaval."

months it was André Cochut who was asked to give some advice regarding an economist who would come to Chile. In this sense, it seems that he was quick to earn a good name in Chile.[22] On the other hand, the mention of Gustave de Molinari comes as a surprise to me. I should explain, however, that I do not know whether Cochut or Blanco Encalada (or Marcó del Pont) ever contacted him. What I do know is that at this time he was on the market, so to speak, since, like many other liberal thinkers, he was not feeling comfortable with the current political situation in France.[23]

In any case, a decision was soon made. In mid-February of 1855, Minister Varas informed Marcó del Pont of the selection of "Mr. Courcelles Seneuil" and stipulated that, "in accordance with the ideas stated in the enclosed memorandum, you will complete this contract in representation of the Chilean Government."[24] The contract signed between Marcó del Pont and Courcelle-Seneuil turned out to be identical to the memorandum sent by Varas.[25] As noted earlier, Fuentealba (1945) transcribed this document, although he failed to state in which of the numerous collections (and corresponding volumes) of the Archivo Nacional he found this document.[26] But, since I have already

22. It is interesting to note that, although he was hired in mid-1854, the first contribution we find by Cochut in *El Araucano* is in December of that year. We then find his more regular contributions on current events in Europe from April 1855. This may be due to the fact that the work of the collaborator for *El Araucano* was viewed as one not only of collaborating in Chilean periodicals but also of writing about Chile in European journals (Varas to Blanco Encalada, 31 October 1853, Varas 1919, #9; and Blanco Encalada to Varas, 30 December 1853, Varas 1919, #14). In any case, the fact that the *Revue des deux mondes* also seems to have been read in Chile may provide the missing link as to how Cochut was known in the country.

23. Although Gustave de Molinari (1819–1912) was Belgian by birth, he lived in France most of his life and was a member of the French School of Political Economy. After Louis-Napoleon Bonaparte's coup of December 1851 and the establishment of the Second Empire, he left for Belgium where he was named professor of political economy at the Royal Belgium Museum of Belgian Industry and later at the Institut Supérieur du Commerce in Antwerp. Eventually, in 1860, he returned to Paris. On this, see Guyot 1912.

24. Varas to Marcó del Pont, 14 February 1855, Chile, AH MINREL, *Fondo Histórico,* 11c, #70. It seems that we should not read anything into the fact that Varas addressed the Chilean consul instead of Blanco Encalada, the minister. In a letter to the latter, Varas explained that he had addressed Marcó del Pont because he thought Blanco Encalada would be out of town by the time his instructions reached France (Varas to Blanco Encalada, 14 February 1855, Varas 1919, #48).

25. I should note, incidentally, that it seems that not everything went as smoothly as planned with this deal; in June 1855, Varas wrote the Blanco Encalada that he was "glad that you have solved the problems that had detained Marco in his agreement with Courcelle" (Varas to Blanco Encalada, 14 June 1855, Varas 1919, #55). Unfortunately, we do not know what problems this referred to.

26. To correct this failure, I will explicitly state that I found this document at the Archivo Nacional, *Fondo MINEDUC,* vol. 50, #24. The document consulted was a translation of the contract, in Spanish, accompanying a letter from Minister Antonio Varas to Minister Silvestre Ochagavía, dated 5 September 1855, informing him of the hiring of J. G. Courcelle-Seneuil (a similar letter was sent to Minister José María Berganza, of Finance, but the enclosed copy of the contract is missing) (Varas to

referred to the main terms of this contract, I will not spend more time on it here.[27]

This account suggests that, while the original instructions for the hiring of a professor and economic adviser referred to finding someone in Europe, as far as I can tell the search process took place exclusively in France. For instance, neither the United States nor Spain nor England, which one would also imagine to be some natural reference points for Chile, seems to have even been considered as places in which to search for a foreign expert. Moreover, note that the expert finally selected did not even speak Spanish.[28] Yet this does not seem to have been a problem. The really important point to keep in mind is that in the postindependence era the main foreign influences in Chile were British and French. In terms of trade and commerce, Great Britain was the leader in almost all of Spanish America. Nonetheless,

> the new influences playing on Chilean (especially upper-class) life were neither exclusively British nor exclusively commercial. [Soon after independence] France was beginning to exert her commercial sway, not least through imported reading matter. (Collier and Sater 1996, 45)

At the same time, it has been argued by Jean-Pierre Blancpain that "[based on] its programs, its teachers and its ideology, prior to 1880 the Chilean educational system was a copy of the French model" (1987, 92). Blancpain adds that the French community in Chile was especially influential in the liberal professions and the development of medicine (on this see footnote 27) as opposed to artisanship or trade (98). On the other hand, we also know that during the 1840s and 1850s France was a source of instructors, as well as weapons, for the Chilean army (Aran-

Berganza, 5 September 1855, Chile, AN, *Fondo Ministerio de Hacienda* (*MINHA*), vol. 239, n.f.). In decrees in the following days, President Manuel Montt approved the terms of the contract and officially named Courcelle-Seneuil a professor of political economy and adviser to the Minister of Finance (13 September 1855, AN, *Fondo Ministerio de Educación* (*MINEDUC*), vol. 50, #25; and 24 September 1855, AN, *Fondo MINHA*, vol. 239, n.f., respectively). In these documents, we also find that Courcelle-Seneuil's salary was in Chilean pesos. Thus, the FF$18,000 was translated into Ch$3,600.

27. That said, an interesting point regarding this document is the establishment of compensation clauses in case of a unilateral termination of the contract by the Chilean government. We can presume that the fact that by this time the Chilean government had hired foreign experts in other areas may have given government officials some experience in this sense. On this, see, for example, Roberto Hernández's (1990–91) review of the hiring of the French doctor Laurent Sazie as a professor in a school of medicine in Chile in 1833.

28. On this, see Barros Arana, who adds that Courcelle-Seneuil studied Spanish and by the time he arrived to Chile "spoke [Spanish] with fluency and understood the meaning of all its idioms and locutions" ([1892] 1914, 197).

cibia 2002). All of this, then, would explain why France was considered the natural place to undertake a search for an expert in a field such as economics.[29]

Another point worth noting is the fact that nowhere in the correspondence we are examining do we find any ideological type of requirement for the hiring of a foreign expert. In this sense, it seems that, indeed, there was no ex ante discussion about the nature of the advice the expert was to give in Chile. To be sure, there may have been a tacit understanding between Manuel Blanco Encalada and Minister Varas or Minister Ochagavía that the search would focus on a liberal economist. Or, even plainer, maybe a communication that contains more explicit requirements for the job is missing from the Archivo Nacional in Santiago. While both of these points may well be true, they cannot lead us to change our preliminary judgment. Of course, we know that Jean Gustave Courcelle-Seneuil was influential in advancing a liberal economic agenda, so these notions must have had some type of political support. However, this only happened ex post, when, given his prestige, Courcelle-Seneuil was able to impose his preferences, so to speak. Thus, and as a more general conclusion, it is important to be cautious with the straightforward use of revealed-preference types of arguments in analyzing historical narratives. As we have seen in the case under examination, just because a liberal foreign adviser was hired does not mean that being liberal was a requirement of the job.

The Problem of Selecting an Economic Adviser

The framework I have adopted in this essay treats the problem of selecting a foreign expert as a two-sided problem. Both experts and those who demand their services have preferences about the work to be delivered. But so far I have not found any evidence that Chilean officials may have imposed ideological requirements on the person to be hired as a foreign economic adviser and professor of political economy. This still leaves us with the problem of considering the ideological leanings an expert may have. Indeed, experts may differ in terms of a series of characteristics and attributes unknown to advice seekers, which makes the problem of hiring an expert even harder. At any rate, note that here we are assuming that the country selecting an economic adviser recognizes that advisers have policy preferences even though they may not know what the policy issues are. And in this case advice seekers will face a problem that

29. This point is underscored by the fact that M. Blanco Encalada was the Chilean minister to both France and Great Britain while in most of the other European countries relations were conducted by consular offices only.

may be both serious and urgent. The seriousness of this problem should be apparent; hiring a biased expert who might be able to indulge these biases could lead to serious externalities.[30] Regarding its urgency, note that this is a problem that should be tackled ex ante, that is, before the adviser is hired, because when advice seekers discover the expert's beliefs it may be too late to prevent serious evils. Of course, these problems may occur even though the expert is intellectually honest because when we refer to bias we are really referring to the fact that the adviser is advocating one position in a contested issue. Thus, it is in this sense that one would like to assure that the hiring process of a foreign adviser is as unbiased as possible. The relevance of these points for the problem of the hiring of an expert should by now be clear; it is precisely when advice seekers are searching for an unbiased expert, and when they have an imperfect knowledge about the field in which they want to acquire expertise, that the dangers referred to earlier are most serious.[31] And it is in this respect that one would like to consider the implementation of a selection process that would minimize these risks.

Before discussing some alternative processes that may achieve such a goal, it is interesting to note that nowadays the kind of choice Chilean officials faced in the mid–nineteenth century is almost nonexistent in practice. The selection of a foreign expert is mostly tied to the acceptance of foreign assistance by multilateral agencies (such as the International Monetary Fund) or of foreign aid by individual countries (the U.S. Alliance for Progress initiative of the 1960s is a particularly clear example in this respect). In this context, the problems facing advice-seeking countries are essentially neglected (see, however, Drake 1989). Therein lies an additional interest for the problem we are examining here.

Given the development of the narrative so far, it should come as no surprise that the case of Chile in the nineteenth century will be our working example for an analysis of alternative processes for the hiring of a foreign adviser. And it should also come as no surprise if our starting point is a competitive process. A priori it is easy to imagine that a process of this type would be a good way to distinguish between "good" and "bad" potential experts and thus assist in the selection of an expert in a field such as economics.

---

30. A way out of this problem would be to design an incentive-compatible mechanism to constrain the behavior of the foreign adviser. In the case we are examining, however, there is no evidence that any specific mechanism of this type was designed, although such concepts may have been discarded because they were considered unnecessary, as will discussed later.

31. To be sure, if we assume that experts are homogeneous in the sense that their "preferences" are alike, the problem we are examining here would be virtually nonexistent. But, then, it is the consequences of deviations from these instances of best-case thinking that are the situations we most want to avoid.

A first type of competitive process for the hiring of a foreign expert one can imagine could be the option of inserting an invitation to apply for a position in Chile in an international journal in Europe. Journals for this purpose could include the *Revue des deux mondes,* the *Edinburgh Review,* or maybe the *Economist,* all of which were influential journals during the nineteenth century. Yet browsing through some of these journals I find that they do not carry these types of advertisements. This would suggest that, while the alternative under consideration is appropriate today, it seems to have been unsuited for the mid–nineteenth century. More seriously, even if such announcements could have been a viable alternative how would Chilean officials have judged who was the best specialist from all of the submissions they received?

Given the imperfect knowledge Chileans had regarding political economy, they would not have been able to judge the qualities of a good expert and so would have had to find someone to judge the potential candidates for them. But then a different process would have had to take place for the selection of the judges, and we would have the same problem at a different level.

On careful examination it should be apparent that this problem is common to all types of competitive processes. Thus, this would leave out the interesting proposals advanced in this sense by Jeremy Bentham in the 1820s and 1830s. In his *Constitutional Code* ([1830] 1983) Bentham proposed competitive processes in the comprehensive examination for entry into the civil service (IX, §16) and in the pecuniary competition system for obtaining public jobs (IX, §17). A priori this seems a promising alternative for addressing the problem at hand. Yet, even if we assume that Bentham's works were well known in Chile in the mid–nineteenth century,[32] this system clearly gives rise to the problems mentioned earlier. How to judge the results of the comprehensive examination process would also be an obstacle.

An additional problem with the alternatives examined so far, as well as with other, more complicated alternatives (e.g., a lottery à la Tullock 1980 or some other incentive-compatible mechanism one could devise) is one of transaction costs intensified by the lack of information. Even if one assumes that the information that was lacking could be obtained, such that an advice seeker could perfectly differentiate among potential experts, such a process would take time (and money). Note, of course, the similarity of this argument to the case for representative democracy. The idea of representative democracy is that a democratically elected government (or parliament) saves on the transaction costs of governance

32. It seems, however, that Bentham's work on penal law was better known than his work on constitutionalism; see de Avila 1979.

vis-à-vis direct democracy (see, e.g., Mueller 1996). In this sense, then, it would seem reasonable to argue in favor of much simpler and straightforward alternatives for the problem under consideration.

One such alternative available to an advice seeker could be to ask the professor of political economy at the Collège de France, or Oxford or at any other well-known center of higher education, for guidance in this matter. And yet note the similarity of this process to the steps that were followed in Chile. In essence, the steps followed by Chilean officials involved some kind of trust in the judgment of Félix Frías and then André Cochut. But this process acquired a personal dimension. It was people who were known who were asked for advice, as opposed to relying on the judgment of a famous, but unknown, foreign professor. In a more fundamental sense, note that the system utilized for the hiring of a foreign expert in Chile contained important random elements. The decision to ask for Félix Frías's advice, at least when viewed from our present standpoint, seems random, although I should also explain that it was in some sense constrained by and limited to the number of people known by Chilean officials who were in Europe at the time. In any case, it is very likely that had someone other than Frías been asked to give a recommendation Chileans would never have heard of André Cochut or Jean Gustave Courcelle-Seneuil. Of course, note that if you follow such a course you can end up hiring a noneconomist for an economist's job (as would have been the case with Cochut). Thus the importance of constraining, or regulating, this random process such that it looks more like a sequential decision. This is of vital importance if we wish to avoid worst-case prospects, and, indeed, this has been the motivating force throughout the discussion in this section: devising mechanisms to find an unbiased adviser and thus avoid potentially disastrous consequences. By mere chance, this is what happened in Chile, where first Frías and then Cochut were consulted. And this seems to be an improvement over the alternative of consulting a famous professor, who, one would imagine, would not have liked to be cross-checked and, further, would not have been (in general) personally known by the advice seekers.

Of course, it seems pretty risky to rely on a random process for the selection of a foreign adviser, especially if the stakes are as high as I have suggested.[33] But it seems important to ask ourselves whether Chilean officials visualized the hiring of a foreign expert as a really important matter in which the stakes were actually that high. As we saw, Manuel

33. Indeed, as Levy (1992) has reminded us, even in ancient Athens, which is probably the best-known instance of the use of random elections, the lot was only used for minor issues; for important issues, direct democracy was resorted to.

Blanco Encalada was encouraged to "pursue this matter very seriously." But we also have evidence that hiring foreign experts was not an extraordinary event for Chilean officials (on this see, for example, footnote 27). Moreover, one can easily imagine that as the minister of the interior and foreign affairs Antonio Varas had many more important things to worry about than the hiring of a professor of political economy. And the same can be said of Silvestre Ochagavía, whose full title (and attendant responsibilities) was of minister of justice, church affairs, and education.[34] What about Blanco Encalada? He surely had many things on his mind, as the correspondence in the *Fondo Legación Chile—Francia y Gran Bretaña* at the Archivo Nacional can attest, and he probably saw this as one more job to do, nothing more and nothing less. In any case, recall that the contacts with first Frías and then Cochut came through Minister Ochagavía and not from Blanco Encalada, who, in the main, turned out to be the executor of orders he received from Santiago. Probably, then, it was thought that, regarding the teaching of political economy, any candidate with good "recommendations" would be preferable to the status quo situation. In this sense, it would seem safe to assume that the influence of the expert as an adviser to the government may have been visualized as easy to constrain due to the political nature of the job, which was above the realm of an adviser.

We have seen that during the mid–nineteenth century France was the main reference point for Chilean cultural and intellectual life. Does this suggest that, given that Chileans were searching for an expert there, they would only find a liberal economist? In other words, is it possible to argue that since the selection of the foreign expert was bound to take place in France the selection of a liberal economist was almost predetermined? Several comments are in order here. On the one hand, it is not true that you would only have found liberal economists in France during this time (on this see, e.g., Gide and Rist 1915). But, even if this were the case, there are some important points I should like to make. In the first place, considering the individual attributes of an economist would still be an important problem. Second, it is important to stress that there was no covenant, so to speak, that forced Chileans to search for an economist in France; had Chilean officials had some definite preferences they well could have looked elsewhere, for example, in the United States, if they were looking for a protectionist-type economist. Last, and more generally, the reliance on only one source of new ideas carries with it the danger of

34. All of these responsibilities were allotted to one minister. Thus, in the 1850s the president's cabinet was composed of only five ministries: Interior; Foreign Affairs; Finance; War and Navy; and Justice, Church Affairs, and Education. On this, see Valencia Avaria 1986.

intellectual cascades when we believe a claim because it is believed. In this case it may well be that whatever ideas or fashions are in vogue in a metropolis will be introduced into a country looking for inspiration almost independent of their objective content. As should be clear, this is a problem very similar to the dangers referred to in this essay.

At any rate, even if we recognize that the implementation of a competitive procedure has important practical difficulties, it seems fair to ask ourselves why Chileans would disregard considerations of accountability, as they seem to have done by not considering a competitive process. The relevant question then seems to be: was accountability as big an issue in mid-nineteenth-century Chile as it is now in Chile and elsewhere? For the likes of Jeremy Bentham, accountability and transparency were very important points, but what about Chile? Is it possible that Bentham's stance on accountability was one of the many reasons why some of his ideas were deemed almost exotic in many countries, including his own? To put matters differently, when do we start seeing a greater demand for transparency in the types of matters we have examined in this essay? I venture to suggest that it was when foreign loans were involved; foreign creditors have been an important source of demand for more accountability in terms of public sector management, in particular when the creditors are multilateral agencies.[35]

To sum up, here I have provided a rationale of sorts for the selection process for the hiring of a foreign expert as undertaken in nineteenth-century Chile, which culminated with the employment of Jean Gustave Courcelle-Seneuil as a foreign economic adviser and professor of political economy. I have described the tradeoff Chilean officials faced in terms of the transaction costs involved in learning more about the economist to be hired, the potential bias the expert could have, and the ex post criticisms of his work precisely because he was viewed as biased. In this respect, Chilean officials decided to take a risk in terms of not gathering all the possible background information on the adviser they were to hire. This, however, can be interpreted as a rational calculus given their preferences and the constraints they faced.

Conclusion and Implications

In this essay, I have discussed the problem of selecting an economic adviser that a country involved in such a task faces. This work is grounded

35. For the issuance of sovereign bonds, on the other hand, their prices, which provide a signal of country risk and quasi symbolizes the possibility of further such emissions, would fluctuate with the extent of the problems the countries face, thus providing a built-in incentive for these nations to act "responsibly."

on the conviction that one should not only consider the political constraints within which economic advisers act but should also recognize that they are agents who have ideological preferences. Thus, here we have a principal-agent problem of sorts that may be very important for an advice seeker who does not know what type of agent he or she is hiring. When the country looking for an expert discovers the expert's beliefs only after he or she has been hired, it may be too late to prevent serious evils. And even if no disastrous consequences come about from the work of the expert, historiography will not be kind to the biased adviser. While an advice seeker may not have the necessary knowledge to discriminate and, to put it plainly, indulge his or her preferences ex ante (since they could be assumed to be nonexistent), ex post we have a different story. Once we start learning about a subject, we come to realize that there are two sides to everything. Clearly this is what happened in Chile. While Jean Gustave Courcelle-Seneuil taught classical economics, through his lessons Chileans also became aware that this was not the only economic doctrine in existence.[36] All of these problems may occur, I am ready to argue, even though the adviser may be intellectually honest (see the earlier discussion on the relevance of this comment to Jean Gustave Courcelle-Seneuil). When I talk about bias here I am really referring to the fact that the adviser is seen as advocating one position in a contested issue. And such was, indeed, the case with Jean Gustave Courcelle-Seneuil in Chile.

This framework, it seems to me, can also be used to examine other experiences in the transfer of expertise. In particular, I believe that it seems to explain the experience of the "Chicago Boys" in Chile and the evaluation of their legacy.[37] While some differences are evident, the general correspondence between this episode and the hiring of Jean Gustave Courcelle-Seneuil is straightforward since both represented, in essence, the transfer of economic ideas and expertise.

As an opening for the discussion in this sense, the following com-

36. On this, see the following comments by P.N. Urzúa: "Let us listen to List, who while not the holder of the flattering title of *Newton of Political Economy,* as Adam Smith, carries the no less greater title of *founder of German protectionism*" (1884, 14; italics in the original). See also Courcelle-Seneuil's *Tratado* (1859).

37. Edwin Walter Kemmerer of Princeton headed a mission whose recommendations helped create an independent central bank and a period of monetary stability. The case of the Kemmerer mission to Chile in 1925, on the other hand, is different in the sense that here the advice seekers (i.e., the Chilean government) had some very distinct ideas about what could be done regarding the economic problems of the country (Drake 1989; Hirschman 1963). Thus, as Hirschman has argued, in this case "the mission served principally as an umpire or perhaps even as a random device: in other words, it was the means for choosing one out of a number of competing proposals" (1963, 177). In particular, these proposals referred to the precise institutional and economic environment for the establishment of a central bank.

ments by Luis Escobar Cerda, who was recollecting his experience as dean of the School of Economics of the Universidad de Chile in the mid 1950s, are highly illuminating.

> One day an official from the U.S. Embassy in Chile came to my office to present me with a "present." It concerned the possibility of sending students, on a scholarship program, to study in the U.S., together with the possibility of receiving American teachers in whatever fields we required. The Department of State, which managed the U.S. foreign aid programs, had selected the University of Chicago to administer the program. I liked the idea, contingent on the fact that I were granted the liberty to send my students to study in the American university that we chose. . . . I remember that I once asked John K. Galbraith, one of my professors at Harvard, what he thought about Chicago, and he answered: "It is a luxury that the U.S. can afford." . . . Thus, I explained [to the U.S. official] that I could not send all my students to Chicago, that represents a very definite "school of thought." It would be like sending them all to Patrice Lumumba University in Moscow. What would happen in Chile in the next twenty years or so? (Escobar 1991, 33–34)

The exchange process Escobar felt uneasy about did, however, end up taking place as had been proposed, though through the Universidad Católica de Chile.[38] And the Chilean economists educated at Chicago were highly influential during the presidency of Augusto Pinochet. Here, however, I will leave aside questions regarding the authoritarian nature of the Pinochet regime, as well as the issue of whether or not there really were ideological considerations in this transfer of ideas. (This latter factor, incidentally, is a controversial issue; see Valdés 1995; and Vial 1999). The point I wish to stress, instead, is that one of the main

38. The exchange programs between the University of Chicago and the Universidad Católica de Chile were instituted in 1956 within the context of the Point Four Agreement (which involved technical cooperation) with the U.S. International Cooperation Administration. Their purpose was to modernize the (university-level) study of economics in Chile. This implied the establishment of a Centro de Investigaciones Económicas at the Universidad Católica and the institution of a scholarship program under which Chilean graduates studied economics at Chicago and return to work at the university. The project, which was originally planned to last three years yet ended up lasting till 1964, seems to have come as a "present" from the U.S. Agency for International Development, as Escobar argues. For more on these issues, see Valdés 1995; and Vial 1999.

differences that economists opposed to the Pinochet regime, such as Alejandro Foxley (1983),[39] had with the Chicago Boys during the 1980s had to do with their models.

For instance, in his discussion regarding the (anti-inflationary) stabilization policies implemented in Chile during the 1970s and early 1980s, Foxley writes:

> Most current views would agree that contemporary inflation is a complex process of interaction among demand, cost, and expectation factors. An approach that ignores some of these factors is likely to result in an unnecessarily long transition period and one that will generate deeper recession and more unemployment than necessary. (1983, 201)

As it should probably be unnecessary to explain, Foxley is contesting the basic monetarist view of inflation (and its open-economy version of the monetary approach to the balance of payments), which served as the theoretical foundation for the ("orthodox") stabilization policies implemented by the Chicago Boys. In this sense, it can be said that within the Chilean policy-watchers community the Chicago Boys were considered biased in a scientific sense because they advocated the undiluted implementation of policies that followed from models that were considered contested in a theoretical sense. According to Foxley, the fact that the policies as implemented produced a severe economic contraction in Chile in the period under consideration gives further credence to his argument. In all, therein lies an important rationale for quarreling with the Chicago Boys, especially when one also recalls how the relationship between the Chilean economists and the University of Chicago was established. Doubtless, this is an incomplete account as to the evaluation of the Chicago Boys in Chile, but I believe the point raised is valid nevertheless, and, more important, the situation seems very similar to that of the hiring of a foreign adviser in the 1850s.

Bibliography

Alcouffe, Alain. 1989. "The Institutionalization of Political Economy in French Universities, 1819–1896." *History of Political Economy* 21:313–44.

39. Alejandro Foxley was to be the minister of finance of the first democratically elected government following the Pinochet regime. The fact that he was the leader of the economists opposed to Pinochet while serving as director of Corporación de Investigaciones Económicas para América Latina, an academic/public policy think tank in Santiago, was the main basis for his appointment.

Anguita, Ricardo. 1912–1916. *Leyes Promulgadas en Chile desde 1810 hasta el 1o. de Junio de 1912.* 4 vols. plus supplement. Santiago: Imprenta, Litografía i Encuadernación Barcelona.

Arancibia Clavel, Roberto. 2002. *La Influencia del Ejército Chileno en América Latina, 1900–1950.* Santiago: Centro de Estudios e Investigaciones Militares.

Barros Arana, Diego. [1892] 1914. "Don Juan Gustavo Courcelle Seneuil (1813–1892)." In *Obras Completas,* 13:193–241. Santiago: Imprenta Litografía i Encuadernación Barcelona.

Bello, Andrés. [1853] 1982. "Memoria Correspondiente al Curso de los Estudios Universitarios en 1852." In *Obras Completas,* 18:81–100. Caracas: Fundación La Casa de Bello.

Bentham, Jeremy. [1830] 1983. *Constitutional Code.* Volume 1 of *The Collected Works of Jeremy Bentham.* Edited by F. Rosen and J. H. Burns. Oxford: Clarendon.

Blancpain, Jean-Pierre. 1987. *Francia y los Franceses en Chile (1700–1980).* Translated by L. E. Jara. Santiago: Ediciones Pedagógicas Chilenas.

Chile, Archivo General Histórico del Ministerio de Relaciones Exteriores (AH, MINREL). *Fondo Histórico.* Several volumes.

Chile, Archivo Nacional (AN). *Fondo Legación Chile—Francia y Gran Bretaña.* Several volumes.

Chile, Archivo Nacional (AN). *Fondo Ministerio de Hacienda* (Fondo MINHA). Several volumes.

Chile, Archivo Nacional (AN). *Fondo Ministerio de Justicia, Culto e Instrucción Pública* (Fondo MINEDUC). Several volumes.

Collier, Simon, and William F. Sater. 1996. *A History of Chile, 1808–1994.* Cambridge: Cambridge University Press.

Coquelin, Charles, and C. Guillaumin. 1864. *Dictionnaire de l'économie politique.* 3rd ed., 2 vols. Paris: Librairie de Guillaumin.

Cortés, José Domingo. 1875. *Diccionario Biográfico Americano.* Paris: Tipografía Lahure.

Courcelle-Seneuil, Jean Gustave. 1840. *Le crédit et la banque, étude sur les réformes à introduire dans l'organisation de la Banque de France et des banques départementales, contenant un exposé de la constitution des banques américaines, écossaises, anglaises et françaises.* Paris: Pagnerre.

Courcelle-Seneuil, Jean Gustave. 1853. *Traité théorique et pratique des opérations de banque.* Paris: Guillaumin.

Courcelle-Seneuil, Jean Gustave. 1856. *Examen Comparativo de la Tarifa i Lejislación Aduanera de Chile con las de Francia, Gran Bretaña, i Estados Unidos.* Santiago: Imprenta Nacional.

Courcelle-Seneuil, Jean Gustave. 1857a. "Bancos de Circulación." *Revista de Ciencias y Letras* 1 (Santiago): 37–50.

Courcelle-Seneuil, Jean Gustave. 1857b. "Estudios sobre la Crisis Económica." *Revista de Ciencias y Letras* 1 (Santiago): 507–25.

Courcelle-Seneuil, Jean Gustave. 1858. *Traité théorique et pratique des opérations de banque.* Paris: Guillaumin.

Courcelle-Seneuil, Jean Gustave. 1859. *Tratado Teórico i Práctico de Economía Política.* 2 vols. Paris: Librairíe de Guillaumin.

Courcelle-Seneuil, Jean Gustave. 1860. "Economía Política: Programa formado por el profesor del ramo en la Sección Universitaria don Juan Gustavo Courcelle Seneuil, i que ha obtenido la aprobación del Consejo de la

Universidad para los exámenes que sobre esta materia se rindan." *Anales de la Universidad de Chile* 18:327–32.

Cruchaga, Miguel. 1870. *Tratado Elemental de Economía Política.* 2nd ed., rev. Santiago: Imprenta de El Independiente.

de Avila, Alamiro. 1979. "The Influence of Bentham in the Teaching of Penal Law in Chile." *Bentham Newsletter* 5:13–28.

Drake, Paul W. 1989. *The Money Doctor in the Andes: The Kemmerer Missions, 1923–1933.* Durham: Duke University Press.

Drake, Paul W., ed. 1994. *Money Doctors, Foreign Debts, and Economic Reforms in Latin America from the 1890s to the Present.* Wilmington, DE: Scholarly Resources.

Escobar Cerda, Luis. 1991. *Mi Testimonio.* Santiago: Editorial Ver.

Foxley, Alejandro. 1983. *Latin American Experiments in Neoconservative Economics.* Berkeley: University of California Press.

Fuentealba Hernández, Leonardo. 1945. *Courcelle-Seneuil en Chile: Errores del Liberalismo Económico.* Santiago: Prensas de la Universidad de Chile.

Gide, Charles, and Charles Rist. 1915. *A History of Economic Doctrines from the Time of the Physiocrats to the Present Day.* Boston: Heath. Translation of the second revised edition of 1913.

Guyot, Yves. 1912. Obituary for Gustave de Molinari. *Economic Journal* 85:152–56.

Hernández, Roberto. 1990–91. "José Miguel de la Barra contrata en París al médico Lorenzo Sazie." *Diplomacia* (Academia Diplomática de Chile) 54–55:22–23.

Hirschman, Albert O. 1963. *Journeys toward Progress: Studies of Economic Policy-Making in Latin America.* New York: Twentieth Century Fund.

Hirschman, Albert O. 1987. "Jean Gustave Courcelle-Seneuil." In *The New Palgrave: A Dictionary of Economics,* edited by J. Eatwell, M. Milgate, and P. Newman, 1:706–8. London: Macmillan.

Jakšić, Iván, and Sol Serrano. 1990. "In the Service of the Nation: The Establishment and Consolidation of the Universidad de Chile, 1842–79." *Hispanic American Historical Review* 70:139–71.

Jevons, W. Stanley. 1965. *The Theory of Political Economy, with Preface and Notes and an Extension of the Bibliography of Mathematical Economic Writings by H. S. Jevons.* New York: Kelley.

Journal des Économistes. 1892. "Nécrologie: J.-G. Courcelle-Seneuil." *Journal des Économistes* 5e. S., no. 11: 70–81. (Includes comments by M. Tétreau, M. Georges Picot, and M. G de Molinari.)

Juglar, Clément. 1895. "Notice sur la vie et les travaux de M. J.-G. Courcelle-Seneuil." *Séances et Travaux de L'Académie des Sciences Morales et Politiques* 144:850–82.

Krishna, Vijay, and John Morgan. 2001. "A Model of Expertise." *Quarterly Journal of Economics* 116:747–75.

Le grande encyclopédie, inventaire raisonné des sciences, des lettres et des artes, par une societé de savants et de gens de lettres. 1886?–1902. 31 vols. Paris: Larousse.

Letort, Charles. 1890. "Compte Rendu: Société d'Economie Politique, Réunion du 5 Février 1890." *Journal des Économistes* 5e. S: 260–62.

Levy, David M. 1992. *The Economic Ideas of Ordinary People: From Preferences to Trade.* London: Routledge.

Levy, David M. 2001. *How the Dismal Science Got Its Name: Classical Economics and the Ur-Text of Racial Politics.* Ann Arbor: University of Michigan Press.

Marco, Luc. 1991. "Jean-Gustave Courcelle-Seneuil, 1813–1892: L'orthodoxe intrasigeant." In *L'Économie politique en France au XIXe siècle,* edited by Y. Breton and M. Lutfalla, 141–61. Paris: Economica.

Morris, Stephen. 2001. "Political Correctness." *Journal of Political Economy* 109:231–65.

Mueller, Dennis C. 1996. *Constitutional Democracy.* Oxford: Oxford University Press.

Ottaviani, Marco, and Peter N. Sørensen. 2003. "Professional Advice: The Theory of Reputational Cheap Talk." London Business School discussion paper.

Passy, Hippolyte. 1859. "Rapport de M. Passy a l'Academie des Sciences Morales et Politiques sur l'ouvrage de M. Courcelle Seneuil, intitulé *Traité Théorique et Pratique d'Économie Politique.*" *Journal des Économistes* 2e. S, no. 23: 64–67.

Pinto, Aníbal. 1962. *Chile: Un caso de desarrollo frustrado.* 2nd ed. Santiago: Editorial Universitaria.

Rodríguez, Zorobabel. 1889. "Un capítulo sobre la enseñanza de la economía política en la Universidad de Chile, sacado del libro *Páginas Sueltas* de don Domingo Amunátegui Solar." *Revista Económica* (Valparaíso) 31:75–80.

Rodríguez, Zorobabel. 1893. *Estudios Económicos.* Valparaíso: Imprenta del Comercio.

Rodríguez, Zorobabel. 1894. *Tratado de Economía Política.* Valparaíso: Imprenta del Comercio.

Romero, Ambrosio, and Juan I. Quesada. 1995. *Vida y Testimonio de Félix Frías.* Buenos Aires: Boletín de la Academia Nacional de Derecho y Ciencias Sociales de Buenos Aires.

Schneider, Ben Ross. 1998. "The Material Bases of Technocracy: Investor Confidence and Neoliberalism in Latin America." In *The Politics of Expertise in Latin America,* edited by M. A. Centeno and P. Silva, 77–95. London: Macmillan.

Subercaseaux, Guillermo. 1922. *Monetary and Banking Policy of Chile.* Oxford: Clarendon.

Subercaseaux, Guillermo. 1924. *Historia de las Doctrinas Económicas en América Latina y en Especial en Chile.* Santiago: Sociedad Imprenta y Litografia Universo.

Tullock, Gordon. 1980. "Efficient Rent Seeking." In *Toward a Theory of the Rent Seeking Society,* edited by J. M. Buchanan, R. D. Tollison, and G. Tullock, 97–112. College Station: Texas A&M University Press.

Universidad de Chile. *Anales de la Universidad de Chile.* Several volumes, 1853–55.

Urzúa, Pedro N. 1884. *Zorobabel Rodríguez o las exajeraciones del libre cambio.* Santiago: Imprenta Cervantes.

Valdés, Cristóbal. [1850] 1993. "Observaciones sobre la enseñanza de la economía política en el Instituto Nacional." In *Ensayistas Proteccionistas del Siglo XIX,* edited by S. Villalobos and R. Sagredo, 225–31. Santiago: Dirección de Bibliotecas Archivos y Museos.

Valdés, J. Gabriel. 1995. *Pinochet's Economists: The Chicago School in Chile.* Cambridge: Cambridge University Press.

Valencia Avaria, Luis. 1986. *Anales de la República.* 2nd ed. Santiago: Editorial Andrés Bello.

Varas, Antonio. 1919. *Correspondencia de don Antonio Varas con el Almirante Manuel Blanco Encalada sobre su misión en Europa, 1853–1857.* Santiago: Imprenta Universitaria.

Vial, Gonzalo, with Angel C. Morales and Federico G. Hugo. 1999. *Una Trascendental Experiencia Académica: Una Historia de la Facultad de Ciencias Económicas y Administrativas de la Pontificia Universidad Católica de Chile y la Nueva Visión Económica.* Santiago: Fundación Facultad de Ciencias Económicas y Administrativas de la Pontificia Universidad Católica de Chile.

Villalobos, Sergio, and Rafael Sagredo. 1987. *El Proteccionismo Económico en Chile.* Vol. 19. Santiago: Instituto Blas Cañas.

Will, Robert M. 1960. "La Política Económica de Chile, 1810–64." *El Trimestre Económico* 27:238–57.

Will, Robert M. 1964. "The Introduction of Classical Economics into Chile." *Hispanic American Historical Review* 44:1–21.

Zilci, Sonia. 1990. "La Ordenanza de Aduanas de 1864." *Cuadernos de Historia* (Departamento de Ciencias Históricas de la Universidad de Chile) 10:109–25.

PART 4 • Literature, Biology, and Economics

15 • Is a Novel a Model?

Tyler Cowen

I defend the relevance of fiction for social science investigation. Novels can be useful for making some economic approaches—such as behavioral economics or signaling theory—more plausible. Novels are more like models than is commonly believed. Some novels present verbal models of reality. I interpret other novels as a kind of simulation, akin to how simulations are used in economics. Economics can, and has, profited from the insights contained in novels. Nonetheless, while novels and models lie along a common spectrum, they differ in many particulars. I attempt a partial account of why we sometimes look to models for understanding and other times look to novels.

"Why don't those authors just come right out and *say* what they mean?" One of my economist colleagues offered this query when we were discussing the so-called Great Books. Shortly thereafter the question came as to why we need the classics when we can work with formal models. Few economists today read Homer much less work on the problems he raised. On the other side of the divide stand many individuals from the humanities. These individuals spend much of their careers reading the Great Books. They may not reject the idea of formal modeling in the social sciences, but it is distant from their concerns. These individuals believe that models are forced to oversimplify in a way that a literary text does not.

Addressing this difference in perspectives, I consider how novels and stories differ from formal models. By novels I mean written, full-length, fictional stories that are designed to inspire, entertain, or otherwise stimulate the reader. I do not mean to dismiss the distinctions among various fictional forms or the importance of those distinctions for literary theory. Nonetheless, I start by posing the question in the grossest possible way, namely, by comparing models and a generic concept of fictional stories as represented here by novels. While there is a massive

The author wishes to thank Bryan Caplan, Robin Hanson, Mary Hirschfeld, David Levy, Russ Roberts, and Alex Tabarrok for very useful comments and discussions.

literature on what novels are all about, there is virtually nothing comparing novels to models.[1]

By models I mean economic models with a formal mathematical structure, most typically in the form of exact assumptions about utility functions and production technologies or, in the case of game theory, behavioral conjectures. These models typically embody a social science mechanism about how a series of initial conditions give rise to a final result. Models are not typically realistic in their details or degrees of abstraction, but rather they attempt to portray some stylized features of how the world works. I will not consider every possible kind of economic model (the possibilities are vast), but rather I will focus on the kind of rational models taught in the first year or two of a typical graduate sequence in economics. These models form the core of the discipline.[2]

I will draw on two additional concepts. I refer to *data* as facts, numbers, or true stories about the real world. I refer to *simulations* as artificially generated ("false") data produced by estimating a model. Models, data, and simulations hardly exhaust the entirety of social science, but they form my initial categories for asking where and how novels relate to the social sciences.

My inquiry has several purposes. First, I wish to argue for the benefits and long-run complementarity of novels and models. Of course, at any single point in time they are substitutes—today should I read a novel or study a model? But in the larger picture social scientists should consider, for research reasons, spending time reading novels and humanities professors should consider spending time with formal models. The two methods of investigation, despite notable and persisting differences, have more in common than is commonly supposed. Since this

1. Morgan (2001) and Ingrao (2001) both argue that economists can learn something from literature. Morgan stresses how models are embodied in a broader narrative, which I discuss later. Ingrao (2001) considers the lessons in some particular novels. Watts (2002) considers the use of implicit models in literary works; see also the collection edited by Watts (2003). Henderson (1995) studies the presentation of economic ideas, through the literary medium, by such classical economists as Maria Edgeworth, and Harriet Martineau. Roback (1985) examines the economics of George Orwell. Rockoff (1990) draws out the monetary economics in *The Wizard of Oz*. Levy and Peart (2004) have been working on how pictures, images, and paintings might differ from formal models. Paulos (2002) offers some very brief remarks comparing stories to mathematical logic. On novels alone, Booth (1961) is one classic place to start. See also Frye ([1957] 1990), Hirsch (1967), Lentricchia (1980), and Gadamer (1989) among many others. Norris (1982) surveys deconstruction. Shell (1993) studies the use of economic metaphors in literature. Oatley (1994) treats the novel as analogous to a computer simulation and argues that this view has its roots in Aristotle's theory of mimesis. On the comparison between literature and the law, see the essays in Ledwon 1996. The neo-Kantian philosopher Vaihinger (1924) argued that the fundamental constructs of science resemble fictions; see also van Fraassen 1980.

2. Morgan (2001) surveys some contrasting definitions of *model*. For the debate on the realism of economic models, see Mäki 2003.

chapter is directed at social scientists, it should be thought of as pronovel, relative to economic science as a whole, although individuals from the humanities may experience discomfort at seeing novels compared to models at all.

Two hundred years ago the social sciences and the humanities were very closely linked, but they have moved increasingly apart. I hope to make some progress in reuniting these disparate fields of investigation. Similarly, we find a battle, often vitriolic in form, in American law schools. The so-called law and economics movement uses models to analyze the law. The alternative critical legal studies tradition rejects these models and places greater stress on narratives and the methods of the humanities. "Law and literature" classes are now commonplace, but there is no consensus among rational choice theorists on what kind of value they add.[3]

A comparison of novels and models might start with categories from literary criticism (allegory, metaphor, mimesis, etc.) and see how they relate to models or how they might be found in models. Deirdre McCloskey (1985, 1990), for instance, argues that economic techniques have more in common with rhetoric than is commonly acknowledged.[4] In contrast, I start with categories from the modeling literature (models, data, and simulations) and see how novels fit into those categories. This is the investigation of an economist not a literary theorist.

The presumption that novels ought to be given justification in terms of social science categories may offend some, but I do not see this question as reflecting skepticism about novels or discriminating against novels relative to models. Nor am I attempting to "reduce" the value of novels to economic or rational choice categories. We can recognize that novels stand on their own as works of art while still wishing to focus on how novels fit into rational choice categories. My account seeks to *add* to the value of novels rather than explaining that entire value in reductionist terms or forcing all of that value into the boxes of rational choice social science. I also will consider why we should read "false" novels instead of concentrating on the true descriptions of historical research.

An investigation of novels and models also may help us better understand how the public thinks about economic issues. Economists typically use formal models to think about the world. We cannot help but notice that most members of the general public do not appear to think very scientifically about policy in the sense of deferring to the estab-

3. Posner's (1998) account of law and literature is an eclectic, pragmatic, and sometimes skeptical account of how literature helps us understand jurisprudence.

4. Ankersmit (1996) argues that many political models rely ultimately on aesthetic concepts.

lished expert bodies of knowledge. Instead most citizens are heavily influenced by stories, movies, and popular culture. They think in terms of narrative, often false narrative, and spend little time learning economics. Economists naturally wonder whether citizens and voters spend too much time thinking in terms of stories and not enough time thinking in terms of models.

How should we think about this difference in approach? Is model-based thinking unpopular for some specific reason or is it simply too hard for most people? Or does the "common man" in fact use a different model rather than rejecting model-based thinking altogether? To pursue these questions, we need a better sense of exactly how models and stories differ.[5]

What Exactly Do We Learn from Novels?

I will proceed by citing three points—all relevant for economics—that we might learn from novels. After discussing each point briefly, I will then return to the more foundationalist question of exactly how novels might have brought us to these insights.

Assessing Behavioral Economics

A large literature on behavioral economics has arisen over the last twenty years (see Rabin 1998 for a survey). This line of research suggests that human behavior is far more complex than standard models of utility maximization dictate. More important, behavioral economists argue that understanding the complexity of choice will give us a better grasp of many economic phenomena.

A familiarity with novels increases the plausibility of behavioral economics. Most characters in novels have complex motivations and show a variety of behavioral quirks. For instance, Flaubert's characters often exhibit a "grass is always greener" approach to romantic choice rather than rationally assessing their current and future prospects. Madame Bovary seems to want every man but the one, her husband, who adores her. The lead characters in Brontë's *Wuthering Heights* (Heathcliff and Catherine) consider themselves connected by a sense of

5. The reader will notice, of course, that I am trying to construct a "model" of the difference between models and stories. Had I been born with different talents or inclinations, I might have written a novel about the difference between models and novels. The economist Russell Roberts (2001) has in fact written a novel, *The Invisible Heart: An Economic Romance,* contrasting economistic and literary ways of approaching the world. Or perhaps I should produce (better yet, commission) a painting of the differences between novels and models. At the same time this chapter is asking how much and why those alternative approaches would differ.

common fate and destiny, and they pursue disastrous courses of action. Captain Ahab, in Melville's *Moby-Dick,* is obsessed with taking his revenge against the white whale, which eventually leads to his death.

Utility maximization may describe the behavior of these characters ex post, but it does not help us understand or predict their behavior very much. Instead their behavior appears best described in terms of complex psychological mechanisms. Their biographies, and the social contexts they live in, lead them to perceive realities in ways that are not captured by traditional economic models. Their behaviors appear irrational in some regards, but we are supposed to imagine, for instance, that Ahab faces an utterly compelling sense of mission to hunt down the white whale.

The standard criticism of behavioral economics is that it offers too many varying accounts of human behavior with no unified framework or no ability to offer useful ex ante predictions. A reader of novels, who is used to complex portraits of multifaceted characters, is less likely to find such a criticism persuasive. Such a reader is less likely to see simplicity as an explanatory virtue and less likely to look for unified accounts of complex social phenomena.

Novels also may point our attention to some behavioral mechanisms rather than others. Homer's *Odyssey* portrays a world where most people are struck with self-deception and confusion about their motives; Rabin and Schrag (1999) and Benabou and Tirole (2002) have integrated the self-deception idea into behavioral economics. Ingrao (2001) surveys writings of Dickens, Melville, Dostoyevsky, and Balzac, in support of the claim that people choose their own budget constraints; this idea runs contrary to standard theory but is familiar to behavioral economists (e.g., Thaler 1994).

Welfare Economics and Human Welfare

At the margin, pure Pareto improvements are scarce. For this reason, applied welfare economics typically focuses on some form of the Kaldor-Hicks compensation rule. If the gainer's gains, as measured in dollars, exceed the loser's losses, economists are inclined to recommend the policy. This rule can be modified to take distribution into account, thus weighting the dollars of the poor more heavily, but economists still link wealth and welfare.

A separate literature has developed on the empirics of happiness (see Oswald 1997 and Frey and Stutzer 2002 for surveys). Drawing on techniques of empirical psychology, researchers ask individuals to report their subjective well-being. These subjective measures are then correlated, for purposes of reliability, with more objective measures of happiness, including health, propensity to smile, expected longevity, reports from peers, and number of friends.

These researchers find that more wealth, above a certain baseline level, does not make most individuals much happier. Employment (after adjusting for wealth), health, marital status, volunteer work, and religious participation, among other variables, have a positive correlation with happiness. Insofar as a wealth effect is found, it tends to be for relative wealth. People enjoy having more wealth than their neighbors. This wealth effect, of course, does not translate into net social value since one person's loss is another person's gain.

When evaluating economic welfare, the question remains as to whether we should use a wealth-based view or a happiness view. Novels make the happiness-based view more plausible both by portraying the complexities of human welfare and by showing how the rich are not always happy. When the very poor escape extreme poverty, they are better off. It is never fun to starve. Yet literary figures are not generally happier as they become wealthier. Instead we often find that money and avarice corrupt happiness, as expressed in tales by Balzac, Dickens, Proust, Flaubert, and many other writers. Less intellectual, "popular" novels, such as Harlequins, focus on love and togetherness as a source of happiness, not money. More generally, when literary characters report their happiness, or lack thereof, they rarely cite changes in wealth as a reason, again barring the case of escape from extreme poverty and privation.

These novelistic portraits suggest that readers find it plausible that happiness does not increase much with wealth, at least above a certain level. Readers presumably have experienced the same phenomenon in their lives. So reading novels increases our skepticism about the relevance of the Kaldor-Hicks rule for economic welfare and increases our appreciation for the happiness measures of welfare.

The Plausibility of Signaling Models

Many famous fictional characters take great care to control the presentation of their image to the outside world. They invest significant resources so that other people will have a more favorable opinion of them. We find this theme in the works of George Eliot, Jane Austen, Tolstoy, Proust, and numerous other novels of note. Proust's aristocrats go to great trouble to show that they are accepted in the proper social circles. Austen portrays elaborate mechanisms for signaling properness, chastity, upbringing, and property. Tolstoy presents an explicit recognition of the signaling mechanism. *War and Peace* presents the characters of Sonya, the Count, and the Countess as fussing over the health of Natasha (chap. 16). They wish to show that they are doing something and to signal their status as caring people. Hanson (2002) modeled this idea many years later.

Again, it is plausible to think that novelists use descriptions that resonate with the intuitions of their readers. The fictional depictions of signaling illuminate our own behavior to ourselves and make us more aware of how others around us are signaling as well. So reading novels will make us more receptive to the signaling arguments used in economic theory. We are more likely to see those models as intuitive rather than as requiring some leap of the imagination.

The bottom line can be explained as follows. Economic theory is rigorous, or at least it attempts to be. Yet how we evaluate economic theory, and how we choose economic theories, is often highly intuitive. A knowledge of novels can refine our intuitions in these tasks.

Novels as Models?

Having outlined some insights from novels that are relevant for economics, how should we think about the sources of this knowledge? How can we put both novels and models into a broader spectrum of how human understanding is generated?

Clearly novels are not data as a social scientist would use that term. By definition novels do not narrate true events. A novel may be "true data" about the mind of its creator and the proclivity of that mind to draw connections and tell stories. But a novel remains a constructed tale. If novels cannot be data, I therefore consider two other major categories in economic theorizing—models and simulations—to see how novels might fit in.

Novels as Models

Some kinds of fiction resemble models. Some science fiction stories, for instance, embody model-like thinking. The author writes down a description of some new technologies to be found in a hypothetical world. The author then traces through the effects of these technologies and outlines how things would work or outlines an equilibrium in economic terminology. That equilibrium is then "disturbed" by some new change such as alien invasion or a new technology. The bulk of the novel then traces through the effects of the change, performing a kind of comparative statics exercise. The works of Ayn Rand, which portray capitalistic and collectivistic societies, offer a similar exercise, although they focus on changes in individual freedom rather than on technologies more narrowly.[6]

In other cases the behavior of a particular character fits an economic model. Defoe's Moll Flanders, for instance, appears to maximize wealth. When one line of activity promises higher returns, she is keener to pursue that activity. Another major character of Defoe, Robinson Crusoe, responds to incentives and property rights. The treatment of signaling in Tolstoy, mentioned earlier, fits this category as well.[7]

I take these novels (or parts of them) to literally be models, albeit of the informal sort. They use a stylized setting to show how one set of causes leads to particular effects, working through a mechanism of some generality. The mechanism is not always spelled out explicitly but can be seen in the examples. They are like the models from early in the history of economics. Before the mathematization of the economics profession, economists offered verbal models without explicit mathematical forms and rigorous proofs. It is no accident that contemporary model builders sometimes refer to earlier, nonformal economists as "telling stories."

Nonetheless these model-like novels are not the primary cases for our comparison. Despite the examples given earlier, most novels do not offer much in the way of model-like reasoning. Most novels relate many particulars but make no overall theoretical pronouncements about the motivation of their characters or the results of those motivations. If we look, for instance, at James Joyce's *Ulysses,* it is hard to model any of the particular behaviors. We read about a character doing forty-seven different things. The actions may fit together to form a coherent portrait in our minds, but we are given no general account, in the sense required by the economist, of how all those behaviors fit together. What are we to make of this kind of novel?

Novels as Simulations

Many novels are more like economic simulations than models. In other words, the novel is made-up data. To see why studying made-up data

---

6. Ingrao (2001) considers some anticommercial examples from Zola and Balzac, and Watts (2002) surveys some examples more generally. Cowen (1998, chap, 2) considers some examples from eighteenth-century British fiction. On the didactic functions of novels, see Boyd 1980, especially chapter 7, which examines the views of Samuel Johnson in this regard.

7. *Murder at the Margin,* written under the pseudonym Marshall Jevons (a compendium of two nineteenth-century economists' names, Alfred Marshall and William Stanley Jevons, but actually William Breit and Kenneth G. Elzinga), has every character behaving in terms of an explicit logic of choice. This novel, written by two economists, then uses economic reasoning to solve the murder.

may be useful, let us first step back and consider some basic information about simulations.

In economics a simulation typically takes a previous model and assigns particular values to the open parameters. One of the free variables is then tweaked or changed so that the results may be traced. Imaginary time is played out, and the simulation generates information on prices, quantities, and other measurable economic variables.

It is now well understood that the difference between a regression and a simulation is one of degree rather than kind (Hansen and Heckman 1996). Any regression contains an implicit simulation. Consider, for instance, $y = 2x + k$ as a least squares estimation fitted around actual data points. This regression also suggests imaginary, simulated, alternate histories based on varying values for the independent variable. Similarly, simulations contain implicit (or explicit) regressions. The assigned parameter values for the simulation are typically taken from real data or econometric estimates of that data. We make the regression a simulation simply by exploring alternative realizations for the independent variables. To put this point in other words, the regression fits the data points we know, and the simulation uses that information to speculate about the data points we do not observe.

Economists use simulations in two different ways either to resolve uncertainty about possible data or to resolve uncertainty about the explanatory power of a model. In the first case economists trust the underlying estimated model but wish to obtain information about alternative scenarios for the independent variables. We might, for instance, have an acceptable model and then ask what will happen if the price of oil goes to sixty dollars a barrel, seventy dollars a barrel, and so on. I will refer to simulations of this kind as estimations.

Second, economists may already know the data and wonder whether a particular model can describe that reality. For instance, economists already know the data series for a macroeconomic downturn. Inventories move so much, the unemployment rate moves so much, investment moves so much, interest rates move so much, and so on. These facts are rarely disputed. It remains a question, however, whether any theory can account for that data. By simulating a theory we see whether it can generate and thus perhaps explain the magnitudes in question. This second use of simulation is sometimes called calibration, or calibrating an artificial economy, and is common in contemporary macroeconomics.[8]

Simulations thus require either a good sense of the model, to judge

8. For discussions of simulations in macroeconomics, see Prescott 1986; Hoover 1995; Kydland and Prescott 1996; Hansen and Heckman 1996; and Sims 1996.

the data (estimation), or a good sense of the data to judge an underlying model (calibration). Simulations do not require a firm sense of both data and model, and, indeed, they would be superfluous if we knew both the data and the proper model.

Along these lines, if we are to fit novels into the boxes offered by rational choice theory, they can count as either estimations or calibrations. Let us consider each in turn.

Simulation Estimations

We have a novelistic estimation when the author plays out the implications of his or her underlying worldview. It may be a political worldview but is more likely some understanding of society, psychology, and human behavior. Think of a novel as resulting when that worldview is filled in with particular characters, a particular historical era, a particular conflict or choice, and so on.[9]

A novelist, for instance, might believe in the universal human desire for status and recognition. He or she can then ask, as did Proust, how this desire will play itself out in French social circles at the time of the Dreyfus Affair. The resulting story then offers us some vision of how an underlying worldview applies to a particular setting. Similarly, we can think of Tolstoy's *Anna Karenina,* in part, as a story of the prevalence of self-deception set among the Russian nobility.

The portrayal of happiness in many novels, as noted earlier, fits into this category. In Charles Dickens's *Bleak House,* for instance, the pursuit and prospect of a sizable inheritance damages the well-being of a number of characters, most of all Richard. The text suggests that the happy characters (such as Esther in the latter part of the story) learn to come to terms with what they have and set their expectations accordingly. Modesty, a core minimum of autonomy, and freedom from legal hassles are all shown as more important for happiness than is money.

So we might learn by studying a novel just as we might learn from running an estimation simulation. The analogy is not exact since the starting framework of "the novelist's worldview" does not correspond exactly to the alternate starting framework of "an economic model." Nonetheless in both cases general principles and insights are used to generate more specific outcomes, namely, stories that do not describe reality directly. We look at the stories, which are of interest in their own right, to illuminate some underlying general principles. Novels and sim-

9. Levy and Peart (2004) remark that a painting is a model without the error term. Perhaps this point can be understood within the context of simulation. Economic simulations never have error terms because the theorist is creating the "data." The same is true for a novel.

ulations—both false in the literal sense of that term—give us ideas of how differing scenarios are likely to play themselves out.

Simulation Calibrations

Alternatively, readers may use novels to test underlying theories, as with calibration. Readers, for instance, may feel they already know what is a plausible story and what is not. In other words, readers may know what kind of replicated data a novel needs to generate. If the worldview behind a novel can generate plausible data, that worldview will increase in plausibility, otherwise not.

To return to Marcel Proust, he portrayed many of his characters as receiving their primary pleasures from anticipations and memories, rather than actual events, and drew our attention to the distinction between voluntary and involuntary memory. His novel *Remembrance of Things Past* strikes a chord with many readers and therefore has increased the plausibility of models that embody the enjoyment of memories and anticipations such as the work of George Loewenstein (1987). We can think of the Proustian account as providing one piece of evidence for behavioral economics, as discussed earlier. If the story of the novel resonates with our intuitions, we will see the author's postulates as relevant.

Along similar lines, the novels of Camus and Sartre have convinced many readers of the philosophic virtues (and vices) of existentialism. Camus's *The Stranger* and Sartre's *The Age of Reason* reflect elements of the existentialist worldview. If a reader finds the final psychological portraits convincing, and to match his intuitions, he may conclude there is something to existentialism after all as an account of the human condition.

We again see an imperfect analogy with economic models. If, in the economic context, simulated data do not look right (imagine a model in which a dollar a gallon rise in the price of oil would cut the gross domestic product in half), we conclude that something is wrong with the model. In the novelistic context, if we find the story implausible we discriminate against the worldview of the novelist. In the novelistic case the link of course is looser. In economics, short of scientific fraud or computer error, we know that ridiculous estimates reflect a problem with a well-specified model. But say that we do not find Sartre's *The Age of Reason* to be either plausible or interesting. How sure can we be that existentialism is at fault? Perhaps Sartre is simply bad at writing characters, bad at dialogue, or whatever. Our ability to judge inputs by the plausibility of outputs is much looser when we are looking at a novel compared to examining a simulated economic model.

The Novelistic Narrative as False

It is not unusual to defend the use of narrative in the social sciences (see Mink 1970; and Roth 1989), and indeed this topic is prominent in the philosophy of history and elsewhere. But the value of novels suggests a more radical position, defending the use of *deliberately false* narrative.[10]

Given our earlier discussion, we now have a better sense of why we should study novels and not just some combination of models and history. First, the number of possible constructed stories is far larger than the number of true stories. Fiction allows us to consider new and different possibilities. Novelists therefore run many more simulations than would be found in history. A novel can construct settings that are not possible or easily accessible in historical investigation. Even when a novel is set in a historical era, the novelist can create new masses of detail and narrative. History, by definition, attempts to present only true scenarios. This is an obvious virtue, but it also limits the use of history to create simulations, as discussed earlier. A novel, for instance, can offer the stream of consciousness reasoning of its characters, whereas history usually cannot.

Second, a constructed story, by its nature, sheds light on the author's underlying worldview. The plausibility of the story allows us to "test" the plausibility of the author's framework. A true historical narrative cannot, by its construction, do the same, as we already know that historical stories are both possible and real. Historical *interpretation* allows for a test of a historian's underlying worldview, but history per se does not. Models, like novels, but unlike history, are fictions. And this use of fiction gives us insight into the abstract constructions behind the fictions.

The Dangers of Novels and Models

Viewing novels as simulations draws our attention to some of their virtues and flaws relative to models.

On the negative side, many readers judge the plausibility of novels by using their introspection. If we believe that self-deception is rife in human affairs (see Cowen 2005), this test is not in every way a good one. We will tend to like those novels that affirm what we think we already know and reject novels that provide disconfirming messages. Novels also can mislead when introspection provides no guide to truth. It is easy to point to novelistic simulations (just about any novelistic utopia will do, from Thomas More to Edward Bellamy) that are plain, flat-out wrong about how individual human behavior translates into social out-

10. Of course, many novels also contain true historical facts. To this extent the case for learning social science from novels is straightforward.

comes. Readers are nonetheless attracted by the emotional resonance of the story. An introspective test *may* be able to distinguish true and false propositions about human behavior, but certainly it cannot judge factual claims about the world very well. Similarly, Upton Sinclair's *The Jungle* continues to convince people of the merits of food and meat regulation (for better or worse) despite its openly fictional status.

Novel reading runs the risk of confirmation bias in this regard. No one reader can read any more than a small fraction of the published novels; few people have enough time to read even most of the classics. So what one takes away from novels will depend, in part, on which novels one chooses to read. To some extent we can expect people to read novels that confirm their ideologies and preconceptions. So a left-wing reader may prefer Upton Sinclair while a libertarian may read Ayn Rand.

An economic model attempts to provide a cluster of related qualities, including mathematical formality, transparency, simplicity, and clarity. By no means do all models succeed in offering these qualities. Game-theoretic models, for instance, are known for their messiness and multiple equilibria. That being said, such qualities are usually held against game theory. Economic models are considered successful to the extent that they provide transparency and clarity, and, of course, some models succeed in this endeavor. Simple models, for instance, help us understand the difference between an income and a substitution effect, and such a distinction can be considered a triumph of economics and the model-building method. Clear models thus enable the modeler to state some general principles of behavior with a relatively small number of well-defined assumptions. Both the model and its simulations are replicable and verifiable.

If we think of economic models as "existence theorems," telling us "what could possibly happen" (Nelson 1986), we can get some sense of likelihood by examining the underlying assumptions. A model of a Giffen good, for instance, tells us that if price goes up people under some circumstances will buy more not less. Nonetheless playing with the model shows that this can hold only when the price rise is for a necessity and when that necessity takes up a large part of the consumer's budget. A novel cannot easily serve this same function in the same way. We might read a Jane Austen novel and conclude that various kinds of courtship behaviors are indeed possible or plausible. That being said, it is harder to draw out the underlying assumptions, as embedded in the story, needed to generate this kind of behavior.

On the positive side, when we wish to base our simulations on alternative assumptions about human behavior, novels fill gaps that models cannot. They give up formal exactness and transparency to draw our attention to sophisticated motivations, emotional mechanisms, and interpersonal relationships. The insights of novelists usually cannot be expressed in a small number of theoretical or mathematical propositions.[11]

The successful novelist also must make his or her characters live in the mind of the reader. This requires insight into human behavior that goes beyond typical economic postulates about rationality, downward-sloping demand curves, and so on. A novelist must offer the reader an "interior" understanding of what various events, experiences, and stories are like. Novels can appeal to our empathy in a way that models cannot. As noted earlier, the novelist must "test" the story, and the character portraits, against human intuition and introspection. The novelist invents plausible particulars and explores their ramifications with an eye toward deeper generalities, often about the nature of the human condition.

Novels spur readers to ask questions, thereby helping readers increase the value of their human capital. The reader turns his or her implicit, unarticulated knowledge into explicit knowledge. This questioning may generate knowledge above and beyond any particular contribution the author has to offer. In short, novels help generate self-knowledge and help turn self-knowledge into useful forms.

An individual who reads Kafka's *The Trial* may be led to ponder the nature of guilt, responsibility, and punishment. A good novel is memorable, has storylike qualities, and elicits an emotional response, all of which mobilize the human capital and energies of the reader. Devices such as multiple perspectives, changes of voice, and irony all may encourage particular reader questions. Ingrao (2001, 15) notes that "in novels plurality of meaning is the rule." Reader "self-deception"—temporarily thinking the story is more real than it actually is—assists the knowledge generation process. These features also give novels some advantages of factual history.[12]

A variety of questions, ranging from the nature of beauty, the nature of tragedy, the nature of the good or the meaning of life, receive only limited insight from formal models. Economic models (e.g., Arrow's theorem) shed some light on these topics, but they may not elicit reader questions and introspection equally well. The transparency of economic models offers scientific advantages, but the models themselves do not

11. West (1996) argues that characters in novels typically have less rationality than economic man but far greater empathy and sympathy. Ingrao (2001) stresses the complexity of the kind of knowledge found in novels.

12. There is a substantial philosophic literature on the difference between novels and reality. One central question addressed is why a reader might care about the outcome of a novel given that the he or she knows the events are not really happening. On this question, and others, see Hjort and Laver 1997.

interest many people and thus do not motivate those people to ask better questions. Economic models therefore fail to draw out many kinds of internal or introspective knowledge. Novels, in contrast, are most useful where introspection is most likely to provide some insight relative to measurement and formal scientific experimentation. We might read a novel to better understand the emotion of self-righteousness, but we would be ill-advised to read a novel to discover how the labor market works.

We can think of novels and models as relying on tacit knowledge (Polanyi 1974) in differing ways. Both novelists and model builders have tacit knowledge about how the real world works, and they try to articulate that knowledge in the form of either a story or equations. The economist tries to make previously hidden connections more transparent. The hope is that our previously tacit knowledge can be articulated more clearly and that the knowledge will no longer be tacit. The novelist keeps many of the relevant connections in the sphere of tacit knowledge and hopes that his or her initial tacit knowledge can spur some more knowledge, often of the tacit kind, in readers.

For this reason, any account of what we learn from novels is likely more subjective than a comparable account of what we learn from models. What we learn from novels will be person specific and strongly tinged with biographical elements, more than will be the case with models.

Concluding Remarks

Novels are akin to models in at least two ways. Some novels resemble models proper, whereas others can be thought of as simulations of underlying implicit models.

Most of all, I have tried to show that the difference between (economic) models and novels can be modeled. This suggests that we have some broader model about the generation of knowledge and understanding with "economic models," "novels," and other kinds of information as relevant subcategories.

The general advantages of model-based thinking therefore should not be used to discriminate against knowledge production through novels, the Great Books, and the humanities generally. Those methods of knowledge production have their own advantages, and those advantages can be understood through model-based thinking. In many cases reliance on the Great Books may represent the wrong use of models at the wrong point in time, but this is an empirical question to be answered by context. Those who defend economic models simply by citing the general advantages of models are viewing the comparison with the humanities too narrowly. They are also doing injustice to the very broad power of models.[13]

At the same time, we should recognize the power of stories. Many models, especially the most relevant models, are embedded in stories, further illustrating the complementarities between novels and models. Abstract transparency accounts for many of the virtues of the model, but the "sharper" the model is the harder it is to translate the results of the model into a claim about the messy and complex real world. If a model tells us *only* that assumptions A, B, and C lead to result X, this is not useful if A, B, and C do not hold in the real world. If we want to know what our model really means, and how it translates into information about the real world, we often fall back on storylike accounts (McCloskey 1985, 1990; Morgan 2001). Economists, for instance, have storylike accounts of the vices and virtues of markets and often use models (and data) to support one story over another. Similarly, economists offer storylike accounts of the rationality, or irrationality, of individual human agents and again use models in support of their stories about the nature of human beings.

Giambattista Vico ([1744] 1976), in his *New Science,* struck out the extreme position that myth and "poetic wisdom" are more fundamental means of knowledge than is science. He saw politics and economics as flowing from this more primeval source of wisdom. He writes of myth as a kind of "matrix" in which other categories of human understanding, including science, are made intelligible. We need not accept Vico's extreme view about the primacy of story and myth, but nonetheless the two methods of communication and discovery—model and story—are not so neatly separable.[14]

One commentator on this chapter (Alex Tabarrok) suggested that contemporary computer games break down the distinction between novels and models altogether. If the game has enough sophistication, and is sufficiently entertaining or inspiring, the model becomes like a novel as well. Game characters are "produced by" mathematical equations and programs, as we might find in an economic model. Nonetheless, the resulting model has enough storylike properties to make it both a model and novel at once. Arguably, the same might be said about chess, at least as played by grand masters. At the very least the distinctions between models and novels will vary with technologies.

Finally, these categories may help us understand why so many indi-

13. Hume ([1767] 1999, sec. 3) argues for the unity of poetry, storytelling, and other methods of knowledge, claiming that all are based on the idea of resemblances.

14. For a recent interpretation of Vico, see Mazzotta 1999.

viduals fail to find model-based thinking, in the narrow economistic sense, to be so persuasive. These people are not simply the unwashed masses or fuzzy-minded English professors. Rather they are people who, either implicitly or explicitly, recognize that novels have some potential advantages over traditional economic models. No matter how antimodel their rhetoric may be, in reality they prefer models of a different kind.[15]

Many economists believe that people spend too much time thinking in terms of stories and not enough time thinking in terms of models. The more likely problem is that these individuals need better and more informed stories.

Bibliography

Ankersmit, F. R. 1996. *Aesthetic Politics: Political Philosophy beyond Fact and Value.* Stanford: Stanford University Press.

Benabou, Roland, and Jean Tirole. 2002. "Self-Confidence and Personal Motivation." *Quarterly Journal of Economics* 117, no. 3: 871–915.

Booth, Wayne C. 1961. *The Rhetoric of Fiction.* Chicago: University of Chicago Press.

Boyd, John D. 1980. *The Function of Mimesis and Its Decline.* New York: Fordham University Press.

Cowen, Tyler. 1998. *In Praise of Commercial Culture.* Cambridge: Harvard University Press.

Cowen, Tyler. 2005. "The Roots of Political Failure: Self-Deception vs. Imperfect Information." *Public Choice* 124, no. 3–4: 437–51.

Frey, Bruno S., and Alois Stutzer. 2002. "What Can Economists Learn from Happiness Research?" *Journal of Economic Literature* 40, no. 2: 402–35.

Friedman, Milton. 1953. *Essays in Positive Economics.* Chicago: University of Chicago Press.

Frye, Northrop. [1957] 1990. *Anatomy of Criticism: Four Essays.* Princeton: Princeton University Press.

Gadamer, Hans-Georg. 1989. *Truth and Method.* 2nd, rev. ed. New York: Crossroad.

Goodman, Nelson. 1976. *Languages of Art: An Approach to a Theory of Symbols.* Indianapolis: Hackett.

Hansen, Lars Peter, and Heckman, James J. 1996. "The Empirical Foundations of Calibration." *Journal of Economic Perspectives* 10:87–104.

Hanson, Robin. 2002. "Why Health Is Not Special: Errors in Evolved Bioethics Intuitions." *Social Philosophy and Policy* 19, no. 2: 153–79.

Hayek, Friedrich A. 1989. *The Fatal Conceit: The Errors of Socialism.* Chicago: University of Chicago Press.

Henderson, Willie. 1995. *Economics as Literature.* New York: Routledge.

Hirsch, E. D., Jr. 1967. *Validity in Interpretation.* New Haven: Yale University Press.

15. Levy and Peart (2004) consider a different but related question. Should a person with a story trust an expert with a model? They find some circumstances under which the answer is no. Anecdotal evidence, as used by nonexperts, is often a relatively efficient way of estimating the median of a distribution.

Hjort, Mette, and Sue Laver, eds. 1997. *Emotion and the Arts.* New York: Oxford University Press.

Hoover, Kevin D. 1995. "Facts and Artifacts: Calibration and the Empirical Assessment of Real-Business-Cycle Models." *Oxford Economic Papers* 47:24–44.

Hume, David. [1767] 1999. *An Enquiry concerning Human Understanding.* Oxford: Oxford University Press.

Ingrao, Bruna. 2001. "Economic Life in Nineteenth-Century Novels: What Economists Might Learn from Literature." In *Economics and Interdisciplinary Exchange,* edited by Guido Erreygers, 7–40. New York: Routledge.

Jevons, Marshall. 1978. *Murder at the Margin.* Glen Ridge, N.J.: Thomas Horton and Daughters.

Kydland, Finn E., and Edward C. Prescott. 1996. "The Computational Experiment: An Econometric Tool." *Journal of Economic Perspectives* 10, no. 1: 69–85.

Ledwon, Lenora, ed. 1996. *Law and Literature: Text and Theory.* New York: Garland.

Lentricchia, Frank. 1980. *After the New Criticism.* Chicago: University of Chicago Press.

Levy, David M., and Sandra J. Peart. 2004. "Analytical Egalitarianism, Anecdotal Evidence and Information Aggregation." *Journal of Economic Methodology* 11:411–35.

Loewenstein, George. 1987. "Anticipation and the Valuation of Delayed Consumption." *Economic Journal* 97:666–84.

Mäki, Uskali, ed. 2003. *Facts and Fiction in Economics: Models, Realism, and Social Construction.* Cambridge: Cambridge University Press.

McCloskey, Deirdre N. 1985. *The Rhetoric of Economics.* Madison: University of Wisconsin Press.

McCloskey, Deirdre N. 1990. *If You're So Smart: The Narrative of Economic Expertise.* Chicago: University of Chicago Press.

Mazzotta, Giuseppe. 1999. *The New Map of the World: The Poetic Philosophy of Giambattista Vico.* Princeton: Princeton University Press.

Mink, Louis O. 1970. "History and Fiction as Modes of Comprehension." *New Literary History* 1:541–58.

Morgan, Mary S. 2001. "Models, Stories, and the Economic World." *Journal of Economic Methodology* 8, no. 3: 361–84.

Nelson, Alan. 1986. "New Individualistic Foundations for Economics." *Noûs,* 20, no. 4: 469–90.

Norris, Christopher. 1982. *Deconstruction: Theory and Practice.* New York: Methuen.

Oatley, Keith. 1994. "A Taxonomy of the Emotions of Literary Response and a Theory of Identification in Fictional Narrative." *Poetics* 23:53–74.

Oswald, Andrew J. 1997. "Happiness and Economic Performance." *Economic Journal* 107 (November): 1815–31.

Paulos, John Allen. 2002. "What Is Your Question? . . . Why?" Accessed on December 2007 at http://www.edge.org/q2002/q_paulos.html.

Pevear, Richard. 2000. "Introduction." In *Anna Karenina,* by Leo Tolstoy. Translated by Richard Pevear and Larissa Volokhonsky. New York: Penguin.

Plato. 1991. *The Republic of Plato.* Edited and translated by Allan Bloom. New York: Basic Books.

Polanyi, Michael. 1974. *Personal Knowledge: Towards a Post-critical Philosophy.* Chicago: University of Chicago Press.

Posner, Richard A. 1998. *Law and Literature.* Rev. ed. Cambridge: Harvard University Press.

Prescott, Edward C. 1986. "Theory Ahead of Business Cycle Measurement." *Federal Reserve Bank of Minneapolis Quarterly Review* 10:9–22.

Rabin, Matthew. 1998. "Psychology and Economics." *Journal of Economic Literature* 36 (March): 11–46.

Rabin, Matthew, and Joel Schrag. 1999. "First Impressions Matter: A Model of Confirmatory Bias." *Quarterly Journal of Economics* 114, no. 1: 37–81.

Roback, Jennifer. 1985. "The Economic Thought of George Orwell." *American Economic Review* 75, no. 2: 127–32.

Roberts, Russell. 2001. *The Invisible Heart: An Economic Romance.* Cambridge: MIT Press.

Rockoff, Hugh. 1990. "*The Wizard of Oz* as a Monetary Allegory." *Journal of Political Economy* 98, no. 4: 739–60.

Roth, Paul A. 1989. "How Narratives Explain." *Social Research* 56:449–78.

Shell, Marc. 1993. *The Economy of Literature.* Baltimore: Johns Hopkins University Press.

Sims, Christopher A. 1996. "Macroeconomics and Methodology." *Journal of Economic Perspectives* 10, no. 1: 105–20.

Strauss, Leo. 1988. *Persecution and the Art of Writing.* Chicago: University of Chicago Press.

Thaler, Richard H. 1994. *Quasi Rational Economics.* New York: Russell Sage Foundation.

Vaihinger, Hans. 1924. *The Philosophy of "As If."* London: Routledge and Kegan Paul.

Van Fraassen, Bas C. 1980. *The Scientific Image.* Oxford: Clarendon.

Vico, Giambattista. [1744] 1976. *The New Science of Giambattista Vico.* Ithaca: Cornell University Press.

Watts, Michael. 2002. "How Economists Use Literature and Drama." *Journal of Economic Education* 33 (fall): 377–86.

Watts, Michael, ed. 2003. *The Literary Book of Economics.* Wilmington, DE: Intercollegiate Studies Institute.

West, Robin. 1996. "Economic Man and Literary Woman: One Contrast." *In Law and Literature: Text and Theory,* edited by Lenora Ledwon, 127–36. New York: Garland.

16 • Denying Human Homogeneity
Eugenics and the Making of Postclassical Economics

Sandra J. Peart and David M. Levy

Introduction

The question we propose to address is how peace came to the conflict between economics and racism. How did economics move from the classical period characterized by the hardest possible doctrine of initial human homogeneity—all the observed differences among people arise from incentives, luck, and history[1]—to become comfortable with accounts of human behavior that alleged foundational differences among and within races of people (Darity 1995)? In this chapter, we shall argue that early British eugenics thinkers racialized economics in the postclassical period.

Given their stature as mathematical statisticians, we find it odd that the importance of the eugenic writing of Francis Galton and Karl Pearson has been neglected in the secondary literature on postclassical economics.[2] The racial debates of the nineteenth century have been so hidden that many economists still believe the "dismal science" label has something to do with Malthus's views on population and wages. In fact,

---

A lengthier version of this chapter appeared in *Journal of the History of Economic Thought* in 2003. Earlier versions were presented at the History of Economics Society meetings in Vancouver in 2000, the first Summer Institute for the Preservation of the History of Economics in 2000, and the Middlebury College Christian A. Johnson economics conference Race, Liberalism, and Economics in April 2001. We have received helpful comments from David Colander, Sandy Darity, Robert Leonard, Deirdre McCloskey, Larry Moss, and A. M. C. Waterman. Bryan Caplan and Ed McPhail provided valuable references.

1. Smith [1776], 1976, 28.

2. The silence in the commentary on Fisher is noted in the first sentence of Aldrich (1974, 33). Electronic searches allow a systematic, albeit limited, exploration of the scholarship on the subject. Using JSTOR, we find no use of the word *eugenics* in any of the literally hundreds of articles and reviews written by Joseph Schumpeter, George Stigler, and A. W. Coats. The results of the search, conducted on 23 May 2002, are available in HTML form upon request. (The case of Schumpeter's *History of Economic Analysis,* which, as Aldrich notes, pays attention to racist doctrines and as a book is not accessible in JSTOR, will be discussed later). Among the past generation of historians of economics, as far as we can determine, only Spengler systematically paid attention to eugenics (Spengler 1955, 1966). Mirowski (1989) discusses energetics at length with a slight glance at eugenics. The essays in Mirowski (1994) mention eugenics once in connection with Marshall. The eugenic involvement of the neoclassical economists is apparent in specialist accounts of eugenics such as that by Soloway (1995).

classical economics was condemned because it was characterized by a doctrine of homogeneity that abstracted from race. Recent work has shown that the "dismal science" characterization was earned because the classical economists supported the emancipation of West Indian slaves (Persky 1990; Levy 2001a, 2001b; Levy and Peart 2001–2).

Early eugenics thinking emerged in direct opposition to the classical account of economic decision making entailing homogeneity, and eugenicists temporarily succeeded in moving economics to accounts of competency involving racial difference. To make our case, we trace the opposition to race-blind accounts from Thomas Carlyle and the cofounder (with Francis Galton) of eugenics, W. R. Greg, and then to James Hunt and the Anthropological Society of the 1860s. Hunt is important in our account for his "new"—and devastating—theory of race entailing lack of differentiation within the race, which, we argue, influenced the other cofounder of eugenics, Galton. Next we examine how the early eugenicists' characterization of race influenced economic analysis in the postclassical period in terms of both Hunt's zero-variation theory and the anthropologists' parametric claims about the features of "lower" races. We also show that postclassical economists endorsed each of the three major policy recommendations of the eugenicists. Finally, we note how Ludwig von Mises and the Chicago School revived the classical economists' doctrine of human homogeneity.[3] Perhaps not surprisingly, the Chicago revival began with skepticism about the common link supposed in early neoclassical economics between time preference and race.

Contemporary readers may be surprised that nineteenth-century arguments about racial superiority play out in terms of both the Irish and the former slaves in Jamaica (Curtis 1968, 1997).[4] "Race" was a rather ill-defined notion well into the twentieth century, and in this period *race* is sometimes used to indicate national or vaguely defined ethnic differences. Nonetheless, by 1870 two theories of racial hierarchy can be identified as coexisting in the scientific community and the popular

3. Max Weber, whose influence on Mises is common knowledge, severely criticized the racialization of the social sciences (Proctor 1991, 182). The antiracist connections among Weber, Mises, and Eric Voegelin are in much need of specialist attention. Weber does not make Schumpeter's list of the "three greatest sociologists," but joining Vico and Marx is Francis Galton (Schumpeter 1954, 791).

4. Discussion in the Anthropological Society at this time very much focused on the Irish and on whether a well-defined, separate Irish "race" might be identified. The president of the Anthropological Society of London in 1870, John Beddoe, became well known for developing an "Index of Nigrescence" that could be applied to Celtic "types," as well as the racial category "Africanoid Celts" (Curtis 1997, 20; Beddoe 1870, 212–13). Huxley takes issue with Beddoe over the question of whether the Irish were a separate race. Loring Allen notes that eugenicists were also unclear on the meaning of *race* (1993, 150).

press.[5] The more devastating view of the owner of the *Anthropological Review,* James Hunt, held that there were races whose physical development had been arrested prematurely, dead races incapable of elevation.

> We now know it to be a patent fact that there are races existing which have no history, and that the Negro is one of these races. From the most remote antiquity the Negro race seems to have been what they are now. We may be pretty sure that the Negro race have been without a progressive history; and that they have been for thousands of years the uncivilized race they are at this moment. (Hunt 1863, 13)

The second theory, which we call "parametric racism," held that the inferior race differed from the superior (Anglo-Saxons) along some parameter(s). W. R. Greg, who is featured later for having cofounded the eugenics movement with Galton, persistently attacked classical political economy for its assumption that the Irishman is an "average human being" rather than an "idiomatic" and "idiosyncratic" man prone to "idleness," "ignorance," "jollity," and "drink" (Greg 1868, 78).

That both types of racial accounts coexisted and were applied to the Irish is evident from these remarks by Thomas Huxley in an 1870 address to the Anthropological Society.

> If the writer means to be civil, the Celt is taken to be a charming person, full of wit and vivacity and kindliness, but, unfortunately, thoughtless, impetuous, and unstable, and having standards of right and wrong so different from those of the Anglo-Saxon that it would be absurd, not to say cruel, to treat him in the same way. Or, if the instructor of the public is angry, he takes the Celt as if he were a kind of savage, out of whom no good ever has come or ever will come, and whose proper fate is to be kept as hewer of wood and a drawer of water for his Anglo-Saxon master. This is the picture of the lion by the man. (1870, 197)

Early Eugenics and the Opposition to Classical Economics

Darwin's theory of natural selection profoundly influenced early eugenicists, and the admiration was mutual. But there was a key difference between Darwinism and the "theory" put forward by early eugenicists.

5. Peart and Levy (2002) examine representations of the Negro and the Irish in the popular press at the time, most notably in *Punch.*

Darwinism, applied to humans, predicted that the fit would survive, *without intervention,* naturally. Yet A. R. Wallace made the case early on that the doctrine of natural selection did not apply to humans. Recognizing that humans could not count on such a tendency, eugenicists recommended that human (state) action should used to obtain it.

In 1864, Wallace argued that the doctrine of natural selection did not apply to humans because of ethical concerns generated by human sympathy. Our morals do not allow us to let the infirm perish (1864, clxii). W. R. Greg responded that sympathy blocked the "salutary" effects of the survival of the fittest and therefore such sentiments should be suppressed (1875, 119).[6]

In his *Enigmas of Life*—now informed by Galton's "Hereditary Genius"—Greg focused his attack on the homogeneity doctrine implicit in T. R. Malthus's recommendation of delay of marriage. Malthus is concerned only that, on average, marriage be postponed, whereas Greg is concerned that the "improving element" will be outbred by the "more reckless."

> Malthus's "prudential check" rarely operates upon the lowest class; the poorer they are, usually, the faster do they multiply; certainly the more reckless they are in reference to multiplication. It is the middle classes, those who form the energetic, reliable, improving element of the population, those who wish to rise and do not choose to sink, those in a word who constitute the true strength and wealth and dignity of nations,—it is these who abstain from marriage or postpone it. (Greg 1875, 129)

In a chapter entitled "Malthus Notwithstanding," Greg emphasizes a new law in opposition to Malthus's, "namely, THE TENDENCY OF CEREBRAL DEVELOPMENT TO LESSEN FECUNDITY" (1875, p. 103, typography in original).

To see the eugenics movement pick up the racist challenge to classical economics in Carlyle's "Negro question," we begin with the two cofounders of eugenics: Galton and Greg. Galton's 1865 "Hereditary Talent and Character" announces his adherence to the doctrine of national characters (1865, 320). The generating mechanism Galton posits for racial hierarchy is a conjunction of the argument that Thomas Carlyle advanced in his quarrel with the economists (Levy 2001b; Levy and Peart 2001–2)—labor makes us fully human—conjoined with the principle of natural selection (Galton 1865, 325).

6. Darwin cites Greg approvingly (1989, 138–39). In the later *Enigmas of Life,* Greg seems rightly pleased to report this endorsement (1875, 137).

Next we juxtapose Carlyle's *Shooting Niagara*—the defense of Governor Eyre and the attack on democratic movements in America and Great Britain—with Greg on the survival of native races.

There is a difference in style, of course, between Carlyle and Greg.

The connection between Carlyle and the eugenics movement can be appreciated more deeply by considering the substantial claims advanced in *Shooting Niagara* and Galton's 1872 "Gregariousness in Cattle and in Men" (table 16.2).[7]

James Hunt Converts Francis Galton

Galton's criticism of economics as practiced in section F of the British Association has been heavily discussed.[8] Testimony from Nassau Senior

Table 16.1. Carlyle and Greg on Race

Carlyle	Greg
One always rather likes the Nigger; evidently a block-head with good dispositions, with affections, attachments,—with a turn for Nigger Melodies, and the like:—he is the only Savage of all the coloured races that doesn't die out on sight of the White Man; but can actually live beside him, and work and increase and be merry. The Almighty Maker has appointed him to be a Servant (1867, 5).	The Indians of the Antilles, the Red man of North America, the South Sea Islanders, the Australians, even the New Zealanders (the finest and most pliable and teachable of savages), are all alike dying out with rapidity—in consequence of the harshness, or in spite of the forbearance and protection, of the stronger and more capable European. The negro alone survives— and, but for the observation of what is now going on in our sugar islands and in the United States we should say, seems likely to survive. He only has been able to hold his own in a fashion, and to live and flourish, side by side with masterful and mightier races (1868, 357).

7. Our intention here is to highlight how Carlyle's racism influenced early eugenics thinking. Elsewhere, we have demonstrated how the Governor Eyre controversy served to harden attitudes about race (Levy 2001a; Levy and Peart 2001–2; Peart and Levy 2002). The advocates of the social importance of racial hierarchy, those who supported Governor Eyre's brutal actions against former slaves in Jamaica, include some of the greatest prose stylists of Victorian Britain: Thomas Carlyle, Charles Dickens, Charles Kingsley, and John Ruskin. By contrast, all the economists we have found—J. S. Mill, John Bright, J. E. Cairnes, H. Fawcett, H. Spencer, and T. Rodgers—were on the other side (Semmel 1962).

8. See Stone 1980; Henderson 1994; and Porter 1986, 135–36.

suffices to demonstrate that the ideal was infrequently observed.[9] But what was the feasible alternative to economics as practiced? One such, of which Galton evidently approved, was anthropology and in particular the anthropological reasonings of Dr. James Hunt.[10]

The modern theory of statistical racism as first explained by Arrow (1972) and Phelps (1972) supposes that groups will be divided on the basis of sample means. The race α will differ from race β on the basis of an estimate of location. On the contrary, we argue that, at least as an approximation, the racists we consider, Hunt first and foremost, distin-

Table 16.2. Carlyle and Galton Compared

Carlyle	Galton
[T]here soon comes that singular phenomenon . . . "*Swarmery*," or the "Gathering of Men in Swarms," and what prodigies they are in the habit of doing and believing, when thrown into that miraculous condition. Some big Queen Bee is in the centre of the swarm; but any commonplace stupidest *bee* . . . whatever of palpable incredibility and delirious absurdity, universally believed, can be uttered or imagined on these points, "the equality of men," any man equal to any other; Quashee Nigger to Socrates or Shakespeare; Judas Iscariot to Jesus Christ;—and Bedlam and Gehenna equal to the New Jerusalem, shall we say? If these things are taken up, not only as axioms of Euclid, but as articles of religion burning to be put in practice for the salvation of the world,—I think you will admit that *Swarmery* plays a wonderful part in the heads of poor Mankind (1867, 4–5).	I propose, in these pages, to discuss a curious and apparently anomalous group of base moral instincts and intellectual deficiencies, to trace their analogies in the world of brutes, and to examine the conditions, through which they have been evolved. I speak of the slavish aptitudes, from which the leaders of men, and the heroes and the prophets, are exempt, but which are irrepressible elements in the disposition of average men. I refer to the natural tendency of the vast majority of our race to shrink from the responsibility of standing and acting alone, to their exaltation of the *vox populi*, even when they know it to be the utterance of a mob of nobodies, into the *vox Dei*, to their willing servitude to tradition, authority and custom (quoted in Pearson 1924, 72).

9. Nassau Senior (1860, 357; Henderson 1994, 499) adds: "Any number of the early arguments defending the continued existence of Section F are curious and fail to confront directly Galton's primary argument that the section dealt with unscientific matters."

10. Spencer (1986, 154) reports that Hunt's *The Negro's Place in Nature* served as the "model for 'scientific' writing on the subject for the remainder of the century." Hunt's importance is stressed in Curtis 1968; Banton 1977; Lorimer 1978; Rainger 1978; Stepan 1982; Desmond 1994; Young 1995; and Levy 2001b. Another theme common to Hunt and Galton is their disdain for the presence of women at academic meetings. This aspect of Galton's attack on section F is discussed by Henderson 1994. Hunt separated himself from the Ethnological Society over its admission of women.

guish race α from race β on the basis of an estimate of scale. "Inferior" is a judgment applied to a race β, which is supposed with zero variance. The sample mean of some race, its stereotype in Arrow-Phelps terminology, *is* the "inferior" race. The reader who thinks the first β that deviated from the stereotype would falsify this hypothesis has insufficiently reflected on the "mixed race" immunization strategy. The intelligent "β" is not a real "β."[11]

The generating mechanism for this preposterous claim is actually elegantly simple. Both the mean and variance of intelligence and other moral characteristics are said to be functions of the length of time during which one's mind develops. Development of the "lesser" races stops sooner.[12]

The first issue of Hunt's *Anthropological Review* contains abstracts of anthropological papers presented at a section E meeting of the British Association along with reports of the floor discussion. The third paper is Hunt's "On the Physical and Mental Characters of the Negro." This occasion generated considerable discussion because it was at this time that the escaped slave and abolitionist writer William Craft rose to challenge Hunt.[13] But before Craft spoke Galton pointed out the stupidity of the zero-variance assertion based on his own experience in Africa.[14]

How did Galton's ideas "evolve" from a full recognition of the diversity of African peoples to his 1865 articles in *Macmillan's*?[15] Before his encounter with Hunt, Galton's views represent his African experience viewed through the lens of a theory not too distant from that held by the classical economists. After his encounter with Hunt, he reads, in the passages from the articles that we will quote, as if he were seeing the world through the theory provided by Hunt.

How is this possible? Hunt was, by contemporary judgments, a

11. The details are provided in Desmond 1994, 353; Young 1995; and Levy 2001b. Hunt (1863, 16) provides an example of how this works.

12. Reade (1864, 399): "[T]he growth of the brain in the negro, as in the ape, is sooner arrested than in those of our race."

13. Lorimer (1978, 47–8) discusses Craft and the confrontation with Hunt. Levy (2001b) transcribes Charles Kingsley's letter to Hunt about the event. It is illuminating that Mill's most technically proficient disciple, J. E. Cairnes (1865, 336) cites "William Crafts, the African explorer, the eloquent defender of the humanity of his race, and now the leading merchant and reformer in the kingdom of Damoney," along with Frederick Douglass and others, as a counterexample to the zero-variance claim.

14. Galton "Anthropology at the British Association" (1863, 386). We find no discussion of this report in any of the secondary literature even though Pearson's *Life* (1924) devotes an extensive section to Galton's anthropological writings.

15. Stepan (1982, 127): "Galton clearly recognized the variety in physical character, language and social organization of the various African tribes he encountered; once home, however, the tribal distinctions became merged in a single Negro race."

"quack."[16] Galton's integrity is beyond reproach.[17] But Galton had a weakness. Here was a result he really wanted to believe: the positive correlation between the physicality of a man and his intellect. And many years after Hunt's death he admits that he really wants to believe in the uniformity of the Negro.[18]

All that has been written on Hunt describes him as having enormous vitality and energy.[19] When Galton defended anthropology in the British Association from the type of charges he levied against economics, he cited the qualities of the anthropologists not their procedures.[20] Galton would not be the first intellectual, nor would he be the last, to have been seduced by charisma. Nor would he be the only African explorer to learn to see the world through Hunt's eyes.[21] By 1865 Galton on savages in general reads just like Hunt on the Negro.

It is important to note that Galton never—as far as we know—employed the "mixed race" immunization strategy. Thus, he lacks Hunt's device for dealing with the difference between the theorized "Negro" and observed people of color. Hunt never denied that people of color had considerable variation. He insisted that all the variation was the result of their white ancestors. Without this quackery to distinguish between the theorized Negro and actual people of color, Galton later assumes that variance is a constant across observed races.[22] Nonetheless,

16. For some of his more bizarre arguments, see Hunt 1863, 19. Hunt's language slur resurfaced early in the twentieth century when Commons (1916, 94) asserted that the Yiddish spoken by Russian Jews was "scarcely a language—it is a jargon without syntax, conjugation, or declension."

17. At the age of eighty-five, he found technical reasons to believe that majoritarian decision making had desirable properties. And he called attention to this "unexpected" result with great clarity, choosing to title the first of a pair of articles "*Vox Populi,*" explicitly challenging his Carlylean assertions quoted earlier! See Galton 1907a, 1907b. Levy and Peart (2002) reprint the articles and call attention to Pearson's judgment that Galton chose to publish these results in *Nature* to maximize their contemporary (policy?) impact. Porter (1986, 130) notes Galton's anti-egalitarianism in the years before these essays were published.

18. Pearson 1924, 94; Galton 1892, 195–96.

19. See the obituary in the *New York Weekly Day-Book* of 6 November 1869, reprinted in the *Anthropology Review* (under "Anthropological News," 1870, 97): "Dr. Hunt, in his own clear knowledge and brave enthusiasm, was doing more for humanity, for the welfare of mankind, and for the glory of God, than all the philosophers, humanitarians, philanthropists, statesmen, and, we may say, bishops and clergy of England together. He was teaching them what they are in *fact*—what God has made them, what their relations to other *species* of human kind, Mongols, Malays, Negroes, etc., and thus preparing them for the fulfilment of their duties to each other, and to the dependent races that were, or might be, in juxtaposition with them." Cf. Keith 1917, 19; Stocking 1971, 377; Banton 1977, 77; and Desmond 1994, 320.

20. Galton, "Economic Science and the British Association" (1877, 471–72).

21. Reade 1864, 399.

22. In the book version of *Hereditary Genius,* Galton assumes for exposition that races have the same variance ([1892] 1978, 337). More pointed, he asserts that there is considerable overlap in the abilities of blacks and whites (338). We thank Bryan Caplan for the reference.

in 1865 his words give warrant to the supposition that the "Savage" is without variation (table 16.3).

Race, Economics, and Breeding Policy

By the late nineteenth century, a common language and racial argument became evident in postclassical economics, suggesting that the influence of early racial theorizing was persistent and wide. More, it took on the two forms outlined earlier: the model that posited that the "inferior" race differed in terms of some parameter(s) such as work effort or time preference; and the other—more devastating—model, which held that the Other was a dead race with zero variance.

So postclassical economists made statements concerning the lack of differentiation among "lower races." They also argued that inferior races

Table 16.3. Hunt and Galton Compared

Hunt	Galton
M. Gratiolet has also observed that in the anterior races the sutures of the cranium do not close so early as in the occipital or inferior races. From these researches it appears than in the Negro the growth of the brain is sooner arrested than in the European. The premature union of the bones of the skull may give a clue to much of the mental inferiority which is seen in the Negro race. There can be no doubt that in puberty a great change takes place in relation to physical development; but in the Negro there appears to be an arrested development of the brain, exactly harmonizing with the physical formation. Young Negro children are nearly as intelligent as European children; but the older they grow the less intelligent they become. They exhibit, when young, an animal liveliness for play and tricks, far surpassing the European child (1863, 8).	Another difference, which may either be due to natural selection or to original difference of race, is the fact that savages seem incapable of progress after the first few years of their life. The average children of all races are much on a par. Occasionally, those of the lower races are more precocious than the Anglo-Saxon; as a brute beast of a few weeks old is certainly more apt and forward than a child of the same age. But, as the years go by, the higher races continue to progress, while the lower ones gradually stop. They remain children in mind, with the passions of grown men. Eminent genius commonly asserts itself in tender years, but it continues long to develop. The highest minds in the highest races seem to have been those who had the longest boyhood (1865, 326).
With the Negro, as with some other races of man, it has been found that the children are precocious, but that no advance in education can be made after they arrive at the age of maturity (1863, 12).	

are characterized by lower work effort,[23] improvidence, alcoholism, inability to control sexual passion, and overall carelessness.[24] Throughout, some imprecision exists as to whether the economist has in mind the lower classes or a racial or ethnic type. British economists typically focused on the lower classes and argued that members of the working classes are creatures of passion unable to plan for the future and unusually susceptible to alcoholism (Peart 2000). Yet when the Irish are involved class signifies race (as Jevons [1870] reveals; see also Peart 2001a). For Marshall, the "industrial" classes are racially inferior: as conquest and the intermixture of races occurred, the inferior (yet still white) races sort themselves into the lower ranks of industrial society ([1890] 1930, 195). The legacy of slavery looms large in the work of early-twentieth-century American writers. Among both British and American postclassical economists, an overriding fear of the dysgenic effects of immigration is present.

Eugenicists urged that selective breeding be used to improve the genetic makeup of the race. Without intervention, they argued, the quality of the genetic pool would decline over time. What was required, then, was a wide-ranging program to counteract eugenic tendencies, what Sidney Webb referred to as the "social machinery" of eugenic intervention (1910, 237). The implication for national greatness was stressed repeatedly.[25] Eugenicists—biologists and social scientists alike—who endorsed eugenic policies made their case in explicit opposition to utilitarian economists of the nineteenth century for whom the happiness of one counts as that of another (Hankins 1923, 398) and in opposition to democratic theory (395).

---

23. As in Carlyle (1849), climate is often offered as an explanation for reduced work effort among the "lower races" (and, since lack of work effort implies that simple and then more complex tasks are neither attempted nor mastered, climate is also associated with lack of differentiation within the race). See Marshall [1890] 1930, 195, 205, 528; and Commons 1916, 212–13. Jevons was also struck by the relationship between climate and race (1869). For an application of Jevons's argument to the American context, see F. Walker [1881] 1995. Thus, an economic explanation is provided for "facts" of anthropology.

24. While we find no discussion of lack of variation in the secondary literature, there are several good discussions of parametric racism in postclassical thinking. See Collard 1996 for an examination that links Pigou's "faulty telescopic tendency" to the distribution of resources over time. White (1994) discusses issues of race and gender in Jevons. Peart (2000) discusses racial determinants of rationality in Jevons, Marshall, Pigou, and Fisher. Levitt (1976) mentions Marshall on eugenics. Aldrich (1975) discusses Fisher's economic analysis and eugenics.

25. Leonard Darwin claims that the limitation of family size by those who can afford children is both "immoral" and "unpatriotic" (1916a, 173). Macbride, discussing Darwin, "regrets" to admit that eugenics is taking greater hold in the United States than in England, a fact that leads him to the conclusion that America "would beat them [England] in the race for commercial supremacy" (Darwin 1919, 31). Pearson also linked eugenics with national welfare, arguing in 1925 that Galton's phrase "national eugenics" was well chosen (Pearson and Moul 1925, 3–4).

Among economists, as among the anthropologists, the argument was often that the Irish overbreed while Anglo-Saxons reproduce at relatively low rates. In America, the Irish are frequently offered as an example of an inferior race, but the "Negro" and "immigration problems" formed the central backdrop to discussions of eugenics policies. Waves of immigration drawn predominantly from genetically inferior races were said to have reduced the genetic quality of the nation (Commons 1916, pp. 200ff). Since such immigrants multiplied at high rates, the deterioration would be ongoing.[26]

Marshall endorsed the differential fertility rate argument. He writes about a "cause for anxiety" and "some partial arrest of that selective influence of struggle and competition which in the earliest stages of civilization caused those who were strongest and most vigorous to leave the largest progeny behind them; and to which, more than any other single cause, the progress of the human race is due" ([1890] 1930, p. 201).[27] Advances in public health that saved the "feeble" and "unfit" served to reduce the quality of the genetic pool (201).[28]

Pigou also accepted that the lower classes reproduce at relatively high rates, while the "higher classes" delay marriage and have few children (1907, 364–65).[29] The "injurious" effects of such relatively high reproductive rates among the poor might be counteracted by policies designed to improve the well-being of low-income people (cf. Webb 1910). But the biological question remained: is there reason to believe that bad original properties and poverty are closely related? Pigou answers affirmatively (1907, 365).

26. In England, economists such as Marshall feared that such deterioration would occur within cities (Marshall 1883). Here the argument is that the Irish form a relatively large and (due to high birthrates) growing constituency in cities (see Jevons 1870; and Peart 2001a). Cf. "The slums and courts of our large cities are chiefly inhabited by the unfit, who are recruited by the failures in the industrial struggle; and among these early marriages and illegitimate intercourse is more common than among the saner and more intelligent class."

27. The argument was specified in the common terminology of low fertility rates among the "upper classes" and high birthrates among the poor. At least in Marshall's case, however, the racial element is quite clear (see [1890] 1930, 195).

28. Ibid., 201n1. Galton's argument concerning the inheritance of traits of genius is endorsed in this context, as well (202, 206). The contention that, without sterilization or segregation, saving the "feeble" entails a reduction in genetic quality is common; see Fisher [1909] 1976; Darwin 1916a; and Webb 1910.

29. Pigou is singled out by Leonard Darwin (1916b, 311), who writes, "as far as I know, [Pigou] is almost the only economist who has paid serious attention to eugenics in connection with economics." Indeed, a JSTOR search on *eugenics* in the economics list finds Pigou (1907) and Fetter (1907) as the earliest. Schumpeter (1954, 790): "Economists entirely failed to bestow on these problems ["the quality of the human stock"] the amount of attention they deserve: flippant phrases pro or con form the bulk of their contribution; the only one of the leading men to take more trouble was Pigou."

In America, the argument regarding relatively low fertility rates among the highly civilized became known as "race treason," a phrase that elicited no small amount of resentment among the educated and well-to-do. For economists, eugenics provided at least a partial solution to two related problems, the "relative decrease of the successful strains of the population" and the racial mix of the existing population that resulted from slavery and ongoing immigration (Fetter 1916, 366).[30] For Fetter the "most grave" population problem, the Negro problem, was "insoluble." The alternatives of intermixture of races, existence in separate geographical regions, and extinction are said to be "repugnant," "impractical," and unrealistic. Fetter concludes with "futile expressions of regret" (366–68).

Three sets of eugenics policies were endorsed by economists to improve the genetic makeup of the economic unit (generally, in this context, the nation):[31] (1) positive measures to encourage fertility among those with "superior" genetic stock; (2) negative policies to reduce fertility among those of "inferior" natural ability; and (3) immigration restrictions, which increasingly became central to these discussions. Irving Fisher, Frank Fetter, and J. R. Commons each argued that without such restrictions on immigration, the race treason problem in America would only worsen.[32]

While Pigou finds a "heavy burden of proof" for advocates of genetic selection (1907, 366), he nevertheless favored policies to alter the incentives for family formation. The positive proposal by McDougall (1907) is said to have "much to recommend it" (Pigou 1907, 368). Accepting that the evidence on the heredity of defects is strong, Pigou also favored a policy of "permanent segregation" or sterilization to improve "the general economic welfare of the community" (1920, 112; cf. 1920, 110; and 1907, 269).[33]

30. Black population growth was low relative to that of whites. But there was still cause for alarm. Commons (1916, 60), argued that the difference resulted from high mortality rates among blacks (attributed in large measure to the effects of "sexual immorality and debauchery"), differences that could be eliminated and even reversed in the event of improved public health standards.

31. As Collard (1996) has noted regarding Pigou, economists typically favored a combination of eugenics and environmental policy. See Pigou 1907; and 1920, 120–25. The purported relative efficacy of eugenics proposals is made clear in a series of papers presented at the School of Economics and Political Science, University of London, in 1904, 1905, and 1906, of which that by Archdall Reid is particularly representative for its nationalistic overtones and the concern with alcoholism (1906, 22).

32. See Cherry [1976] 1995; and Commons 1916, 198ff.

33. Fisher ([1909] 1976) also endorsed government "bounties" to encourage births among the "vital" classes (673). Proposals ranged from sterilization and German-style marriage tests to developing social prejudice against such reproduction, as well as a fuller appreciation of women's rights (Thomson 1906, 179).

In their massive study on Jewish immigration in the first several issues of the *Annals of Eugenics,* Pearson and Moul explain in detail why immigration is the central matter in eugenics policy (1925, 7).

Economists also focused on the need to be selective in order to reduce the number of immigrants from the "inferior," "defective," and "undesirable" classes (Commons 1916, 230).[34] The practical measure seized on by Commons in this context was the simple device of a literacy test, which would "raise the average standard" of immigrants (235). Fetter argued for an overall reduction in immigration, as well as the eugenic selection of immigrants in order to "improve the racial quality of the nation by checking the multiplication of the strains defective in respect to mentality, nervous organization, and physical health, and by encouraging the more capable elements of the population to contribute in due proportion to the maintenance of a healthy, moral, and efficient population" (1916, 378).

A popular representation of the eugenic aspects of immigration can be found in the image in *Punch* reproduced in figure 16.1.

Return to Fixed Human Nature

Whatever disputes remain about how economic theory changed with the transition to neoclassicism, it is widely accepted that the boundary of economic science was narrowed throughout the late nineteenth century (Winch 1972). The 1870s in particular were characterized by often intense disputes over the nature and scope of economic "science." By the turn of the century it became clear that the historical school would not prevail and the profession would follow the lead of W. S. Jevons in his calls for narrowing economic science through subdivision and specialization (Jevons [1871] 1911; Peart 2001b). Jevons's subdivision idea rendered economic *theory* unassailable but severely incomplete; he recognized all sorts of cases in which the theory required modification—and these, he argued, should be taken into account in *applications* (Peart 2001b). This chapter has examined one example of such narrowing in terms of the "race" to which economics might be applied: late in the century economists began to argue that the intertemporal decision making of a higher race might not be applicable to a lower one.

This chapter has demonstrated that, for a time at least, the classical economists' postulate of homogeneity lost the day and racial theories prevailed in economics. Hierarchical, often racial accounts won the day

34. Pearson also favored restrictions on immigration, arguing that it should be restricted to those who are at least 25 percent above the mean for natives in intelligence and physical characteristics (Pearson and Moul 1925, 127).

SOME UNTAXED IMPORTS FROM ITALY

WHO WEAR AN UNWONTED AIR OF GAIETY JUST NOW.

we can't swallow that, can we? Even an editor wouldn't go and do a silly thing like that, would he? No, how the money came there I can't imagine, but there it was, and BROWN found it, and the moral of *that* story is, if you must play practical jokes, stick to the old-fashioned apple-pie bed, and don't try to be too original. G'night."

And he vanished.

SOMEWHAT TOO PROGRESSIVE.

(*A Reactionary Protest.*)

"PROGRESSIVE dinners" are described in last week's *Gentlewoman.* After the first course the hostess rings a little bell. Each man seizes his bread and napkin and moves two paces to the left. A servant follows him with his wine-glasses. In this way each man can chat with each lady.

This is excellent discipline for "Little MARY." If the twentieth-century digestive apparatus will stand a two yards' spurt, an obstacle race, an introduction to a new partner, a re-adjustment of ideas, and a fresh inventory of glassware and other portables at intervals of five minutes, say, throughout the course of a Progressive dinner, it (or she) will stand anything. By the end of the entertainment the male portion of the guests—it appears that they only are to circulate—will be in a state of wonderment whether they have been assisting at a table-turning performance, an earthquake, or a game of musical chairs. If to the householder three removes are equal to a fire, this particular meal should have the effect of a volcanic eruption on a modern sybarite. As to knowing who 's who, or who 's where, after boxing the compass once round the dinner-table, this would have to be given up as a bad job when the convives are so very cinematographic and mixed. But, perhaps, Little MARY will put her foot down and revolt against such treatment.

There is, indeed, a danger that the "progressive" mania may extend in other directions. Next week we shall be hearing of a progressive clothes party, where every one assumes his neighbour's costume, and discards in turn for some one else. This will be all right for a "quick-change" artist, but we fear that the portly City man and the elegant West-Ender will have difficulties with their environment.

Let us be warned in time, too, against "progressive" evenings at the theatre. This would mean consecutive visits to the fifty odd (but legitimate) temples of the drama in the metropolis between 8 and 11 P.M., or an average of about three-and-a-half minutes at each. This would be too much for the Highest of Tea-ites or the Squarest of Mealers.

And in view of the appalling statement of a lady writer that ninety-nine out of a hundred women wear wigs, some wicked leader of the so-called "Smart Set" may start the game of "Progressive Coiffures." The fashion would have to be followed, of course, but it would be too "diskie" for words, though amusing enough for us other males and the hundredth lady whose locks are irremovable.

Lastly, some irresponsible *mésallié* is sure to suggest the variation of "Progressive Households"—but here we are treading on delicate ground. We shall leave it, it is to be hoped, severely alone. We are not a German regiment.

"Progressive Dinners," in fact—to make a salad of metaphors—are the thin end of a wedge which must be nipped in the bud before they get out of hand and involve us in a social, or rather unsocial, Feast of Misrule.

Fig. 16.1. *Punch,* 18 November 1903.

well into the twentieth century.[35] Near the middle of the century the classical tradition of equal competence (homogeneity) was revived at the University of Chicago. Not surprisingly, given the racial characterization focused on intertemporal decision making, time preference was central in the Chicago revival. In his 1931 review of Irving Fisher's *Theory of Interest,* Frank Knight voiced his skepticism about the common link supposed in economists' accounts between time preference and race. Knight, and after him George Stigler and Gary Becker, questioned myopic accounts of intertemporal decision making. As the Chicago School revived the classical doctrine of homogeneity it also (and by no coincidence) revived the presumption of competence even in political activity.

When Knight reviewed Fisher's theory of interest, he saw no difference in the motivations of different sorts of people (1931, 177).[36] There is nothing here about the "curious lack of variation" of savages but instead an illustration of economic problems across time, culture, and race. And the antirace argument was made even more emphatically, perhaps, by Ludwig von Mises.

> [The ethnologists] are utterly mistaken in contending that these other races have been guided in their activities by motives other than those which have actuated the white race. The Asiatics and the Africans no less than the peoples of European descent have been eager to struggle successfully for survival and to use reason as the foremost weapon in these endeavors. (1949, 85)

The Stigler and Becker attack on the postulate of positive time preference (Stigler and Becker 1977) continued the argument Stigler made in his dissertation: positive time preference has no role in the making of abstract economic man.[37] In this stigmatization of positive time preference, Stigler remained a faithful student of Frank Knight.

Was the Chicago revival in some sense motivated by the racialist attacks on classical economics and the widespread acceptance of racial ac-

35. The new translation of omitted material from Schumpeter's *Theory of Economic Development* (Schumpeter 2002) makes it clear that Schumpeter's entrepreneur is Carlyle's Hero.

36. Knight objected to how "this discussion has been cluttered up and the issue beclouded by theorizing (mostly quite bad) regarding the ultimate motivations involved in the choice between present and future ('spending' and 'saving'—or 'investing,' which is not the same thing), on the one hand, and, on the other hand (not nearly so bad), regarding the technological nature and implications of the investing progress" (1931, 198).

37. Stigler 1941, 213: "The second ground for valuing present goods more highly is that '. . . to goods which are destined to meet the wants of the future, we ascribe a value which is really less than the true intensity of their future marginal utility.' This is a failure of perspective, an irrationality in human behavior—the only irrationality, it may be noted, that Böhm-Bawerk introduces into his 'economic man.'"

counts of human behavior that we have demonstrated? Here one must be cautious, but it is surely no coincidence that the reading list for Stigler's history of economics classes in the 1960s included Walter Bagehot's *Postulates of English Political Economy.* In this work, which impressed Marshall enough that he wrote the introduction to a student edition (Bagehot 1885), Bagehot "explained" the classical doctrines by appealing to the "race" of classical theorists. Individuals were optimizers because Adam Smith was a Scot; they were careful with money because David Ricardo was a Jew. Marshall was, of course, not the only one taken with Bagehot. Bagehot seems to have obtained his editorship of the *Economist* through the intervention of a close friend of the *Economist*'s owner, James Wilson—none other than W. R. Greg (Barrington 1933).

Bibliography

Aldrich, Mark 1975. "Capital Theory and Racism: From Laissez-Faire to the Eugenics Movement in the Career of Irving Fisher." *Review of Radical Political Economics* 7:33–42.

Allen, Robert Loring. 1993. *Irving Fisher: A Biography.* Cambridge, Mass., and Oxford: Blackwell.

"Anthropological News: Death of the Best Man in England." 1870. *Anthropological Review* 8:97.

"Anthropology at the British Association." 1863. *Anthropological Review* 1:379–89.

Arrow, Kenneth J. 1972. "The Theory of Discrimination." In *Discrimination in Labor Markets,* edited by Orley Ashenfelter and Albert Rees, 3–33. Princeton: Princeton University Press.

Bagehot, Walter. 1885. *The Postulates of English Political Economy.* Introduced by Alfred Marshall. Student ed. New York and London: G. P. Putnam's Sons.

Banton, Michael. 1977. *The Idea of Race.* London: Tavistock.

Barrington, Mrs. Russell, ed. 1933. *The Love-letters of Walter Bagehot and Eliza Wilson Written from 10 November 1857 to 23 April 1858.* London: Faber and Faber.

Beddoe, John. 1870. "Anthropology and Politics: Kelts and Saxons." *Anthropological Review* 8:211–13.

Cairnes, [J. E.]. 1865. "The Negro Suffrage." *Macmillan's* 12:334–43.

[Carlyle, Thomas]. 1849. "Occasional Discourse on the Negro Question." *Fraser's Magazine for Town and Country* 40:670–79.

Carlyle, Thomas. 1867. *Shooting Niagara: And After?* London: Chapman and Hall.

Cherry, Robert. [1976] 1995. "Racial Thought and the Early Economics Profession." *Review of Social Economy* 34, no. 2: 147–62. Reprinted in *Economics and Discrimination,* edited by William Darity Jr., 17–32. Brookfield, Vt.: Edward Elgar.

Collard, David. 1996. "Pigou and Future Generations: A Cambridge Tradition." *Cambridge Journal of Economics* 20 (September): 585–97.

Commons, J. R. 1916. *Races and Immigration in America.* New York: Macmillan.

Curtis, L. P., Jr. 1968. *Anglo-Saxons and Celts.* Bridgeport: Conference on British Studies at the University of Bridgeport.

Curtis, L. P., Jr. 1997. *Apes and Angels: The Irishman in Victorian Caricature.* Rev. ed. Washington, D.C.: Smithsonian Institution Press.

Darity, William, Jr. 1995. "Introduction." In *Economics and Discrimination,* edited by William Darity Jr., xiii–li. Brookfield, Vt.: Edward Elgar.

Darwin, Charles. 1989. *The Descent of Man and Selection in Relation to Sex.* Volume 21 of *The Works of Charles Darwin.* Edited by Paul H. Barrett and R. B. Freeman. New York: New York University Press.

Darwin, Leonard. 1916a. "On the Statistical Studies Needed after the War in Connection with Eugenics." *Journal of the Royal Statistical Society* 79, no. 2: 159–88.

Darwin, Leonard. 1916b. "Quality Not Quantity." *Eugenics Review* 8 (April): 297–321.

Darwin, Leonard. 1919. "Eugenics in Relation to Economics and Statistics." *Journal of the Royal Statistical Society* 82, no. 1: 1–27. Includes a discussion by E. W. Macbride, 30–31.

Desmond, Adrian. 1994. *Huxley: The Devil's Disciple.* London: M. Joseph.

Duff, M. E. Grant. 1881. "Address of the President of Section F, Economics Science and Statistics, of the British Association." *Journal of the Statistical Society of London* 44 (December): 649–59.

"Economic Science and the British Association." 1877. *Journal of the Statistical Society of London* 40:468–76.

Fetter, Frank A. 1916. *Modern Economic Problems.* New York: Century.

Fetter, Frank A., William B. Bailey, Henry C. Potter, Emily Balch, L. M. Rubinow, C. W. A. Veditz, and Walter E. Willcox. 1907. "Western Civilization and Birth-Rate Discussion." *Publications of the American Economic Association.* 3rd ser., 8:90–93.

Fisher, Irving. 1907. *The Rate of Interest.* New York: Macmillan.

Fisher, Irving. [1909] 1976. *National Vitality, Its Wastes and Conservation.* New York: Arno.

Fisher, Irving. [1930] 1986. *The Theory of Interest.* Fairfield, N.J.: Augustus M. Kelley.

Galton, Francis. 1865. "Hereditary Talent and Character." *Macmillan's* 12 (June–August): 157–66, 318–27.

Galton, Francis. 1892. *Finger Prints.* London: Macmillan.

Galton, Francis. 1904. "Eugenics: Its Definition, Scope, and Aims." *American Journal of Sociology* 10 (July): 1–6.

Galton, Francis. 1907a. "One Vote, One Value." *Nature* 75 (28 February): 414. Letter to the editor.

Galton, Francis. 1907b. "*Vox Populi.*" *Nature* 75 (7 March): 450–51.

Galton, Francis. 1908. *Memories of My Life.* London: Methuen.

Galton, Francis. [1892] 1978. *Hereditary Genius: An Inquiry into Its Laws and Consequences.* London: Julian Friedmann.

[Greg, W. R.]. 1868. "On the Failure of 'Natural Selection' in the Case of Man." *Fraser's Magazine for Town and Country* 78 (September): 353–62.

[Greg, W. R.]. 1869. "The Realities of Irish Life." *Quarterly Review* 126:61–80.

Greg, W. R. 1875. *Enigmas of Life.* Boston: James R. Osgood.

Greg, W. R. 1876. *Mistaken Aims and Attainable Ideals of the Artizan Class.* London: Trubner.

Hankins, F. H. 1923. "Individual Differences and Democratic Theory." *Political Science Quarterly* 38, no. 3: 388–412.

Henderson, James P. 1994. "The Place of Economics in the Hierarchy of the Sciences: Section F from Whewell to Edgeworth." In *Natural Images in Economic Thought: "Markets Read in Tooth and Claw,"* edited by Philip Mirowski, 484–535. Cambridge, New York, and Melbourne: Cambridge University Press.

Hunt, James. 1864. *The Negro's Place in Nature: A Paper Read before the London Anthropological Society.* New York: Van Evrie, Horton, and Co.

[Hunt, James]. 1866. "Race in Legislation and Political Economy." *Anthropological Review* 4:113–35.

Huxley, T. W. 1870. "Professor Huxley on Political Ethnology." *Anthropological Review* 8:197–204.

Jevons, William Stanley. 1869. "A Deduction from Darwin's Theory." *Nature* 1 (30 December): 231–32.

Jevons, William Stanley. 1870. "Opening Address of the President of Section F (Economic Science and Statistics), of the British Association for the Advancement of Science." *Journal of the Royal Statistical Society of London* 33, no. 3: 309–26.

Jevons, William Stanley. [1871] 1911. *Theory of Political Economy.* 4th ed. London: Macmillan.

Keith, Arthur. 1917. "Presidential Address. How Can the Institute Best Serve the Needs of Anthropology?" *Journal of the Royal Anthropological Institute of Great Britain and Ireland* 47:12–30.

Keith, Arthur. 1920. "Galton's Place among Anthropologists." *Eugenics Review* 12 (April): 14–28.

Keynes, J. M. 1937–38. "Some Economic Consequences of a Declining Population." *Eugenics Review* 29 (April 1937–January 1938):13–17.

Knight, Frank H. 1931. "Professor Fisher's Interest Theory: A Case in Point." *Journal of Political Economy* 39:176–212.

Levitt, Theodore. 1976. "Alfred Marshall: Victorian Relevance for Modern Economics." *Quarterly Journal of Economics,* 90, no. 3: 425–43.

Levy, David M. 2001a. "Economics Texts as Apocrypha." In *Reflections on the Classical Canon: Essays in Honor of Samuel Hollander,* edited by Evelyn L. Forget and Sandra J. Peart, 400–450. London: Routledge.

Levy, David M. 2001b. "How the Dismal Science Got Its Name: Debating Victorian Racial Quacks." *Journal of the History of Economic Thought* 23:5–35.

Levy, David M., and Sandra J. Peart. 2001–2. "The Secret History of the Dismal Science." Accessed on 18 December 2007 at www.econlib.org.

Levy, David M., and Sandra J. Peart. 2002. "Galton's Two Papers on Voting as Robust Estimation." *Public Choice* 113, nos. 3–4: 357–65.

Lorimer, Douglas. 1978. *Colour, Class, and the Victorians.* Leicester: Leicester University Press.

Marshall, Alfred. 1883. "The Housing of the London Poor." *Contemporary Review* 45 (February): 224–31.

Marshall, Alfred. [1890] 1930. *Principles of Economics.* 8th ed. London: Macmillan.

McDougall, William. 1907. "A Practicable Eugenic Solution." *Sociological Papers* 3:55–89.

Mill, John Stuart. [1848] 1965. *The Principles of Political Economy.* Volume

2 of *Collected Works of John Stuart Mill.* Edited by J. M. Robson. Toronto: University of Toronto Press.

Mirowski, Phillip. 1989. *More Heat Than Light.* Cambridge: Cambridge University Press.

Mirowski, Phillip, ed. 1994. *Natural Images in Economic Thought: "Markets Read in Tooth and Claw."* Cambridge: Cambridge University Press.

Mises, Ludwig von. 1949. *Human Action.* London: William Hodge.

Myres, John L. 1944. "A Century of Our Work." *Man* (January–February): 2–9.

Pearson, Karl. 1924. *The Life, Letters, and Labours of Francis Galton.* Cambridge: Cambridge University Press.

Pearson, Karl, and Ethel M. Elderton. 1925. "Foreword." *Annals of Eugenics* 1:1–4.

Pearson, Karl, and Margaret Moul. 1925. "The Problem of Alien Immigration into Great Britain Illustrated by an Examination of Russian and Polish Jewish Children. *Annals of Eugenics* 1:5–127.

Peart, Sandra J. 2000. "Irrationality and Intertemporal Choice in Early Neoclassical Thought." *Canadian Journal of Economics* 33:175–88.

Peart, Sandra J. 2001a. "'Facts Carefully Marshalled' in the Empirical Studies of William Stanley Jevons." In *The Age of Measurement: Annual Supplement to Volume 33 of the History of Political Economy,* edited by Judy L. Klein and Mary S. Morgan, 252–76. Durham: Duke University Press.

Peart, Sandra J. 2001b. "Theory, Application, and the Canon: The Case of Mill and Jevons." In *Reflections on the Classical Canon in Economics: Essays in Honor of Samuel Hollander,* edited by Evelyn L. Forget and Sandra J. Peart, 356–78. London: Routledge.

Peart, Sandra J., and David M. Levy. 2002. "Modeling Non-abstract Economic Man: Victorian Anthropology, *Punch,* and Piltdown." Paper presented at the meetings of the European Conference on the History of Economics, March 2002, Montreal.

Persky, Joseph. 1990. "Retrospectives: A Dismal Romantic." *Journal of Economic Perspectives* 4:165–72.

Phelps, Edwin S. 1972. "The Statistical Theory of Racism and Sexism." *American Economic Review* 62:659–61.

Pigou, A. C. 1907. "Social Improvement and Modern Biology." *Economic Journal* 17, no. 3: 358–69.

Pigou, A. C. 1920. *The Economics of Welfare.* 3rd ed. London: Macmillan.

Porter, Theodore M. 1986. *The Rise of Statistical Thinking.* Princeton: Princeton University Press.

Proctor, Robert N. 1991. "Eugenics among the Social Sciences." In *The Estate of Social Knowledge,* edited by JoAnne Brown and David K. van Keuren, 175–208. Baltimore: Johns Hopkins University Press.

Rainger, Ronald. 1978. "Race, Politics, and Science: The Anthropological Society of London in the 1860s." *Victorian Studies* 22:51–70.

Reade, W. Winwood. 1864. *Savage Africa: Being the Narrative of a Tour in Equatorial, Southwestern, and Northwestern Africa; with Notes on the Habits of the Gorilla; on the Existence of Unicorns and Tailed Men; on the Slave-Trade; on the Origin, Character, and Capabilities of the Negro, and on the Future Civilization of Western Africa.* New York: Harper and Brothers.

Reid, B. Archdall. 1906. "The Biological Foundations of Sociology."*Sociological Papers* 3:3–51. Paper read to the Sociological Society, 24 October 1905, with comments by C. W. Saleeby, H. Ashby, and H. Bernard.

Schumpeter, Joseph A. 1954. *History of Economic Analysis.* New York: Oxford University Press.

Schumpeter, Joseph A. 2002. "New Translations from *Theorie der wirtschaftlichen Entwicklung.*" Translated by Markus C. Becker and Thorbjørn Knudsen. *American Journal of Economics and Sociology* 61:405–37.

Semmel, Bernard. 1962. *The Governor Eyre Controversy.* London: Macgibbon and Kee.

Senior, Nassau W. 1860. "Opening Address of Nassau W. Senior, Esq., as President of Section F (Economic Science and Statistics), at the Meeting of the British Association, at Oxford, 28th June, 1860." *Journal of the Statistical Society of London* 23:357–61.

Smith, Adam. [1776] 1976. *An Inquiry into the Nature and Causes of the Wealth of Nations.* Edited by W. B. Todd. Oxford: Clarendon.

Soloway, Richard A. 1995. *Demography and Degeneration: Eugenics and the Declining Birthrate in Twentieth-Century Britain.* Chapel Hill: University of North Carolina Press.

Spencer, Frank. 1986. *Ecce Homo: An Annotated Bibliographic History of Physical Anthropology.* New York: Greenwood.

Spengler, J. J. 1955. "Marshall on the Population Question, Part II." *Population Studies* 9, no. 1: 55–66.

Spengler, J. J. 1966. "The Economist and the Population Question." *American Economic Review* 56:1–24.

Stepan, Nancy. 1982. *The Idea of Race in Science.* Hamden, Conn.: Archon.

Stigler, George J. 1941. *Production and Distribution Theories.* New York: Macmillan.

Stigler, George J., and Gary S. Becker. 1977. "De Gustibus Non Est Disputandum." *American Economic Review* 67:76–90.

Stocking, George W., Jr. 1971. "What's in a Name? The Origins of the Royal Anthropological Institute (1837–71)." *Man* 6 (September): 369–90.

Stone, Richard. 1980. "Political Economy, Economics, and Beyond." *Economic Journal* 90, no. 360:719–36.

Thomson, J. Arthur. 1906. "The Sociological Appeal to Biology." *Sociological Papers* 3:157–94. Paper read to the Sociological Society, 14 March.

Walker, Francis A. [1881] 1995. "The Colored Race in the United States." *Forum* 2:501–9. Reprinted in *Economics and Discrimination,* edited by William Darity Jr., 33–41. Brookfield, Vt.: Edward Elgar.

Wallace, A. R. 1864. "The Origin of Human Races and the Antiquity of Man Deduced from the Theory of 'Natural Selection.'" *Journal of the Anthropology Society* 2:clviii–cixx.

Webb, Sidney. 1910. "Eugenics and the Poor Law: The Minority Report." *Eugenics Review* 2 (November): 233–41.

Wells, H. G. 1904. "Discussion of Galton 'Eugenics: Its Definition, Scope, and Aims.'" *American Journal of Sociology* 10 (July): 10–11.

White, Michael V. 1994. "Bridging the Natural and the Social: Science and Character in Jevons's Political Economy." *Economic Inquiry* 32 (July): 429–44.

Winch, Donald. 1972. "Marginalism and the Boundaries of Economic Science." *History of Political Economy* 4, no. 2: 325–43.

Young, Robert J. C. 1995. *Colonial Desire: Hybridity in Theory, Culture, and Race.* London: Routledge.

17 • More Merciful and Not Less Effective
Eugenics and American Economics in the Progressive Era

Thomas C. Leonard

Oliver Wendell Holmes was made a progressive lion upon his pithy dissent to the U.S. Supreme Court's landmark decision to overturn a New York statute restricting (male) bakers' working hours. "The 14th Amendment," said Holmes famously, "does not enact the *Social Statics* of Mr. Herbert Spencer."[1] Twenty-two years later, in another well-known case, Holmes wrote for the majority, which upheld the constitutionality of a Virginia law proposing involuntary sterilization of persons believed to be mentally retarded—the "feebleminded" in the jargon of the day. "The principle that sustains compulsory vaccination is broad enough to cover cutting the Fallopian tubes," Holmes wrote in *Buck v. Bell* (1927). "Three generations of imbeciles," Holmes volunteered, "is enough."

How does an opponent of Spencerian social Darwinism come to endorse eugenic sterilization of the unfit? This essay argues that, as a matter of history, there is no contradiction in the views that underwrite the two opinions. It is not merely that both statutes proposed to subordinate individual rights to a putatively greater social good.[2] Progressive thought, it turns out, did not have to travel far when it moved from labor statutes conceived as protecting society from social Darwinism to eugenic legislation conceived as protecting society from persons deemed biologically unfit. The heart of the Progressive enterprise—to improve

Correspondence may be addressed to Thomas C. Leonard, Department of Economics, Fisher Hall, Princeton University, Princeton, N.J. 08544; e-mail: tleonard@princeton.edu. I acknowledge with gratitude the constructive criticisms of Malcolm Rutherford, Deirdre McCloskey, David Levy, Sandy Peart, Bob Goldfarb, and seminar participants at the Summer Institute, the annual meetings of the Eastern Economic Association and of the History of Economics Society.

1. *Lochner v. New York,* 198 U.S. 45, 76 (1905) (USSC). As popular as his *Lochner* dissent was with Progressives, Holmes was no Progressive. He did not share their political program; he merely believed in a kind of judicial restraint—that "general propositions do not decide concrete cases" (*Lochner v. New York,* 77). Holmes's *Lochner* dissent explicitly disavows any economic theory, Progressive or otherwise. On the sources of Holmes's jurisprudence, see Menand 2001.

2. Said Holmes: "We have seen more than once that the public welfare may call upon the best citizens for their lives. It would be strange if it could not call upon those who already sap the strength of the State for these lesser sacrifices, often not felt to be such by those concerned, in order to prevent our being swamped with incompetence" (*Buck v. Bell,* 274 U.S. 200, 207 [1927] [USSC]).

society by uplifting the industrial poor—was not the whole of the Progressive enterprise. In fact, in the Progressive era especially, eugenic treatment of those deemed biologically inferior was promoted *as a means* to the end of uplifting the worthy poor.

The history of eugenics and the history of American economics remain mostly unacquainted. Historians of eugenics have shown little interest in Progressive era political economy. And histories of Progressive era American economics routinely fail to even mention eugenics or scientific racism, movements with widespread intellectual and political influence.[3] This essay, which considers the influence of eugenics on American economics in the Progressive era, begins an attempt to fill this historical lacuna.

The notion that groups of human beings—especially blacks, Asians, Southern and Eastern Europeans, and mental and physical "defectives"—should be seen as innately different and inferior was not new in the Progressive era. Race prejudice may be as old as human history. What was new in the Progressive era was the increasingly systematic use of a biological, deterministic discourse to explain and remedy, often using racial categories, the root causes of economic problems, especially labor and immigration. Progressive era prejudice, having acquired the imprimatur of science, was used to buttress the reformist thought and legislation that was so characteristic of the time. Progressive era economists not only appealed to eugenics; they also developed and espoused theories that helped promote eugenics by offering a newfound scientific respectability to the garden variety prejudices already deeply rooted in American soil.

Eugenics and Scientific Racism

Racial science begins with the view that human racial differences are real, significant, scientifically measurable, and heritable. Scientific racism is racial science premised on racial hierarchy—the idea that different races can be ranked by innate fitness. Racists could differ in their views of the implications of racial hierarchy. Thomas Jefferson, for example, believed that blacks were innately inferior, although he wrote that "whatever be their degree of talents, it is no measure of their rights."[4] John R. Commons ([1897] 1907), in contrast, regarded blacks' immutable inferiority as justifying slavery. In Commons's view, poor

3. Important exceptions are Hodgson 1991, to which the present article, especially the race-suicide discussion, is indebted, and Ross 1991.

4. Thomas Jefferson to Henri Grégoire, February 25, 1809, http://www.loc.gov/exhibits/jefferson/jeffrep.html.

Appalachian whites, owing to their racial fitness as Anglo-Saxons, could be educated and thereby assimilated into American life. Poor blacks could not be so uplifted; black inferiority, Commons believed, could be remedied only by interbreeding with superior races (213).

Progressive era racial scientists, like their mid-nineteenth-century predecessors, were both imprecise and inconsistent when defining race. Sometimes the term *race* referred to all of humankind—the human race—and sometimes it denoted something like its modern sense—a group roughly defined by skin color and geographic ancestral origin. More commonly, *race* meant nationality, especially when distinguishing among Europeans. Progressive era usage routinely treated the English, for example, as a race biologically distinct from, say, the Irish or the Swiss or the Poles.[5]

Measurement was essential to racial science; measurement offered a tool for determining racial differences and a potential means for ranking the separate races. Before the advent of intelligence testing, which had its origins in the Progressive era, racial scientists relied on anthropometric measurement, especially skull measurement, or craniometry.[6]

William Z. Ripley, an economist trained at the Massachusetts Institute of Technology (where he was a favorite of Francis Amasa Walker) and Columbia, and who spent a long career at Harvard studying railroad economics, wrote perhaps the most influential racial taxonomy of the Progressive era, *The Races of Europe* (1899). Ripley employed a well-established and easily obtained measure—the cranial index or ratio of skull width to skull length—to classify European Caucasians into three distinct races. The Teutonic (northern) race was long-skulled (dolichocephalic), tall in stature, and pale in eyes and skin; the Mediterranean (southern) race was also dolichocephalic but shorter in stature and dark in eyes and skin; and people of the Alpine (central) race were round skulled (brachycephalic), stocky, and intermediate in eye and skin color. Ripley's racial categories were not hard and fast; he was not sure what to

5. Some Progressive era racists, such as Madison Grant, the author of *The Passing of the Great Race* ([1916] 1921), went so far as to claim that different races (in the sense of nationality) were distinct biological subspecies of *Homo sapiens.* Grant's view was extreme even in the heyday of eugenics and scientific racism but historically quite continuous with mid-nineteenth-century science, an influential faction of which (the polygenists) regarded races as distinct biological species.

6. Scientific racists had been for some years measuring skull volumes to determine brain size, which was thought to be a proxy for intelligence. Samuel Morton, a Philadelphia physician, meticulously measured the cranial volumes of the hundreds of skulls in his famous collection, and, after some egregious finagling of already unreliable data, found that Caucasian brains are larger than American Indian brains, which are larger than Negro brains (1839). For a debunking of Morton, see Gould 1981, 30–72. See also Menand 2001, 102–10.

do with the Jews, and in later work he placed the Slavs into a separate racial category.

By the standards of the day, Ripley was more a racial scientist than a scientific racist. His book explains racial difference on the basis of geography, social factors, and physical attributes such as the cephalic index and skin color. His imitators were less restrained. Madison Grant's *The Passing of the Great Race* ([1916] 1921) borrowed Ripley's taxonomy and serves up a catalog of ugly stereotypes, finding not merely inferior races but inferior social classes, inferior religions (Catholicism), and the inferior sex (women). Grant's screed essentially abandons the scientific part of scientific racism, but his book went into four editions and was a national best seller widely taught in universities.

Eugenics derives from the Greek for "wellborn" and describes a movement to improve human heredity by the social control of human breeding based on the assumption that differences in human intelligence, character, and temperament are largely due to differences in heredity (Paul 2001). The term *eugenics* first appears in Francis Galton's *Inquiries into Human Faculty* (1883), although Galton had already published several eugenicist articles, which become a book, *Hereditary Genius* (1869), arguing that human traits are heritable and manipulable for social ends. Galton, a well-known polymath and cousin of Charles Darwin, defined *eugenics* as the social program that aims "to replace natural selection by other processes that are more merciful and not less effective." Eugenics' "first object," says Galton (1908, 323), "is to check the birth rate of the unfit instead of allowing them to come into being. . . . [T]he second object is the improvement of the race by furthering the productivity of the fit by early marriages and the healthful rearing of children." Reducing the children born to the unfit is sometimes called negative eugenics; increasing the children born to the fit is positive eugenics.

Eugenics does not require racism; biological superiority need not be premised on racial hierarchy. In fact, early eugenic research in the United States studied white families thought to have "degenerate" attributes; criminality, pauperism, alcoholism, and prostitution were the chief worries. Richard Dugdale's (1877) famous *The "Jukes"* considers the family history of an Anglo-Saxon clan and, moreover, gives weight to environmental as well as hereditary causes of degeneracy.

During the Progressive era, however, American eugenic thought became racist. The rise of hereditarian science likely reinforced the trend. The German biologist August Weismann's watershed finding in 1889—that mice with their tails cut off do not bear short-tailed progeny—was intended as a refutation of Lamarckism, the idea that parents' acquired characteristics can be inherited by offspring. Weismann's result—which showed only that acquired characteristics are not inherited—was commonly read as a brief for the idea that bad blood would undermine the social improvement of bad homes. The rediscovery in 1900 of Gregor Mendel's work gave eugenicists hope that the laws of human heredity would be discovered and exploited.

American eugenics in the Progressive era tended to be racist, but the catalog of unfit persons included far more than inferior races. Fitness was also applied to sex and class. Women and the "lower orders," whatever their race, were commonly regarded as biologically inferior. There is, for example, an entire eugenics subgenre dedicated to the worry that upper-crust college men and women were being outbred by their socioeconomic inferiors. Scholars from traditionally black colleges worried about the lower fertility of the Howard University professoriate—"the higher element of the negro race"—compared to the average African American (Miller 1917).

With so many unfit types to be contended with, it is not surprising that eugenicists found it congenial to treat all human attributes as the product solely of heredity. The research of Charles Davenport, perhaps the leading American eugenicist of the day, provides an example. Davenport, an experienced chicken breeder, collected family pedigrees in *The "Jukes"* vein. His extensive collection of family records found that albinism, deafness, insanity, epilepsy, alcoholism, manic depression, pauperism, criminality, nomadism, shiftlessness, and thalassophilia run in families, which he read as establishing hereditary cause.[7]

The story of how eugenics came to inform political economy is a complex one. At work are three complementary and reinforcing themes. The first theme is the one just sketched: the rise of scientific racism and other theories of degeneracy as tools for explaining the conditions of groups on the socioeconomic margins of American life.

The second theme is the advent of the regulatory state. The U.S. government created the Federal Reserve, instituted the income tax, applied antitrust law to firms and labor unions, and restricted immigration while state governments regulated working conditions, working hours, and minimum wages. Historians increasingly regard the Progressive era as a vital precursor—in thought and policy—to the American welfare state (Rodgers 1998; Skocpol 1992). The expansion of state power meant that

7. Thalassophilia—love of the sea—Davenport concluded, must be a sex-linked recessive trait because it was almost always expressed in male naval officers (Kevles 1995, 49). This paragraph is indebted to Kevles 1995, 44–49.

it was now possible to have not only eugenic thought but also eugenic practice.

The third theme—the professionalization of American social science—helps explain the increased policy influence of academic experts and legislative activists, who were often one and the same. American Progressive era economists, in their overlapping roles as academics and activists, played an important role in the enactment of immigration and labor legislation. What is less well known is that these economists, especially the Progressives among them, made their case for exclusionary laws by joining economic theory to eugenic thought. Progressive era reform legislation invidiously excludes whole groups of persons from citizenship or labor force participation on grounds that exclusion would ameliorate the adverse economic effects of permitting biologically inferior groups to work and live in the United States.

Immigration and Race Suicide

In the late 1880s and into the 1890s, when the U.S. frontier "closed," scholars increasingly viewed population growth with alarm. The economists who wrote on immigration, however, did not make a strictly Malthusian case for too many mouths to feed. What worried the economists was not excess population but the population's changing *racial* composition. They well understood the difference; "the cry of race suicide has replaced the old fear of overpopulation," said Simon Patten (1912, 64).[8] The problem, as some Progressive era economists saw it, was not that Malthus was at work but that Darwin was not. Because these economists feared race degradation more than Malthusian conflict, they founded their arguments for immigration restriction on grounds of blood not numbers.

Fear and dislike of immigrants certainly were not new to the United States. But professional economists—notably Francis Amasa Walker (1891, 1892), Frank Fetter (1899), and Edward A. Ross (1901a)—were among the first to provide scientific respectability for race-based immigration restrictions.[9] Race-based immigration restriction was justified by

8. Frank Fetter's presidential address to the American Economic Association (entitled "Population or Prosperity"), for example, is at pains to characterize his argument against immigration as Malthusian, thus "without race prejudice" and valid whatever the truth of the claim that "present immigration is inferior in racial quality to that of the past" (1913, 13). Fetter is being coy; in Fetter 1899 he opposes immigration on race suicide grounds.

9. See also Mayo-Smith 1888a, 1888b, 1888c; and Bemis 1888. Mayo-Smith (1888c, 411) says: "It is the right of the higher civilization to make the lower give way before it. It was this right that the nations of Europe felt was their justification in taking possession of this new country. . . . The higher civilization has a moral right to triumph over the lower, for it is in this way that the world progresses."

what came to be called "race suicide." Race suicide joins scientific racism to differential fertility, naming a process whereby a superior native stock is outbred by prolific, inferior, immigrant stock.

Progressive era economists explained both sides of the differential fertility story. In explaining why poor immigrants were more prolific, they emphasized how economic life under industrial capitalism was increasingly dysgenic, that is, tending to select for the *unfit*. Simon Patten, for example, emphasized the dysgenic effects of industrial capitalism's higher living standards. Technological advancement and increases in productivity had removed the natural discipline of the survival of the fittest, making it more likely that the unfit would survive to reproduce. "Every improvement which simplifies or lessens manual labor," explained Patten, "increases the amount of the deficiencies which the laboring classes may possess without their being thereby overcome in the struggle for subsistence that the survival of the ignorant brings upon society" (quoted in Ross 1991, 197). Patten here emphasizes not the direct effects of capitalism on to the poor but its effects on natural selection: the productivity of capitalism, by making the struggle for existence slightly less desperate, works against natural selection of the fittest.[10]

What to do? Patten ultimately argues for the state taking over the task of selecting the fittest—eugenics. "Social progress is a higher law than equality, and a nation must choose it at any cost," said Patten, and the only way to progress was the "eradication of the vicious and inefficient" (Ross 1991, 199).

Henry Farnam, a Yale economist who cofounded and personally funded the American Association for Labor Legislation (AALL), a leading reform organization, emphasized public assistance as a cause of dysgenic selection.

> Every effort . . . to remove what Malthus called the "positive checks" to populations, without at the same time increasing the preventative checks, must result in an increase of the very classes which are least able to take care of themselves, and render more and more imperative the solution of that exceedingly difficult problem which Mr. Arnold White calls "sterilization of the unfit." (1888, 295)

10. Patten's influence in Progressive circles derives from his role as a protectionist Wharton School leader who viewed big business as an enemy of society and, most especially, as an activist who argued that professional economists had an obligation to lead reform movements—to leave the library, write for the newspapers, "and get their inspiration from the struggle . . . which passing events reveal" (1909, 9). "To be scientific," Patten said, "is to be popular" (8). Students attracted to Philadelphia by Patten's reform activism included many leading Progressive voices, including Scott Nearing, who later joined the Wharton faculty, and Edward Devine, a social work professional.

"We are," worried Farnam, "by means of our very improvements, setting forces in operation which tend to multiply the unfit" (295).

Patten and Farnam see higher living standards and public assistance as less a victory for social justice than as an impediment to Darwinian weeding out. Their response to what they regarded as the dysgenic effects of industrial capitalism was not to argue (as might a social Darwinist) against public assistance but to advocate eugenics, the substitution of social for natural selection of the fittest.

Francis Amasa Walker, the most respected American economist at the beginning of the Progressive era, and the first president of the American Economic Association (AEA), offered a race suicide account that proved especially influential. Walker's race suicide theory begins with the lower fertility of the "superior" "native" stock.[11] Walker argued that immigration itself checked the natural fertility of the native population so that inferior foreign-born stock effectively displaced superior native stock. "The native element failed to maintain its previous rate of increase," says Walker (1899, 423), "*because* the foreigners came in such swarms" (emphasis added).

Why? Walker appealed to the labor problem. "The [native] American shrank from the industrial competition thrust upon him," Walker proposed. "He was unwilling himself to engage with the lowest kind of day labor with these new elements of the population; he was even more unwilling to brings sons and daughters into the world to enter into that competition" (1899, 424). Walker (1896, 828) characterized the new elements of the population ("immigrants from southern Italy, Hungary, Austria, and Russia") as "beaten men from beaten races; representing the worst failures in the struggle for existence. Centuries are against them, as centuries were on the side of those who formerly came to us."

Racism to one side, Walker's race degeneration theory stood on a shaky inferential foundation. In "Immigration and Degradation" (1896), he used early-nineteenth-century population forecasts for 1840 and 1850, forecasts that effectively assume little immigration. Finding the forecasts quite accurate, but noting ex post the large increase in immigration during the 1830s and 1840s, Walker (1899, 422) concludes that the unanticipated immigration must have *induced* a native population decline in fertility, else the forecasts, in assuming little immigration, would have underestimated the total population. Walker's conjecture was not much of a demonstration. It completely fails to consider other likely explanations, for example, that native birthrates declined in re-

11. Walker uses *native* to refer to earlier European immigrants of Anglo-Saxon ethnicity.

sponse to increased urbanization, higher living standards, and later age of marriage.

More sophisticated analyses, such as R. R. Kuczynski's (1901) comparison of birthrates of foreign-born and native-born populations, had similar problems. Race suicide advocates read the higher fertility rates of foreign-born mothers (3.1 to 1.6) as conclusive evidence that the inferior immigrant stock was outbreeding the superior natives. (See, for example, economist Walter Wilcox's 1914 article on "differential fecundity" in the *Journal of Heredity.*) But this reading confuses "native-born" with "native stock," since second-generation immigrants (who, born in the United States, were legal citizens) are combined with the Yankee "natives" in the native-born category, and so the comparison cannot go to the race suicide claim. In fact, Miriam King and Steven Ruggles (1990) show convincingly that second-generation immigrants had *lower* fertility rates than did the Yankee descendants of earlier European immigrants, chiefly because of later age of marriage.[12] Thus was the differential fertility aspect of the race suicide claim factually unfounded.

Race suicide talk was, in any event, typically unburdened with empirical evidence, a point noted by Allyn A. Young (1905, 263). Walker's degeneration via displacement theory, though factually unfounded, thus gained a wide currency in academic and policy circles. Walker's scientific reputation—he had directed the U.S. Census of 1870 and 1880—if not his science, carried the day. Anti-immigrant groups were pleased to invoke Walker. Henry Pratt Fairchild (1911, 263), an anti-immigrant demagogue at Yale, said, "Our immigrants are not additions to our total population, but supplanters of native children, to whom they deny the privilege of being born." Prescott Hall (1904, 182), cofounder with Robert DeCourcy Ward of the Immigration Restriction League, characterized Walker's race degeneration story thus: "The main point is that the native children are murdered by never being allowed to come into existence, as surely as if put to death in some older invasion of the Huns and Vandals."

The term *race suicide* is most often attributed to the economist-turned-sociologist Edward A. Ross, who said, "The higher race quietly and unmurmuringly eliminates itself rather than endure individually the bitter competition it has failed to ward off by collective action" (1901a: 88).[13] Ross was a student of Richard T. Ely and took politics with

12. So, in fact, it was the second generation of the "inferior stock" that accounted for the lower birthrates among the native born. My discussion is indebted to King and Ruggles 1990.

13. Rexford Tugwell (1923, 201) credits his teacher, Simon Patten (without citation), with the coinage.

Woodrow Wilson. Ross was closely affiliated with another pioneering sociologist, Lester Ward, who had made his reputation by attacking William Graham Sumner, the reform economists' bête noire, whose laissez-faire economics Ely invoked as the chief cause for founding the AEA.

Ross's coinage gained enough currency to be used by a sitting president, Theodore Roosevelt, who called race suicide the "greatest problem of civilization" (1907, 550). In that same year, more than forty years after the American Civil War, Ross (1907, 715) wrote, "The theory that races are virtually equal in capacity leads to such monumental follies as lining the valleys of the South with the bones of half a million picked whites in order to improve the conditions of four million unpicked blacks."

During his stormy tenure at Stanford, Ross was well known for his stance against Chinese immigration. Speaking before a group of San Francisco labor leaders, Ross, according to newspaper accounts, said, "Should the worst come to the worst, it would be better for us if we were to turn our guns upon every vessel bringing [Asiatics] to our shores rather than permit them to land" (quoted in Furner 1975, 235–36).

Ross was no outlier. He was a leading public intellectual of his time; his books sold in the hundreds of thousands. Of the many Gilded Age academic freedom cases, Ross's was the one that galvanized fellow academics, not least members of the AEA. It is no small irony that a vigorous opponent of political and economic freedom should today be so closely associated with the cause of academic freedom.

Ross also popularized the term *social control,* which became a catchphrase of Progressive era reformers, as it was for their successors, the institutionalists. Many took *social control* to refer narrowly to state intervention in the economy. But Ross was not referring to regulatory policy per se. He (1901b) employed the term in a broader, sociological sense to describe the various ways in which society makes individuals conform to social ends.

Ross (1901b) conceives of society organically—as prior to the individual—and by society he means natives of Anglo-Saxon (aka Aryan) stock. Ross emphasized not the consequences of industrial capitalism per se but rather the consequences of inferior races—"Latins, Slavs, Asiatics, and Hebrews"—outbreeding the superior Anglo-Saxon race.

Walker had native stock mothers reducing births for fear of their offspring being outcompeted by inferior immigrants. Ross's theory was that native Anglo-Saxons, though biologically well adapted to rural gemeinschaft life, were less well suited to modern conditions, the crowded, urban, industrial gesellschaft life. New immigrant stock, while racially inferior, was better adapted to industrial capitalism.

Like Walker, Ross proposes that persons of "inferior" stock outcompete their biological betters, which turns Darwinism on its head. Darwinism defines fitness as reproductive success, so that those who outcompete their rivals in reproductive success are, by definition, fitter. Ross, like others before him, did not regard his paradoxical conclusion as threatening to his racist premises. Instead, Ross takes his conclusion as evidence that modern society has become dysgenic. Natural selection is no longer working in the society, just as competition is no longer working in the economy, so the state must regulate human reproduction just as it must regulate industry.

The Chicago sociologist Charles Henderson chaired the National Conference of Charities and Corrections—a title that, by itself, nicely captures the tension in the progressive view of economically marginal groups. Henderson (1900, 253), an AALL stalwart, offered banishment to rural labor colonies for the "feebleminded and degenerate" who "are not very numerous, and can all be easily segregated in self-supporting rural colonies." But even segregation was not dire enough for the "obviously unfit." The "insane, feebleminded, and epileptics" must, in the name of the greater good, be coercively sterilized:

> It is clearly and distinctly the right of a commonwealth, when called upon to support a large number of the obviously unfit, to deprive them of liberty and so prevent their propagation of defects and thus the perpetuation of their misery in their offspring. . . . Therefore the policy of painless asexualization is offered. (Henderson 1909, 228–29)

Henderson also harkens to Walker's account in emphasizing racial fitness, not numbers, and in justifying eugenic policy by instancing its putative economic benefits. "This is not an argument against immigration," he says (1909, 232), "but only against the immigration of persons who can never be induced to demand a civilized scale of life." And when the feebleminded and degenerates "are removed, the real workers will more easily rise in earning power" (1900, 253).

The economists' race suicide argument made new and influential intellectual connections. Walker connected perceived fertility trends to immigration and the "labor problem." The use of socioeconomic position and nationality as proxies for heritable fitness was vital in connecting all of these issues to the eugenics movement. Irving Fisher understood the political advantages of selling eugenics to those already predisposed to racial immigration restrictions. In a 1912 letter to Charles Davenport, he wrote, "Eugenics can never amount to anything practically until it has begun, as Galton wanted it, to be a popular movement with a certain amount of religious flavor in it, and as . . . there is already a sentiment in favor of restricting immigration . . . this is a golden opportunity to get people in general to talk eugenics" (quoted in Haller 1984, 144).

In making these connections, and in founding exclusionary regulation on racist eugenics, the race suicide theorists served as precursors of the Progressive economists affiliated with the AALL. Their AALL successors, who influenced the U.S. reform movement of the latter half of the Progressive era, would likewise invoke eugenics to defend reform legislation, notably legal minimum wages, the sine qua non of labor reform.

Sifting the Industrial Residuum: Legal Minimum Wages as Eugenic Policy

Disciplinary opposition to legal minimum wages boasts a pedigree of more than 150 years (Leonard 2000). All along the way, however, there have been dissenters, perhaps no more so than in the Progressive era. Leading supporters of legal minimum wages, certainly the most influential economists among them—Ely, Commons, Henry Rodgers Seager, Sidney Webb, John B. Andrews, and others—were progressive reformers, and many were AALL leaders. Progressive era marginalists—Alfred Marshall, John Bates Clark, Philip Wicksteed, and A. C. Pigou—generally opposed minimum wages (Leonard 2003b).

More surprising than Progressive support for legal minimum wages was the fact that Progressive economists, like their marginalist interlocutors, believed that binding minimum wages would result in job losses. What distinguished supporters of minimum wages from their marginalist opponents was how they regarded minimum-wage-induced job loss. Whereas the marginalists saw disemployment as the principal cost of binding minima—indeed, as the reason to oppose minimum-wage legislation—minimum-wage advocates regarded minimum-wage-induced disemployment as a social *benefit, a eugenic virtue of legal minimum wages.* Sidney and Beatrice Webb (Webb and Webb [1897] 1920, 785) state it plainly: "With regard to certain sections of the population ["unemployables"], this unemployment is not a mark of social disease, but actually of social health."

When Ross (1936, 70) said that "the Coolie cannot outdo the American, but he can underlive him," he was making an economic argument.

Native workers have higher productivity, claims Ross, but because Chinese immigrants will work for lower wages—"underliving"—they displace the native workers. Ross does not say why ostensibly more productive native workers cannot command relatively higher wages. Progressive era labor economics is eclectic on the relation between wages and productivity.

It is often posited that the wage for *all* workers, regardless of their skills, is relentlessly pulled downward by the marginal productivity of the least productive worker—the so-called marginal man—a process sometimes known as destructive competition. The immigrant or woman or "defective" accepts a low wage and thereby ensures that his or her inframarginal betters get paid less than they deserve. The problem is not that workers are paid a wage worth less than the value of their marginal products, the sort of exploitation that the marginalists emphasized, but that workers deemed unworthy undercut their more deserving betters.

The idea that inframarginal workers are exploited—paid less than the value of what they produce—dates to Thünen (1850) at least. What was new was the use of scientific racism to vilify the marginal man. Why vilify the most desperate of the industrial poor? Part of the answer is that Progressive wage theories regarded the marginal man as a cause of low wages not merely for himself but for more skilled workers as well.

A minority of the working poor, the "industrial residuum," as the Fabians called it, was regarded not as victims deserving public aid but as threats needing public restraint. This crude eugenic sorting of the industrial poor into worthy and unworthy categories was reinforced by economic theories of wage determination.

Progressive era marginalists such as John Bates Clark argued, as does modern neoclassical economics, that inframarginal workers (in competitive markets) are not exploited. The inframarginal workers are more productive, Clark argues, because they work with more capital. Diminishing marginal labor productivity, for a class of homogeneous workers, arises from diminishing capital per worker and not from the innately lower skill of workers hired later (1899, 321n1). Workers of different skill levels—nonhomogeneous workers—should thus be regarded as participating in different labor markets. The lower marginal product of the marginal man comes not from biological inferiority but from relatively less capital with which to work.[14]

In the marginalist scheme, moreover, marginal productivity (assum-

14. Sympathetic to Progressive causes, and writing well before neoclassical economics developed a monopsony-based explanation, Clark himself is somewhat unclear on the process by which wages may fall below workers' marginal products. See Leonard 2003a.

ing an elastic labor supply) determines the wage and the wage determines the standard of living. Progressive wage theories often reversed the causality. The standard of living determines the wage; workers with lower standards of living are willing to accept lower wages. Why would some classes of workers willingly accept lower wages? Ignorance, worker immobility, and inability to organize are all cited, but an answer was sometimes found in race. Low-wage "races" are depicted as innately disposed to endure a low standard of living. Racial theories were flexible enough to found a willingness to accept low wages on racial causes that ran from laziness to greed.[15]

Jews were a favorite target. In *Races and Immigrants,* John R. Commons ([1897] 1907, 148) volunteers that "the Jewish sweat-shop is the tragic penalty paid by that ambitious race." Like Ross's coolie, Commons's Jew is industrious but less productive than native workers. The tragedy Commons refers to is the process by which ambition leads to destructive wage competition. Wage competition destroys not only wages; it also, for Commons, is biologically destructive—dysgenic. "But competition has no respect for superior races," he writes, in an echo of the race suicide theorists, for "the race with lowest necessities displaces others" (151).

The progressive muckraker Jacob Riis, a protégé of Theodore Roosevelt and generally regarded as sympathetic to the urban working class, whose conditions he documented in his sensational book *How the Other Half Lives,* provides another example. Riis ([1890] 1997) casually avers to racial causes when explaining the low wages of tenement New York. In chapters titled "Jewtown" and "The Sweaters of Jewtown," Riis argues that Jewish sweatshop bosses, though themselves once sweatshop workers, readily exploit new workers because Jews are incorrigibly greedy.

Riis explains New York's cheap clothing as the product of "the cutter's long knife [a technological innovation] and the Polish Jew," where the latter has "cut deepest into the workman's wages." "The Jew has monopolized the [garment] business," Riis avers, but "not satisfied with having won the field, he strives as hotly with his own [fellow Jews] for the profit of half a cent as he fought with his Christian competitor for the dollar" ([1890] 1997, 92).

15. John R. Commons ([1897] 1907, 136) volunteered that blacks' putative willingness to accept low pay comes from their innate laziness—"in the entire circuit of the globe those races which have developed under a tropical sun are found too indolent and fickle." Innate indolence and fickleness explain why, Commons argues, slavery was required: "The negro could not possibly have found a place in American industry had he come as a free man. . . . [I]f such races are to adopt that industrious life which is a second nature to races of the temperate zones, it is only through some form of compulsion" (136).

Riis explains wage determination as did Commons—using crude racial stereotypes. Jews accept low wages because they accept a low standard of living, and Jews accept a low standard of living because they are thrifty and love money. "[The Jew's] price is not what he can get," says Riis, "but the lowest he can live for and underbid his neighbor" ([1890] 1997, 92).

"Thrift is the watchword of Jewtown, as of its people the world over," says Riis. Thrift is Jewtown's "cardinal virtue and its foul disgrace," for thrift "has enslaved [Jews] in bondage worse than that from which they fled." This is because "money is their God" and life for Jews is "of little value compared with even the leanest bank account" ([1890] 1997, 83).

The example of Columbia University's Henry Rogers Seager, a leading progressive economist, is also instructive.[16] In some places, Seager argues for higher minimum wages on eugenic grounds. In later editions of his successful textbook, for example, he endorses a binding minimum wage (1923, 615–16). Worthy wage earners, he says (1913a, 12), need protection from the "wearing competition of the casual worker and the drifter," as well as from other "unemployables" who unfairly drag down the wages of more deserving higher productivity workers (1913b, 82–83). Says Seager, "The operation of a minimum wage requirement would merely extend the definition of defectives to embrace all individuals, who even after having received special training, remain incapable of adequate self-support" (1913a, 9).[17]

So which workers are deemed unemployable? Seager thought of "unemployables" as workers whose marginal product is worth less than a "living wage," by which he means income to meet all living expenses of a worker independently. But the imprecision of the term *living wage*—what *is* a decent standard of living, should a living wage support a family as well, and, if so, a family of what size?—opened the door to a flexible interpretation of who deserved work. The Webbs ([1897] 1920, 785), for instance, classified as unemployable

> children, the aged, and the child-bearing women . . . the sick and the crippled, the idiots and lunatics, the epileptic, the blind and the deaf and dumb, the criminals and the incorrigibly idle,

16. The remaining discussion in this section borrows from Leonard 2003a, 8–10.

17. He adds, "One important part of the program with reference to those who are defective from birth is to prevent that monstrous crime against future generations involved in permitting them to become the fathers and mothers who must suffer under the same handicap. If we are to maintain a race that is to be made up of capable, efficient and independent individuals and family groups we must courageously cut off lines of heredity that have been proved to be undesirable by isolation or sterilization" (Seager 1913a, 10).

> and all those who are actually "morally deficient" . . . and [those] incapable of steady or continuous application, or who are so deficient in strength, speed or skill that they are incapable . . . of producing their maintenance at any occupation whatsoever.

"Of all ways of dealing with these unfortunate parasites," Sidney Webb (1912, 992) argues, "the most ruinous to the community is to allow them unrestrainedly to compete as wage earners."

Seager and Webb, leading Progressive economists, were not anomalous. Royal Meeker, a Princeton Progressive who served as the third U.S. commissioner of labor, rejects subsidizing the wages of poor workers in favor of the disemployment a minimum wage would induce—an efficient means of culling out the least productive workers.

> It is much better to enact a minimum-wage law even if it deprives these unfortunates of work. Better that the state should support the inefficient wholly and prevent the multiplication of the breed than subsidize incompetence and unthrift, enabling them to bring forth more of their kind. (1910, 544)

Sidney Ball, an Oxford Fabian, also promotes the eugenic virtues of minimum wages. For Ball, the disemployment results from a legal minimum wage demarcates the unfit, something that dysgenic markets cannot do.

> The Socialist policy, so far from favoring the weak, favors the strong. . . . it is a process of conscious social selection by which the industrial residuum is naturally sifted and made manageable for some kind of restorative, disciplinary, or, it may be, surgical treatment. (1896, 295)

A. B. Wolfe, an American reformer, also argues for the eugenic virtues of disemployment. "If the inefficient entrepreneurs would be eliminated [by minimum wages] so would the ineffective workers," he wrote. "I am not disposed to waste much sympathy with either class. The elimination of the inefficient is in line with our traditional emphasis on free competition, and also with the spirit and trend of modern social economics. . . . [These incompetents] are a burden upon society" (1917, 278).

Paul Kellogg, editor of the *Survey,* one of the most influential organs of Progressive ideas, proposes legislation that would deny new immigrants industrial employment by the use of a high legal minimum wage, instead quarantining them in open farming country and villages.

> No corporation would hire Angelo Lucca and Alexis Spivak for $3 [per day] as long as they could get John Smith and Michael Murphy and Carl Sneider for less. It would be the intent and result of such legislation to exclude Lucca and Spivak and other "greeners" from our congregate industries, which beckon to them now. (1913, 75)

Minimum-wage-era Progressives, like their immigration-restriction antecedents Walker and Ross, used the law to invidiously exclude whole classes of persons from the labor force and regarded such exclusion as socially beneficial. And, as with Walker and Ross, the economic basis for exclusion—what made one an unemployable—was explained by a putative biological inferiority.

Not all minimum-wage proponents proposed the most drastic measures—sterilization or segregation—for those who lost their jobs to minimum wages. Some, like Seager, also proposed, at least for some groups, more humane policies, which ranged from public assistance to public employment to training and schooling. But most economists defending exclusionary legislation seem to have believed that some groups were so biologically disadvantaged, and socially dangerous, as to require drastic measures. John R. Commons (1897) estimated that "defectives" constituted fully 5.5 percent of the U.S. population in 1890 and that nearly 2 percent of the population was defective by heredity, thus irredeemable, and candidates for segregation. Commons's estimates do not include other groups he regards as beyond public help such as African Americans.

It is a Whiggish temptation to regard progressive thought of a century ago as akin to contemporary Progressivism. But Progressive era Progressives viewed the industrial poor with great ambivalence. Their goal to uplift the industrial poor was entangled with a view that uplift of the worthy poor required social control of the unworthy poor. Progressive era Progressives believed that the industrial poor should be protected from the depredations of industrial capitalist society, but they also believed that society should be protected from the depredations of the industrial poor.

The obvious tension in this view was released by theoretically separating the industrial poor into worthy and the unworthy categories. Biological fitness determines who is worthy, and thereby entitled to social justice, and who is unworthy and thereby entitled to social control. Groups deemed eugenically unfit—immigrants, blacks, those defective in character and intellect—are treated not as victims but as threats to the health and well-being of the worthy poor and society at large.

Social Justice *and* Social Control

What explains the apparent fact that, in American Progressive era economics, reformers are disproportionately represented among economists influenced by eugenics?[18] It is surely not that Progressives were more likely to hold racist beliefs. The pervasiveness of Progressive era prejudice is remarkable, and economists of quite different politics can be found promoting racist views in the context of eugenics and elsewhere. Writing at the height of Jim Crow, Commons ([1897] 1907, 3–4) said, "It is now nearly forty years since these opportunities and educational advantages were given to the negro, not only on equal terms, but actually on terms of preference over the whites, and the fearful collapse of the experiment is recognized even by its partisans as something that was inevitable in the nature of the race at the stage of its development."

The AEA published in 1896 a three-hundred-page article entitled "Race Traits of the American Negro," by Frederick Hoffman, an insurance company statistician. Hoffman's offering was virtuoso scientific racism. "The presence of the colored population is a serious hindrance to the economic progress of the white race," he wrote, and as such the "white population . . . will not hesitate to make war upon those races who prove themselves useless factors in the progress of mankind" (1896, 328–29). He says of the alleged decline of black America, which he predicts must continue, that "all the facts prove that a low standard of sexual morality is the main and underlying cause of the low and anti-social condition of the race at the present time" (329).

Frank W. Taussig, no reformer but a member of the AALL, endorses, in spectacularly intemperate language, eugenic sterilization of the unfit (1921, 332–33). The American Marxist Scott Nearing, who was removed from the Wharton School faculty for his opposition to child labor in coal mines, published in 1912 a Superman screed that is a virtual museum

18. A useful, if inevitably imperfect, proxy for defining a Progressive economist is affiliation with the AALL, which Ann Orloff and Theda Skocpol (1984, 726) call the "leading association of U.S. social reform advocates in the Progressive Era." Few important Progressive economists did not have ties to the AALL. Richard T. Ely was its first president and his protégé John R. Commons the first executive secretary. The latter position was soon taken over by Commons's own protégé, John B. Andrews, who led the organization for many years. Irene Osgood (who became Irene Osgood Andrews), another Commons disciple, served as the assistant secretary. Henry Rodgers Seager, of Columbia, served as its third and fifth president (Commons was the second to hold the presidency). Charles Richmond Henderson, a Chicago sociologist and social gospeler, was another AALL leader. See Moss 1996; Skocpol 1992; and Leonard 2003a, 8–10.

piece of the brief Nietzschean vogue in eugenicist thought. Charlotte Perkins Gilman, perhaps the most eminent woman economist of the day, produced several articles with racist, eugenicist, and anti-Semitic sentiments. The restless Irving Fisher served as president of the leading U.S. eugenics society from 1922 to 1926 and opposed the First World War on the grounds that it was dysgenic. "War's real tragedy lies not in wrecked cathedrals, filled graves, or gutted treasure boxes," Fisher explained, but in "its waste of the germ plasm" (quoted in Haller 1984, 88; on Fisher's eugenics, see Cot 1989).

What drew progressives to eugenics was the same set of intellectual commitments that drew them to the AALL. The progressive intellectual commitments were (1) a belief in the power of scientific social inquiry; (2) a belief in the legitimacy of social control, which derives from a conception of society as an organism prior to and more important than its constituent individuals; and (3) a belief in the efficacy of social control via state scientific management, in particular faith in the ability of academic experts to suspend their own interests and circumvent (or, better, transcend) the messy business of everyday interest-group politics. As one widely read eugenics text put it, "Government and social control are in the hands of expert politicians who have power, instead of expert technologists who have wisdom. There should be technologists in control of every field of human need and desire" (Albert Wiggam's *New Decalogue* [1923], cited in Ludmerer 1972, 16–17).

This last progressive belief—that modern conditions of industrial capitalism no longer permitted a quaint liberal individualism but demanded wise government by expert elites—we can call technocratic paternalism.[19] The idea is that benignly motivated experts should interpose themselves, in the name of the greater good, to better represent the interests of the industrial poor, for whom many reformers felt contempt as much as pity.[20]

Economists more skeptical of eugenic laws, such as Pigou (1907), were probably no better disposed toward immigrants, the feebleminded, or other allegedly inferior persons, but they were more skeptical about the reliability of eugenic science and about the likelihood that eugenic programs would be carried out wisely by governments.[21] G. K. Chester-

19. The pioneering sociologist Lester Ward called it "sociocracy"—the "scientific control of the social forces by the collective mind of society" (quoted in Fine 1956, 263).

20. Several historians of the Progressive era find a similar strain of elitism in Progressive thought. See, for example, Rodgers 1982.

21. No group as heterogeneous and fractious as the Progressives could be unanimous behind any issue, eugenics included. Father John Ryan, for example, an influential and stalwart advocate of minimum wages and other labor legislation, opposed sterilization of the unfit on slippery-slope grounds.

ton, whose famous opposition to eugenics is usually attributed to his Catholicism, also connected eugenics to Prussianism, says Daniel Kevles, objecting to, in Chesterton's words, the "same stuffy science, the same bullying bureaucracy and the same terrorism by tenth-rate professors that have led the German empire to its recent conspicuous triumphs" (Kevles 1995, 120).

An additional benefit of explaining Progressive enthusiasm for eugenics by reference to a greater enthusiasm for science, social control, and technocratic paternalism is that we avoid a common mistake, conflating social Darwinism and selectionist thought more generally. Progressives certainly opposed social Darwinism (aka conservative Darwinism). But Progressives did not reject "survival of the fittest" ideology. What distinguished the reform Darwinism of Progressives from social Darwinism was the Progressive belief that the state, as guided by expert science, could do better than "nature" in the essential Darwinian task of weeding out the unfit.[22]

Lester Ward provides an illustration. Ward, a Progressive era reformer and eugenicist, made his career by attacking social Darwinism. The state of the human race is "deplorable," argues Ward, but science enables the state to do what nature no longer can. "Are we to accept that modern scientific fatalism known as *laissez faire*?" he asks. No. Since "the end and aim of the eugenists cannot be reproached," he concludes, "it is therefore a question of method rather than of principle" (1913, 746–47).

One hundred years ago, eugenic practice entailed state management of human reproduction. A consistent social Darwinian should prefer the "natural" selection offered by unfettered social competition to the "artificial" selection of the fittest by the state. Sidney Webb, an enthusiastic eugenicist, understood this: "No consistent eugenicist can be a 'Laisser Faire' individualist unless he throws up the game in despair. He must interfere, interfere, interfere!" (1910–11, 237). Havelock Ellis could argue in 1911 that eugenics was "the only method by which Socialism can be enabled to continue on its present path" (quoted in Freeden 1979, 668).[23]

American economists who might be regarded as reform Darwinians likewise insisted that modern conditions required the state to assume control of human reproduction. Just as labor and goods markets could

---

22. Today we associate the term *social Darwinism* with a quasi-biological defense of the late-nineteenth-century social order—emergent industrial capitalism and a limited state role in the economy—which invokes natural selection and the survival of the fittest to explain, and often justify, that social order.

23. I am here indebted to Diane Paul's (1984) pioneering essay on leftist eugenics for quotations and insight.

no longer be left unregulated, so, too, must the state take over from "nature" the project of selecting the fittest human beings. Irving Fisher captured this expansive view of social control when he wrote:

> The world consists of two classes—the educated and the ignorant—and it is essential for progress that the former should be allowed to dominate the latter. . . . [O]nce we admit that it is proper for the instructed classes to give tuition to the uninstructed, we begin to see an almost boundless vista for possible human betterment. (1907, 20)

Race building via scientific state management of the "germ plasm" was not regarded as fundamentally different in kind from other policies designed to protect society from dysgenic modern forces.

Coda

Gunnar Myrdal wrote in *An American Dilemma* (1944), his influential study of race relations, "A handful of social and biological scientists over the last 50 years have gradually forced informed people to give up some of the more blatant of our biological errors. But there still must be other countless errors of the same sort that no living man can yet detect, because of the fog within which our type of Western culture envelops us" (quoted in Gould 1981, 23). In *The Mismeasure of Man,* Steven Jay Gould invokes Myrdal's passage as a commentary on the real difficulties that arise when one tries to disentangle the effects of culture on science from the effects of science on culture.

Gould was perhaps unaware that Myrdal knew whereof he spoke. Both Myrdal and his wife Alva were themselves eugenicists who promoted an expansion of Swedish sterilization laws during the Second World War. More than sixty thousand Swedes, over 90 percent of them women, were sterilized from 1941 to 1975 (Broberg and Tydén 1996, 109–10). The Myrdals' eugenics was not racist. They saw forced sterilization of the unfit, says Daniel Kevles (1999, 437), "as part of the scientifically oriented planning of the new welfare state." Said Alva Myrdal in 1941, "In our day of highly accelerated social reforms the need for sterilization on social grounds gains new momentum. . . . The fact that community aid is accompanied by increased fertility in some groups hereditarily defective or in other respects deficient and also the fact that infant mortality among the deficient is decreasing demands some corresponding corrective" (quoted in Broberg and Tydén 1996, 105).

Gunnar Myrdal's metascientific insight was correct: scientists cannot step wholly outside the culture in which they perform their scientific work. But Myrdal was unable or unwilling to apply this insight to his own scientific advocacy of eugenics. Instead, a rival and ultimately more powerful Progressive idea carried the day; at the end of *An American Dilemma,* Myrdal (1944, 1024) writes, "We have today in social science a greater trust in the improvability of man and society than we have ever had since the Enlightenment."

Bibliography

Ball, Sidney. 1896. "The Moral Aspects of Socialism." *International Journal of Ethics* 6, no. 3: 290–322.

Bemis, Edward W. 1888. "Restriction of Immigration." *Andover Review* 9 (March): 251–64.

Broberg, Gunnar, and Mattias Tydén. 1996. "Eugenics in Sweden: Efficient Care." In *Eugenics and the Welfare State,* edited by Gunnar Broberg and Nils Roll-Hansen, 77–149. East Lansing: Michigan State University Press.

Clark, John Bates. 1899. *The Distribution of Wealth: A Theory of Wages, Interest, and Profits.* New York: Macmillan.

Commons, John R. 1897. "Natural Selection, Social Selection, and Heredity." *Arena* 18:90–97.

Commons, John R. [1897] 1907. *Races and Immigrants in America.* New York: Chautauqua Press.

Cot, Annie L. 1989. "Le gene et l'interet: L'anamorphase d'Irving Fisher." *Economies et Societes* 23, no. 6: 89–107.

Dugdale, Richard. 1877. *The "Jukes": A Study in Crime, Pauperism, Disease, and Heredity.* New York: G. P. Putnam's Sons.

Fairchild, Henry Pratt. 1911. "The Paradox of Immigration." *American Journal of Sociology* 17, no. 2: 254–67.

Farnam, Henry W. 1888. "The State and the Poor." *Political Science Quarterly* 3, no. 2: 282–310.

Fetter, Frank A. 1899. "Social Progress and Race Degeneration." *Forum* 28 (October): 228–38.

Fetter, Frank A. 1913. "Population or Prosperity." *American Economic Review* 3, no. 1 (supplement): 5–19.

Fine, Sidney. 1956. *Laissez-Faire Thought and the General Welfare State: A Study of Conflict in American Thought, 1865–1901.* Ann Arbor: University of Michigan Press.

Fisher, Irving. 1907. "Why Has the Doctrine of Laissez Faire Been Abandoned?" *Science,* new ser., 25, no. 627: 18–27.

Fisher, Irving. 1921. "Impending Problems of Eugenics." *Scientific Monthly* 13, no. 3: 214–31.

Freeden, Michael. 1979. "Eugenics and Progressive Thought: A Study in Ideological Affinity." *Historical Journal* 22, no. 3: 645–71.

Furner, Mary. 1975. *Advocacy and Objectivity: A Crisis in the Professionalization of American Social Science, 1865–1905.* Lexington: University Press of Kentucky.

Galton, Francis. 1869. *Hereditary Genius.* London: Macmillan.

Galton, Francis. 1883. *Inquiries into Human Faculty and Its Development.* London: J. M. Dent and Sons.

Galton, Francis. 1908. *Memoirs of My Life.* London: Methuen.

Gould, Stephen Jay. 1981. *The Mismeasure of Man.* New York: Norton.

Grant, Madison. [1916] 1921. *The Passing of the Great Race; or, the Racial Basis of European History.* 4th ed. New York: Charles Scribner's Sons.

Hall, Prescott. 1904. "Selection of Immigration." *Annals of the American Academy of Political and Social Science* 19:169–84.

Haller, Mark H. 1984. *Eugenics: Hereditarian Attitudes in American Thought.* New Brunswick, N.J.: Rutgers University Press.

Henderson, Charles Richmond. 1900. "Science in Philanthropy." *Atlantic Monthly* 85, no. 508: 249–54.

Henderson, Charles Richmond. 1909. "Are Modern Industry and City Life Unfavorable to the Family?" *American Economic Association Quarterly,* 3rd ser., 10, no. 1: 217–32.

Hodgson, Dennis. 1991. "Ideological Origins of the Population Association of America." *Population and Development Review* 17, no. 1: 1–34.

Hoffman, Frederick L. 1896. "The Race Traits and Tendencies of the American Negro." *Publications of the American Economic Association* 11, nos. 1–3: 1–329.

Kellogg, Paul. 1913. "Immigration and the Minimum Wage." *Annals of the American Academy of Political and Social Science* 48 (July): 66–77.

Kevles, Daniel. 1995. *In the Name of Eugenics.* Cambridge: Harvard University Press.

Kevles, Daniel. 1999. "Eugenics and Human Rights." *British Medical Journal* 318:435–38.

King, Miriam, and Steven Ruggles. 1990. "American Immigration, Fertility, and Race Suicide at the Turn of the Century." *Journal of Interdisciplinary History* 20, no. 3: 347–69.

Kuczynski, R. R. 1901. "The Fecundity of the Native and Foreign Born Population in Massachusetts." *Quarterly Journal of Economics* 16, no.1: 1–36.

Leonard, Thomas C. 2000. "The Very Idea of Applying Economics: The Modern Minimum-Wage Controversy and Its Antecedents." In *Toward a History of Applied Economics,* edited by Roger Backhouse and Jeff Biddle. *History of Political Economy* 32 (supplement): 117–44.

Leonard, Thomas C. 2003a. "'A Certain Rude Honesty': John Bates Clark as a Pioneering Neoclassical Economist." *History of Political Economy* 35, no. 3:521–28.

Leonard, Thomas C. 2003b. "American Progressive-Era Political Economy: The Case of Legal Minimum Wages." Manuscript.

Ludmerer, Kenneth M. 1972. *Genetics and American Society.* Baltimore: Johns Hopkins University Press.

Mayo-Smith, Richmond. 1888a. "Control of Immigration I." *Political Science Quarterly* 3, no. 1: 46–77.

Mayo-Smith, Richmond. 1888b. "Control of Immigration II." *Political Science Quarterly* 3, no. 2: 197–225.

Mayo-Smith, Richmond. 1888c. "Control of Immigration III." *Political Science Quarterly* 3, no. 3: 409–24.

Meeker, Royal. 1910. Review of *Cours d'économie politique. Political Science Quarterly* 25, no. 3: 543–45.

Menand, Louis. 2001. *The Metaphysical Club.* New York: Farrar, Straus and Giroux.

Miller, Kelly. 1917. "Eugenics of the Negro Race." *Scientific Monthly* 5, no. 1: 57–59.

Morton, Samuel G. 1839. *Crania Americana.* Philadelphia: John Pennington.

Moss, David. 1996. *Socializing Security: Progressive-Era Economists and the Origins of American Social Policy.* Cambridge: Harvard University Press.

Myrdal, Gunnar, with the assistance of Richard Sterner and Arnold Rose. 1944. *An American Dilemma.* 2 vols. New York: Harper and Brothers.

Nearing, Scott. 1912. *The Super Race: An American Problem.* New York: B. W. Huebsch.

Orloff, Ann Shola, and Theda Skocpol. 1984. "Why Not Equal Protection? Explaining the Politics of Public Social Spending in Britain, 1900–1911, and the United States, 1880s–1920." *American Sociological Review* 49, no. 6: 726–50.

Patten, Simon N. 1909. "The Making of Economic Literature: Annual Address of the President." *American Economic Association Quarterly,* 3rd ser., 10, no. 1: 1–14.

Patten, Simon N. 1912. "Theories of Progress." *American Economic Review* 2, no. 1: 61–68.

Paul, Diane. 1984. "Eugenics and the Left." *Journal of the History of Ideas* 45, no. 4: 567–90.

Paul, Diane. 2001. "History of Eugenics." In *The International Encyclopedia of Social and Behavioral Sciences,* edited by Neil Smelser and Paul Baltes. Amsterdam: Elsevier.

Pigou, A. C. 1907. "Social Improvement in the Light of Modern Biology." *Economic Journal* 17, no. 67: 358–69.

Riis, Jacob. [1890] 1997. *How the Other Half Lives: Studies among the Tenements of New York.* New York: Penguin.

Ripley, William Z. 1899. *The Races of Europe: A Sociological Study.* New York: D. Appleton.

Rodgers, Daniel T. 1982. "In Search of Progressivism." *Reviews in American History* 10:113–32.

Rodgers, Daniel T. 1998. *Atlantic Crossings: Social Politics in a Progressive Age.* Cambridge: Belknap Press of Harvard University Press.

Roosevelt, Theodore. 1907. "A Letter from President Roosevelt on Race Suicide." *American Monthly Review of Reviews* 35, no. 5: 550–51.

Ross, Dorothy. 1991. *The Origins of American Social Science.* Cambridge: Cambridge University Press.

Ross, Edward Alsworth. 1901a. "The Causes of Race Superiority." *Annals of the American Academy of Political and Social Science* 18, no. 1: 67–89.

Ross, Edward Alsworth. 1901b. *Social Control: A Survey of the Foundations of Order.* New York: Macmillan.

Ross, Edward Alsworth. 1907. "Social Darwinism." *American Journal of Sociology* 12, no. 5: 695–716.

Ross, Edward Alsworth. 1936. *Seventy Years of It.* New York: D. Appleton–Century.

Seager, Henry Roger. 1913a. "The Minimum Wage as Part of a Program for Social Reform." *Annals of the American Academy of Political and Social Science* 48 (July): 3–12.

Seager, Henry Roger. 1913b. "The Theory of the Minimum Wage." *American Labor Legislation Review* 3:81–91.

Seager, Henry Roger. 1923. *Principles of Economics.* 3rd ed., rev. New York: Henry Holt.

Skocpol, Theda. 1992. *Protecting Soldiers and Mothers: The Political Origins of Social Policy in the United States.* Cambridge.: Belknap Press of Harvard University Press.

Taussig, Frank W. 1921. *Principles of Economics.* 3rd ed., rev. Vol. 2. New York: Macmillan.

Thünen, J. H. von. [1850] 1966. *Isolated State: An English Edition of Der isolierte Staat.* Translated by Carla M. Wartenberg. Oxford: Pergamon.

Tugwell, Rexford. 1923. "Notes on the Life and Work of Simon Nelson Patten." *Journal of Political Economy* 31, no. 2: 153–208.

Walker, Francis Amasa. 1891. "Immigration and Degradation." *Forum* 11 (August): 634–44.

Walker, Francis Amasa. 1892. "Immigration." *Yale Review* 1, no. 2: 125–45.

Walker, Francis Amasa. 1896. "Restriction of Immigration." *Atlantic* 77:822–29.

Walker, Francis Amasa. 1899. *Discussions in Economics and Statistics.* Edited by Davis Dewey. Vol. 2. New York: Holt.

Ward, Lester. 1913. "Eugenics, Euthenics, and Eudemics." *American Journal of Sociology* 18, no. 6: 737–54.

Webb, Sidney. 1910–11. "Eugenics and the Poor Law: The Minority Report." *Eugenics Review* 2:233–41.

Webb, Sidney. 1912. "The Economic Theory of a Legal Minimum Wage." *Journal of Political Economy* 20, no. 10: 973–98.

Webb, Sidney, and Beatrice Webb. [1897] 1920. *Industrial Democracy.* London: Longmans Green.

Wilcox, Walter. 1914. "Differential Fecundity." *Journal of Heredity* 5:141–48.

Wolfe, A. B. 1917. "Some Phases of the Minimum Wage: Discussion." *American Economic Review* 7, no. 1: 275–81.

Young, Allyn A. 1905. "The Birth-Rate in New Hampshire." *Publications of the American Statistical Association* 9, no. 71: 263–91.

18 • Evolution and Human Behavior

Gordon Tullock

Introduction: The Evolution of Self-Sacrificing Behavior

Most economists and most biologists believe that at least part of our behavior is inherited. Most economists use theories in which people are assumed to be selfish maximizers. For example Field (2001, 133) says, 'The standard economic model embodies an implicit theory of human nature based on the assumption that individuals are egoistic." A typical support has been Darwinian. Individuals who have predispositions to act otherwise would over the eons have suffered a relative fitness disadvantage (Sober 2001, 132–34).[1] This assumption differs radically from human behavior. When some catastrophe occurs, an earthquake in Turkey or a flood in Guatemala, human beings from all over the world send gifts to the victims.

All humans presumably had common ancestors several hundred thousand years ago, but the gene overlap would be minimal. There also clearly is no chance of direct reciprocation by the victims of these catastrophes to the givers. One might hope that if you yourself suffered a similar catastrophe you also would receive gifts, but this would not be reciprocation from those to whom you had previously made gifts after a catastrophe.

This is not the only place where human beings behave in a nonselfish maximizing way. In 1945 thousands of Japanese committed suicide by attempting to crash their aircraft into American naval vessels. It's hard to see any way in which this could be regarded as selfish maximization. This is particularly true because the nature of Japanese religion, for the bulk of these pilots, did not offer heavenly rewards. In a mild way I went through a similar experience. I landed in Normandy on D plus 7 as a rifle company replacement. That this was extremely dangerous I knew, although I cannot say I realized quite how dangerous it would be. Fortunately, I ended up in a headquarters company and ran

1. In a review of Wilson and Sober 1998, Sober (2001) uses the group selection model, which is presently being revived, notably by the biologist David Sloan Wilson. See his coauthored book (Wilson and Sober 1998). Ghiselin has pointed out to me that there are other possible explanations or reinforcements to this one (1999).

relatively little risk. At the time I landed, however, I had no idea that I would find the war primarily boring and not particularly dangerous. I cannot recall any strong feeling that all this was unjust or that I should do anything about it except go forward and fire my rifle. My colleagues in the replacement package with which I landed seemed to have much the same attitude. In my own case, I wasn't even enthusiastic about the war. I had read Schumpeter and thought the war was three sided. I suspected that the end would leave Russia without any other European country to hold it in check. The fact that American soldiers died to give Warsaw to the Russians did not in any way surprise me. Nevertheless I had no particular doubts about going forward and perhaps being killed. As in the case of the kamikazes, I was clearly not selfishly maximizing.

The purpose of this essay is to explain these particular kinds of behavior, which are not selfishly maximizing. Indeed, they are self-sacrificing. I am particularly interested in human behavior, but the explanation requires a deviation into biology. Human beings are not the only animals that engage in self-sacrifice. The worker bee committing suicide to defend the nest is a more comprehensive example. Biologists and bioeconomists (e.g., Landa 1986), of course, have no difficulty explaining this. The behavior of the bee protects its genes, including the gene that directs it to make the sacrifice, although it does not protect itself. It will have no descendants anyway, and protecting the hive makes it more likely that the gene, which directed the sacrifice, will be present in the future. Neither the bee nor the gene thinks about this; indeed, the gene cannot think, and the bee's ability in that direction is minor.

For the benefit of nonbiologists, let me elaborate a little; any behavior, which is transmitted by biological heredity, goes by way of genes. A gene that directs me to take a 49 percent chance of death in order to save a brother, who has 50 percent of the same genes, from certain death will find itself statistically more numerous after I have done so than it would have been had I not taken the risk. Thus, this kind of gene has survival value, not in the sense that its holder has a higher rate of survival or higher rate of reproduction directly but in the sense that there will be more of that gene in the next generation. Biologists have done a great deal of work with this model, and as far as I know nobody seriously doubts it.

When dealing with behavior, especially human behavior, we should keep in mind that we only know in detail a small part of the development of human beings. Most of the behavioral traits that we study originated many, many generations ago in a society radically different from our present one. As an appendix to this essay I have a discussion of the fairly detailed theories of sexual behavior among humans. These theories are based on a very small sample and a very specialized sample of human behavior, and I doubt their accuracy, but the reader should turn to the appendix for my reasoning.

I, too, am going to run a large risk here because the traits I discuss appear to have been produced by evolution many, many generations ago. Indeed, they appear to have been produced before human beings crossed over from the other primates.

Charity

Let me first take up charity to people who are immensely distant from us and then turn to risking one's life for the group. If we consider chimpanzee bands, or, indeed, other types of animals that live in bands, most of the members of the band will be at least distantly related to the others. This is an effect of the long-continued existence of the band. If we consider those bands that have a more or less continuous existence, so that many individuals spend their whole adult lives in one band associated with much the same comrades, most of them will be moderately related to any randomly selected member of the same band. This would be because they are descendants, with a limitation I will discuss later, of the same collection of members of the previous generation. Thus, the genetic effects just discussed would lead them to make some, though perhaps modest, sacrifice for the benefit of other members of the band. They would, for example, be willing to make small gifts to other members of the band when the sacrifice was not great. The gene that directs this would turn out to be more common in the next generation for the reasons just given.

Of course, this would apply even more strongly to direct relatives. One would anticipate that the gene for gifts to your brother would provide for much larger gifts than a gene for gifts to members of the tribe who are not closely related. Turning to humans, parents make very large sacrifices for their children. Close relatives also receive gifts larger than those given to other members of the tribe. Indeed, by observation, the size of the gifts we give is roughly related to the relationship, and hence the probability, of gene overlaps. Gifts to other members of the tribe or village, where the gene overlap is small, are proportionately small. Of course, this is not the result of conscious calculation but is built into our preference function. Other members of the tribe or band are more distantly related and receive proportionately smaller gifts.

Incest

Here we come to another biological effect. Incest is dangerous, not in the sense that it kills the incestuous animal but in the sense that is likely to accumulate bad genes in the descendants of incestuous pairing. Most nonhuman bands deal with this by having one or the other sex seek mates in other bands. Chimpanzees may, for example, drive out the young males, who then seek mates in other tribes. This has two effects; it does make the dangerous incestuous mating unusual, but it also means that any individual member of the band probably has at least some gene sharing with individuals in the next band over. Since this band also engages in out-breeding, there is a further weakened likelihood that the genes will be shared with other bands that are farther out. Thus, charitable gifts, if they cost very little to the giver, may be evolutionarily selected for the area occupied by a number of bands.

The bands, however, for reasons to be discussed shortly, would tend to have few direct contacts, and the contacts they have would tend to be unfriendly. Human tribes in such situations frequently kill people from the next tribe over if he or she enters their territory. The only real friendly contact they have involves sex, where out-breeding to avoid incest is necessary. Under these circumstances information about members of other tribes would tend to fall very rapidly with distance and would reach zero for tribes farther out. The gene, however, would to some extent be shared for a considerably longer distance. Thus, gifts to people who you have no reason to believe are related to you would be feebly genetically positive. The flood victims in India in 3000 BCE would not come to my attention. Today they do. What we would expect is a gradual falling off in probable relationships and gene sharing from direct close relatives to the members of distant tribes. The size of the gifts and the amount of sacrifice would fall off similarly, and, of course, so we observe today. The difference is that today we know about things happening vast distances away.

The genes, of course, do not actually know the relationship of fellow members of the species. Indeed, the genes do not know anything. A gene that calls for large gifts to close relatives, another gene that calls for modest gifts to more distant relatives, and third that calls for tiny gifts to anyone about whom you have information would have been genetically desirable in primitive conditions and are not dangerous now, so they have not been selected out.

Villages

Of course, we no longer live in tiny hunter-gatherer bands. Most human beings, however, lived in somewhat similar situations until very recently. London was a large city in 1800, but the bulk of the population of England lived in small agricultural villages. The relationship between villages was not much different from that of the relationship between two neighboring hunter-gatherer tribes. Thus, the same genes retain their evolutionary value. Further, large cities like London were not only centers of population; they were also centers of disease. They required immigration from the agricultural villages to retain their populations. Thus, genes that might be desirable in large cities would have little chance of perpetuating themselves.

All of this has changed. Not only do we have information from far off, but also very large numbers of us live safely in cities and we can predict that in the future those backward countries with large populations in the countryside will succumb to the same phenomenon. Further, the cities are not now massive centers of deadly disease, even when their populations do not seem to be increasing or even replacing themselves. Thus, we would expect that with time these genes would be eliminated, but that may be a very long time off.

Extensions

To deviate slightly, people living in small communities with continuous interaction will gain from establishing a favorable reputation. Lying and breaking promises both will tend to lower the reputation and hence would tend to reduce the prosperity of the liar or promise breaker. Whether this would tend to be incorporated in the genes is obviously a difficult problem. Further, we do sometimes lie and sometimes break our promises. There may be some formula that tells how often you should break promises and how often you should lie to get maximum survival possibility. Note, however, that I've not calculated this in any way. It is an interesting but also very difficult problem, which we must leave to the future.

War, Again

Let me now turn to the kamikazes. Many animals and some plants have territories that they defend.[2] They are in essence using resources to preserve other resources for their use. Whether this is a good bargain or not varies a good deal, and by no means all plants or animals are territorial. Most cases of territoriality involve only a breeding pair and sometimes only one individual of either the male or female sex. Animals that live

2. Plants sometimes poison the area around their roots.

in larger groups, however, may defend the territory in which they live, and I'm going to call them tribal territorial. Wolf packs, for example, defend a hunting range, although, due the size of these ranges and the sparse distribution of prey, this is not very intensive.

Origins of Group Conflict

When we turn to the early history of the human race we are necessarily speculating. There are two possible sources of information. One of them is the behavior of our close relatives, particularly the chimpanzees and, probably, also the bonobos. They live in what we can call tribal communities. There is another close relative of ours, the gorilla, which lives in small groups, each containing an adult male, several females in his harem, and perhaps a couple of juvenile males. In all cases they seem to occupy a specific territory, although I cannot say that they have been investigated carefully enough so we can say that they're truly territorial. There is only one case of a war between tribes of chimpanzees, but that one was particularly vicious with the losing tribe being exterminated. Wars, as among human beings, are relatively rare, and the total amount of observation of these primates is limited. Further close observation of gorillas is dangerous and particularly so if you enter their protected space. In the case of the chimpanzees and the bonobos the total observation is also rather limited, especially with the bonobos. In the case of the chimpanzees the first books on them regarded them as peaceful and, indeed, held them out as models for human beings (see Goodall 1990). The apparent reason for this was that the study area was in the middle of the territory of one band. The war came when the population rose to the point where some of the chimpanzees broke off and tried to establish their own tribal area. As mentioned earlier, they were exterminated.

The bonobos are a recently discovered species and have only been moderately investigated. They are once again being held up as models for human beings, but the principal investigator admits he may be wrong (De Waal and Lanting 1997, 84–85). Although he saw no fighting, he reports that many of the males have scars, missing fingers, and even missing hands. Since wars between tribes are probably rare the absence of direct observations does not indicate that they never occur.

Further, students are apt to put their investigative facilities where there are a lot of the animals under investigation. If the species is tribal and territorial that is likely to be in the center of their tribal area. Thus, the rather rare combat between groups would take place some distance from the base camp and might well be missed. In any event it is surely rare, like human wars. That does not mean it is unimportant, once again like human wars.

Territoriality

The general reason for territoriality is the desirability of monopolizing a suitable supply of resources. Since there are changes in resource availability throughout the year and, for that matter, from one year to the next, the area seized should be large enough to support its occupiers even in the down period. Thus, trespassers must be kept out, and this would lead to fighting or at least displays from time to time. Whether the observer would see them is a matter of chance and dependent on the length of the observations.

Territoriality, though not universal among species, is not by any means remarkably rare. Most of this territoriality, however, is either individual or family. Territoriality at the tribal level is unusual, but a number of primates, including humans, use it. Its advantage is, of course, that it is easy for a group to keep individual trespassers out. Its disadvantage is that the division of resources among the members of the group must be determined, and usually is determined, by means of dominance maneuvers. These can be deadly.

The human connection with the other primates was long ago and with different, though related, species. Thus, the likelihood of the same genes must depend on their evolutionary value rather than crossbreeding or other direct sharing of genes. Necessarily, the reasoning given here is speculative but can be reinforced by some further, rather speculative evidence about primitive humans.

Primitive Tribes

We have a good deal in the way of description of tribal societies of humans. Partly that comes from historical documentation of the primitive tribes encountered by literate peoples. Partly it comes from anthropological research on the few surviving primitive tribes in such places as the Amazon Basin. They seem to be territorial in much the same sense as the chimpanzees. They have a territory occupied by each tribe, and, except on special occasions, they keep trespassers out. Usually there is some kind of overarching structure that permits the tribes to provide mates for neighboring tribes in order to avoid incest, and trading facilities may exist. Sometimes a number of villages will have an annual meeting in which nobody kills anyone else. Still relations among the tribes are much like those of the chimpanzees.

Civilizations

Human beings are smarter than chimpanzees, however. They are able to organize larger organizations, sometimes a federation of villages; more commonly the leader of one village conquers neighboring villages and establishes an empire. With time these things get bigger, and we have things like the Persian empire, which tried to add Greece.

It seems likely that these large organizations in net benefited their subject peoples. They were able to prevent local wars, and their ability to mobilize large numbers of people meant that they normally could deal with less well organized neighboring groups with ease. Domestically they normally objected to competition in the form of local thugs or thieves, and of course they tried to prevent foreign competitors, other groups of villages, or other empires from entering. Further, they tended to improve transportation by building roads so that their armies and tax collectors could get around easily. All these things probably benefited their subjects more than the injury inflicted by their taxes.

There was an even greater gain to the people who lived in the early civilized nations. Both in Mesopotamia and Egypt irrigation was of great importance and required the mobilization of large numbers of people. The gain to the population was great, and the need to build pyramids for their rulers was a modest price to pay for water control, which kept them alive.

This may seem like a deviation from my main subject, but it is not. The individual member of the tribal society would gain from the tribe maintaining its territory or even adding some from a neighboring tribe. Of course, if he could get others to do the fighting, holding himself back it would be even better. Tribes that had many members doing that would tend to be eliminated. Whether there would be some kind of internal structure to punish slackers or whether the tribe would itself be eliminated if there were many, with a result that those genes would also be eliminated, I do not know.

Thus, in addition to genes for some types of charitable acts, we would expect to find genes for engaging in group fighting for territory. Thus, my landing in Normandy was simply an expression of my genetic inheritance. Surely I would not have been willing to engage in an individual landing. Landing with part of a large section of my "tribe," however, seemed perfectly normal. Thus, if I'm correct, primates organized in tribes or nations are able to fight to protect their resources or to grab other people's resources.

Primitive Human Tribes

Primitive human tribes seem to have much the same mechanism. In some cases, the Yanamo, for example, belligerence has been carried to what an outside observer is apt to think an almost insane degree. Nevertheless, they have existed for a considerable period of time in a difficult environment. Other tribes are normally not quite as belligerent as the Yanamo, but they still defend their territories and sometimes try to take neighboring territories. It would appear, then, that genes calling for participation in tribal defense or aggression have been selected favorably. The kamikazes and the Americans who landed on the beaches of Normandy can most readily be explained by this mechanism.

Of course, we have ways of punishing slackers, but they are rarely used. Occasionally my coinvaders of Normandy mentioned the first sergeant and his .45 in this connection, but I never heard of it being used and I do not think it was a major influence on their behavior. They were genetically programmed to fight for their tribe. They were also programmed to punish people who did not fight, but the second type of programming seems to have been mainly unnecessary and certainly seldom used. But all of this reasoning is theoretical, and the empirical tests refer to things that happened long ago or to accounts of present-day primitive people. The theory is good, and the outcome seems plausible. Nevertheless, I could easily be wrong granted the immense distance between the theory and actual observation.

Appendix: Sexual Behavior among Humans

As an example of the type of error that might occur, I'm going to annoy other sociobiologists by alleging that they are simply wrong in an important area. Specifically let us consider the current theory of the relation between the sexes.

Women carry the baby before birth and nourish it for considerable periods after birth. This is a sizable capital investment by the mother. The father, however, can go on and fertilize other women freely. This has led to a theory in which the female is very careful to find a father who is a good provider and will stick with her while the male is polygamous. Social institutions intending to make the father responsible are frequently observed, but they rarely prevent extramarital sex on the part of at least some males.

All of this fits what we saw in Europe and America in the latter part of the nineteenth century and early part of the twentieth. It doesn't fit most of history and certainly does not fit European and American behavior in the latter part of the twentieth century. Let us begin abroad.

Most people in the world have arranged the marriages of young people through parental contracts. Frequently there is a material payment. In any event neither the woman nor the man has any real choice. The pattern of behavior found in many articles is simply not realistic.

If we consider the situation in the United States, Sweden, and many other countries today we find that a very large number of women produce children without any permanent arrangement with the father. Further, it is not at all obvious that a permanent arrangement with the father is even legally possible. There are frequently cases in which the male member of the family is changed, although the children usually go with the mother. Today among black families more than half of the children are fatherless. This just doesn't fit the theory discussed earlier.

I've no complaints about the reasoning that was used to deduce these patterns of male and female behavior. It does not, however, fit the real world today. It didn't fit the real world in, let us say, China two hundred years ago. A set of institutions prevailing in the area where most theoretical biologists lived not long ago was used to produce a theory covering the whole world and the whole of history. Further, the biologists do not seem to notice that the changes in family structure today invalidate their theory.

The reason I brought this up is not to attack the very prominent biologists who developed the theory. My point is that this kind of theory is necessarily dubious. I've just produced a new one of my own, and I want to make it clear that I realize it has not been tested. It's also possible that another theory would fit what we know better, and, indeed, it is possible that the whole enterprise is vacuous. Thus, I may have been wasting your time, though I hope you'll take comfort in the view that my wasted time and effort is even more extreme than yours. On the other hand, of course, I hope my theory is correct. If any reader can find a way to test it, I would be deeply grateful. This will be so even if the theory, on testing, turns out the wrong.

Bibliography

De Waal, Frans, and Frans Lanting. 1997. *Bonobo, the Forgotten Ape*. Berkeley: University of California Press.

Field, Alexander. 2001. Review of *Unto Others: The Evolution and Psychology of Unselfish Behavior* by Elliott Sober and David Sloan Wilson. *Journal of Economic Literature* 39:132–34.

Ghiselin, Michael T. 1999. "Institutional Bioeconomics and the Division of Labor: Reflections on Yarbrough and Yarbrough's Paper." *Journal of Bioeconomics* 1:319–22.

Goodall, Jane. 1990. *Through a Window.* Boston: Houghton Mifflin.

Goodall, Jane, and Michael Nicho. 1999. *Brutal Kinship.* New York: Aperture.

Landa, Janet T. 1986. "The Political Economy of Swarming in Honeybees: Voting with-the-Wings, Decision-Making Costs, and the Unanimity Rule." *Public Choice* 51:25–38.

Sober, Elliott. 2001. "Unto Others: The Evolution and Psychology of Selfish Behavior." *Journal of Economic Literature* 40:132–34.

Wilson, David Sloan, and Elliott Sober. 1998. *Unto Others: The Evolution and Psychology of Unselfish Behavior.* Cambridge: Harvard University Press.

PART 5 • The Buchanan-Rawls Correspondence

19 • Introduction and Correspondence

David M. Levy and Sandra J. Peart

Introduction

The intellectual interconnection between John Rawls and James Buchanan is evident in their published work. Buchanan writes:

> This construction in *The Calculus of Consent* was essentially worked out independently of the comparable construction of John Rawls. But discovery of his early paper on "Justice as Fairness" during the course of writing our book served to give us confidence that we were on a reasonable track. . . . The coincidence both in the timing of our initial work and in the basic similarity in analytical constructions has made me share an affinity with Rawls that has seemed mysterious to critics of both of us. (Buchanan [1986] 1999, 23–24)

Buchanan has written about his admiration for Rawls (1958). "Justice as Fairness" resulted in an invitation to Rawls to participate in the meeting that established the Committee for the Study of Non-market Decision Making. That committee would later become the Public Choice Society. In *A Theory of Justice* (1971) and elsewhere Rawls discusses Buchanan's work in public finance and Buchanan and Gordon Tullock's coauthored *The Calculus of Consent* (1962).

The correspondence between Rawls and Buchanan is one episode in a larger discussion between Rawls and the economics community from the 1950s through the 1970s. What makes the Buchanan-Rawls discussion distinct is that both take a historical perspective on the debate. Rawls, in particular, seems to propose a discussion with twentieth-century economists using past debates among economists and philosophers. Buchanan attempts to engage political philosophers through their past in his appendix to *The Calculus of Consent.*

A Theory of Justice is prefaced with Rawls's tribute to the intellectual depth of the great utilitarian economists of the eighteenth and nineteenth centuries.

> During much of modern moral philosophy the predominant systematic theory has been some form of utilitarianism. One reason

> for this is that has been espoused by a long line of brilliant writers who have built up a body of thought truly impressive in its scope and refinement. We sometimes forget that the great utilitarians, Hume and Adam Smith, Bentham and Mill, were social theorists and economists of the first rank; and the moral doctrine they worked out was framed to met the needs of their wider interests and to fit into a comprehensive scheme. Those who criticized them often did so on a much narrower front. (Rawls 1971, xvii)

Buchanan and Rawls's attitude toward the thinkers of the past reflects their attitude toward other people in general. The views from the distant past require serious consideration. Rawls takes the very strong position that if a writer's views seem incorrect, the writer will have realized this and solved the apparent problem.[1]

This shared attitude toward the texts of past scholars stands out in the larger discussion of Rawls and the economists. Even in the 1970s, economics was losing its connection with the past. Was it really necessary to argue for the egalitarian foundations of welfare economics?[2] We suggest that economists do not understand foundational work in welfare economics unless they confront the claim that some people have a higher capacity for happiness than other people. The transition from the utilitarianism of F. Y. Edgeworth and A. C. Pigou to that of Nicholas Kaldor and J. R. Hicks occurs precisely because of Lionel Robbins's worries about how to provide evidence against the argument in Edgeworth, which asserts a differential capacity for happiness.[3]

---

1. Rawls's attitude is quoted in the preface to his *Lectures on the History of Moral Philosophy:* "I took to heart Mill's remark. . . . 'A doctrine is not judged until it is judged in its best form.' I always took it for granted that the writers we were studying were much smarter than I was. If they were not, why was I wasting my time and the students' time by studying them? If I saw a mistake in their arguments, I suppose those writers saw it too and must have dealt with it. But where? I looked for their way out" (2000, xvi). The "best-form" doctrine is important to reading Rawls's take on Lionel Robbins's reformulation of classical utilitarianism.

2. Arrow 1973, 247–48: "This *generalized difference principle,* as Rawls terms it, is no tautology. In particular, it implies that even natural advantages, superiorities of intelligence or strength, do not in themselves create any claims to greater rewards. . . . Personally, I share fully this value judgment; and, indeed it is implied by almost all attempts at full formalization of welfare economics." In a note, Arrow suggested: "See A. Bergson . . . P. A. Samuelson . . . or F. Y. Edgeworth {*Mathematical Psychics*} (London: Kegan Paul, 1881), pp. 56–82." Also see Arrow 1973, 259: "The conflict between incentive and equity occurs in a utilitarian framework and was already noted by Edgeworth (who was really very conservative and was glad to escape from the rigorous egalitarianism to which his utilitarianism led)."

3. Our account of the transition between cardinal and ordinal utilitarianism is through the problem of differential capacity for happiness, which Edgeworth espouses (Peart and Levy 2005, 226–30). Our emphasis on the nature and consequence of Lionel Robbins is consistent with Rawls's reading. Rawls read Robbins very carefully, a reading that shows in Rawls's "Justice as Reciprocity" ([1959] 1999,

Perhaps the best way to appreciate the commonality between Rawls's "justice as fairness" and Buchanan's "politics as exchange" is provided in Rawls's "Justice as Reciprocity" ([1959] 1999).[4]

> It is the requirement of the possibility of mutual acknowledgment of principles by free and equal persons who have not authority over one another which makes the concept of reciprocity fundamental to both justice and fairness. . . . Now, in ordinary speech, the concepts of justice and fairness are distinguished roughly in this way: Fairness applies to practices where persons are cooperating with or competing against one another and which allow a choice whether or not do so. . . . On the other hand, justice applies to practices in which there is no choice whether or not to participate. ([1959] 1999, 209)

Thus, "justice as fairness" turns "politics into exchange" and conversely.

If politics as exchange is equivalent to justice as fairness then we can appreciate the concern for unanimity in both Buchanan and Rawls. This shows that the Pareto principle is far from harmless or weak as is sometimes suggested.[5] Welfare economists responded to Robbins's challenge to find a justification for assumptions about interpersonal capacities for happiness by rediscovering or reviving the Pareto principle of weak unanimity of net benefit. The Pareto principle makes explicit where the individual person fits within a utilitarian calculus: all individuals count equally.

The Correspondence

The bulk of the correspondence concerns the key element of Rawls's theory of justice, impartial regard for the condition of the worst off. Fa-

---

222), in which utilitarianism with the assumption of equal capacity is interpreted as "moral and political principles expressed in a somewhat technical language. . . . More importantly, one could hold that the best way to defend the classical utilitarian view is to interpret these assumptions as moral and political principles. . . . When pressed they might well have invoked the idea of a more or less equal capacity of men in relevant respects if given an equal chance in a just society." Rawls's description of Robbins's reformulation of egalitarian utilitarianism as the "best way to defend the classical utilitarianism" might be read in light of Rawls interpretative principle described in note 1.

4. Freeman (1999, x): "Chapter 10 [of 'Justice as Reciprocity'], though published in 1971, was prepared in the summer of 1959 for teaching purposes at Harvard University, where Rawls was a visiting professor in 1959–60. Chapter 10 is a rewriting and elaboration of Chapter 3 [of 'Justice as Fairness']."

5. The power of the Pareto principle in blocking the eugenic utilitarianism expounded in Edgeworth's *Mathematical Psychics* is considered in Peart and Levy 2005, 230–33.

mously, Rawls offers the "original position," veiled in ignorance, as a vantage point from which to discuss possible constitutional orders. Behind this veil of ignorance, we are uncertain about our status in any realizable state of affairs. Thus, if we were to allow a constitution consistent with chattel slavery we would have no way to know whether we will be master or slave. Out of concern that we might be the slave, it is the principle of *A Theory of Justice* that behind the veil of ignorance we would never allow a system of chattel slavery.[6]

This ignorance about our standing in the order we agree on can be characterized as Knightian uncertainty.[7] In this special context, Rawls argues that it is more plausible to adhere to the principle of maximizing the well-being of the worst off than the principle of maximizing average well-being. In this original position we have no basis in experience for objective probabilities, but we can still appeal to the "maximin" procedure to make decisions.

By the time of the correspondence reproduced here, there had been a flurry of attacks on the maximin principle. Arrow (1973), Alexander (1974), and Harsanyi (1975) challenged Rawls's argument.[8] Here is the rather sharp statement from Harsanyi.

> There are two schools of thought about the decision rule to be used by a rational person under uncertainty. One proposes the *maximin principle,* or some generalization or modification of this principle, as the appropriate decision rule. From the mid-'forties (when the problem first attracted wider attention) to the mid-'fifties this was the prevailing opinion. But then came a growing realization that the maximin principle and all its relatives lead to serious paradoxes because they often suggest

6. The lexical structure of Rawls's argument is prefigured by Frank Knight ([1935], 1951, 28): "We can scarcely imagine a slave society placed under physical compulsion so effective that men would permanently live in it. If they were given the least sight or knowledge of their masters and their masters' way of life, no provision however bountiful for all physical wants would prevent some irrational individual from setting up a cry for 'liberty or death.'" In the margin of Rawls's copy of Knight's *The Ethics of Competition* ([1935] 1951) we find written "Lexical order!"

7. Is Rawls a Knightian in some interesting philosophical sense? *A Theory of Justice* cites Knight's doctrine of the importance of discussion for democratic government (Knight [1935] 1951, 293–95); the moral irrelevance of natural ability (54–57); and legislative discussion as information aggregation (345–47). There is a great deal more commonality that suggests a link between Rawls and Knight. Here, for example, is a position expounded by Knight whose importance might not have been recognized until Rawls work on political liberalism (e.g., Rawls 1993). Knight (1939, 8), writes that: "liberalism is not logically committed to any particular conception of the nature or content of the good, individual or social. The importance of this fact can hardly be too much stressed."

8. Rawls 1974b responded to Arrow 1973 and a prepublication copy of Harsanyi 1975. Rawls 1974a responds to Alexander 1974.

> wholly unacceptable practical decisions. The other—Bayesian—school of thought, which is now dominant, proposes *expected-utility maximization* as decision rule under uncertainty. (1975, 594)

Harsanyi cites Abraham Wald (1950) and Leonard J. Savage (1954) as exemplars of the two contending positions. Harsanyi (1975, 595) claims that a consistent minimax theorist would never cross a street, and Arrow (1973), in much the same vein, characterizes the minimax position as one of infinite risk aversion. We shall return to the Harsanyi-Arrow characterizations of minimax procedures later.

The first letter, Rawls to Buchanan, of 25 February 1975, acknowledges and comments on Buchanan's attempt to find a new foundation for Rawls's concern with the worst off. Buchanan's "Hobbesian Analysis" represents a change from the Spinoza-centric historical appendix to *The Calculus of Consent* (Buchanan and Tullock 1962) toward the worst-case Leviathan models that would characterize his joint work with Geoffrey Brennan beginning with Brennan and Buchanan 1977.

Rawls's 16 July 1976 letter about Buchanan's unhappiness with Robert Nozick's entitlement theory of justice might be read to supplement Rawls's *Justice as Fairness,* which cites Nozick and Buchanan as advancing common libertarian alternatives (Rawls 2001, 16). Rawls does not, of course, say that they are the same alternatives, and it is important not to think he did.

The 27 August 1978 letter from Rawls is perhaps the most revealing of them all. In his first numbered point he is explicit about his unhappiness with the use of "as-if" probabilities as developed by Savage and others in the subjectivist tradition as the basis for agreement on fundamental moral issues. Consistent lunatics have as-if probabilities, so why ought these to count? The third point speaks to the question of reasonable differences among people's theories, the line of argument that was developed in Rawls 1985, and culminated in *Political Liberalism* (Rawls 1993). It is important to note that in Rawls's usage "reasonable" people reciprocate but "rational" people do not (Rawls 2001, 6–7).

Rawls's unhappiness with as-if probabilities ought to have been published. Harsanyi's statement of the issue between maximin and Bayesian estimation is very confusing. Bayesian approaches require a prior probability, but these prior probabilities may or may not be subjective. In particular, in 1950 Wald established that minimax estimators are Bayesian with a "least favorable prior" (Lehmann 1983, 236–90). Perhaps the best-known minimax estimators are those developed by Peter Huber for location and regression (1964, 1981). At the same time that *A*

Theory of Justice was published, statisticians were engaged in the study of estimators by means of a Rawlsian procedure. Behind the veil of distributional uncertainty, statisticians were asked to propose an estimator or family of estimators to deal the unknown (Andrews et al. 1972). The estimator that Savage himself contributed, coded as LJS, was a minimax estimator.[9]

Bibliography

Alexander, Sidney S. 1974. "Social Evaluation through Notional Choice." *Quarterly Journal of Economics* 88:597–624.

Andrews, D. F., P. J. Bickel, F. R. Hampel, P. J. Huber, W. H. Rogers, and J. W. Tukey. 1972. *Robust Estimates of Location.* Princeton: Princeton University Press.

Arrow, Kenneth J. 1973. "Some Ordinalist-Utilitarian Notes on Rawls' Theory of Justice." *Journal of Philosophy* 70:245–63.

Brennan, Geoffrey, and James M. Buchanan. 1977. "Towards a Tax Constitution for Leviathan." *Journal of Public Economics* 8:255–73.

Buchanan, James. 1975. "Utopia, the Minimal State, and Entitlement." *Public Choice* 23:121–26

Buchanan, James. M. 1976a. "A Hobbesian Interpretation of the Rawlsian Difference Principle." *Kyklos* 29:5–25.

Buchanan, James M. 1976b. "The Justice of Natural Liberty." *Journal of Legal Studies* 5:1–16.

Buchanan, James M. 1977a. "The Libertarian Legitimacy of the State. In *Freedom in Constitutional Contract: Perspective of a Political Economist.* College Station: Texas A&M University Press.

Buchanan, James M. 1977b. "Notes on Justice in Contract." In *Freedom in Constitutional Contract: Perspective of a Political Economist.* College Station: Texas A&M University Press.

Buchanan, James M. [1986] 1999. "Better Than Plowing." In *The Logical Foundations of Constitutional Liberty.* Volume 1 of *The Collected Works of James M. Buchanan,* 9–27. Indianapolis: Liberty Fund.

Buchanan, James M., and Roger L. Faith. 1980. "Subjective Elements in Rawlsian Contractual Agreements on Distributional Rules." *Economic Inquiry* 18:23–38.

Buchanan, James M., and Gordon Tullock. 1962. *The Calculus of Consent.* Ann Arbor: University of Michigan Press.

Freeman, Samuel. 1999. "Editor's Preface." In John Rawls: *Collected Papers,* ix–xii. Cambridge: Harvard University Press.

Harsanyi, John C. 1975. "Can the Maximin Principle Serve as a Basis for Morality? A Critique of John Rawls's Theory." *American Political Science Review* 69:594–606.

9. The close relationship between a minimax approach and an expected utility approach is doubtless responsible for Savage's comments on the work leading to Huber (1981). Savage 1972, 291: "An important nonpersonalistic advance in the central problem of statistical robustness." The Huber family of estimators is an explicit solution to a minimax problem (see, e.g., Andrews et al. 1972, 2C1; and Huber 1981. Thus, the estimator LJS, Savage's contribution to Andrews et al. (1972, 2C3), is a Huber estimate for a least favorable distribution.

Huber, P. J. 1964. "Robust Estimation of a Location Parameter." *Annals of Mathematical Statistics* 35:73–101.

Huber, P. J. 1981. *Robust Statistics.* New York: Wiley.

Knight, Frank H. [1935] 1951. *The Ethics of Competition.* New York: Augustus Kelley.

Knight, Frank H. 1939. "Ethics and Economic Reform I: The Ethics of Liberalism." *Economica* 6:1–29.

Lehmann, E. L. 1983. *Theory of Point Estimation.* New York: Wiley.

Peart, Sandra J., and David M. Levy. 2005. *The "Vanity of the Philosopher": From Equality to Hierarchy in Post-classical Economics.* Ann Arbor: University of Michigan Press.

Rawls, John. N.d. Marginal notes on a copy of Frank Knight's *Ethics of Competition.*

Rawls, John. [1958] 1999. "Justice as Fairness." In *Collected Papers.* Edited by Samuel Freeman. Cambridge: Harvard University Press.

Rawls, John. [1959] 1999. "Justice as Reciprocity." In *Collected Papers.* Edited by Samuel Freeman. Cambridge: Harvard University Press.

Rawls, John. 1971. *A Theory of Justice.* Cambridge: Harvard University Press.

Rawls, John. 1974a. "Reply to Alexander and Musgrave." *Quarterly Journal of Economics* 88:633–55.

Rawls, John. 1974b. "Some Reasons for the Maximin Criterion." *American Economic Review* 64:141–46.

Rawls, John. [1985] 1999. "Justice as Fairness: Political Not Metaphysical." In *Collected Papers.* Edited by Samuel Freeman. Cambridge: Harvard University Press.

Rawls, John. 1993. *Political Liberalism.* New York: Columbia University Press.

Rawls, John. 2000. *Lectures on the History of Moral Philosophy.* Edited by Barbara Herman. Cambridge: Harvard University Press.

Rawls, John. 2001. *Justice as Fairness: A Restatement.* Edited by Erin Kelly. Cambridge: Harvard University Press.

Savage, Leonard J. 1954. *The Foundations of Statistics.* New York: Wiley.

Savage, Leonard J. 1972. *The Foundations of Statistics.* Rev. ed. New York: Dover.

Wald, Abraham. 1950. *Statistical Decision Functions.* New York: Wiley.

The Texts

February 25, 1975

Dear Jim

I am very grateful to you for sending me a copy of your paper on the Hobbesian analysis of the difference principle. It pleases me enormously to read it: I found it extremely interesting and greatly appreciated your perceptive interpretation of my view. As you note, people focus on risk aversion and maximin far too much & seem unaware of the main features of the theory, e.g., that the two principles are to apply to the *basic structure,* that the difference principle bears but a relation to the maximin rule of choice, which is something quite *different* & which is at best a guide for deliberation in the original position and *only* because of the very *special* features of that situation, etc. All of which, & more, you so clearly bring out.

I also found your Hobbesian analysis as to how one might arrive at the DP very illuminating. I didn't have anything *quite* like that in mind, but the kind of argument you are making is closely related to what I called the problem of stability, and you noted some of the main places where I mention this (e.g., pp. 15, 175ff, and Reply to A & M, pp. 652f). I introduced this problem by saying that I would divide the argument for the two principles into two stages (pp. 144, 530f): at the *first* stage one would choose principles without worrying about the question of stability and psychological feasibility. At the *second* stage, we take the principles adopted at the 1st stage and see whether they are stable, that is, whether people, or *enough* people, *can* live by them without resentment, hostility, envy, etc. If they *can,* then the argument is complete; if not, then we have to begin again at step one, and revise the initial choice of principles. Since I held that the two prins[1] with the Diff. Principle are stable enough, I just went through each stage once.

I mention this by way of saying that your very instructive analysis fits nicely into the *kind* of inquiry I undertake at stage two. So one could say: if the parties would make your sorts of assumptions at stage two (& they should if they are sufficiently plausible), they would confirm their choice of the two prins. I guess I do think that the social product is very much a joint product; and that while the poorer individuals & groups don't threaten to withdraw cooperation as a tactic, as a rational strategy, so to speak, they do in fact withdraw their cooperation in other ways: by crime, by self-destructive & compulsive behavior and ways of life (e.g., by drug addiction); by acquiring far less constructive capacities for working successfully & cooperatively; by just not developing themselves from loss of self-respect (I am convinced that much low I. Q. scores is the result of large and poor and disorganized families, etc.). So while all this is not done as a threat, it perhaps has much the same destructive effect. The upper classes greatly miscalculate its consequences; though I believe they should take it into account for other reasons as well.

1. Rawls uses "prins" to indicate principles.

Thus I shouldn't reject your analysis as not what I had in mind. The question of stability at the second stage raises just these sort of questions. And while the assumptions you make are not the very ones I had in mind, they point to some of the same considerations. The normative aspect is important for me; but the two-stage structure of the whole theory certainly allows for positive theory to be brought in. Indeed the second stage requires this.

I want to think some more about your analysis. It is most instructive. Perhaps w[h]ere I come closest to it, in addition to the pages you note, is pp. 180f, assuming that lack of self-respect leads to the destructive behavior sketch[ed] above. Also, section 86, last paragraph, is relevant to your remark about getting by with no police.

Many thanks & greetings.

Jack

P. S. This year I am on leave here. (The University of Michigan, Department of Philosophy, 2209 Angell Hall, Ann Arbor, Michigan 48104) I return to Cambridge in the fall, but mail always reaches me via Harvard.

---

27 February 1975

Professor John Rawls
Department of Philosophy
Harvard University
Cambridge, Mass. 02138

Dear Jack:

You may be interested in the enclosed draft review of Nozick, which will appear in *Public Choice.*

Sincerely,
Jim Buchanan

/btr
Enclosure

11 August 1975

Professor John Rawls
Department of Philosophy
Harvard University
Cambridge, Massachusetts 02138

Dear Jack:

I know that you must get far too many drafts of papers commenting on your work, so I do not necessarily expect a reaction to this one.

But if you get the opportunity, I should be interested in knowing whether or not you think my Smith-Rawls comparison is at all reasonable. Admittedly, I read Rawls from my own prejudices, and the interpretation placed on your equal liberty principle may not at all be what you intend.

The paper emerged while I was writing another one on Adam Smith in connection with a celebration next spring at Glasgow.

Sincerely yours,
Jim Buchanan

/btr
Enclosure

---

24 March 1976

Professor John Rawls
Department of Philosophy
Harvard University
Cambridge, Massachusetts 02138

Dear Jack:

I enclose early drafts of two recently-written papers. You may find these of some interest, and especially the one on Nozick. I want to do more with the "social rent" notion, since this is something that is common to your thinking and to my own, but something that has not been fully clarified or explained.

With best regards.

Sincerely,
Jim Buchanan

/btr
Enclosure

July 16th, 1976

Dear Jim

Thanks ever so much for the copy of your paper for the symposium in Ohio. As always, I find it very instructive. Two observations may clear up a thing or two:

(1) You query the suggestion, which you believe I make, that the deliberations in the initial contract situation *must always* settle on the two prins of justice

But actually, that is not how I proceed. I always assume that the choice of prins is made by the parties from some *list* with which they are *presented*. They decide between the two prins of justice (as I state them, say) vs the prins of utility, or equality of distribution, or whatever. I take up only a few *pair-wise* comparisons. With other lists of prins, other choices would be made; and conceivably the two prins may *not* win in *all* comparisons, probably will not (on this, see p. *581*). In the section on mixed conceptions (§49) I felt the case for the two prins was considerably weaker than the case for them in a contest with the prins of utility (without any qualifications etc). So I think that the actual procedure in the book is more cautious than you indicate. Of course, I do think the two prins have many supporting grounds; it is *conceivable* that they are pretty close to the best one could ever do, but I don't know how one could claim, or argue for, any thing so ambitious as that! (Argue rigorously & respectably, that is.

(2) With the above in mind, your idea to use the initial contract situation to argue *contra* Nozick's view, & his principles of transactions, etc. by *rejecting* them: That is, showing that they would be rejected in that situation—this idea fits in very nicely. The way to make this idea fit the book's procedure would be to find *some* other principles that would be chosen over Nozick's prins in a pair-wise comparison. Once we find such prins, we know that his prins cannot be the *best* we can do, & so are to be rejected. I think the two prins would be chosen in favor of Nozick's prins; so we can use these prins to reject his. And we can do this without either accepting the two prins as the best possible, or holding that the two prins are the only possible outcome of the initial contractual situation. I had hoped I was careful not to say the latter, but no doubt long stretches of the text read differently, & perhaps fail to note this background view sufficiently.

Let me say how much I appreciate your comments on the text & the greater understanding of the problems of contract theory that I have gained from your papers.

Best wishes for an enjoyable visit to Ohio!

Yours

Jack

P.S. I inclose [sic] a copy (xerox) of the letter I wrote you last February a year ago regarding your Hobbesian derivation, or argument, for the difference prins; should you care to recall what I thought about that. I guess I would still say roughly the same.

---

3 May 1977

Professor John Rawls
Department of Philosophy
Harvard University
Cambridge, Massachusetts 02138

Dear Jack:

Last year at the Alpach European Forum in Austria, I met a very interesting young philosopher, Peter Koslowski, from the University of Munich. He had been head of the students at Munich, and he was just finishing his work in philosophy. He has now been appointed to the faculty to replace Dr. Ottfried Höffe, with whom you might be familiar because of his edition of some of your papers.

He is interested in the various intersections between philosophy and public choice, and he has been spending the past six weeks here at our Center. We have enjoyed having him around.

Before he returns to Germany, he is interested in visiting Harvard, and he would very much like to meet you. Hence, the purpose of my letter. He plans to visit Harvard sometime around the end of this month and the first of next month. If you are planning to be in town, I think you would find him to be a very nice young man. And, of course, he would consider it one of the highlights of his whole American visit to meet you. In any case, if you can talk with him, he can try to contact you directly in Cambridge, or, if you want to indicate some dates as to possibilities, you can drop him a note here at the Center or, alternatively, through me directly.

All the best.

Sincerely yours,
Jim Buchanan

/btr

P.S. Jointly with Geoff Brennan, who has been visiting us this year from Canberra, I have been working recently on some very interesting Rawls-like applications to normative tax theory. We have tried to get at the question: Behind the veil of ignorance, just what tax rules or tax arrangements would we want to assign to government? With fascinating results to this point.

May 27

Dear Jim

Thanks for your letter of May 3; I'll be seeing Peter Koslowski this coming Wednesday. I look forward to meeting him.

I enclose a short thing which pulls together a few points I made re an assumption in my book. Sometime I hope you'll send me some of your conclusions re taxes etc that you've worked out, or are in the process thereof, with Brennan.

with best regards
Jack

951–5501

29 June 1978

Professor John Rawls
Department of Philosophy
Harvard University
Cambridge, Massachusetts 02138

Dear Jack:

I think that you will at least like the overall thrust of the enclosed draft paper. It represents an attempt to derive the difference principle from the contractual process under certain specified conditions, and the argument does, we think, offer a good response to some of your critics. Admittedly, in developing the argument we depart at certain points from your strictures, but not from the spirit of your original position notion, as we interpret it. The last part of the argument is related to the earlier paper I did on "A Hobbesian Interpretation . . . ," but, overall, this is a more complete argument.

We should be especially interested in your reactions-comments and we hope that you will have time to look the draft over.

Sincerely yours,
Jim Buchanan

/btr
Enclosure

August 27, 1978

Dear Jim:

I am extremely grateful to you for sending me a copy of your paper with Faith on the subjective elements in veil of ignorance bargaining. I apologize for the fact that you have had to wait so long for a reply; I have been on leave & away off & on, & more in disarray than usual. But now I have read it through carefully. You are quite right in thinking I would like its overall tendency; the argument does, as you say, fit nicely the idea of the original position & does offer a reply to some basic criticisms. More than that, I think your argument is very ingenious; you've noted a fundamental matter I ignored & seen that it does introduce genuine contractual elements into the original position. So good: This certainly can be done, as you propose. In general, I agree with the conclusions of your paper & find them plausible & valuable, even if I might make certain points differently (*now* that I understand them, thanks to you).

There are only minor matters, so minor in fact they don't affect your argument; [but] relate mainly to what I originally said. The *first* re the remark p. 9 that you accept Harsanyi's view that decision processes can always be analyzed & discussed on the "as-if" assumptions that probabilities are assigned, in some subjective sense. In *Theory Justice* I did not intend to deny this. I take it to be a consequence of the Ramsay-de Finetti-Savage Theorem (actually formulated by Savage & proved by Savage but the ideas have a longer history). The theorem can't be denied; it is a consequence of some math plus consistent choices over lotteries (as prospects). But the probabilities are "as-if" probabilities; an intelligent & consistent paranoiac will have them much as the most rational & informed realist. In *TJ* I took the view that Savage's theorem expresses *necessary* but *not sufficient* conditions for *reasoned* beliefs: those that are *reasons* for choice. And that by hypothesis in the orig. position there are no grounds for more than mere as-if probs as to our own particular place in society etc. Mere as-if probs are *not* reasons; hence the decision must either ignore probs altogether or discount them heavily. Unless one thinks that mere as-if probs are reasons, one does not disagree. But how *can* they be reasons if consistent lunatics have them as much as the rest of us?

In your paper you need not get into this, I think. You can use the as-if equi-probable calculations to work out your numerical examples.

Second: I am not quite sure about some language you use on p. 20. In the paragraph in middle page you say: suppose i assigns some positive *value* to the prospect that A etc. I understand what you mean on this page but what is positive value? Is it some probability greater than 0? Or is it that value counts as a reason for thinking that? You must mean the former, as the latter doesn't fit quite. So why not say: probability. Since this probability is based solely on general beliefs, or so it appears, it is an allowed estimate in the orig. position. What would be excluded is probs based upon some *particular* facts about j. Actually, all of the likelihood estimates used in your sustainability argument are based on general beliefs etc & so allowed in the orig. position.

Third: there is a distinction that you don't make & which you need not go into but which might sometime be useful to explore; namely, between differences in predictions about how in general institutions will work & distribute things, all based on the *same* social theory but arising from the inevitable inexactness of the theory & how one must allow for various parameters & elements it ignores. These are *reasonable* differences between people holding common views. But another sort of difference in predictions arises from people holding different views & *theories all* of which are *reasonable* (in the present state of knowledge). A more realistic conception of original position bargaining should allow, if possible, for both cases, although you appear to have in mind only or mainly the first. Of course, to keep the account manageable, we must draw the line at what counts (or could count) as a reasonable scientific doctrine given accepted opinions on scientific procedure. The second ground of differences in predictions might weaken your arguments for maximin as given on pp. 16f, since differences might now be larger, although they would not have the kind of grounds that are excluded.

I am afraid none of this is very helpful. My writing these comments is really just a way of saying that I think you have found a second way, consistent with (as you say) the spirit of the original position argument, to introduce genuine contractual elements into the picture. This is, I think, very important & helps greatly to account for the contract notion, which is basic. I tended to lose sight of this & have not be[en] able [to] include enough such elements to make a convincing case. Also very significant is that your argument does not depend upon risk aversion, since pessimism in the sense explained in your argument is a different matter: it derives, as I interpret it, from the *leeway* allowed by all existing & probably future social theories in making *reasonable* predictions from them. That is, within some *range,* no prediction is held with grounds & estimates of the ususal sort with our understanding of the theory, can be declared *un*reasonable. Pessimism just describes a certain, as it were, lower range of reasonable predictions. These predictions are subjective only in the sense that they cannot be shown unreasonable, or to violate sound prins of method or to contradict plain facts. (Perhaps it is worth a word or two more why pessimism is not risk aversion, although you make it clear enough).

I am grateful for your paper & plan to think about [it] some more. Best regards to you & your colleague Roger Faith.

Sincerely,
Jack Rawls

Dear Jim,

Thanks ever so much for your Nobel Lecture. It gives an excellent statement of your views as a whole. I'm very pleased to have a copy. I trust you're flourishing & well.

Yours
Jack

Contributors

James M. Buchanan is Distinguished Professor Emeritus of Economics at George Mason University and University Distinguished Professor Emeritus of Economics and Philosophy at Virginia Polytechnic and State University, Blacksburg, Virginia. He received the Alfred Nobel Memorial Prize in Economic Sciences in 1985. Some of his well-known major works include *Better than Plowing: And Other Personal Essays* (1992); *The Economics and the Ethics of Constitutional Order* (1991); *The Reason of Rules* (with Geoffrey Brennan, 1985); *The Power to Tax* (with Geoffrey Brennan, 1980); *Freedom in Constitutional Contract* (1978); *Democracy in Deficit* (with Richard E. Wagner, 1977); *The Limits of Liberty* (1975); *The Calculus of Consent* (with Gordon Tullock. 1962). A twenty-volume *Collected Works of James M. Buchanan* was published from 1999–2004. His latest publications include *Why I, Too, Am Not a Conservative: The Normative Vision of Classical Liberalism* (2005) and an expanded edition of *Better than Plowing.*

Juan Pablo Couyoumdjian received his Ph.D. in Economics from George Mason University in 2004. He works at the School of Business and the School of Government at the Universidad del Desarrollo, in Santiago, Chile, where he has a joint appointment.

Tyler Cowen is Professor of Economics at George Mason University and author of numerous books on economics and culture, including *In Praise of Commercial Culture, Creative Destruction: How Globalization is Changing the World's Cultures, Markets and Cultural Voices,* and *Good and Plenty: The Creative Success of American Arts Funding.* He co-writes a blog at www.marginalrevolution.com.

Eric Crampton is Senior Lecturer in Economics at the University of Canterbury in Christchurch, New Zealand. His work with Andrew Farrant on the benevolence assumption in the socialist calculation has been published in the *Review of Austrian Economics;* other work has appeared in *Constitutional Political Economy, The Independent Review,* and the *Journal of Private Enterprise.*

Andrew Farrant teaches economics at Dickinson College. His research interests include: Political Economy, British Economic History (1945–1951), and nineteenth-century Philosophic Radicalism.

Samuel Hollander is University Professor Emeritus at the University of Toronto where he served on the faculty from 1963 to 1998 and is currently attached to Ben-Gurion University of the Negev, Israel. He is an Officer of the Order of Canada and a Fellow of the Royal Society of Canada, and he holds an honorary Doctorate of Laws from McMaster University, Ontario, Canada. He was Research Director at the Centre National de la Recherche Scientifique of France from 1999–2000. His major books are devoted to studies of Adam Smith, David Ricardo, John Stuart Mill, Thomas Robert Malthus, Jean-Baptiste Say, and Karl Marx.

M. Ali Khan is Abram Hutzler Professor of Economics at Johns Hopkins University. His work addresses those situations in which an individual agent is "numerically negligible" but is nevertheless influenced by actions, or summary statistics of actions, of all other agents in the game, and where individual and social outcomes are uncertain. Interest in development economics alongside those in methodology and the history of ideas leads to consider the relationship between economic development and cultural change. This in turn led to the Scottish Enlightenment, and to the economics of the eighteenth century.

Thomas (Tim) C. Leonard is Lecturer in Economics at Princeton University. His current research interests lie at the intersection of economics with history, ethics and law. He is at work on a book about the influence of eugenic ideas upon American economic reform during the Progressive Era. Many of his papers can be found at www.princeton.edu/~tleonard/research.

David M. Levy is Professor of Economics and Research Associate of the Center for Study of Public Choice at George Mason University. He is co-director and coffee maker at the Summer Institute. His work with Sandra Peart ranges from statistical ethics to the history of eugenics and to the sources of Adam Smith's concepts.

Deirdre McCloskey teaches economics, history, English, and communication at the University of Illinois at Chicago, and is a sometime professor at the University of the Free State, South Africa, and the Academia Vitae, Deventer, The Netherlands. She has written sixteen books on economics, rhetorical criticism, economic history, and philosophy, among them *The Bourgeois Virtues: Ethics for an Age of Commerce* (2006) and, with Stephen Ziliak, *The Cult of Statistical Significance: How the Standard Error Costs Us Jobs, Justice, and Lives* (University of Michigan Press, 2008). Educated at Harvard, she was for twelve years in Economics at the University of Chicago, and taught for many years at the University of Iowa. She describes herself as a "quantitative, literary, historical, postmodern, Episcopalian, female economist with a past."

Leonidas Montes is Civil Engineer, Licenciate in Philosophy and Master in Political Science from Pontificia Universidad Católica de Chile. He obtained his M.Phil. and Ph.D. in the Faculty of Economics at King's College, University of Cambridge. He is the author of *Adam Smith in Context* (2004), has co-edited with Eric Schliesser *New Voices on Adam Smith,* and has published different articles on Adam Smith and the Scottish Enlightenment. Leonidas is currently Dean of the School of Government at Universidad Adolfo Ibáñez, Chile.

Maria Pia Paganelli is an Assistant Professor of Economics at Yeshiva University and an Adjunct Associate Professor of Economics at New York University. She specializes in the history of economic and monetary thought and currently works on Adam Smith and eighteenth-century monetary theories.

Sandra J. Peart is Dean of the Jepson School of Leadership Studies at the University of Richmond. She is President of the History of Economics Society and co-director of the Summer Institute. With David Levy, she has begun to sketch out two books: on experts and expertise in economics; and on the economist in cartoons. She is preparing the new edition of F. A. Hayek's *John Stuart Mill and Harriet Taylor: Their Friendship and Subsequent Marriage* for the *Collected Works of F. A. Hayek.* Her history of economic thought blog is AdamSmithLives!

Warren J. Samuels is Professor Emeritus of Economics at Michigan State University. His contributions beginning with the *Classical Theory of Economic Policy* (1966) continue to address the economic role of government and the history of economics. A five-volume collection of his *Essays* (1992) include these concerns as well as the issue of methodology and economic discourse.

Eric Schliesser (Ph.D., The University of Chicago, 2002) is a four-year VENI post-doctoral research fellow (2006–2009), funded by Netherlands Organisation for Scientific Research and an Universitair Docent at the Philosophy Department, Leiden University. He is also a Research Associate, Amsterdam Research Group in History and Methodology of Economics, University of Amsterdam. He has published widely in seventeenth- and eighteenth-century philosophy and science (especially Newton, Huygens, Spinoza, Hume, and Adam Smith), political philosophy, and philosophy of economics. He is co-editor (with Leonidas Montes) of a collection of papers, *New Voices on Adam Smith*

Gordon Tullock is University Professor of Law and Economics at George Mason University. He holds a joint teaching position in the Department of Economics and the School of Law. A ten-volume *Selected Works of Gordon Tullock* (2004–2006) contains his contributions in many fields, beginning with the 1962 *Calculus of Consent* (with James Buchanan) continuing into voting theory, the economics of predation, and other forms of rational action beyond exchange.

Index